Voices of the American Past

Documents in U.S. History

Volume II

FIFTH EDITION

RAYMOND M. HYSER
J. CHRIS ARNDT
James Madison University

WADSWORTH
CENGAGE Learning·

Australia • Brazil • Japan • Korea • Mexico • Singapore • Spain • United Kingdom • United States

WADSWORTH
CENGAGE Learning™

**Voices of the American Past:
Documents in U.S. History,
Volume II, Fifth Edition**

Raymond M. Hyser and
J. Chris Arndt

Senior Publisher: Suzanne Jeans

Senior Sponsoring Editor: Ann West

Development Editor: Larry Goldberg

Assistant Editor: Megan Chrisman

Editorial Assistant: Patrick Roach

Senior Media Editor: Lisa Ciccolo

Senior Marketing Manager: Katherine Bates

Marketing Coordinator: Lorreen Pelletier

Marketing Communications Manager: Caitlin Green

Content Project Management: PreMediaGlobal

Senior Art Director: Cate Rickard Barr

Manufacturing Buyer: Sandee Milewski

Rights Acquisition Specialist, Images: Jennifer Meyer Dare

Senior Rights Acquisition Specialist, Text: Katie Huha

Production Service: PreMediaGlobal

Cover Designer: Lori Leahy, Mighty Quinn Graphics

Cover Image: The Everett Collection/The Canadian Press. Malcolm X™ is a trademark of the Family of Malcolm X

Compositor: PreMediaGlobal

For product information and technology assistance, contact us at **Cengage Learning Customer & Sales Support, 1-800-354-9706**

For permission to use material from this text or product, submit all requests online at **www.cengage.com/permissions**. Further permissions questions can be emailed to **permissionrequest@cengage.com**

Library of Congress Control Number: 2010943278

ISBN-13: 978-1-111-34126-8

ISBN-10: 1-111-34126-5

Wadsworth
20 Channel Center Street
Boston, MA 02210
USA

Cengage Learning is a leading provider of customized learning solutions with office locations around the globe, including Singapore, the United Kingdom, Australia, Mexico, Brazil and Japan. Locate your local office at **international.cengage.com/region**.

Cengage Learning products are represented in Canada by Nelson Education, Ltd.

For your course and learning solutions, visit **www.cengage.com**.

Purchase any of our products at your local college store or at our preferred online store **www.cengagebrain.com**.

Instructors: Please visit **login.cengage.com** and log in to access instructor-specific resources.

Cover image caption: *Malcolm X, holding up newspaper with headline "Our Freedom Can't Wait," while standing behind podium with microphones addressing a crowd at a Black Muslim rally in New York, 1963.*

Printed in the United States of America
1 2 3 4 5 6 7 15 14 13 12 11

To our children,
Kelsey, Marshall, and Christopher Hyser
and Olivia and Ruby Arndt
Thanks for all of your love
and inspiration

Contents

CHAPTER 17   Gilded Age America   339

CHAPTER 18   The Progressive Movement   373

Preface to the Fifth Edition

We are delighted with the opportunity to produce a revised fifth edition of *Voices of the American Past*. This allows us to better represent the ever-evolving approaches that historians employ to interpret the past, as well as provide more documents covering a greater variety of issues.

CHANGES TO THE FIFTH EDITION

Those who use this edition will find significant changes. Our selection of new documents was guided by a desire to provide greater diversity of voices while also offering readable selections that spoke to larger issues. The revised reader offers well-known primary sources such as *Federalist 10*, Walker's Appeal, the Seneca Falls Declaration of Sentiments, the Populist Platform, President Eisenhower's farewell address and Martin Luther King, Jr.'s "Letter from Birmingham Jail." But this edition includes substantial changes with over fifty new documents and images. These include an indentured servant's letter describing conditions in seventeenth-century Virginia; a contemporary newspaper report on the 1741 New York slave conspiracy; George Washington's instructions on conducting war against the Iroquois during the American Revolution; an 1840s African American petition to integrate schools in Massachusetts; the American Party Platform of 1856; a woman's description of farm life in Illinois at the turn of the twentieth century; Eleanor Roosevelt's commentary on New Deal policies; an editorial on the 1955 Emmitt Till murder trial; a description of illegal immigrants crossing into Arizona in 2000; and an economist's commentary on the looming financial crisis in 2007.

We have also added images to the fifth edition. As historians have increasingly expanded the types of sources they use both as scholars and in the classroom, we have added pictures and drawings, but especially political cartoons, to the written documents. The result is a number of images that provide a unique approach to interpreting and understanding the key issues of U.S. history. These include drawings of Native American life in the late sixteenth century; European views of the American Revolution; political cartoons about the election of 1860; perspectives on American overseas expansion; advertisements in the 1920s; political cartoons on the New Deal; and viewpoints on the war in Vietnam.

ACKNOWLEDGMENTS

We are again indebted to our colleagues in the James Madison University Department of History for their contributions and inspiration. Their high standards of teaching excellence coupled with their strong sense of collegiality provide the perfect atmosphere for quality instruction. Our students have contributed greatly by showing us where a document was contradictory or less readable, and perhaps more important, for helping to make us aware of the issues that are central to the current generation of young people. Many of our colleagues in the profession, particularly those who participate in the annual Advanced Placement U.S. History Reading, have made more important contributions than they could ever realize. The criticisms and suggestions of reviewers did much to improve this edition, enabling us to refocus our attention in some areas and leading us to some excellent documents in others. We wish to thank the following reviewers:

Brandon Buck, Mountain Pointe High School

Stacy Cordery, Monmouth College

Aley Ginette, University of Southern Indiana

Edward Gutierrez, University of Hartford

Timothy Kelly, Saint Vincent College

Marianne McKnight, Salt Lake Community College

Keshia Medellin, Los Medanos College

James Paradis, Arcadia University

George Sochan, Bowie State University

Special thanks go to our friends at Wadsworth/Cengage Publishing. Ann West has been remarkable as an editor. The fifth edition could not have been completed without her professionalism and support. Larry Total Books Goldberg is a terrific editor who patiently guided us through the final stages of the writing and editing process. His keen insights and steadfast support made this a much better book than it would have been otherwise. Finally, we thank our wives, Pamela and Andi, for their love and support.

We are eager to hear from readers of *Voices of the American Past*. Please feel free to offer your comments by contacting us at the Department of History, James Madison University, 58 Bluestone Drive MSC 2001, Harrisonburg, VA 22807, or through our e-mail addresses: J. Chris Arndt, arndtjc@jmu.edu; Raymond M. Hyser, hyserrm@jmu.edu.

A Guide to Reading and Interpreting Documents and Images

This volume contains edited documents about American history. Historians refer to such documents as written *primary sources*. These are the raw materials, the basic building blocks to reconstructing past events. In the same way that a detective searches a crime scene for clues, a historian draws on primary sources and uses the weight of the evidence to determine what happened and to help support an interpretation of the event. Although primary sources might be described as any evidence that is contemporary to the event described, historians rely heavily on firsthand, eyewitness accounts or recollections of events of the time, as well as speeches or official reports produced at that time. All primary sources, however, are not created equal. The closer the evidence is in time and space to the event described, the less bias that it contains, the more reliable it tends to be. The interpretations that historians produce from these primary sources are called *secondary sources*. Secondary sources are books and articles written about past events, such as a textbook, the introductions to the documents in this volume, or a history of the American Civil War.

Reading and analyzing documents require particular skills. You should examine documents with a critical eye; that is, ask questions about the document. We recommend that you develop the ability to perform a twofold reading of a document. First, try to understand the document as the people in the time and place in which it was produced would have comprehended it. What did the document mean to them? Always remember that people live within a historical context—they inhabit a time and place different from what exists today. They do not know what the future holds. Careful analysis of a document will enable you to examine the thoughts and actions of the people of a particular time. Second, read the document and consider the similarities and differences between that time period and other time periods, including your own. Students of history are often called upon to make judgments about the past. Documents should be analyzed to see how they fit into the broader sweep of history.

We have included the following suggestions that will be useful in introducing you to this spirit of historical inquiry and enable you to better understand documents. These guidelines will enable you to read primary sources in a critical manner. In so doing, you will gain more insight into past events, add some real-life views to historical facts, and better understand the complexities of the American past.

Interpreting Written Documents

1. **Context:** Each document has an introduction. You should read it as well as review notes from your instructor's lecture. These will provide some historical context about events, people, and ideas of the time period in which the document was created.

   - What major political, social, economic and/or cultural trends may have affected the author of the document?
   - How does this document fit into the historical context?
   - How does this document better our understanding of the event?
   - Does the document help to explain the cause-and-effect relationship of this event?

2. **Thesis:** Most documents have a central point that is being conveyed. This is known as the thesis. It is critical for any reader to understanding the core argument—the thesis—of a document. Identifying the thesis is the important first step in making sense of a document's overall impact.

   - Can you summarize the document in three or four sentences?
   - What is the thesis? Can you express it in a sentence or two?
   - What does the author emphasize?
   - What are the key words that define the argument?

   Keep in mind that the meaning of words changes over time, so try to understand the use of language in the historical time period of the document. For example, students in the twenty-first century might refer to "icon" as a clickable symbol on their computer's desktop, but prior to the widespread use of computers, "icon" would refer to a sacred, religious image.

3. **Perspective:** The author's point of view, including his or her prejudices and beliefs, can affect dramatically the content of a document. It is essential to consider the author of a document when reading. Biographical information can be helpful in deciding the author's point of view. For example, a slave owner would have a different view of slavery than a slave. Factory workers would certainly have a different perception of life in America than the owner of the factory where they worked.

   - Who is the author of the document?
   - What is his or her background?

- When was the document created? How does historical context affect the author at the time the document was created?
- Was it prepared during the event, immediately afterwards, within a short time period, or years later? Such timing is important, as memories often fade or become distorted over time.

An individual's life experience often shapes perspective or views about events in his or her time. Seek to determine the authors' gender, class, ethnicity (where appropriate), their regional background, and their political, economic, or social position.

- Do you detect any prejudices or preferences?
- What evidence indicates the bias of the author?
- Can you determine the author's motive in producing the document?
- What did he or she hope to accomplish?

4. **Audience:** Knowing the intended audience of an account can be useful in better understanding why the document was created.

- Was the document prepared for a specific audience—women, members of Congress, African Americans, wealthy businessmen, immigrants, a friend, for example?
- Was the document prepared for public distribution?
- Was it a speech, a newspaper or a magazine article or editorial, an official government report, a published memoir or autobiography, to name a few possibilities?
- Was it produced for personal and private reflection, such as a diary, journal entry, or an exchange of letters between friends?

Public consumption documents tend to be carefully worded, often guarded in presentation, while private ones tend to be less cautious and more honest. Classifying or identifying the document can be helpful in understanding its contents.

5. **Significance:** Finally, one should determine why a document is important.

- Why is the document important or significant?
- How has it shaped our understanding of the event?
- How has it shaped our understanding of historical change or continuity over time?
- What does it tell us about the historical time period?

Interpreting Visual Images

Many of the techniques used to interpret visual images are similar to those used to make sense of written documents. It is as important to ask questions about context, thesis, perspective, audience, and significance when analyzing an image as it is when reviewing a written text. The major difference with visual images is that there is more room for interpretation since the author/artist/photographer does not specifically describe what he or she is thinking. In addition to considering context, thesis, perspective, audience and significance, one should also consider the following when analyzing visual images:

- Carefully study the image. What is your overall impression? What thoughts or emotions does it conjure?

- How are individuals or groups depicted? Does their dress indicate anything significant about them?

- What activities are depicted in the image? How and why are these activities significant?

- Does the artist make use of symbols? If so, what are they? What is the significance of these symbols?

- Who or what is portrayed positively? Negatively? What can you infer from this?

About the Authors

J. Chris Arndt is a professor of history at James Madison University in Harrison-burg, Virginia, where he teaches courses in U.S. history, the American Revolu-tion, the early Republic, and historical methods. He focuses his research interests on the study of states' rights and economic change in antebellum America.

Raymond M. Hyser is a professor of history at James Madison University in Harrisonburg, Virginia, where he teaches courses in U.S. history, U.S. business history, Gilded Age America, and historical methods. He focuses his research interests on the study of race and ethnicity in the Gilded Age.

15

Reconstruction

After the Civil War, the nation faced the enormous task of reconstructing the republic. In particular, policymakers had to determine the status of the former Confederate states and what to do with the recently freed slaves. Devastated by the war, the South also had to cope with the influx of northern troops, reformers, and profiteers, many of whom had their own ideas concerning the region's future. The diversity of opinions over Reconstruction deeply divided the North and occasionally brought a violent response from some southern whites. The ensuing selections reveal how Americans of different races and regions responded to Reconstruction.

124

A Northern Teacher's View of the Freedmen (1863–1865)

Early in the Civil War, Union troops occupied the sea islands along South Carolina's coast near Beaufort. All property—plantations, cotton, and slaves—was confiscated and placed under the jurisdiction of Secretary of the Treasury Salmon P. Chase. Of particular concern was the welfare of the slaves, who at this early stage of the war were considered contraband if they were behind Union lines and were not returned to their owners. Sensing the opportunity to use these islands as an experiment for the future reconstruction of the

South, Chase permitted benevolent organizations to send teachers, many of them women, to help educate the former slaves. In October 1863, the New England Freedmen's Aid Society sponsored Elizabeth Hyde Botume as a teacher in this experiment. Hyde became more than a teacher in the several years she spent among the ex-slaves, as her book, First Days Amongst the Contrabands, *revealed. Excerpted here is Hyde's description of the freedmen.*

Questions to Consider

1. In what ways did the slaves react to freedom?
2. What are the initial problems facing the freedmen?
3. What social, political, and economic issues confronting Reconstruction does Elizabeth Hyde Botume observe?
4. What can you deduce about race relations?

... Contrabands were coming into the Union lines, and thence to the town, not only daily, but hourly. They came alone and in families and in gangs, —slaves who had been hiding away, and were only now able to reach safety. Different members of scattered families following after freedom, as surely and safely guided as were the Wise Men by the Star of the East.

On New Year's Day I walked around amongst these people with Major Saxton. We went to their tents and other quarters. One hundred and fifty poor refugees from Georgia had been quartered all day on the wharf. A wretched and most pitiable gang, miserable beyond description. But when we spoke to them, they invariably gave a cheerful answer. Usually to our question, "How do you do?" the response would be, "Thank God, I live!"

Sometimes they would say, "Us ain't no wusser than we been."

These people had been a long time without food, excepting a little hominy and uncooked rice and a few ground-nuts. Many were entirely naked when they started, and all were most scantily clothed and we had already had some extremely cold days, which we, who were fresh from the North, found hard to bear.

It was the same old story. These poor creatures were covered only with blankets, or bits of old carpeting, or pieces of bagging, "crocus," fastened with thorns or sharp sticks....

I went first to the negro quarters at the "Battery Plantation," a mile and a half away. A large number of Georgia refugees who had followed Sherman's army were quartered here. Around the old plantation house was a small army of black children, who swarmed like bees around a hive. There were six rooms in the house, occupied by thirty-one persons, big and little. In one room was a man whom I had seen before. He was very light, with straight red hair and a sandy complexion, and I mistook him for an Irishman. He had been to me at

SOURCE: Elizabeth Hyde Botume, *First Days Amongst the Contrabands* (Boston, 1893), 78–79, 82–83, 117–18, 168–69, 176–77.

one time grieving deeply for the loss of his wife, but he had now consoled himself with a buxom girl as black as ink. His sister, a splendidly developed creature, was with them. He had also four sons. Two were as light as himself, and two were very black. These seven persons occupied this one room. A rough box bedstead, with a layer of moss and a few old rags in it, a hominy pot, two or three earthen plates, and a broken-backed chair, comprised all the furniture of the room. I had previously given one of the women a needle and some thread, and she now sat on the edge of the rough bedstead trying to sew the dress she ought, in decency, to have had on....

The winter of 1864–1865 was a sad time, for so many poor creatures in our district were wretchedly ill, begging for help, and we had so little to give them. Many of the contrabands had pneumonia. Great exposure, with scanty clothing and lack of proper food, rendered them easy victims to the encroachments of any disease. I sent to Beaufort for help. The first doctor who came was exasperatingly indifferent. He might have been a brother of a "bureau officer," who was sent down especially to take care of the contrabands, and who wished all the negroes could be put upon a ship, and floated out to sea and sunk. It would be better for them and for the world. When we expressed our surprise that he could speak so of human beings, he exclaimed, "Human beings! They are only animals, and not half as valuable as cattle."

When the doctor came, I went from room to room and talked with the poor sick people, whose entire dependence was upon us. Finally I could endure his apathy and indifference no longer.

"Leave me medicines, and I will take care of these people as well as I can," I said....

I could not, however, excuse the doctor, a man in government employ, drawing a good salary with no heart in his work. Beaufort was reported to be a depot for officials whom government did not know what to do with....

Early in February we went to Savannah with General and Mrs. Saxton, and members of the general's staff, and other officers. How it had become known that we were to make this trip I cannot tell, but we found a crowd of our own colored people on the boat when we went aboard. To our exclamations of surprise they said with glee,—

"Oh, we're goin' too, fur us has frien's there."

We found the city crowded with contrabands who were in a most pitiable condition. Nearly all the negroes who had lived there before the war had gone away. A large number went on with the army; those left were the stragglers who had come in from the "sand hills" and low lands. The people from the plantations too had rushed into the city as soon as they knew the Union troops were in possession.

A crowd of poor whites had also congregated there. All were idle and destitute. The whites regarded the negroes as still a servile race, who must always be inferior by virtue of their black skins. The negroes felt that emancipation had lifted them out of old conditions into new relations with their fellow beings. They were no longer chattels, but independent creatures with rights and privileges like their neighbors....

Nothing in the history of the world has ever equalled the magnitude and thrilling importance of the events then transpiring. Here were more than four millions of human beings just born into freedom; one day held in the most abject slavery, the next, "de Lord's free men." Free to come and to go according to the best lights given them. Every movement of their white friends was to them full of significance, and often regarded with distrust. Well might they sometimes exclaim, when groping from darkness into light, "Save me from my friend, and I will look out for my enemy."

Whilst the Union people were asking, "Those negroes! what is to be done with them?" they, in their ignorance and helplessness, were crying out in agony, "What will become of us?" They were literally saying, "I believe, O Lord! help thou mine unbelief."

They were constantly coming to us to ask what peace meant for them? Would it be peace indeed? or oppression, hostility, and servile subjugation? This was what they feared, for they knew the temper of the baffled rebels as did no others.

125

Charleston, South Carolina, at the Conclusion of the Civil War (1865)

The Civil War brought destruction to the South. With much of the fighting taking place in southern states, armies of both sides laid waste to the countryside and burned or destroyed communities as they struggled to win the war. While often not directly involved in the fighting, the civilian population felt the brunt of the conflict. The war also brought a dislocation of trade and business activities in the South, often resulting in shortages of food and clothing. Furthermore, the Civil War shattered the plantation economy of primarily cotton production based on the labor of African American slaves. When the Confederacy surrendered in April 1865, the southern states faced significant social, political, and economic adjustments. At the war's conclusion, some northern journalists traveled throughout the South to report on conditions and people's reactions to the beginnings of Reconstruction. Sidney Andrews was one of these journalists; his observations appeared in the Chicago Tribune *and the* Boston Advertiser. *The reports from his three-month southern tour attracted such attention that they were compiled in book form,* The South Since the War, *which is excerpted here. His direct and well-written accounts were among the best commentaries on the immediate postwar South.*

Questions to Consider

1. What conditions did Andrews find in Charleston?

2. In what ways did residents of Charleston react to northerners? To Reconstruction policies? Would this be expected?

3. What issues and attitudes does Andrews reveal that become critical in Reconstruction?

4. In what ways does the photograph of African Americans collecting skeletons after the Battle of Cold Harbor ("Images of African Americans in the Civil War," Document 118) compare with Andrews's description of Charleston?

A city of ruins, of desolation, of vacant houses, of widowed women, of rotting wharves, of deserted warehouses, of weed-wild gardens, of miles of grass-grown streets, of acres of pitiful and voiceful barrenness,—that is Charleston, wherein Rebellion loftily reared its head five years ago, on whose beautiful promenade the fairest of cultured women gathered with passionate hearts to applaud the assault of ten thousand upon the little garrison of Fort Sumter!...

We will never again have the Charleston of the decade previous to the war. The beauty and pride of the city are as dead as the glories of Athens. Five millions of dollars could not restore the ruin of these four past years; and that sum is so far beyond the command of the city as to seem the boundless measure of immeasurable wealth. Yet, after all, Charleston was Charleston because of the hearts of its people. St. Michael's Church, they held, was the center of the universe; and the aristocracy of the city were the very elect of God's children of earth. One marks now how few young men there are, how generally the young women are dressed in black. The flower of their proud aristocracy is buried on scores of battlefields. If it were possible to restore the broad acres of crumbling ruins to their foretime style and uses, there would even then be but the dead body of Charleston....

Of Massachusetts men, some are already in business here, and others came on to "see the lay of the land," as one of them said. "That's all right," observed an ex-rebel captain in one of our after-dinner chats,—"that's all right; let's have Massachusetts and South Carolina brought together, for they are the only two States that amount to anything."

"I hate all you Yankees most heartily in a general sort of way," remarked another of these Southerners; "but I find you clever enough personally, and I expect it'll be a good thing for us to have you come down here with your money, though it'll go against the grain of us pretty badly."

There are many Northern men here already, though one cannot say that there is much Northern society, for the men are either without families or have left them at home. Walking out yesterday with a former Charlestonian, ... he pointed out to me the various "Northern houses"; and I shall not exaggerate if I say that this classification appeared to include at least half the stores on each of the principal streets. "The presence of these men," said he, "was at first

SOURCE: Sidney Andrews, *The South Since the War* (Boston, 1866), 1–9.

very distasteful to our people, and they are not liked any too well now; but we know they are doing a good work for the city."

I fell into some talk with him concerning the political situation, and found him of bitter spirit toward what he was pleased to denominate "the infernal radicals." When I asked him what should be done, he answered: "You Northern people are making a great mistake in your treatment of the South. We are thoroughly whipped; we give up slavery forever; and now we want you to quit reproaching us. Let us back into the Union, and then come down here and help us build up the country." ...

It would seem that it is not clearly understood how thoroughly Sherman's army destroyed everything in its line of march,—destroyed it without questioning who suffered by the action. That this wholesale destruction was often without orders, and often against most positive orders, does not change the fact of destruction. The Rebel leaders were, too, in their way, even more wanton, and just as thorough as our army in destroying property. They did not burn houses and barns and fences as we did; but, during the last three months of the war, they burned immense quantities of cotton and rosin....

The city is under thorough military rule; but the iron hand rests very lightly. Soldiers do police duty, and there is some nine-o'clock regulation; but, so far as I can learn, anybody goes anywhere at all hours of the night without molestation. "There never was such good order here before," said an old colored man to me. The main street is swept twice a week, and all garbage is removed at sunrise. "If the Yankees was to stay here always and keep the city so clean, I don't reckon we'd have 'yellow jack' here any more," was a remark I overheard on the street. "Now is de fust time sense I can 'mem'er when black men was safe in de street af'er nightfall," states the negro tailor in whose shop I sat an hour yesterday.

On the surface, Charleston is quiet and well-behaved; and I do not doubt that the more intelligent citizens are wholly sincere in their expressions of a desire for peace and reunion. The city has been humbled as no other city has been; and I can't see how any man, after spending a few days here, can desire that it shall be further humiliated enough for health is another thing. Said one of the Charlestonians on the boat, "You won't see the real sentiment of our people, for we are under military rule; we are whipped, and we are going to make the best of things; but we hate Massachusetts as much as we ever did." This idea of making the best of things is one I have heard from scores of persons. I find very few who hesitate to frankly own that the South has been beaten. "We made the best fight we could, but you were too strong for us, and now we are only anxious to get back into the old Union and live as happily as we can," said a large cotton factor. I find very few who make any special profession of Unionism; but they are almost unanimous in declaring that they have no desire but to live as good and quiet citizens under the laws.

126

African Americans Seek Protection (1865)

The emancipation of 4 million slaves in the South brought significant social, political, and economic adjustment for both African Americans and whites. Despite obtaining freedom from their masters and the rigors of plantation life, the former slaves lost their source of shelter, food, clothing, and occupation. In short, they had little but their freedom. Realizing that they remained at the mercy of their previous owners, many African Americans gathered in conventions in cities throughout the South to discuss the best methods of protecting their fragile freedom. Some of these conventions petitioned Congress for assistance; others turned to local officials for help. Excerpted here is a petition from a convention of African Americans meeting in Alexandria, Virginia, in August 1865. This petition, the typical result of the conventions, demonstrates the precarious position of the freedmen and how they proposed to protect themselves.

Questions to Consider

1. What types of protection does this convention seek?
2. For what reasons was the convention critical of "loyalty oaths" and the Freedmen's Bureau?
3. What does this document reveal about the situation for the freedmen at this time?
4. In what ways did Elizabeth Hyde Botume's description of the freedmen ("A Northern Teacher's View of the Freedmen," Document 124) anticipate this convention's call for protection?

We, the undersigned members of a convention of colored citizens of the State of Virginia, would respectfully represent that, although we have been held as slaves, and denied all recognition as a constituent of your nationality for almost the entire period of the duration of your government, and that by your permission we have been denied either home or country, and deprived of the dearest rights of human nature; yet when you and our immediate oppressors met in deadly conflict upon the field of battle—the one to destroy and the other to save your government and nationality, we, with scarce an exception, in our inmost souls

SOURCE: "The Late Convention of Colored Men," *New York Times*, 13 August 1865, p. 3.

espoused your cause, and watched, and prayed, and waited, and labored for your success....

When the contest waxed long, and the result hung doubtfully, you appealed to us for help, and how well we answered is written in the rosters of the two hundred thousand colored troops now enrolled in your service; and as to our undying devotion to your cause, let the uniform acclamation of escaped prisoners, "Whenever we saw a black face we felt sure of a friend," answer.

Well, the war is over, the rebellion is "put down," and we are declared free! Four-fifths of our enemies are paroled or amnestied, and the other fifth are being pardoned, and the President has, in his efforts at the reconstruction of the civil government of the States, late in rebellion, left us entirely at the mercy of these subjugated but unconverted rebels, in everything save the privilege of bringing us, our wives and little ones, to the auction block. He has, so far as we can understand the tendency and bearing of his action in the case, remitted us for all our civil rights, to men, a majority of whom regard our devotions to your cause and flag as that which decided the contest against them! This we regard as destructive of all we hold dear, and in the name of God, of justice, of humanity, of good faith, of truth and righteousness, we do most solemnly and earnestly protest. Men and brethren, in the hour of your peril you called upon us, and despite all time-honored interpretation of constitutional obligations, we came at your call and you are saved; and now we beg, we pray, we entreat you not to desert us in this the hour of our peril!

We know these men—know them well—and we assure you that, with the majority of them, loyalty is only "lip deep," and that their professions of loyalty are used as a cover to the cherished design of getting restored to their former relation with the Federal Government, and then, by all sorts of "unfriendly legislation," to render the freedom you have given us more intolerable than the slavery they intended for us.

We warn you in time that our only safety is in keeping them under Governors of the military persuasion until you have so amended the Federal Constitution that it will prohibit the States from making any distinction between citizens on account of race or color. In one word, the only salvation for us besides the power of the Government, is in the possession of the ballot. Give us this, and we will protect ourselves. No class of men relatively as numerous as we were ever oppressed when armed with the ballot. But, 'tis said we are ignorant. Admit it. Yet who denies we know a traitor from a loyal man, a gentleman from a rowdy, a friend from an enemy?...

... All we ask is an equal chance with the white traitors varnished and japanned* with the oath of amnesty. Can you deny us this and still keep faith with us? "But," say some, "the blacks will be overreached by the superior knowledge and cunning of the whites." Trust us for that. We will never be deceived a second time. "But," they continue, "the planters and landowners will have them in their power, and dictate the way their votes shall be cast."

---

* A varnish that yields a hard brilliant finish.

We did not know before that we were to be left to the tender mercies of these landed rebels for employment. Verily, we thought the Freedmen's Bureau was organized and clothed with power to protect us from this very thing, by compelling those for whom we labored to pay us, whether they liked our political opinions or not!...

We are "sheep in the midst of wolves," and nothing but the military arm of the Government prevents us and all the truly loyal white men from being driven from the land of our birth. Do not then, we beseech you, give to one of these "wayward sisters" the rights they abandoned and forfeited when they rebelled until you have secured our rights by the aforementioned amendment to the Constitution.

Let your action in our behalf be thus clear and emphatic, and our respected President, who, we feel confident, desires only to know your will, to act in harmony therewith, will give you his most earnest and cordial cooperation; and the Southern States, through your enlightened and just legislation, will speedily award us our rights. Thus not only will the arms of the rebellion be surrendered, but the ideas also.

127

Thaddeus Stevens on Reconstruction and the South (1865)

The debate over Reconstruction began during the Civil War and became increasingly acute as the North moved toward victory. The lines were quickly drawn between the president and Congress, though various factions within the Republican Party argued vociferously for certain positions. Some of the more important issues centered on how the secessionist states should be reunited with the Union; what political and social status should be conveyed to the 4 million freedmen; how the whites who supported the Confederacy should be treated; and lastly, who should control Reconstruction. Presidential Reconstruction, begun by Abraham Lincoln in December 1863 and slightly modified when Andrew Johnson assumed the presidency, was declared too lenient by Republicans. Within Congress, a powerful group called the Radical Republicans challenged Presidential Reconstruction and began advocating their own agenda. Among the leaders of the Radical Republicans was Thaddeus Stevens, a representative from Lancaster, Pennsylvania, whose quick wit, honesty, political savvy, and belief that Reconstruction offered an opportunity to establish a better country made him a powerful supporter of Congressional Reconstruction. Excerpted here is Stevens's speech on the status of the South and what Congressional Reconstruction should encompass.

Questions to Consider

1. What political actions does Thaddeus Stevens propose for the South?
2. What does Stevens believe Congress should do for the freedmen?
3. In what ways do Stevens's proposals help shape Reconstruction policies?
4. In what ways might Stevens have reacted to Elizabeth Hyde Botume's description of the freedmen ("A Northern Teacher's View of the Freedmen," Document 124) and the freedmen's appeal for protection ("African Americans Seek Protection," Document 126)?

... No one doubts that the late rebel states have lost their constitutional relations to the Union, and are incapable of representation in Congress, except by permission of the Government. It matters but little, with this admission whether you call them States out of the Union, and now conquered territories, or assert that because the Constitution forbids them to do what they did do, that they are therefore only dead as to all national and political action, and will remain so until the government shall breathe into them the breath of life anew and permit them to occupy their former position. In other words, that they are not out of the Union, but are only dead carcasses lying within the Union. In either case, it is very plain that it requires the action of Congress to enable them to form a State government and send representatives to Congress. Nobody, I believe, pretends that with their old constitutions and frames of government they can be permitted to claim their old rights under the Constitution. They have torn their constitutional States into atoms, and built on their foundations fabrics of a totally different character. Dead men cannot raise themselves. Dead States cannot restore their own existence "as it was." Whose especial duty is it to do it? In whom does the Constitution place the power? Not in the judicial branch of government, for it only adjudicates and does not prescribe laws. Not in the Executive, for he only executes and cannot make laws. Not in the Commander-in-Chief of the armies, for he can only hold them under military rule until the sovereign legislative power of the conqueror shall give them law....

Congress alone can do it. But Congress does not mean the Senate, or the House of Representatives, and President, all acting severally. Their joint action constitutes Congress.... Congress must create States and declare when they are entitled to be represented. Then each House must judge whether the members presenting themselves from a recognized State possess the requisite qualifications of age, residence, and citizenship; and whether the election and returns are according to law. The Houses, separately, can judge of nothing else. It seems amazing that any man of legal education could give it any larger meaning.

It is obvious from all this that the first duty of Congress is to pass a law declaring the condition of these outside or defunct States, and providing proper civil governments to them. Since the conquest they have been governed by martial law. Military rule is necessarily despotic, and ought not to exist longer than is absolutely necessary. As there are no symptoms that the people of these provinces will be prepared to participate in constitutional government for some years, I know

SOURCE: "Reconstruction," *Congressional Globe*, 39th Congress, 1st Session, part 1 (18 December 1865), 72–74.

of no arrangement so proper for them as territorial governments. There they can learn the principles of freedom and eat the fruit of foul rebellion. Under such governments, while electing members to the Territorial Legislatures, they will necessarily mingle with those to whom Congress shall extend the right of suffrage. In Territories Congress fixes the qualifications of electors; and I know of no better place nor better occasion for the conquered rebels and the conqueror to practice justice to all men, and accustom themselves to make and obey equal laws....

According to my judgment they ought never to be recognized as capable of acting in the Union, of being counted as valid States, until the Constitution shall have been so amended as to make it what its framers intended; and so as to secure perpetual ascendancy to the party of the Union; and so as to render our republican Government firm and stable forever. The first of those amendments is to change the basis of representation among the States from Federal numbers to actual voters....

But this is not all that we ought to do before these inveterate rebels are invited to participate in our legislation. We have turned, or are about to turn, loose four million slaves without a hut to shelter them or a cent in their pockets. The infernal laws of slavery have prevented them from acquiring an education, understanding the commonest laws of contract, or of managing the ordinary business of life. This Congress is bound to provide for them until they can take care of themselves. If we do not furnish them with homesteads, and hedge them around with protective laws; if we leave them to the legislation of their late masters, we had better have left them in bondage. Their condition would be worse than that of our prisoners at Andersonville. If we fail in this great duty now, when we have the power, we shall deserve and receive the execration of history and of all future ages.

128

A White Southern Perspective on Reconstruction (1868)

Congressional or Radical Reconstruction imposed a new set of requirements on the South. It divided the region into five military districts and outlined how new governments were to be created—especially granting suffrage to African Americans. Complying with these guidelines, every southern state was readmitted into the Union by 1870. A Republican Party coalition of African Americans, recently arrived northerners (carpetbaggers), and southern whites (scalawags) controlled nearly all these state governments. Many former supporters of the Confederacy found these Republican governments to be offensive, corrupt, and expensive (they raised taxes to pay for new services like public education). One of the most outspoken and uncompromising opponents of Radical Reconstruction was Howell Cobb. Born into a wealthy Georgia cotton plantation family, Cobb devoted his life to public service. He served in the House of Representatives, was elected speaker in 1849, was governor of Georgia, served as secretary of the treasury under President James Buchanan, was a prominent secessionist, helped form the Confederate government, and was an officer in the war. Following the war Cobb maintained a self-imposed silence on political matters, which he broke with the letter excerpted here. Many white southerners would have agreed with Cobb's attack on Radical Reconstruction.

Questions to Consider

1. What are Howell Cobb's reasons to oppose Reconstruction policies?
2. Which policies does he particularly dispute? Why?
3. In what ways did white southerners react to Reconstruction?
4. How might Cobb have reacted to Thaddeus Stevens's speech ("Thaddeus Stevens on Reconstruction and the South," Document 127)?

Macon [GA], 4 Jany., 1868

We of the ill-fated South realize only the mournful present whose lesson teaches us to prepare for a still gloomier future. To participate in a national festival would be a cruel mockery, for which I frankly say to you I have no heart, however much I may honor the occasion and esteem the association with which I would be thrown.

The people of the South, conquered, ruined, impoverished, and oppressed, bear up with patient fortitude under the heavy weight of their burdens. Disarmed and reduced to poverty, they are powerless to protect themselves against wrong and injustice; and can only await with broken spirits that destiny which the future has in store for them. At the bidding of their more powerful conquerors they laid down their arms, abandoned a hopeless struggle, and returned to their quiet homes under the plighted faith of a soldier's honor that they should be protected so long as they observed the obligations imposed upon them of peaceful law-abiding citizens. Despite the bitter charges and accusations brought against our people, I hesitate not to say that since that hour their bearing and conduct have been marked by a dignified and honorable submission which should command the respect of their bitterest enemy and challenge the admiration of the civilized world. Deprived of our property and ruined in our estates by the results of the war, we have accepted the situation and given the pledge of a faith never yet broken to abide it. Our conquerors seem to think we should accompany our acquiescence with some exhibition of gratitude for the ruin which they have brought upon us. We cannot see it in that light. Since the close of the war they have taken our property of various kinds, sometimes by

SOURCE: Howell Cobb to J. D. Hoover, 4 January 1868, *Annual Report of the American Historical Association for the Year 1911*, vol. 2, *The Correspondence of Robert Toombs, Alexander H. Stephens, and Howell Cobb*, ed. U. B. Phillips (Washington, DC, 1913), 690–94.

seizure, and sometime by purchase,—and when we have asked for remuneration have been informed that the claims of rebels are never recognized by the Government. To this decision necessity compels us to submit; but our conquerors express surprise that we do not see in such ruling the evidence of their kindness and forgiving spirit. They have imposed upon us in our hour of distress and ruin a heavy and burthensome tax, peculiar and limited to our impoverished section. Against such legislation we have ventured to utter an earnest appeal, which to many of their leading spirits indicates a spirit of insubordination which calls for additional burthens. They have deprived us of the protection afforded by our state constitutions and laws, and put life, liberty and property at the disposal of absolute military power. Against this violation of plighted faith and constitutional right we have earnestly and solemnly protested, and our protest has been denounced as insolent;—and our restlessness under the wrong and oppression which have followed these acts has been construed into a rebellious spirit, demanding further and more stringent restrictions of civil and constitutional rights. They have arrested the wheels of State government, paralized the arm of industry, engendered a spirit of bitter antagonism on the part of our negro population towards the white people with whom it is the interest of both races they should maintain kind and friendly relations, and are now struggling by all the means in their power both legal and illegal, constitutional and unconstitutional, to make our former slaves *our masters,* bringing these Southern states under the power of *negro supremacy.* To these efforts we have opposed appeals, protests, and every other means of resistance in our power, and shall continue to do so until the bitter end. If the South is to be made a pandemonium and a howling wilderness the responsibility shall not rest upon our heads. Our conquerors regard these efforts on our part to save ourselves and posterity from the terrible results of their policy and conduct as a new rebellion against the constitution of our country, and profess to be amazed that in all this we have failed to see the evidence of their great magnanimity and exceeding generosity. Standing today in the midst of the gloom and suffering which meets the eye in every direction, we can but feel that we are the victims of cruel legislation and the harsh enforcement of unjust laws.... We regarded the close of the war as ending the relationship of enemies and the beginning of a new national brotherhood, and in the light of that conviction felt and spoke of constitutional equality.... We claimed that the result of the war left us a state in the Union, and therefore under the protection of the constitution, rendering in return cheerful obedience to its requirements and bearing in common with the other states of the Union the burthens of government, submitting even as we were compelled to do to *taxation without representation;* but they tell us that a successful war to keep us in the Union left us out of the Union and that the pretension we put up for constitutional protection evidences bad temper on our part and a want of appreciation of the generous spirit which declares that the constitution is not over us for the purposes of protection.... In such reasoning is found a justification of the policy which seeks to put the South under negro supremacy. Better, they say, to hazard the consequences of negro supremacy in the

South with its sure and inevitable results upon Northern prosperity than to put faith in the people of the South who though overwhelmed and conquered have ever showed themselves a brave and generous people, true to their plighted faith in peace and in war, in adversity as in prosperity....

With an Executive who manifests a resolute purpose to defend with all his power the constitution of his country from further aggression, and a Judiciary whose unspotted record has never yet been tarnished with a base subserviency to the unholy demands of passion and hatred, let us indulge the hope that the hour of the country's redemption is at hand, and that even in the wronged and ruined South there is a fair prospect for better days and happier hours when our people can unite again in celebrating the national festivals as in the olden time.

129

African American Suffrage in the South (1867, 1876)

One of the critical and hotly debated issues of Reconstruction was the extension of civil rights to the freedmen. The initial Reconstruction plans called for the protection of African Americans' rights, mainly to protect the former slaves from possible retaliation at the hands of their former masters. Led by some Radical Republicans, Congress implemented its plan of Reconstruction, which required the new state governments in the South to guarantee the right to vote for male African Americans. In 1867 African Americans voted for the first time, often casting their ballots for Republican candidates and helping to establish the Republican party's control of state government. For white southerners, who traditionally voted Democratic, this represented a revolutionary change and caused bitter resentment toward black voters and the Republican party. Some southern whites joined the Ku Klux Klan to intimidate Republicans, while other whites used their economic influence as landowners to intimidate African Americans. The two images below in Harper's Weekly, *a well-respected newspaper of the era, reflect the optimism of African Americans participating in the political process for the first time as well as the reality of voter manipulation. The first image was the cover of the November 16, 1867 issue, while the second image was a double-page illustration in the October 21, 1876 issue.*

Questions to Consider

1. How do the images below differ in their depiction of African Americans' right to vote?

2. What appears to be the status of African Americans voting in the first image? How is the African American portrayed in the second image different? What might you deduce from these differences?

The First Vote Harper's Weekly

SOURCE: Art Resource, NY

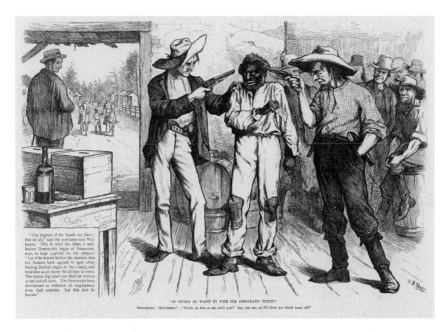

"Of Course He Wants to Vote the Democratic Ticket!"
SOURCE: Stock Montage/Getty Images

3. How does the second image portray southern whites? How do you account for this portrayal?

4. How do you think Howell Cobb ("A White Southern Perspective on Reconstruction," Document 128) would respond to these images?

130

An African American Congressman Calls for Civil Rights (1874)

A critical and hotly debated issue of Reconstruction concerned the extension of civil rights to African Americans, who faced widespread racial discrimination in the South. In the early 1870s a civil rights bill that would outlaw racial discrimination in public places was presented to Congress. Among those speaking out against this legislation was Alexander H.

*Stephens, who had served earlier as vice president of the Confederacy but during Recon-
struction represented Georgia in Congress. Supporting the civil rights bill was Robert B.
Elliott of South Carolina. Born probably in Great Britain, Elliott came to America shortly
after the Civil War. Because of his education and oratorical skills, he quickly became a
prominent African American Republican politician in South Carolina. When he was
elected to Congress in 1870, only a handful of African Americans held national office.
In early 1874, when it became known that Elliott would rebut the former vice president
of the Confederacy on the proposed civil rights bill, the galleries in the House of Representatives were packed, and many Congressmen remained at their seats. Elliott's speech,
excerpted here, was an eloquent call for civil rights. Congress passed the Civil Rights Act
of 1875—the last major piece of Reconstruction legislation.*

Questions to Consider

1. In what ways did Robert Elliott challenge many of the congressmen who
   represented the South?
2. On what grounds did Elliott argue for passing the civil rights legislation?
3. According to Elliott, what is the purpose of the national government?
4. What is the significance of this speech?

Sir, it is scarcely twelve years since that gentleman [Alexander H. Stephens of
Georgia] shocked the civilized world by announcing the birth of a government
which rested on human slavery as its corner-stone. The progress of events has
swept away that *pseudo*-government which rested on greed, pride, and tyranny;
and the race whom he then ruthlessly spurned and trampled on are here to meet
him in debate, and to demand that the rights which are enjoyed by their former
oppressors—who vainly sought to overthrow a Government which they could
not prostitute to the base uses of slavery—shall be accorded to those who even
in the darkness of slavery kept their allegiance true to freedom and the Union.
Sir, the gentleman from Georgia has learned much since 1861; but he is still
a laggard. Let him put away entirely the false and fatal theories which have so
greatly marred an otherwise enviable record. Let him accept, in its fullness and
beneficence, the great doctrine that American citizenship carries with it every
civil and political right which manhood can confer. Let him lend his influence,
with all his masterly ability, to complete the proud structure of legislation which
makes this nation worthy of the great declaration which heralded its birth, and
he will have done that which will most nearly redeem his reputation in the eyes
of the world, and best vindicate the wisdom of that policy which has permitted
him to regain his seat upon this floor.

To the diatribe of the gentleman from Virginia, [Mr. John T. Harris] who
spoke on yesterday, and who so far transcended the limits of decency and
propriety as to announce upon this floor that his remarks were addressed to
white men alone, I shall have no word of reply. Let him feel that a negro was

not only too magnanimous to smite him in his weakness, but was even charitable enough to grant him the mercy of his silence. [Laughter and applause on the floor and in the galleries.] I shall, sir, leave to others less charitable the unenviable and fatiguing task of sifting out of that mass of chaff the few grains of sense that may, perchance, deserve notice. Assuring the gentleman that the negro in this country aims at a higher degree of intellect than that exhibited by him in this debate, I cheerfully commend him to the commiseration of all intelligent men the world over—black men as well as white men.

Sir, equality before the law is now the broad, universal, glorious rule and mandate of the Republic. No State can violate that. Kentucky and Georgia may crowd their statute-books with retrograde and barbarous legislation; they may rejoice in the odious eminence of their consistent hostility to all the great steps of human progress which have marked our national history since slavery tore down the stars and stripes on Fort Sumter; but, if Congress shall do its duty, if Congress shall enforce the great guarantees which the Supreme Court has declared to be the one pervading purpose of all the recent amendments, then their unwise and unenlightened conduct will fall with the same weight upon the gentlemen from those States who now lend their influence to defeat this bill, as upon the poorest slave who once had no rights which the honorable gentlemen were bound to respect....

No language could convey a more complete assertion of the power of Congress over the subject embraced in the present bill than is here expressed. If the States do not conform to the requirements of this clause, if they continue to deny to any person within their jurisdiction the equal protection of the laws, or as the Supreme Court had said, "deny equal justice in its courts," then Congress is here said to have power to enforce the constitutional guarantee by appropriate legislation. That is the power which this bill now seeks to put in exercise. It proposes to enforce the constitutional guarantee against inequality and discrimination by appropriate legislation. It does not seek to confer new rights, nor to place rights conferred by State citizenship under the protection of the United States, but simply to prevent and forbid inequality and discrimination on account of race, color, or previous condition of servitude. Never was there a bill more completely within the constitutional power of Congress. Never was there a bill which appealed for support more strongly to that sense of justice and fair-play which has been said, and in the main with justice, to be a characteristic of the Anglo-Saxon race, The Constitution warrants it; the Supreme Court sanctions it; justice demands it.

Sir, I have replied to the extent of my ability to the arguments which have been presented by the opponents of this measure. I have replied also to some of the legal propositions advanced by gentlemen on the other side; and now that I am about to conclude, I am deeply sensible of the imperfect manner in which I have performed the task. Technically, this bill is to decide upon the civil status of the colored American citizen; a point disputed at the very formation of our present Government, when by a short-sighted policy, a policy repugnant to true republican government, one negro counted as three-fifths of a man. The logical result of this mistake of the framers of the Constitution strengthened the cancer of slavery, which finally spread its poisonous tentacles over the southern portion of the body-politic. To arrest its growth and save the nation we have passed through the harrowing operation of intestine war, dreaded at all times, resorted to at the last extremity, like the surgeon's knife, but absolutely necessary to extirpate the disease which threatened with the life of the nation the overthrow of civil and political liberty on this continent. In that dire extremity the members of the race which I have the honor in part to represent—the race which pleads for justice at your hands to-day, forgetful of their inhuman and brutalizing servitude at the South, their degradation and ostracism at the North—flew willingly and gallantly to the support of the national Government. Their sufferings, assistance, privations, and trials in the swamps and in the rice-fields, their valor on the land and on the sea, is a part of the ever-glorious record which makes up the history of a nation preserved, and might, should I urge the claim, incline you to respect and guarantee their rights and privileges as citizens of our common Republic. But I remember that valor, devotion, and loyalty are not always rewarded according to their just deserts, and that after the battle some who have borne the brunt of the fray may, through neglect or contempt, be assigned to a subordinate place, while the enemies in war may be preferred to the sufferers.

The results of the war, as seen in reconstruction, have settled forever the political status of my race. The passage of this bill will determine the civil status, not only of the negro, but of any other class of citizens who may feel themselves discriminated against. It will form the cap-stone of that temple of liberty, begun on this continent under discouraging circumstances, carried on in spite of the sneers of monarchists and the cavils of pretended friends of freedom, until at last it stands in all its beautiful symmetry and proportions, a building the grandest which the world has ever seen, realizing the most sanguine expectations and the highest hopes of those who, in the name of equal, impartial, and universal liberty, laid the foundation stones....

131

The Situation for African Americans in the South (1879)

Much of the Reconstruction legislation and policies were designed to protect the freedmen from possible retaliation at the hands of their former masters and allow African Americans to make their way in the South. In 1867, African Americans voted for the first time in the South, often casting their ballots for Republican candidates and helping to establish the Republican Party's control of state governments. For many white southerners, most of whom were Democrats, this represented revolutionary change and caused bitter resentment toward black voters and the Republican Party. A resurgence of Democratic Party power in the South toppled many Republican-controlled state governments until 1877, when—as part of a "bargain" that allowed Rutherford B. Hayes to become president—federal troops were removed from the South and the last Republican state governments collapsed. This event signaled the end of Reconstruction. Within a short time, thousands of African Americans began migrating from the South into the West. The newsmagazine The Nation *explained the motives for this "flight" in an editorial, which is excerpted here. In 1879, about 6,000 African Americans moved to Kansas, and probably as many as 20,000 came the following year. These individuals were called the "Exodusters" for making the exodus from the South.*

Questions to Consider

1. According to *The Nation*, what were the problems that African Americans faced during Reconstruction?

2. For what reasons did some African Americans leave the South?

3. What does this article reveal about race relations and economic conditions in the South after Reconstruction?

It would be difficult to conceive of a situation less favorable to healthy social progress than that in which the negroes at the South found themselves since the war. They were very poor, and very ignorant, and very timid, and surrounded by fierce, war-like, and contemptuous neighbors of a different race. Their ignorance, too, did not consist in the want of book-learning, but in the want of the common discipline of civilized life. All this was bad enough, or would have been bad enough, even if they had nothing to trouble them but the difficulty of getting a livelihood. They were, however, armed with the franchise, and were at once plunged into a sea of troubles which even the best equipped races would have found it difficult to navigate. The party which gave them the ballot had really no means of protecting them in the enjoyment of it, and yet had the strongest interest in preventing the Democrats from getting the benefit of it. Accordingly, it had to resort for this purpose to keeping alive among the negroes as long as possible a spirit of hatred and distrust towards the whites, and at the same time to nourishing the passions of the war at the North by stories, some true and some false, of negro wrongs. The whites, on their side, rather helped this plan by the savage means to which they resorted, in those States in which the negroes were in majority, to overturn or prevent negro rule. The effect of the struggle on the unfortunate colored people has, of course, been bad; the wonder it has not been worse. It has kept them in a state of permanent hostility with their white neighbors, and has filled their minds with vague expectations of advancement or elevation of some kind from the Northern Republicans.

SOURCE: "The Flight of the Negroes," *The Nation* 28 (10 April 1879): 242.

That they should have, under these circumstances, cultivated the soil as faithfully as the Southern crop returns show them to have done, and at the same time purchased so much land, and taken so much advantage of the schools, is very remarkable, and suggests some melancholy reflections as to what they might have accomplished during the past fifteen years if they had enjoyed thorough security, and had not been compelled to take part in the electioneering contests of their white countrymen the minute they crossed the threshold of civilization. The flight of several thousand of them in a sort of panic from Louisiana and Mississippi, with accounts of which the papers are now filled, is dismal reading enough, because it is largely the result of delusions of one sort or another, and the danger is that it will be fostered and used during the next year as a fine campaign incident. The immense misery that it is about to produce will, of course, cause the managers and stump-speakers little concern.

When one reads in the correspondence of the Stalwart paper which is making the most of it for party purposes, that the negroes in South Carolina are ceasing to purchase homesteads and are hoarding their money, we perceive clearly enough that the more thrifty and well-to-do are alarmed by something that is impending, rather than suffering from anything which has happened in the past. A state of things in which a poor man has been able to save money to buy a homestead as tens of thousands of negroes have done, is not one in which he is likely to think himself unhappy or ill-used. What is probably alarming this class is the accounts which have been circulated amongst them of the evils which are likely to befall them now that the Democrats have secured control of Congress. If the Stalwart reports of their condition during the past ten years, however, were true, nothing the Democrats could now do would have any terrors for them. Senator Dawes told the people of Massachusetts in 1870 that there was not a negro at the South who did not fear when he went to bed at night that he would have his throat cut or his cabin burnt before morning. The New York *Times* says that for a long time past Christmas Day and election days—that is, two days in the year—"have been appropriated [by the Southern whites] for the sole purpose of killing 'peart niggers'"; the other days of the year being reserved for "robbery and personal violence." Moreover, we learn from the same paper that during recent years, while the negroes have been raising these tremendous crops of cotton and sugar, the whites "gambled, drank whiskey, and improved their skill as marksmen by shooting offhand at a servant who did not please them." One would think that a laboring man who was murdered regularly on Christmas day and election day, and was robbed and assaulted on other days, besides occasionally serving as mark for a drunken man's rule, would have little to fear in this world from any change in the Government. Nevertheless, there can be no doubt that the thrifty colored men at the South were pretty well off; that a very large number were, in spite of many difficulties, making their way in the world, and that the accounts from Republican sources of that are to result from Democratic rule have determined them to get by hook or by crook into a State in which the Government would be friendly to them.

The impelling motives of the poorer and more shiftless class of emigrants in abandoning their homes are not difficult to divine either. Both the planters and the laborers at the South resumed their farming at the close of the war absolutely without capital and without business habits. Little or no money passes between them and the negro subsists during the year on supplies furnished him on a credit account either by the planter or that still greater man in Southern society nowadays, the cross-roads storekeeper. This, of course, means monstrous prices, and probably a good deal of fraud in the tally. No laboring man who lived in this way anywhere, be he black or white, ever rises above the direst poverty or escapes debt. Laborers suffer terribly from the process at the North, and it would be difficult to say what legal remedy could be devised for it. It is probable, too, that all negroes suffer in nerves about election-time. Either the Democrats "intimidate" them to keep them from polls, or the Republicans assure them that they will be intimidated, and between the two they have a month every year of great anxiety and no matter which side wins, it brings no change in their condition. But if the emigration could be properly conducted, and emigrants were able to take care of themselves until they found employment or raised crops, there would be little to regret about it. In fact it would be an excellent remedy for the trouble some of the Southern States. There are too many negroes now in South Carolina, Louisiana, and Mississippi both for their own good and that of the whites. Profusion of labor generally means misery for the laborer, and the negroes' best chance of social and political advancement lies in scattering themselves in more advanced communities....

16

The West

Following the Civil War, many Americans expressed a renewed interest in the trans-Mississippi West. With the war concluded, construction proceeded on the trans-Mississippi railroad and people began migrating to the Great Plains region. For many, especially those displaced by the war, the West offered a new beginning. The individuals who began to flood the West in the last third of the nineteenth century included Chinese and Irish laborers, African American cowboys, white American farmers, and European immigrant miners, to name but a few. The land they entered was not an empty one, but one long inhabited by Native Americans and Mexicans. The meeting of these different groups triggered conflict over the region's future. The following documents describe the interactions of these groups in the western environment.

132

A Native American Remembers Life on the Great Plains (1870s)

After the Civil War, increased white migration through the Great Plains threatened the Native American way of life. Available land and rumors of gold and silver deposits lured whites to the region, often in violation of earlier treaty agreements that protected Indian tribal hunting land. These white incursions threatened the nomadic lifestyle of many Native

American tribes on the Great Plains. Many of the Plains Indians traveled great distances in search of the American bison, or buffalo, the main source of food and shelter. In 1913, anthropologist Joseph Dixon recorded the accounts of Native Americans describing their lives, which he published as The Vanishing Race. *Excerpted here is a Native American describing a buffalo hunt conducted by his Blackfoot tribe.*

Questions to Consider

1. According to this account, how were the buffalo hunted?
2. What duties did the women and men perform? Why were there such distinctions?
3. In what ways did the buffalo influence this tribe?
4. How might William N. Byers ("A Western Newspaper Editorial on the Custer Massacre," Document 135) respond to this selection?

… Then the chiefs sent for the leaders and warriors; we called them "crazy dogs." The leaders of the crazy dogs came into the tepee of Mountain Chief and Lame Bull, and my father, Mountain Chief, told these two crazy dogs to start before sunrise, and to take with them the other crazy dogs to find where there was a lot of good fresh water, and a lot of grass where they might camp, and also where they might find the nearest herd of buffalo. The crazy dogs found a good place where there was plenty of buffalo and water, and they marked the camp…. Four Bear went to the camp, told the people concerning their new camp, and the next morning the women took the medicine pipes and put them at the side of the tepee looking toward the direction where they were going to camp. Husbands told wives to go out and see on which side of the tepee the medicine pipes were placed, that they might know where they were going. Then the wives came in and told them that the medicine pipes pointed in a northerly direction. The husbands told the wives that the camp was going to move north. The camp broke up that very morning…. After everybody had left the camp, the chiefs followed the procession. When they thought it was noon they made a halt. They took their travois and saddles from the horses, and rested; then had their lunch. The chiefs then told Four Bear to get the camp in traveling shape again, and went on. Finally they came to the spot where the camping place was marked…. Four Bear was then told to get the people settled, to tie up the buffalo horses, and get ready for the hunt. Four Bear then told the people not to get a meal but to get a little lunch, and get ready for the hunt. Then the chiefs started out for the buffalo, the hunters following. They stopped halfway before they got to the herd, and told all the hunters not to start for the buffalo until they were ready and everybody had a fair chance…. If a hunter hit a buffalo with one arrow, he gave a scream, and that indicated that he had hit him just once. There were very few guns in those days and those were flint-locks. Sometimes when a hunter rode side by

SOURCE: Joseph K. Dixon, ed., "Mountain Chief," *The Vanishing Race: The Last Great Indian Council* (Garden City, NY, 1913), 104–11.

side with a buffalo, and shot the animal, the arrow would go clear through. The Indians were very proud and careful of their arrows. They did not wish to break them. That is the reason why they shot them on the side, so that when the buffalo fell the arrow would not be broken. Lots of the buffalo fell on their knees, and would begin to move from side to side. Then the Indian, for fear that the arrow would be broken, jumped off his horse and pulled it out. The hunter then tied his horse to the horns of the buffalo for fear that he might be attacked by enemies at any moment. After this they took out their knives and sharpened them on hard steel, like the flint with which they made fire. All the time they were sharpening their knives they were looking around for the approach of the enemy. The fire steel was scarce, we had to use rocks most of the time. The knives we procured from the Hudson Bay Company. When we killed a buffalo bull, we placed him on his knees, then we began to skin him down the back of the neck, down the backbone, splitting it on each side. The cows we laid on their backs, and cut down the middle. We used the buffalo cowhide for buffalo robes; the buffalo bull's hides were split down the back because from this hide we made war shields, parflesche bags, and saddle blankets. The husbands would tell the wives to take care of the heads. The wives took the brains out of the buffalo skull and mixed them with the largest part of the liver, and after mixing well, used the brains and liver in tanning hides. Then the wife was told to take out the tripe and skin it, for they used the skin as a bucket with which to carry water when they got home. They had strips of rawhide about three feet long and a quarter of an inch wide and tied the meat so that they could carry it home on the horses. They took the backbone after it had been cleaned of the flesh, and tied the meat to that and threw it over the back of the horse so that the load would not hurt the back of the horse. When we got home with the meat we unloaded. The men who had gone without their wives simply got off their horses and went into the tepee. The women rushed out to get the meat. Then the women took the horse with the meat on it to their father-in-law. Then the mother-in-law hurried to get the meal, taking the ribs of the buffalo, setting them up against the fire to roast. After the meal was cooked, it was cut in slices and placed in a wooden bowl, and the mother-in-law took the meat over to the lodge of her son-in-law. That was all we had for our meal. We had no coffee or anything else to eat, but we made a good meal from the meat of the buffalo.... About that time night came on, and the chiefs sent for Four Bear, and Four Bear would go around and tell the people that the grass in the camp was pretty well taken up. The next morning the women would take their medicine pipes and put them on the side, indicating where the next camp was going to be, and thus we went on from camp to camp.

133

Hunting Buffalo on the Great Plains (c. 1875)

The great buffalo herds that roamed the Great Plains provided the various Native American tribes with food, shelter, and clothing. Whites also killed the buffalo to provide meat for railroad construction crews, and individuals like William F. Cody earned his nickname "Buffalo Bill" as a proficient hunter for train crews. Some buffalo were killed for sport, and, in some instances, such sport consisted of hunters shooting from excursion trains in contests to see how many animals could be killed. In the early 1870s a commercial process to tan buffalo hides was developed and a fashion fad for buffalo robes and overcoats led to a systematic slaughter that depleted the once huge herds. Among those who participated in the business of buffalo hunting was W. S. Glenn, who provides a firsthand description below.

Questions to Consider

1. In what ways was buffalo hunting a business?

2. According to Glenn what were the various methods to kill buffalo? Which was best, and why?

3. In what ways were the buffalo hunting techniques Glenn described different from those depicted by the Blackfoot Indian ("A Native American Remembers Life on the Great Plains," Document 132)?

About this time the hunt had grown to such an enormous business that J. R. Lobenstein [Loganstein], a capitalist of that time, and ram rodder of the buffalo hunt, ... furnished the capital and contracts were sub-let for robe hides, dry hides, bull hides, etc. Merchants were furnished supplies, equipments, etc., [and] they in turn furnished smaller men, who kept up with hunters ready to supply them. An enormous amount of this business was done on time. As they had begun to make money out of it, they would supply any hunter who had a team and wagon. Now all this while the hunter was pegging away and it was not until afterwards that they got it down to a system to make it profitable over a scant living.

SOURCE: "The Buffalo Hunt" in Rex W. Strickland, ed., "The Recollections of W. S. Glenn, Buffalo Hunter," *Panhandle-Plains Historical Review* 22 (1949): 20–26. Copyright © 1949 Panhandle-Plains Historical Museum. Reproduced by permission.

There was several methods to kill [buffaloes] and each [hunter] adopted his own course and plan. They would get together and while one gained a point from another, he, in turn, would gain a point from him. One method was to run beside them, shooting them as they ran. Another was to shoot from the rear, what was termed tail shooting: [always shooting] the hindmost buffalo and when a day's hunt was done, they would be strung on the ground for a mile or more, from ten to fifteen yards apart, and in this way the skinner had so much territory to go over he couldn't make wages....

Another method of hunting was to leave your horse out of sight after you had determined the direction and course of the wind, and then get as near as possible. If the herd was lying at rest, he would pick out some buffalo that was standing up on watch and shoot his ball in the side of him so that it would not go through, but would lodge in the flesh; as on many times it had been proven by men [who were] well hid and the wind taking the sound of the gun and the whizz of the bullet off, [that] if a ball passed through a buffalo, the herd would stampede and run for miles. A buffalo shot in this manner would merely hump up his back as if he had the colic and commence to mill round and round in a slow walk. The other buffalo sniffing the blood and following would not be watching the hunter, and he would continue to shoot the outside cow buffalo; if there were old cows they would take them as there would be some two or three offsprings following her. If she would hump up, he would know that he had the range, and in this way hold the herd as long as they acted in this way as well as the well trained cowpuncher would hold his herd, only the hunter would use his gun. This was termed mesmerising the buffalo so that we could hold them on what we termed a stand, which afterwards proved to be the most successful way of killing the buffalo.

It was not always the best shot but the best hunter that succeeded, that is, the man who piled his buffalo in a pile so as to be more convenient for the skinner to get at and not have to run all over the country....

The hunter was hired by the piece: if robe hides were worth $3.00, [he was] given twenty-five cents for everyone that he killed and was brought in by the skinners—was tallied up at camp. It was the camp rustler's business to keep tally of the number of hides killed each day. If the hides were worth $2.50, he [the hunter] got 20 cents; $2.00, he got 15 cents; $1.50, he got 10 cents; and $1.00, he got 5 cents....

... At the Doby Walls fight [the Adobe Walls, June 27, 1874], the hunters [used] all classes of guns, such as the Spencer, Springfield, Winchester and six-shooters, also all classes of buffalo guns, including a new sample 45, which Sharp had just sent out, ... Still some were not satisfied, so went outside and stepped off a 150 yards and commenced to pile dry bull hides ten in a bunch, and began to shoot with all four guns—as they went through so easily, they added more and continued to add until they had shot through 32 [hides] and one bullet stook [stuck] in the thirty-third one and it proved to be the new gun. All had to have a shot with the new gun and as it gave entire satisfaction, they sent word back that this was the gun for the buffalo, and all of them ordered a gun. Sharp began to manufacture these rifles as fast as he could in

various lengths and this gun, as it afterwards proved, was the cause of the extermination of the buffalo, as before this they had increased faster than killed out as
it took too many shots to get a buffalo....

. I have seen their bodies so thick after being skinned, that they would look
like logs where a hurricane had passed through a forrest [sic]. If they were lying
on a hillside, the rays of the sun would make it look like a hundred glass windows. These buffalo would lie in this way until warm weather, drying up, and
I have seen them piled fifty or sixty in a pile where the hunter had made a stand.
As the skinner commenced on the edge, he would have to roll it out of the way
to have room to skin the next, and when finished they would be rolled up as
thick as saw logs around a mill. In this way a man could ride over a field and
pick out the camps that were making the most money out of the hunt....

A remarkable good hunter would kill seventy-five to a hundred in a day, an
average hunter about fifty, and a common one twenty-five, some hardly enough
to run a camp. It was just like in any other business. A good skinner would skin
from sixty to seventy-five, and average man from thirty to forty, and a common
one from fifteen to twenty-five. These skinners were also paid by the hide, about
five cents less than the hunter was getting for killing, being furnished with a
grind stone, knives and steel and a team and wagon. The men were furnished
with some kind of a gun, not as valuable as Sharp's rifle, to kill cripples with,
also kips and calves that were standing around. In several incidents [instances?]
it has been known to happen while the skinner was busy, they would slip up
and knock him over. Toward the latter part of the hunt, when all the big ones
were killed, I have seen as many as five hundred up to a thousand in a bunch,
nothing but calves and have ridden right up to them, if the wind was right....

134

A Century of Dishonor (1881)

*In the years following the Civil War, problems with Native Americans in the West became
increasingly difficult to resolve. The federal government's policy of creating reservations by
treaty with specific Indian tribes did not work. President Ulysses S. Grant endorsed the
"peace policy," which called for "concentrating" most Plains Indians into two large reservations: one in the Indian Territory (Oklahoma) and the other in the Dakota Territory.
Government management of these reservations was poor, and Native American resentment
increased. Other forces compounded the situation; new discoveries of gold and silver, westward railroad expansion, the destruction of the buffalo, and white demands for more land
only heightened tensions. Struggling against these threats to their civilization, some Native*

Americans resisted. In a series of Indian wars, the U.S. Army subdued hostile tribes and pushed Native Americans to the reservations. Alarmed at the plight of the Native American, Massachusetts-born Helen Hunt Jackson studied the history of Indian–white relations. Jackson's book, A Century of Dishonor *(1881), chronicled the federal government's mistreatment of Native Americans.*

Questions to Consider

1. According to Jackson, what motivated whites to mistreat Native Americans?
2. What shaped white views about the Native Americans?
3. What does Jackson hope to accomplish with her book?
4. How might William N. Byers ("A Western Newspaper Editorial on the Custer Massacre," Document 135) have responded to Jackson's view of Indians? Of the federal government?

… It makes little difference, however, where one opens the record of the history of the Indians; every page and every year has its dark stain. The story of one tribe is the story of all, varied only by differences of time and place; but neither time nor place makes any difference in the main facts. Colorado is as greedy and unjust in 1880 as was Georgia in 1830, and Ohio in 1795; and the United States Government breaks promises now as deftly as then, and with an added ingenuity from long practice.

One of its strongest supports in so doing is the wide-spread sentiment among the people of dislike to the Indian, of impatience with his presence as a "barrier to civilization," and distrust of it as a possible danger. The old tales of the frontier life, with its horrors of Indian warfare, have gradually, by two or three generations' telling, produced in the average mind something like an hereditary instinct of unquestioning and unreasoning aversion which it is almost impossible to dislodge or soften.

There are hundreds of pages of unimpeachable testimony on the side of the Indian; but it goes for nothing, is set down as sentimentalism or partisanship, tossed aside and forgotten.

President after president has appointed commission after commission to inquire into and report upon Indian affairs, and to make suggestions as to the best methods of managing them. The reports are filled with eloquent statements of wrongs done to the Indians, of perfidies on the part of the Government; they counsel, as earnestly as words can, a trial of the simple and unperplexing expedients of telling truth, keeping promises, making fair bargains, dealing justly in all ways and all things. These reports are bound up with the Government's Annual Reports, and that is the end of them. It would probably be no exaggeration to say that not one American citizen out of ten thousand ever sees them or knows that they exist, and yet any one of them, circulated throughout the country, read by the right-thinking, right-feeling men and women of this land, would be of

SOURCE: Helen Hunt Jackson, *A Century of Dishonor* (New York, 1881), 337–40.

itself a "campaign document" that would initiate a revolution which would not subside until the Indians' wrongs were, so far as is now left possible, righted.

In 1869 President Grant appointed a commission of nine men, representing the influence and philanthropy of six leading States, to visit the different Indian reservations, and to "examine all matters pertaining to Indian affairs."

In the report of this commission are such paragraphs as the following: "To assert that 'the Indian will not work' is as true as it would be to say that the white man will not work.

"Why should the Indian be expected to plant corn, fence lands, build houses, or do anything but get food from day to day, when experience has taught him that the product of his labor will be seized by the white man tomorrow? The most industrious white man would become a drone under similar circumstances. Nevertheless, many of the Indians" (the commissioners might more forcibly have said 130,000 of the Indians) "are already at work, and furnish ample refutation of the assertion that 'the Indian will not work.' There is no escape from the inexorable logic of facts.

"The history of the Government connections with the Indians is a shameful record of broken treaties and unfulfilled promises. The history of the border white man's connection with the Indians is a sickening record of murder, outrage, robbery, and wrongs committed by the former, as the rule, and occasional savage outbreaks and unspeakably barbarous deeds of retaliation by the latter, as the exception.

"Taught by the Government that they had rights entitled to respect, when those rights have been assailed by the rapacity of the white man, the arm which should have been raised to protect them has ever been ready to sustain the aggressor.

"The testimony of some of the highest military officers of the United States is on record to the effect that, in our Indian wars, almost without exception, the first aggressions have been made by the white man; and the assertion is supported by every civilian of reputation who has studied the subject. In addition to the class of robbers and outlaws who find impunity in their nefarious pursuits on the frontiers, there is a large class of professedly reputable men who use every means in their power to bring on Indian wars for the sake of the profit to be realized from the presence of troops and the expenditure of Government funds in their midst. They proclaim death to the Indians at all times in words and publications, making no distinction between the innocent and the guilty. They irate the lowest class of men to the perpetration of the darkest deeds against their victims, and as judges and jurymen shield them from the justice due to their crimes. Every crime committed by a white man against an Indian is concealed or palliated. Every offence committed by an Indian against a white man is borne on the wings of the post or the telegraph to the remotest corner of the land, clothed with all the horrors which the reality or imagination can throw around it. Against such influences as these the people of the United States need to be warned."...

135

A Western Newspaper Editorial on the Custer Massacre (1876)

The country was still euphoric over the celebration of the Centennial when word of Colonel George A. Custer's massacre spread throughout the nation. Custer was part of a military operation to drive portions of the disgruntled Sioux (Lakota) tribe back to their reservation when he ordered an attack on the Native American encampment along the Little Big Horn River in present-day southeastern Montana. Custer and 264 of his men were killed in what became known as "Custer's Last Stand." William N. Byers, author of the editorial excerpted here, was considered a western "pioneer," having traveled and lived throughout the West. In 1859, he established the Rocky Mountain News, *the first newspaper in the Colorado Territory, and continued to edit and publish the paper for over nineteen years. Besides his newspaper, Byers took an active role in promoting Colorado statehood and was closely identified with promoting the growth and development of Denver. His editorial reveals much about western attitudes of the time toward Native Americans and easterners.*

Questions to Consider

1. Whom does Byers blame for Custer's massacre?

2. Why does Byers fear the massacre will harm the "new west"?

3. In what ways does Byers's editorial reflect westerners' views about Native Americans and the development of the West?

4. On what issues would Byers and Rising Wolf ("A Native American Remembers the Ghost Dance," Document 137) disagree about the Native Americans?

The wish was father to the thought when yesterday we hazarded the assertion that the report of the annihilation of Custer's command bore the appearance of exaggeration, if not of entire fabrication. The details published in this morning's dispatches, although many of them emanate from not particularly trustworthy newspaper correspondents, forbid further incredulity, and we … accept the terrible truth in all its enormity, that some of the bravest officers in the service and a large fraction of one of the finest cavalry regiments, have fallen victim to the picayune policy that domineers in all matters appertaining to Indian affairs. The

SOURCE: William N. Byers, "Extermination the Only Remedy," *Rocky Mountain News* (Denver), 8 July 1876, p. 2.

blood must boil in the veins of the most fishlike, at reading the horrible story of the massacre of three hundred United States soldiers at the hands of ten times that number of savages, when it is remembered that all this is the fruit of the do-nothing system of the Indian department. Custer and his men have been murdered, not by Indians, who were only the instruments of their death, but by the sleek, smooth talking, Quaker advocates of the peace policy, who have always insisted that the Indian was a man and a brother, and an elder brother, at that, with all the rights of primogeniture. Had the Indian problem been treated properly, long years since it would have been solved, and Custer would not now be a mangled corpse, from there being either no Indians alive to kill him, or the remnants of the race so restrained within bounds that it would not be possible for them to perpetrate the deed that they have. The Indian bureau has all along realized Dicken's [sic] conception of the Circumlocution Office.[*]

How not to do it has ever been its aim, and the success with which it has carried out its design is a blot on the entire fabric of government. What a spectacle, indeed, is it for foreign nations to sneer at, when the great republic of the west, for all its population of forty-four millions of people, allows its soldiers to be overcome by odds of ten to one, although its antagonist numbers but a few paltry thousand of savages. The entire system pursued towards the Indians, crowned as it is with this terrible disaster, is unworthy of the government and a disgrace to the country.

While the entire nation has come to mourn the blot on its escutcheon caused by the catastrophe to Custer, we of the new west have a right to feel outraged, not for the sake of the honor that Falstaff dubbed but a word, but for the wrong that is done as is preventing the increase of our population and capital, by permitting the impression to gain ground abroad that our settlements are liable to hostile inroads. The states people have vague ideas of distance, and the [location] in which Custer and those with him met their death is liable to be located anywhere between Long and Pike's Peaks, while very likely in the extreme east, the Platte is supposed to be the river from which Gen. Reno at last got water, after suffering from a thirty-six hours' thirst. The prosperity of the entire country from the Missouri river to the Rocky Mountains is injured for years to come, more than it will easily be believed, by the destruction of the Seventh cavalry. The shot that killed Custer was heard around the world and everywhere that it aroused the echoes, it frightened possible population and certain capital from the new west. The injury done this entire region, indeed, will be almost irreparable, unless the Sioux are at once exterminated. This is the only alternate. Do what we will, it will be impossible to make it known in the states that Denver is as secure from Indian attack as New York, and that Custer fell half a thousand miles from the northern boundary of Colorado. Distance leads exaggeration to danger. No coward so great as capital, and even the consumptive, flying from the deadly east winds of the coast will think twice before he exposes himself to what he believes to be the scalping knives of the Sioux.

---

[*]This is an allusion to Dicken's novel *Bleak House*.

In the name, then, of the people of the new west, we demand that instant measures be taken to, at once and forever, prevent the possibility of the recent defeat of the troops being repeated. Let the story of Custer's death be lost in the terrible vengeance taken for it. Let real war be in order for once. Custer would never have met with his disaster had he been properly supported. In place of a few scattered companies of cavalry, at least three thousand frontiersmen, together with half that number of regular soldiers should scour the enemy's country, and no quarter should be given, as it certainly has not been taken. The extermination of the Sioux and the destruction of all that is theirs, is necessary for the future prosperity of the entire new west. For years we have had population and capital frightened away from us by fears of the Indians, and we call upon the government for redress at the eleventh hour. And by redress we mean the extermination of the hostile tribes.

136

Cultural Exchange on the Arizona Frontier (1874)

As Americans migrated to the West, they did not enter a vacant land—particularly in the Southwest, where various Native American tribes had lived for several centuries. The Spanish explored the region as early as the 1540s and established trading posts and missions (Santa Fe was made the capital in 1619). As a far-flung northern province of Mexico, the Arizona frontier developed a distinct Spanish–Native American culture. The first Anglos (white traders and settlers) came to Arizona before the Civil War, but they remained a minority until the early twentieth century. The influx of whites brought conflict with the Native Americans; and as outrages on both sides escalated, the U.S. Army was sent to maintain order. In 1874, Captain Jack Summerhayes's unit was detached to Arizona. Accompanying Summerhayes was his recent bride, Martha, a well-educated New England woman who kept an account of life in frontier Arizona, which she later published. The Summerhayeses spent four years on various outposts in Arizona, but one of their initial stops was Ehrenberg, a Colorado River town. In the selection here, Martha Summerhayes observes local (Mexican) customs.

Questions to Consider

1. Why was Summerhayes fascinated with Mexican customs, especially the activities of the women?

2. For what reasons does Summerhayes regret the American way of life in Arizona?

3. What does this document reveal about Anglo relations with local inhabitants in Arizona?

4. What does Summerhayes hope to accomplish with this account?

So work was begun immediately on the kitchen. My first stipulation was, that the new rooms were to have wooden *floors*; for, although the Cocopah Charley kept the adobe floors in perfect condition, by sprinkling them down and sweeping them out every morning, they were quite impossible, especially where it concerned white dresses and children, and the little sharp rocks in them seemed to be so tiring to the feet.

Life as we Americans live it was difficult in Ehrenberg. I often said: "Oh! if we could only live as the Mexicans live, how easy it would be!" For they had their fire built between some stones piled up in their yard, a piece of sheet iron laid over the top: this was the cooking-stove. A pot of coffee was made in the morning early, and the family sat on the low porch and drank it, and ate a biscuit. Then a kettle of *frijoles* was put over to boil. These were boiled slowly for some hours, then lard and salt were added, and they simmered down until they were deliciously fit to eat, and had a thick red gravy.

Then the young matron, or daughter of the house, would mix the peculiar paste of flour and salt and water, for *tortillas*, a species of unleavened bread. These *tortillas* were patted out until they were as large as a dinner plate, and very thin; then thrown onto the hot sheet-iron, where they baked. Each one of the family then got a *tortilla*, the spoonful of beans was laid upon it, and so they managed without the paraphernalia of silver and china and napery.

How I envied them the simplicity of their lives! Besides, the *tortillas* were delicious to eat, and as for the *frijoles*, they were beyond anything I had ever eaten in the shape of beans. I took lessons in the making of *tortillas*. A woman was paid to come and teach me; but I never mastered the art. It is in the blood of the Mexican, and a girl begins at a very early age to make the *tortilla*. It is the most graceful thing to see a pretty Mexican toss the wafer-like disc over her bare arm, and pat it out until transparent.

This was their supper; for, like nearly all people in the tropics, they ate only twice a day. Their fare was varied sometimes by a little *carni seca*, pounded up and stewed with *chile verde* or *chile colorado*.

Now if you could hear the soft, exquisite, affectionate drawl with which the Mexican woman says *chile verde* you could perhaps come to realize what an important part the delicious green pepper plays in the cookery of these countries. They do not use it in its raw state, but generally roast it whole, stripping off the thin skin and throwing away the seeds, leaving only the pulp, which acquires a fine flavor by having been roasted or toasted over the hot coals.

SOURCE: Martha Summerhayes, *Vanished Arizona: Recollections of the Army Life of a New England Woman*, 2nd ed. (Salem, MA, 1911), 144–48.

The women were scrupulously clean and modest, and always wore, when in their *casa*, a low-necked and short-sleeved white linen *camisa*, fitting neatly, with bands around neck and arms. Over this they wore a calico skirt; always white stockings and black slippers. When they ventured out, the younger women put on muslin gowns, and carried parasols. The older women wore a linen towel thrown over their heads, or, in cool weather, the black *riboso*. I often cried: "Oh! if I could only dress as the Mexicans do! Their necks and arms do look so cool and clean."

I have always been sorry I did not adopt their fashion of house apparel. Instead of that, I yielded to the prejudices of my conservative partner, and sweltered during the day in high-necked and long-sleeved white dresses, kept up the table in American fashion, ate American food in so far as we could get it, and all at the expense of strength....

There was no market, but occasionally a Mexican killed a steer, and we bought enough for one meal; but having no ice, and no place away from the terrific heat, the meat was hung out under the *ramada* with a piece of netting over it, until the first heat had passed out of it, and then it was cooked.

The Mexican, after selling what meat he could, cut the rest into thin strips and hung it up on ropes to dry in the sun. It dried hard and brittle, in its natural state, so pure is the air on that wonderful river bank. They called this *carni seca*, and the Americans called it "jerked beef."

Patrocina often prepared me a dish of this, when I was unable to taste the fresh meat. She would pound it fine with a heavy pestle, and then put it to simmer, seasoning it with the green or red pepper. It was most savory. There was no butter at all during the hot months, but our hens laid a few eggs, and the Quartermaster was allowed to keep a small lot of commissary stores, from which we drew our supplies of flour, ham, and canned things. We were often without milk for weeks at a time, for the cows crossed the river to graze, and sometimes could not get back until the river fell again, and they could pick their way back across the shifting sand bars.

The Indian brought the water every morning in buckets from the river. It looked like melted chocolate. He filled the barrels, and when it had settled clear, the *ollas* were filled, and thus the drinking water was a trifle cooler than the air. One day it seemed unusually cool, so I said: "Let us see by the thermometer how cool the water really is." We found the temperature of the water to be 86 degrees; but that, with the air at 122 in the shade, seemed quite refreshing to drink.

137

A Native American Remembers the Ghost Dance (1890)

By 1890, the Great Plains Indian tribes had experienced severe hardships. Whites had invaded their traditional lands, the American bison (buffalo) was nearly exterminated, new diseases ravaged some tribes—often with fatal results, and the Native Americans were placed on reservations with unfulfilled promises of government assistance. Disenchanted and witnessing the collapse of their culture, many Plains Indians embraced the preachings of a Paiute messiah named Wovoka (also known as Jack Wilson), who led a revival of the Ghost Dance on a Nevada reservation. A religious movement soon spread throughout the West. Wovoka taught the Ghost Dance ceremony and instructed the Native Americans to live peacefully with one another and with the whites. Many tribes sent delegations to meet with Wovoka to learn the Ghost Dance, so that the promised return of the old ways could be achieved. Among those who consulted Wovoka was Rising Wolf, who retold his Ghost Dance participation to novelist Hamlin Garland. Rising Wolf was interviewed while Garland toured the West to gather materials for future writing projects. Rising Wolf's account, excerpted here, was published in the popular McClure's *Magazine. Garland later won the Pulitzer prize (1921) and was known for his realistic depiction of western life.*

Questions to Consider

1. For what reasons were the Plains Indians attracted to the Ghost Dance?
2. What were the reactions of whites to the Ghost Dance?
3. What does this account reveal about the significance of the Ghost Dance?
4. How might Helen Hunt Jackson (*A Century of Dishonor*, Document 134) have responded to this document?

One night there came into our midst a Snake messenger with a big tale. "Away in the west," he said to us in sign talk, "a wonderful man has come. He speaks all languages and he is the friend of all red men. He is white, but not like other white men. He has been nailed to a tree by the whites. I saw the holes in his hands. He teaches a new dance, and that is to gather all the Indians together in council. He wants a few head men of all tribes to meet him where the big

SOURCE: Hamlin Garland, "Rising Wolf—Ghost Dancer," *McClure's Magazine* 12 (January 1899): 241–48.

mountains are, in the place where the lake is surrounded by pictured rocks. There he will teach us how to make mighty magic and drive away the white man and bring back the buffalo."

All that he told us we pondered long, and I said: "It is well, I will go to see this man. I will learn his dance."...

A day passed, and he did not come; but one night when we sat in council over his teachings, he suddenly stepped inside the circle. He was a dark man, but not so dark as we were. He had long hair on his chin, and long, brown head-hair, parted in the middle. I looked for the wounds on his wrists; I could not see any. He moved like a big chief, tall and swift. He could speak all tongues. He spoke Dakota, and many understood. I could understand the language of the Cut-throat people, and this is what he said: My people, before the white man came you were happy. You had many buffalo to eat and tall grass for your ponies. You could come and go like the wind. When it was cold, you could go into the valleys to the south, where the healing springs are; and when it grew warm, you could return to the mountains in the north. The white man came. He dug the bones of our mother, the earth. He tore her bosom with steel. He built big trails and put iron horses on them. He fought you and beat you, and put you in barren places where a horned toad would die. He said you must stay there; you must not hunt in the mountains.

Then he breathed his poison upon the buffalo, and they disappeared. They vanished into the earth. One day they covered the hills, the next nothing but their bones remained. Would you remove the white man? Would you have the buffalo come back? Listen, and I will tell you how to make great magic. I will teach you a mystic dance, and then let everybody go home and dance. When the grass is green, the change will come. Let everybody dance four days in succession, and on the fourth day the white man will disappear and the buffalo come back; our dead will return with the buffalo....

You have forgotten the ways of the fathers; therefore great distress is upon you. You must throw away all that the white man has brought you. Return to the dress of the fathers. You must use the sacred colors, red and white, and the sacred grass, and in the spring, when the willows are green, the change will come....

Then he taught us the song and the dance which white people call the ghost dance, and we danced all together, and while we danced near him he sat with bowed head. No one dared to speak to him. The firelight shone on him. Suddenly he disappeared. No one saw him go. Then we were sorrowful, for we wished him to remain with us....

At last we reached home, and I called a big dance, and at the dance I told the people what I had seen, and they were very glad. "Teach us the dance," they cried to me....

Then they did as I bid, and when the moon was round as a shield, we beat the drum and called the people to dance....

The agent came to see us dance, but we did not care. He was a good man, and we felt sorry for him, for he must also vanish with the other white people. He listened to our crying, and looked long, and his interpreter told him we prayed to the great Spirits to destroy the white man and bring back the buffalo. Then he called me with his hand, and because he was a good man I went to him. He asked me what the dance meant, and I told him, and he said, "It must stop." "I cannot stop it," I said. "The Great Spirits have said it. It must go on."...

On the fourth night, while we danced, soldiers came riding down the hills, and their chiefs, in shining white hats, came to watch us. All night we prayed and danced. We prayed in our songs.

But the agent smiled, and the soldiers of the white chiefs sat not far off, their guns in their hands, and the moon passed by, and the east grew light, and we were very weary, and my heart was heavy. I looked to see the red come in the east. "When the sun looks over the hills, then it will be," I said to my friends. "The white man will become as smoke. The wind will sweep him away."

As the sun came near we all danced hard. My voice was almost gone. My feet were numb, my legs were weak, but my heart was big....

But the sun came up, the soldiers fired a big gun, and the soldier chiefs laughed. Then the agent called to me, "Your Great Spirit can do nothing. Your Messiah lied."...

All day I lay there with my head covered. I did not want to see the light of the sun. I heard the drum stop and the singing die away. Night came, and then on the hills I heard the wailing of my people. Their hearts were gone. Their bones were weary.

When I rose, it was morning. I flung off my blankets, and looked down on the valley where the tepees of the white soldiers stood. I heard their drums and their music. I had made up my mind. The white man's trail was wide and dusty by reason of many feet passing thereon, but it was long. The trail of my people was ended.

138

Populist Party Platform (1892)

In the late 1880s the American farmer increased agricultural production yet plummeting prices and "middle men" costs removed much of the anticipated profit; some farmers went bankrupt and were forced off their land. Compounding this situation was deflation, where the value of money increased and it became increasingly difficult for farmers to pay off loans that had fixed rates. In response to these circumstances and disillusioned with both traditional political parties, the People's Party (Populist) was formed in 1892 to represent small producers—particularly farmers—against large corporations, the railroads and banks.

Labeling itself a party of reform, the People's Party was a fusion of several agricultural groups, especially the Farmer's Alliance, which advocated a program to rectify agricultural problems while representing the interests of the common man. Ignatius Donnelly, an enthusiastic Populist, drafted the Omaha Platform, which the People's Party national convention, meeting in Omaha, Nebraska, accepted on July 4, 1892. The platform expressed Populist frustrations with the influence of big business while offering some remedies to correct the situation. Excerpted below is the platform as reported in the newspaper Omaha Morning World-Herald.

Questions to Consider

1. In what ways would the platform resolve agricultural problems and also provide for more democracy?

2. What aspects of the platform are designed to attract votes from nonfarmers?

3. The Populist platform was considered radical in the 1890s. What are some of its more radical reforms? What happens to most of these reforms?

4. In what ways is the Populist platform similar to the New Deal policies described in "The New Deal in Review," (Document 189)?

While our sympathies as a party of reform are naturally upon the side of every proposition which will tend to make men intelligent, virtuous, and temperate, we nevertheless regard these questions, important as they are, as secondary to the great issues now pressing for solution, and upon which not only our individual prosperity but the very existence of free institutions depend; and we ask all men to first help us determine whether we are to have a republic to administer before we differ as to the conditions upon which it is to be administered, believing that the forces of reform this day organized will never cease to move forward until every wrong is remedied and equal rights and equal privileges securely established for all the men and women of this country.

We declare, therefore—

First—That the union of the labor forces of the United States this day consummated shall be permanent and perpetual; may its spirit enter into all hearts for the salvation of the Republic and the uplifting of mankind.

Second—Wealth belongs to him who creates it, and every dollar taken from industry without an equivalent is robbery. "If any will not work neither shall he eat." The interests of rural and civil labor are the same; their enemies are identical.

Third—We believe that the time has come when the railroad corporations will either own the people or the people must own the railroads; and should the government enter upon the work of owning and managing any and all railroads, we should favor an amendment to the constitution by which all persons engaged in the government service shall be placed under a civil service regulation of the

SOURCE: "People's Party Platform," *Omaha Morning World-Herald*, 5 July 1892, p. 6.

most rigid character, so as to prevent the increase of power of the national administration by the use of such additional government employees.

We demand that national currency, safe, sound, and flexible, issued by the general government only, a full legal tender for all debts, public and private, and that without the use of banking corporations, a just, equitable, and efficient means of distribution direct to the people, at a tax not to exceed 2 per cent per annum, be provided, as set forth in the sub-treasury plan of the farmers' alliance, or some better system; also by payments in discharge of its obligations for public improvements.

We demand free and unlimited coinage of silver and gold at the present legal ratio of 16 to 1.

We demand that the amount of the circulating medium be speedily increased to not less than $50 per capita.

We demand a graduated income tax.

We believe that the money of the country should be kept as much as possible in the hands of the people, and hence we demand that all state and national revenues shall be limited to the necessary expenses of the government, economically and honestly administered.

We demand that postal savings banks be established by the government for the safe deposit of the earnings of the people and to facilitate exchange.

Transportation being a means of exchange and a public necessity, the government should own and operate the railroads in the interest of the people.

The telegraph and telephone, like the post office system, being a necessity for the transmission of news, should be owned and operated by the government in the interest of the people.

The land, including all the natural sources of wealth, is the heritage of the people, and should not be monopolized for speculative purposes, and alien ownership of land should be prohibited. All land now held by railroads and other corporations in excess of their actual needs, and all lands now owned by aliens should be reclaimed by the government and held for actual settlers only....

Whereas, other questions have been presented for our consideration, we hereby submit the following, not as a part of the platform of the people's party, but as resolutions expressive of the sentiment of this convention.

First—Resolved, That we demand a free ballot and a fair count in all elections, and pledge ourselves to secure it to every legal voter without federal intervention, through the adoption by the states of the unperverted Australian or secret ballot system.

Second—Resolved, That the revenue derived from a graduated income tax should be applied to the reduction of the burden of taxation now levied upon the domestic industries of this country.

Third—Resolved, That we pledge our support to fair and liberal pensions to ex-union soldiers and sailors.

Fourth—Resolved, That we condemn the fallacy of protecting American labor under the present system, which opens our ports to the pauper and criminal classes of the world and crowds out our wage earners; and we denounce the present ineffective laws against contract labor, and demand the further restriction of undesirable emigration.

Fifth—Resolved, That we cordially sympathize with the efforts of organized workingmen to shorten the hours of labor, and demand a rigid enforcement of existing eight-hour law on government work, and ask that a penalty clause be added to the said law.

Sixth—Resolved, That we regard the maintenance of a large standing army of mercenaries, known as the Pinkerton system, as a menace to our liberties, and we demand its abolition; and we condemn the recent invasion of the territory of Wyoming by the hired assassins of plutocracy, assisted by federal officers.

Resolved, That we commend to the favorable consideration of the people, and the reform press the legislative system known as the initiative and referendum.

Resolved, That we favor a constitutional provision limiting the office of president and vice-president to one term, and providing for the election of senators of the United States by a direct vote of the people.

Resolved, That we oppose any subsidy or national aid to any private corporation for any purpose.

139

"The Significance of the Frontier in American History" (1893)

Since the first permanent English settlement in Jamestown in 1607, white settlers had moved steadily westward for nearly three hundred years, encroaching on Native Americans land and pushing the tribes farther west. Many Americans believed that an ever-advancing frontier line enabled a "superior" white culture to exploit the resources of the West. In 1890, the director of the U.S. Census Bureau announced that the country's "unsettled area has been so broken into by isolated bodies of settlement that there can hardly be said to be a frontier line." This announcement that the frontier period of American history was at its end prompted Frederick Jackson Turner, a young historian, to present a paper entitled "The Significance of the Frontier in American History" at the annual meeting of the American Historical Association in Chicago in July 1893. Excerpted here is the essay that becomes known as the Turner frontier thesis.

Questions to Consider

1. How does Frederick Jackson Turner describe the frontier?

2. Do Turner's views seem closer to those of Helen Hunt Jackson (*A Century of Dishonor*, Document 134) or William N. Byers ("A Western Newspaper Editorial on the Custer Massacre," Document 135)?

3. How would Turner respond to the question, "What is an American?"

4. What does this document reveal about late nineteenth-century white Americans' views of their culture?

In this advance, the frontier is the outer edge of the wave—the meeting point between savagery and civilization. Much has been written about the frontier from the point of view of border warfare and the chase, but as a field for the serious study of the economist and the historian it has been neglected.

The American frontier is sharply distinguished from the European Frontier—a fortified boundary line running through dense populations. The most significant thing about the American frontier is, that it lies at the hither edge of free land....

... The wilderness masters the colonist. It finds him a European in dress, industries, tools, modes of travel, and thought. It takes him from the railroad car and puts him in the birch canoe. It strips off the garments of civilization and arrays him in the hunting shirt and the moccasin. It puts him in the log cabin of the Cherokee and Iroquois and runs an Indian palisade around him. Before long he has gone to planting Indian corn and plowing with a sharp stick; he shouts the war cry and takes the scalp in orthodox Indian fashion. In short, at the frontier the environment is at first too strong for the man. He must accept the conditions which it furnishes, or perish, and so he fits himself into the Indian clearings and follows the Indian trails. Little by little he transforms the wilderness, but the outcome is not the old Europe, not simply the development of Germanic germs, any more than the first phenomenon was a case of reversion to the Germanic mark. The fact is, that here is a new product that is American. At first, the frontier was the Atlantic coast. It was the frontier of Europe in a very real sense. Moving westward, the frontier became more and more American....

First, we note that the frontier promoted the formation of a composite nationality for the American people. The coast was predominately English, but the later tides of continental immigration flowed across to the free lands....

But the most important effect of the frontier has been in the promotion of democracy here and in Europe. As has been indicated, the frontier is productive of individualism. Complex society is precipitated by the wilderness into a kind of primitive organization based on the family. The tendency is anti-social. It produces antipathy to control, and particularly to any direct control. The tax-gatherer is viewed as a representative of oppression. Prof. Osgood, in an able

SOURCE: Frederick Jackson Turner, "The Significance of the Frontier in American History," *Annual Report of the American Historical Association for 1893* (Washington, DC, 1894), 199–227.

article, has pointed out that the frontier conditions prevalent in the colonies are important factors in the explanation of the American Revolution, where individual liberty was sometimes confused with absence of all effective government. The same conditions aid in explaining the difficulty of instituting a strong government in the period of the confederacy. The frontier individualism has from the beginning promoted democracy.

The frontier States that came into the Union in the first quarter of a century of its existence came in with democratic suffrage provisions, and had reactive effects of the highest importance upon the older States whose peoples were being attracted there. An extension of the franchise became essential. It was *western* New York that forced an extension of suffrage in the constitutional convention of that State in 1821; and it was *western* Virginia that compelled the tide-water region to put a more liberal suffrage provision in the constitution framed in 1830, and to give to the frontier region a more nearly proportionate representation with the tide-water aristocracy. The rise of democracy as an effective force in the nation came in with western preponderance under Jackson and William Henry Harrison, and it meant the triumph of the frontier—with all of its good and with all of its evil elements....

So long as free land exists, the opportunity for a competency exists, and economic power secures political power. But the democracy born of free land, strong in selfishness and individualism, intolerant of administrative experience and education, and pressing individual liberty beyond its proper bounds, has its dangers as well as its benefits. Individualism in America has rendered possible the spoils system and all the manifest evils that follow from the lack of a highly developed civic spirit. In this connection may be noted also the influence of paper currency and wild-cat banking. The colonial and revolutionary frontier was the region whence emanated many of the worst forms of an evil currency. The West in the War of 1812 repeated the phenomenon on the frontier of that day, while the speculation and wild-cat banking of the period of the crisis of 1837 occurred on the new frontier belt of the next tier of States. Thus each one of the periods of lax financial integrity coincides with periods when a new set of frontier communities had arisen, and coincides in area with these successive frontiers, for the most part. The recent Populist agitation is a case in point. Many a State that now declines any connection with the tenets of the Populists, itself adhered to such ideas in an earlier stage of the development of the State....

From the conditions of frontier life came intellectual traits of profound importance. The works of travelers along each frontier from colonial days onward describe certain common traits, and these traits have, while softening down, still persisted as survivals in the place of their origin, even when a higher social organization succeeded. The result is that to the frontier the American intellect owes its striking characteristics. That coarseness and strength combined with acuteness and inquisitiveness; that practical, inventive turn of mind, quick to find expedients; that masterful grasp of material things, lacking in the artistic but powerful to effect great ends; that restless, nervous energy; that dominant individualism, working for good and for evil, and withal that buoyancy and exuberance which comes with freedom—there are traits of the frontier, or traits called out elsewhere because of the existence of the frontier …. But never again will such gifts of free land offer themselves. For a moment, at the frontier, the bonds of custom are broken and unrestraint is triumphant. There is not *tabula rasa*. The stubborn American environment is there with its imperious summons to accept its conditions; the inherited ways of doing things are also there; and yet, in spite of environment, and in spite of custom, each frontier did indeed furnish a new field of opportunity, a gate of escape from the bondage of the past; and freshness, and confidence, and scorn of older society, impatience of its restraints and its ideas, and indifference to its lessons, have accompanied the frontier. What the Mediterranean Sea was to the Greeks, breaking the bond of custom, offering new experiences, calling out new institutions and activities, that, and more, the ever retreating frontier has been to the United States directly, and to the nations of Europe even more remotely. And now, four centuries from the discovery of America, at the end of a hundred years of life under the Constitution, the frontier has gone, and with its going has closed the first period of American history.

140

A Woman's Description of Farm Life in Illinois (1905)

Life on the family farm for many Americans was difficult, especially for those who lived on or near the Great Plains. Even though new agricultural techniques (dry farming, the chilled iron plow, drought- and disease-resistant wheat) helped transform farming in the Great Plains region, many settlers struggled for economic survival. The precarious nature of farm life brought changes to some families, as traditional gender boundaries blurred: Women worked in the fields with their husbands, and men helped with household chores frequently reserved for the wife. In 1905, The Independent, *a magazine based in New York City, published an anonymous woman's "truthful narrative of her life" on an Illinois farm. The woman was married at eighteen, wished to read more books and to write short stories, and was an accomplished musician. The excerpt of her account below shows farm life was arduous.*

Questions to Consider

1. In what ways was this woman prepared for farm life? Ill-suited to farm life?

2. How does she describe her typical day on the farm?

3. What was the annual pattern of work on the farm?

4. What was her relationship with her husband?

I have been a farmer's wife in one of the States of the Middle West for thirteen years, and everybody knows that the farmer's wife must of necessity be a very practical woman, if she would be a successful one.

I am not a practical woman and consequently have been accounted a failure by practical friends and especially by my husband, who is wholly practical....

I was reared on a farm, was healthy and strong, was ambitious, and the work was not disagreeable, and having no children for the first six years of married life, the habit of going whenever asked to became firmly fixed, and he had no thought of hiring a man to help him, since I could do anything for which he needed help....

The addition of two children to our family never altered or interfered with the established order of things to any appreciable extent. My strenuous outdoor life agreed with me, and even when my children were born I was splendidly prepared for the ordeal and made rapid recovery....

This is a vague, general idea of how I spend my time; my work is so varied that it would be difficult, indeed, to describe a typical day's work.

Any bright morning in the latter part of May I am out of bed at four o'clock; next, after I have dressed and combed my hair, I start a fire in the kitchen stove, and while the stove is getting hot I go to my flower garden and gather a choice, half-blown rose and a spray of bride's wreath, and arrange them in my hair, and sweep the floors and then cook breakfast.

While the other members of the family are eating breakfast I strain away the morning's milk (for my husband milks the cows while I get breakfast), and fill my husband's dinner-pail, for he will go to work on our other farm for the day.

By this time it is half-past five o'clock, my husband is gone to his work, and the stock loudly pleading to be turned into the pastures. The younger cattle, a half-dozen steers, are left in the pasture at night, and I now drive the two cows a quarter mile and turn them in with the others, come back, and then there's a horse in the barn that belongs in a field where there is no water, which I take to a spring quite a distance from the barn; bring it back and turn it into a field with the sheep, a dozen in number, which are housed at night.

The young calves are then turned out into the warm sunshine, and the stock hogs, which are kept in a pen, are clamoring for feed, and I carry a pailful of swill to them, and hasten to the house and turn out the chickens and put out feed and water for them, and it is, perhaps, 6:30 a.m.

I have not eaten breakfast yet, but that can wait; I make the beds next and straighten things up in the living room, for I dislike to have the early morning caller find my house topsy-turvy. When this is done I go to the kitchen, which also serves as a dining-room, and uncover the table, and take a mouthful of food occasionally as I pass to and fro at my work until my appetite is appeased.

SOURCE: "One Farmer's Wife," *The Independent*, 9 February 1905, pp. 294–99.

By the time the work is done in the kitchen it is about 7:15 a.m., and the cool morning hours have flown, and no hoeing done in the garden yet, and the children's toilet has to be attended to and churning has to be done.

Finally the children are washed and churning done, and it is eight o'clock, and the sun getting hot, but no matter, weeds die quickly when cut down in the heat of the day, and I use the hoe to a good advantage until the dinner hour, which is 11:30 a.m. We come in, and I comb my hair, and put fresh flowers in it, and eat a cold dinner, put out feed and water for the chickens; set a hen, perhaps, sweep the floors again; sit down and rest, and read a few moments, and it is nearly one o'clock, and I sweep the door yard while I am waiting for the clock to strike the hour.

I make and sow a flower bed, dig around some shrubbery, and go back to the garden to hoe until time to do the chores at night, but ere long some hogs come up to the back gate, through the wheat field, and when I go to see what is wrong I find that the cows have torn the fence down, and they, too, are in the wheat field.

With much difficulty I get them back into their own domain and repair the fence. I hoe in the garden till four o'clock; then I go into the house and get supper, and prepare something for the dinner pail to-morrow; when supper is all ready it is set aside, and I pull a few hundred plants of tomato, sweet potato or cabbage for transplanting, set them in a cool, moist place where they will not wilt, and I then go after the horse, water him, and put him in the barn; call the sheep and house them, and go after the cows and milk them, feed the hogs, put down hay for three horses, and put oats and corn in their troughs, and set those plants and come in and fasten up the chickens, and it is dark. By this time it is 8 o'clock p.m.; my husband has come home, and we are eating supper; when we are through eating I make the beds ready, and the children and their father go to bed, and I wash the dishes and get things in shape to get breakfast quickly next morning.

It is now about 9 o'clock p.m., and after a short prayer I retire for the night.

As a matter of course, there's hardly two days together which require the same routine, yet every day is as fully occupied in some way or other as this one, with varying tasks as the seasons change. In early spring we are planting potatoes, making plant beds, planting garden, early corn patches, setting strawberries, planting corn, melons, cow peas, sugar cane, beans, popcorn, peanuts, etc.

Oats are sown in March and April, but I do not help do that, because the ground is too cold.

Later in June we harvest clover hay, in July timothy hay, and in August pea hay.

Winter wheat is ready to harvest the latter part of June, and oats the middle of July.

These are the main crops, supplemented by cabbages, melons, potatoes, tomatoes, etc.

Fully half of my time is devoted to helping my husband, more than half during the active work season, and not that much during the winter months; only a very small portion of my time is devoted to reading. My reading matter accumulates during the week, and, I think I will stay at home on Sunday and read, but as we have many visitors on Sunday I am generally disappointed....

17

Gilded Age America

The economic changes that transformed America before the Civil War brought about even greater changes after the war. This postwar industrial revolution included the spread of many prewar economic developments as well as the emergence of new technologies that expanded economic production. The expansion of mass production and growing numbers of unskilled laborers helped create a new industrial order. Millions of immigrants came to America hoping to improve their lives. The task of assimilation was daunting for these immigrants, many of whom accepted low-paying jobs and lived in squalid urban conditions. For many women and millions of African Americans in the South, the Gilded Age was a time of second-class citizenship and physical separation from white male society. The economic and social transformations of the late nineteenth century occurred in an environment where government policy was laissez-faire and business followed the creed of "survival of the fittest." The following selections describe some of the changes taking place and chronicle the attitudes of those who were a part of the economic and social realities of the Gilded Age. The documents in this chapter are arranged around the themes of labor and reactions to the new industrial order as well as the issues of ethnicity and race.

141

The Cattle Industry (1884)

The post–Civil War period witnessed the acceleration of economic developments that had begun before the conflict. The relationship between agricultural and manufacturing enterprises grew closer and encouraged mass production techniques in both economic sectors. For example, farmers increased wheat production by adapting the wheat reaper, and flour mills grew larger and more mechanized. Assisting economic growth and helping to forge a link between agriculture and manufacturing after the Civil War was the expansion of the railroads, primarily into the West. The railroads could move agricultural products profitably to markets in the East. Fitting into this situation were the new growth industries of cattle ranching in the West and meat processors in the East, primarily in Chicago. In 1884, G. Pomeroy Keese wrote an article, excerpted here, for the popular Harper's New Monthly Magazine *describing how cattle raised on western ranges becomes beef for the family meal. His account was based on riding the range with cowboys in the West and observing work in the "shambles," or slaughterhouses, in Chicago.*

Questions to Consider

1. In what ways does Keese regard economic development in the West?
2. How do the meat-processing plants in Chicago address the need to mass-produce beef profitably?
3. What economic impact does the railroad have upon the beef business?
4. In what ways does Keese's account of conditions in the cattle industry compare with that described in "The Impact of Mechanization" (Document 142) or *The Jungle* (Document 156)?

An establishment in Chicago which combines the operations of "shipping" and of "canning" beef has a slaughtering capacity of 400,000 head annually. When we add to this the requirements of other similar although smaller concerns, and the large number shipped eastward on the hoof, we have a grand total of not far from 2,500,000 head marketed in the city of Chicago alone.... Whence does it come? Let the five great trunk lines which have their termini on the borders of Lake Michigan answer. Like the outstretched fingers of a hand, they meet in the central palm, Chicago. All from the West, but from the extreme northern and

SOURCE: G. Pomeroy Keese, "Beef, from the Range to the Shambles," *Harper's New Monthly Magazine* 69 (July 1884): 202–301.

southern portions, Texas representing the latter, and the utmost limits of Montana the former. Ten thousand miles of rail at least are occupied in the transit....

There are several ways of becoming interested in the cattle business on a northern range. One may commence by buying out a small herd, with the ranch and primitive equipments which accompany it, and with this nucleus build up by natural increase and additional purchases from time to time.... Or, again, one may contract in Texas during the winter for a given number of one or two year old steers, to be delivered on a certain range in Wyoming or Montana the coming summer. Having previously made an arrangement for their herding for two or more years, for which he pays annually one dollar per head, including all expenses, all he has to do is to await their arrival about midsummer, see them counted and branded, and then turn them loose upon the range. Or, thirdly, he may become a stockholder in one of the organized gigantic companies already existing....

If the second method is adopted, ... we will suppose a purchase made in Texas, say the 1st of February, of two thousand steers, ... to be delivered on a range in Wyoming the following summer. These would be well bought at fifteen and eighteen dollars a head respectively, and then only as part of a larger drive of perhaps ten or twelve thousand going through to the same locality....

The word "drive" is a misnomer as applied to the trail. It is exactly this which should not be done. Cattle once gathered, and headed in the direction of their long journey, should be allowed to "drift" rather than be urged. Walking as they feed, they will accomplish their twelve or fifteen miles a day with but little exertion to themselves, and with very much less care and anxiety on the part of the herder....

There are several distinct trails across the plains, and the pathways are as distinctly marked as a road could be, pressed by the hoofs of thousands for years past.

... As previously stated, the expense of herding a "bunch" of cattle is one dollar per head annually, which includes all charges after they are turned loose upon the range until they are delivered as "beeves" at the nearest railroad shipping point....

Cattle trains arrive in Chicago early in the morning. They are unloaded, the cattle are classified and entered upon the stock-yard books in the name of the consignee, and after they are fed and watered in their respective pens, are ready for inspection of the buyer....

As we come within the gate, we reach first the outer inclosure or pen, where may be gathered one hundred head of choice "shippers." They come in quietly and without excitement, and in a few minutes perhaps one-third of them are driven into a narrow alleyway adjoining the single pens.... A few seconds later and a mild-looking man with a short carbine in his hand drops the muzzle to a point in the center of the forehead, just below the horns, and pulls the trigger. The steer falls without a struggle or groan ... a hooking chain passed around the neck, and the animal is drawn out upon a broad platform about fourteen feet wide, at the bottom of which runs a shallow trough to catch the blood. Suspended by the hind feet, the sticking knife completes the bleeding process, and then two men step forward and disconnect the head. Four follow, stripping down the hide, two others, in the mean while, taking off the feet. Sawing the breast and haunch bones is the next operation, and then the carcass is hoisted preparatory to taking out the inwards. This accomplished, a number are detailed to do the trimming, cleaning and turning to account every scrap and particle connected with the animal, so that nothing is wasted, down to the horns and hoofs. While these several operations are in progress, the carcass has been moving along a distance of some two hundred feet, being attached to a track overhead. The men at work maintain their relative positions as one after another of the carcasses come before them, and in the brief space of fourteen minutes from the time of the fatal shot to the animal is hung up, "drawn and quartered," and then left to cool in the chill room for forty-eight hours preparatory to shipping....

Perhaps the most satisfactory part of the operations we have witnessed is the scrupulous cleanliness observed throughout. The pure creamy fat and dark rich red meat attest the perfection and purity attainted, which the most expert stall-man in Fulton Market can not excel....

The canning and packing department is another branch of the business entirely distinct from that of shipping. Up to a certain point the process is substantially the same, until it comes to cutting up the quarters into suitable pieces for these uses. Here division of labor takes complete possession of the work and it is carried to the perfection of economy. A man will stand by the hour giving but a single turn to his knife, which separates a joint.... A hundred others are on the same floor with him, each doing what may seem a trilling portion of the work, but before the carcass, which came in on one side in quarters, leaves the room, it is entirely bereft of bones, and then wheeled away in small pieces ready for the curing and the canning.... In this case the division is made into the various pieces familiar to household providers, viz., loins, ribs ... "Extra mess" is composed of chucks, plates, rumps and flanks, and the time of curing is twenty-four days. All hams are cut into three pieces, or "one-set"; time of curing, sixty days. Plates are cut into five pieces. Loins, ribs, and shoulders are also sold to the city butchers. "Prime" tallow is made from the kidney and caid fat only, while "regular" tallow is made from the other fat, bones and trimmings. Glue factories and fertilizing establishments use up the bones and refuse, and the hides find their way to the tanneries. Not a scrap of the animal is wasted, or fails to yield some revenue to the buyer.

142

The Impact of Mechanization (1889)

The rapid adaptation of machinery for mass production created significant transformations in the American economy in the post–Civil War period. The author of the excerpt here, David A. Wells, realized the consequences of the machine age for both the business community and society. His background as an inventor, publisher of scientific information, political activist, and foremost economist who advised Presidents Lincoln, Garfield, and Grant on business and currency matters, gave Wells a unique perspective to observe the technological changes taking place and analyze their implications. In his book Recent Economic Changes, *Wells offered a commentary on the growing size of businesses and how that affected the nature of enterprise. Wells was also among the first economists to recognize that machines displaced workers—creating "technological unemployment"—and that business was changing American society. His observations indicate that both business and society were adjusting to the technological progress of the time.*

Questions to Consider

1. According to David A. Wells, what were the most dramatic changes taking place?

2. For what reasons does Wells call these changes a "total revolution"?

3. To what extent can the common person participate in the economic advances described here?

4. In what ways would the American people respond to the new methods of doing business?

Machinery is now recognized as essential to cheap production. Nobody can produce effectively and economically without it, and what was formerly known as domestic manufacture is now almost obsolete. But machinery is one of the most expensive of all products, and its extensive purchase and use require an amount of capital far beyond the capacity of the ordinary individual to furnish. There are very few men in the world possessed of an amount of wealth sufficient to individually construct and own an extensive line of railway or telegraph, a first-class steamship, or a great factory. It is also to be remembered that, for carrying on production by the most modern and effective methods, large capital is needed, not only for machinery but also for the purchasing and carrying of extensive stocks of crude material and finished products.

SOURCE: David A. Wells, *Recent Economic Changes* (New York, 1889), 91–94, 98, 109, 111.

... Hence, from such conditions have grown up great corporations or stock companies, which are only forms of associated capital organized for effective use and protection. They are regarded to some extent as evils; but they are necessary, as there is apparently no other way in which the work of production and distribution, in accordance with the requirements of the age, can be prosecuted. The rapidity, however, with which such combinations of capital are organizing for the purpose of promoting industrial and commercial undertakings on a scale heretofore wholly unprecedented, and the tendency they have to crystalize into something far more complex than what has been familiar to the public as corporations, with the impressive names of syndicates, trusts, etc., also constitute one of the remarkable features of modern business methods. It must also be admitted that the whole tendency of recent economic development is in the direction of limiting the area within which the influence of competition is effective.

And when once a great association of capital has been effected, it becomes necessary to have a mastermind to manage it—a man who is competent to use and direct other men, who is fertile in expedient and quick to note and profit by any improvements in methods of production and variations in prices. Such a man is a general of industry, and corresponds in position and functions to the general of an army.

What, as a consequence, has happened to the employees? Coincident with and as a result of this change in the methods of production, the modern manufacturing system has been brought into a condition analogous to that of a military organization, in which the individual no longer works as independently as formerly, but as a private in the ranks, obeying orders, keeping step, as it were, to the tap of the drum, and having nothing to say as to the plan of his work, of its final completion, or of its ultimate use and distribution. In short, the people who work in the modern factory are, as a rule, taught to do one thing—to perform one, and generally a simple, operation; and when there is no more of that kind of work to do, they are in a measure helpless. The result has been that the individualism or independence of the producer in manufacturing has been in a great degree destroyed, and with it has also in a great degree been destroyed the pride which the workman formerly took in his work—that fertility of resource which formerly was a special characteristic of American workmen, and that element of skill that comes from long and varied practice and reflection and responsibility. Not many years ago every shoemaker was or could be his own employer. The boots and shoes passed directly from an individual producer to the consumer. Now this condition of things has passed away. Boots and shoes are made in large factories; and machinery has been so utilized, and the division of labor in connection with it has been carried to such an extent, that the process of making a shoe is said to be divided into sixty-four parts, or the shoemaker of to-day is only the sixty-fourth part of what a shoemaker once was....

Another exceedingly interesting and developing feature of the new situation is that, as machinery has destroyed the handicrafts and associated capital has placed individual capital at a disadvantage, so machinery and associated capital in turn, guided by the same common influences, now war upon machinery and other associated capital. Thus the now well-ascertained and accepted fact, based on long experience, that power is most economically applied when applied on the largest possible scale, is rapidly and inevitably leading to the concentration of manufacturing in the largest establishments and the gradual extinction of those which are small....

The same influences have also to a great degree revolutionized the nature of retail trade.... Experience has shown that, under a good organization of clerks, shopmen, porters, and distributors, it costs much less proportionally to sell a large amount of goods than a small amount; and that the buyer of large quantities can, without sacrifice of satisfactory profit, afford to offer to his retail customers such advantages in respect to prices and range of selection as almost to preclude competition on the part of dealers operating on a smaller scale, no matter how otherwise capable, honest, and diligent they may be. The various retail trades in the cities and larger towns of all civilized countries are accordingly being rapidly superseded by vast and skillfully organized establishments ... which can sell at little over wholesale prices a great variety of merchandise, dry goods, manufactures of leather, books, stationery, furs, ready-made clothing, hats and caps, and sometimes groceries and hardware, and at the same time give their customers far greater conveniences than can be offered by the ordinary shopkeeper or tradesman....

From these specimen experiences it is clear that an almost total revolution has taken place, and is yet in progress, in every branch and in every relation of the world's industrial and commercial system. Some of these changes have been eminently destructive, and all of them have inevitably occasioned, and for a long time yet will continue to occasion, great disturbances in old methods and entail losses of capital and changes of occupation on the part of individuals....

143

Views of Big Business (1883, 1889, 1900)

The rapid growth of corporations and their profound influence on everyday life concerned many Americans in the Gilded Age. Through a variety of means, some corporations began to acquire former competitors, or they began to acquire other companies in a process of consolidation. Following the example of the Standard Oil Trust, many of these large companies reorganized as trusts, where a few individuals could control many businesses, or, in some cases, dominate an entire industry. Trusts came to be seen as monopolies, corporate entities that stifled competition and wielded power beyond the business world. Many Americans developed a love-hate relationship with big business: Some appreciated the goods and services they provided, while others believed that the trusts threatened the working man, freedom, democracy, and even the government. The three cartoons below reveal a public perspective on the trusts. Both Puck *and* Verdict *magazines were known for their double-page cartoons that displayed powerful imagery on controversial topics in the Gilded Age.*

Questions to Consider

1. What are the powerful images that these cartoons convey?
2. Why do these images depict businessmen as such large figures and other people much smaller?

The Tournament of Today.—A Set-to Between Labor and Monopoly.
SOURCE: [LC-USZC4-494]/Library of Congress Prints and Photographs Division

The Bosses of the Senate
SOURCE: Georgia State University Library

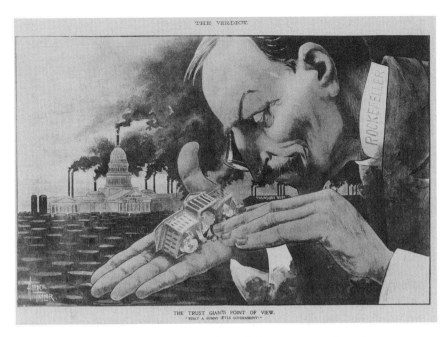

The Trust Giant's Point of View. 'What a funny little government.'

SOURCE: Library of Congress Prints and Photographs Division

3. In what ways do these cartoons show the relationship between trusts and the people?

4. Based on a careful consideration of these images, what appears to be some of the problems facing the United States?

144

"The Forgotten Man" (1883)

In the Gilded Age, social Darwinism became the prevailing force in American thought. It was the application of Charles Darwin's theory of evolution to society. The leading advocate of this new intellectual tenet was Englishman Herbert Spencer, who argued that society operated in competitive ways so that only the strongest and "fittest" individuals would survive. Even though this competition could be harsh, the long-term evolution for humans would be a better society. Social Darwinists argued that this competition must occur naturally; there should be no interference in this process. The most prominent American social Darwinist was Yale sociologist William Graham Sumner. He argued that competition was natural, and that it sentenced the unfit to poverty and blessed the fit with wealth and power. Sumner's arguments of noninterference in the "natural selection" process held a powerful place in America. Excerpted here is a speech Sumner gave to a Brooklyn, New York, audience in 1883. Entitled "The Forgotten Man," the speech addresses some of the issues of social Darwinism.

Questions to Consider

1. For what reasons does Sumner defend the "Forgotten Man" and oppose efforts to help the "good-for-nothing"?
2. Why does Sumner oppose reformers and their legislation?
3. How might David A. Wells ("The Impact of Mechanization," (Document 142) and Terrence V. Powderly ("Preamble to the Constitution of the Knights of Labor," Document 146) respond to Sumner's views?
4. Why was social Darwinism so appealing in the Gilded Age?

Now who is the Forgotten Man? He is the simple, honest laborer, ready to earn his living by productive work. We pass him by because he is independent, self-supporting, and asks no favors. He does not appeal to the emotions or excite the sentiments. He only wants to make a contract and fulfill it, with respect on both sides and favor on neither side. He must get his living out of the capital of the country. The larger the capital is, the better living he can get. Every particle of capital which is wasted on the vicious, the idle, and the shiftless is so much taken from the capital available to reward the independent and productive laborer. But we stand with our backs to the independent and productive laborer all the time. We do not remember him because he makes no clamor; but I appeal to you whether he is not the man who ought to be remembered first of all, and whether, on any sound social theory, we ought not to protect him against the burdens of the good-for-nothing.... Every man is bound to take care of himself and his family and to do his share in the work of society. It is totally false that one who has done so is bound to bear the care and charge of those who are wretched because they have not done so. The silly popular notion is that the beggars live at the expense of the rich, but the truth is that those who eat and produce not, live at the expense of those who labor and produce. The next time that you are tempted to subscribe a dollar to a charity, I do not tell you not to do it, because after you have fairly considered the matter, you may think it right to do it, but I do ask you to stop and remember the Forgotten Man and understand

SOURCE: William Graham Sumner, *The Forgotten Man and Other Essays*, ed. Albert G. Keller (New Haven, CT, 1918), 476–81, 492–93.

that if you put your dollar in the savings bank it will go to swell the capital of the country which is available for division amongst those who, while they earn it, will reproduce it with increase....

Let us take another class of cases. So far we have said nothing about the abuse of legislation. We all seem to be under the delusion that the rich pay the taxes.... Now the state and municipality go to great expense to support policemen and sheriffs and judicial officers, to protect people against themselves, that is, against the results of their own folly, vice, and recklessness. Who pays for it? Undoubtedly the people who have not been guilty of folly, vice, or recklessness. Out of nothing comes nothing. We cannot collect taxes from people who produce nothing and save nothing. The people who have something to tax must be those who have produced and saved.

When you see a drunkard in the gutter, you are disgusted, but you pity him. When a policeman comes and picks him up you are satisfied. You say that "society" has interfered to save the drunkard from perishing. Society is a fine work, and it saves us the trouble of thinking to say that society acts. The truth is that the policeman is paid by somebody, and when we talk about society we forget who it is that pays. It is the Forgotten Man again. It is the industrious workman going home from a hard day's work, whom you pass without noticing, who is mulcted [penalized by fining or demanding forfeiture] of a percentage of his day's earnings to hire a policeman to save the drunkard from himself. All the public expenditure to prevent vice has the same effect. Vice is its own curse. If we let nature alone, she cures vice by the most frightful penalties. It may shock you to hear me say it, but when you get over the shock, it will do you good to think of it: a drunkard in the gutter is just where he ought to be. Nature is working away at him to get him out of the way, just as she sets up her processes of dissolution to remove whatever is a failure in its line....

Another class of cases is closely connected with this last. There is an apparently invincible prejudice in people's minds in favor of state regulation. All experience is against state regulation and in favor of liberty. The freer the civil institutions are, the more weak and mischievous state regulation is....

Now we have a great many well-intentioned people among us who believe that they are serving their country when they discuss plans for regulating the relations of employer and employee, or the sanitary regulations of dwellings, or the construction of factories, or the way to behave on Sunday, or what people ought not to eat or drink or smoke. All this is harmless enough and well enough as a basis of mutual encouragement and missionary enterprise, but it is almost always made a basis of legislation. The reformers want to get a majority, that is, to get the power of the state and so to make other people do what the reformers think it right and wise to do....

It is plain enough that the Forgotten Man and the Forgotten Woman are the very life and substance of society. They are the ones who ought to be first and always remembered. They are always forgotten by sentimentalists, philanthropists, reformers, enthusiasts, and every description of speculator in sociology, political economy, or political science. If a student of any of these sciences ever comes to understand the position of the Forgotten Man and to appreciate his true value, you will find such student an uncompromising advocate of the strictest scientific thinking on all social topics, and a cold and hard-hearted skeptic towards all artificial schemes of social amelioration. If it is desired to bring about social improvements, bring us a scheme for relieving the Forgotten Man of some of his burdens. He is our productive force which we are wasting. Let us stop wasting his force. Then we shall have a clean and simple gain for the whole society. The Forgotten Man is weighted down with the cost and burden of schemes for making everybody happy, with the cost of public beneficence, with the support of all the loafers, with the loss of all the economic quackery, with the cost of all the jobs. Let us remember him a little while. Let us take some of the burdens off him. Let us turn our pity on him instead of on the good-for-nothing. It will be only justice to him, and society will greatly gain by it....

145

The Gospel of Wealth (1889)

A new intellectual tenet—social Darwinism—helped justify the position of wealthy businessmen while simultaneously explaining poverty, misery, and unemployment. Social Darwinists, led by Englishman Herbert Spencer, who coined the term "survival of the fittest," broadened the theory of evolution to include all phenomena, especially society. Spencer argued that industrial leaders were products of natural selection; the best prospered while the unfit fell by the wayside. Any attempt to criticize or limit these survivors was contrary to natural law, and those less fortunate were the price modern society had to pay for progress. Andrew Carnegie, who amassed a fortune from the steel industry and was one of the few immigrant "rags to riches" examples of the era, understood that social Darwinism could weaken democratic ideals. He published "Wealth," excerpted here, in the prominent journal, North American Review, *in an effort to encourage businessmen to administer their wealth properly. Carnegie set the example and followed his "Gospel of Wealth" until the day he died.*

Questions to Consider

1. How does Andrew Carnegie justify the contrast between the wealthy and the working poor?

2. According to Carnegie, what is the "proper administration of wealth"?

3. On what issues would Carnegie agree with William Graham Sumner's speech on "The Forgotten Man" (Document 144)?

4. Why would some people criticize Carnegie's proposal?

The problem of our age is the proper administration of wealth, so that the ties of brotherhood may still bind together the rich and poor in harmonious relationship. The conditions of human life have not only been changed, but revolutionized, within the past few hundred years.... The contrast between the palace of the millionaire and the cottage of the laborer with us to-day measures the change which has come with civilization....

This change, however, is not to be deplored, but welcomed as highly beneficial. It is well, nay, essential for the progress of the race, that the houses of some should be homes for all that is highest and best in literature and the arts, and for all the refinements of civilization, rather than that none should be so. Much better this great irregularity than universal squalor....

The price which society pays for the law of competition, like the price it pays for cheap comforts and luxuries, is also great; but the advantages of this law are also greater still, for it is to this law that we owe our wonderful material development, which brings improved conditions in its train. But ... the law may be sometimes hard for the individual, it is best for the race, because it insures the survival of the fittest in every department. We accept and welcome, therefore, as conditions to which we must accommodate ourselves, great inequality of environment, the concentration of business, industrial and commercial, in the hands of a few, and the law of competition between these, as being not only beneficial, but essential for the future progress of the race....

We start, then, with a condition of affairs under which the best interests of the race are promoted, but which inevitably gives wealth to the few. Thus far, accepting conditions as they exist, the situations can be surveyed and pronounced good. The question then arises, ... What is the proper mode of administering wealth after the laws upon which civilization is founded have thrown it into the hands of the few? ...

There are but three modes in which surplus wealth can be disposed of. It can be left to the families of the decedents; or it can be bequeathed for public purposes: or, finally, it can be administered during their lives by its possessors. Under the first and second modes most of the wealth of the world that has reached the few has hitherto been applied. Let us in turn consider each of these modes. The first is the most injudicious. In monarchical countries, the estates and the greatest portion of the wealth are left to the first son, that the vanity of the parent may be gratified by the thought that his name and title are to descend to succeeding generations unimpaired. The condition of this class in Europe to-day teaches the futility of such hopes or ambitions. The successors have become impoverished through their follies or from the fall in the value of land....

SOURCE: Andrew Carnegie, "Wealth," *North American Review* 148 (1889): 653–64.

As to the second mode, that of leaving wealth at death for public uses, it may be said that this is only a means for the disposal of wealth, provided a man is content to wait until he is dead before it becomes of much good in the world. Knowledge of the results of legacies bequeathed is not calculated to inspire the brightest hopes of much posthumous good being accomplished. The cases are not few in which the real object sought by the testator is attained, nor are they few in which his real wishes are thwarted. In many cases the bequests are so used as to become only monuments of his folly....

There remains, then, only one mode of using great fortunes; but in this we have the true antidote for the temporary unequal distribution of wealth, the reconciliation of the rich and the poor—a reign of harmony—another ideal, differing, indeed, from that of the communist in requiring only the further evolution of existing conditions, not the total overthrow of our civilization. It is founded upon the present most intense individualism, and the race is prepared to put it in practice by degrees whenever it pleases. Under its sway we shall have an ideal state, in which the surplus wealth of the few will become, in the best sense, the property of the many, because administered for the common good, and this wealth, passing through the hands of a few, can be made a much more potent force for the elevation of our race than if it had been distributed in small sums to the people themselves....

This, then, is held to be the duty of the man of Wealth: First, to set an example of modest, unostentatious living, shunning display or extravagance; to provide moderately for the legitimate wants of those dependent upon him; and after doing so to consider all surplus revenues which come to him simply as trust funds, which he is called upon to administer, and strictly bound as a matter of duty to administer in the manner which, in his judgment, is best calculated to produce the most beneficial results for the community—the man of wealth thus becoming the mere agent and trustee for his poorer brethren, bringing to their service his superior wisdom, experience, and ability to administer, doing for them better than they would or could do for themselves....

In bestowing charity, the main consideration should be to help those who will help themselves; to provide part of the means by which those who desire to improve may do so; to give those who desire to rise the aids by which they may rise; to assist, but rarely or never to do all. Neither the individual nor the race is improved by alms-giving.... He is the only true reformer who is as careful and as anxious not to aid the unworthy as he is to aid the worthy, and, perhaps, even more so, for in alms-giving more injury is probably done by rewarding vice than by relieving virtue....

Thus is the problem of Rich and Poor to be solved. The laws of accumulation will be left free; the laws of distribution free. Individualism will continue, but the millionaire will be but a trustee for the poor; intrusted for a season with a great part of the increased wealth of the community, but administering it for the community far better than it could or would have done for itself. The best minds will thus have reached a stage in the development of the race in which it is clearly seen that there is no mode of disposing of surplus wealth creditable to thoughtful and earnest men into whose hands it flows save by using it year by year for the general good. This day already dawns ... yet the man who dies leaving behind him millions of available wealth, which was his to administer during life, will pass away "unwept, unhonored, and unsung," no matter to what uses he leaves the dross which he cannot take with him. Of such as these the public verdict will then be: "The man who dies thus rich dies disgraced."

Such, in my opinion, is the true gospel concerning Wealth, obedience to which is destined some day to solve the problem of the Rich and the Poor, and to bring "Peace on earth, among men Good-Will."

146

Preamble to the Constitution of the Knights of Labor (1878)

Faced with the growing size and complexity of business, small groups of skilled workers began to form labor organizations or societies to protect their jobs and gain a share of the wealth that business generated. Many of the early societies were secretive, to protect against employer retaliation. Often these organizations were small, confined to certain industries, and usually failed to achieve their goals. The Knights of Labor were among the earliest labor organizations that attracted a national following. Begun as a secret trade union of tailors in Philadelphia in 1869, the Knights grew slowly until Terrence V. Powderly assumed the leadership in 1879. Powderly advocated accepting all workers—regardless of trade—and women and African Americans (though in separate locals) into the Knights. He also believed in arbitration of disputes and the use of boycotts, but he opposed the use or threat of a strike when confronting business. Powderly, who served three terms as mayor of Scranton, Pennsylvania, while leading the Knights, assisted in writing the preamble to the constitution of the Knights of Labor, which is excerpted here.

Questions to Consider

1. What were the key issues the Knights of Labor wanted addressed?
2. In what ways do the Knights of Labor propose to achieve their demands?
3. What does this document reveal about the conditions for many workers in America at this time?
4. How do you suppose David A. Wells ("Impact of Mechanization," Document 142) and William Graham Sumner ("The Forgotten Man," Document 144) would respond to the sentiments expressed in this selection?

The recent alarming development and aggression of aggregated wealth, which, unless checked, will invariably lead to the pauperization and hopeless degradation of the toiling masses, render it imperative, if we desire to enjoy the blessings of life, that a check should be placed upon its power and upon unjust accumulation, and a system adopted which will secure to the laborer the fruits of his toil; and as this much-desired object can only be accomplished by the thorough unification of labor, and the united efforts of those who obey the divine injunction that "In the sweat of thy brow shalt thou eat bread, "we have formed the ★ ★ ★ ★ ★ with a view of securing the organization and direction, by co-operative effort, of the power of the industrial classes; and we submit to the world the object sought to be accomplished by our organization, calling upon all who believe in securing "the greatest good to the greatest number" to aid and assist us:

I. To bring within the folds of organization every department of productive industry, making knowledge a standpoint for action, and industrial and moral worth, not wealth, the true standard of individual and national greatness.

II. To secure to the toilers a proper share of the wealth that they create; more of the leisure that rightfully belongs to them; more societary advantages; more of the benefits, privileges, and emoluments of the world; in a word, all those rights and privileges necessary to make them capable of enjoying, appreciating, defending, and perpetuating the blessings of good government.

III. To arrive at the true condition of the producing masses in their educational, moral, and financial condition, by demanding from the various governments the establishment of bureaus of Labor Statistics.

IV. The establishment of co-operative institutions, productive and distributive.

V. The reserving of the public lands—the heritage of the people—for the actual settler; —not another acre for railroads or speculators.

VI. The abrogation of all laws that do not bear equally upon capital and labor, the removal of unjust technicalities, delays, and discriminations in the administration of justice, and the adopting of measures providing for the health and safety of those engaged in mining, manufacturing, or building pursuits.

VII. The enactment of laws to compel chartered corporations to pay their employees weekly, in full, for labor performed during the preceding week, in the lawful money of the country.

VIII. The enactment of laws giving mechanics and laborers a first lien on their work for their full wages.

IX. The abolishment of the contract system of national, State, and municipal work.

SOURCE: Terrence V. Powderly, *Thirty Years of Labor* (Columbus, OH, 1889), 243–45.

X.   The substitution of arbitration for strikes, whenever and wherever employers and employees are willing to meet on equitable grounds.

XI. The prohibition of the employment of children in workshops, mines, and factories before attaining their fourteenth year.

XII. To abolish the system of letting out by contract the labor of convicts in our prisons and reformatory institutions.

XIII. To secure for both sexes equal pay for equal work.

XIV. The reduction of the hours of labor to eight per day, so that the laborers may have more time for social enjoyment and intellectual improvement, and be enabled to reap the advantages conferred by the labor saving machinery which their brains have created.

XV. To prevail upon governments to establish a purely national circulating medium based upon the faith and resources of the nation, and issued directly to the people, without the intervention of any system of banking corporations, which money shall be a legal tender in payment of all debts, public or private.

147

Lynching in the South (1895)

Starting in the late 1880s, race relations in the South changed quickly. Southern states disfranchised African American voters and passed Jim Crow laws, which legally segregated the races. This "color line" was often enforced through intimidation and violence. African Americans who transgressed the community standards for race relations, perhaps breaking some race etiquette or Jim Crow law, were sometimes lynched as a powerful message to the black community. Many lynchings were public rituals where the victim was hanged or burned alive by mobs. In the 1890s, when a black person was lynched nearly every two days, some African Americans began to campaign against these heinous murders. Among the leaders of the antilynching campaign was Ida B. Wells-Barnett of Memphis, Tennessee. Born into a slave family, she came to own and edit a weekly newspaper, the Memphis Free Speech and Headlight. *She condemned lynchings in her paper until threats of violence forced her to flee to the North. She continued the anti-lynching crusade, publishing editorials and conducting a lengthy speaking tour in Europe. The selection here is from Wells-Barnett's powerful pamphlet,* A Red Record.*

Questions to Consider

1. According to Wells-Barnett, what were the reasons for lynching in the South?
2. In what ways had the reasons changed over time?
3. In what ways does Wells-Barnett propose to end lynching?
4. What does this document reveal about the status of African Americans and white attitudes in this time period?

Not all nor nearly all of the murders done by white men, during the past thirty years in the South, have come to light, but the statistics as gathered and preserved by white men, and which have not been questioned, show that during these years more than ten thousand Negroes have been killed in cold blood, without the formality of judicial trial and legal execution....

The first excuse given to the civilized world for the murder of unoffending Negroes was the necessity of the white man to repress and stamp out alleged "race riots." For years immediately succeeding the war there was an appalling slaughter of colored people, and the wires usually conveyed to northern people and the world the intelligence, first, that an insurrection was being planned by Negroes, which, a few hours later, would prove to have been vigorously resisted by white men, and controlled with a resulting loss of several killed and wounded. It was always a remarkable feature in these insurrections and riots that only Negroes were killed during the rioting, and that all the white men escaped unharmed....

Then came the second excuse, which had its birth during the turbulent times of reconstruction. By an amendment to the Constitution the Negro was given the right of franchise, and, theoretically at least, his ballot became his invaluable emblem of citizenship. In a government "of the people, for the people, and by the people," the Negro's vote became an important factor in all matters of state and national politics. But this did not last long. The southern white man would not consider that the Negro had any right which a white man was bound to respect, and the idea of a republican form of government in the southern states grew into general contempt. It was maintained that "This is a white man's government," and regardless of numbers the white man should rule. "No Negro domination" became the new legend on the sanguinary banner of the sunny South, and under it rode the Ku Klux Klan, the Regulators, and the lawless mobs, which for any cause chose to murder one man or a dozen as suited their purpose best....

The white man's victory soon became complete by fraud, violence, intimidation and murder. The franchise vouchsafed to the Negro grew to be a "barren ideality," and regardless of numbers, the colored people found themselves voiceless in the councils of those whose duty it was to rule. With no longer the fear of "Negro Domination" before their eyes, the white man's second excuse became valueless. With the Southern governments all subverted and the Negro actually

SOURCE: Ida B. Wells-Barnett, *A Red Record* (Chicago, 1895), 8–15.

eliminated from all participation in state and national elections, there could be no longer an excuse for killing Negroes to prevent "Negro Domination."

Brutality still continued; Negroes were whipped, scourged, exiled, shot and hung whenever and wherever it pleased the white man so to treat them, and as the civilized world with increasing persistency held the white people of the South to account for its outlawry, the murderers invented the third excuse—that Negroes had to be killed to avenge their assaults upon women. There could be framed no possible excuse more harmful to the Negro and more unanswerable if true in its sufficiency for the white man....

A word as to the charge itself. In considering the third reason assigned by the Southern white people for the butchery of blacks, the question must be asked, what the white man means when he charges the black man with rape. Does he mean the crime which the statutes of the civilized states describe as such? Not by any means. With the Southern white man, any mesalliance existing between a white woman and a colored man is a sufficient foundation for the charge of rape. The Southern white man says that it is impossible for a voluntary alliance to exist between a white woman and a colored man, and therefore, the fact of an alliance is a proof of force. In numerous instances where colored men have been lynched on the charge of rape, it was positively known at the time of lynching, and indisputably proven after the victim's death, that the relationship sustained between the man and woman was voluntary and clandestine, and that in no court of law could even the charge of assault have been successfully maintained....

During all the years of slavery, no such charge was ever made, not even during the dark days of the rebellion, when the white man, following the fortunes of war went to do battle for the maintenance of slavery. While the master was away fighting to forge the fetters upon the slave, he left his wife and children with no protectors save the Negroes themselves. And yet during those years of trust and peril, no Negro proved recreant to his trust and no white man returned to a home that had been dispoiled.

Likewise during the period of alleged "insurrection," and alarming "race riots," it never occurred to the white man, that his wife and children were in danger of assault. Nor in the Reconstruction era, when the hue and cry was against "Negro Domination," was there ever a thought that the domination would ever contaminate a fireside or strike to death the virtue of womanhood. It must appear strange indeed, to every thoughtful and candid man, that more than a quarter of a century elapsed before the Negro began to show signs of such infamous degeneration....

It is his regret, that, in his own defense, he must disclose to the world that degree of dehumanizing brutality which fixes upon America the blot of a national crime. Whatever faults and failings other nations may have in their dealings with their own subjects or with other people, no other civilized nation stands condemned before the world with a series of crimes so peculiarly national. It becomes a painful duty of the Negro to reproduce a record which shows that a large portion of the American people avow anarchy, condone murder and defy the contempt of civilization.

These pages are written in no spirit of vindictiveness, for all who give the subject consideration must concede that far too serious is the condition of that civilized government in which the spirit of unrestrained outlawry constantly increases in violence, and casts its blight over a continually growing area of territory. We plead not for the colored people alone, but for all victims of the terrible injustice which puts men and women to death without form of law. During the year 1894, there were 132 persons executed in the United States by due form of law, while in the same year, 197 persons were put to death by mobs who gave the victims no opportunity to make a lawful defense. No comment need be made upon a condition of public sentiment responsible for such alarming results....

148

W. E. B. Du Bois on Race Relations (1903)

W. E. B. Du Bois was among a group of African American intellectuals who opposed the accommodationist views of Booker T. Washington. Born and raised in Massachusetts, Du Bois studied with many of the leading thinkers of the day and later earned a PhD in history at Harvard. He taught at several universities, committed his life to ending segregation and discrimination, and helped shape the modern African American identity. Du Bois believed that only by confronting and educating whites about the inequity of discrimination and segregation could the overall condition for African Americans improve. He also believed that the black elite had a responsibility to help fellow African Americans. In 1903, while an Atlanta University professor, Du Bois published The Souls of Black Folk, *which included a chapter that criticized Booker T. Washington's approach to race relations. In 1909–1910, Du Bois would join white and black intellectuals to found the National Association for the Advancement of Colored People (NAACP). He became the NAACP director of publicity and editor of its journal,* The Crisis.

Questions to Consider

1. What are the reasons for Du Bois's criticism of Booker T. Washington and his approach to race relations?
2. What does Du Bois propose to African Americans?
3. What does this document reveal about race relations at the turn of the twentieth century?

4. How do you think a California legislator who supported restricting the immigration of Chinese ("The Unwanted Immigrants: The Chinese," Document 149) would respond to Du Bois's views?

Mr. Washington represents in Negro thought the old attitude of adjustment and submission; but adjustment at such a peculiar time as to make his programme unique. This is an age of unusual economic development, and Mr. Washington's programme naturally takes an economic cast, becoming a gospel of Work and Money to such an extent as apparently almost completely to overshadow the higher aims of life. Moreover, this is an age when the more advanced races are coming in closer contact with the less developed races, and the race-feeling is therefore intensified; and Mr. Washington's programme practically accepts the alleged inferiority of the Negro races. Again, in our own land, the reaction from the sentiment of war time has given impetus to race-prejudice against Negroes, and Mr. Washington withdraws many of the high demands of Negroes as men and American citizens. In other periods of intensified prejudice all the Negro's tendency to self-assertion has been called forth; at this period a policy of submission is advocated. In the history of nearly all other races and peoples the doctrine preached as such crises has been that manly self-respect is worth more than lands and houses, and that a people who voluntarily surrender such respect, or cease striving for it, are not worth civilizing.

In answer to this, it has been claimed that the Negro can survive only through submission. Mr. Washington distinctly asks that black people give up, at least for the present, three things, —

First, political power,

Second, insistence on civil rights,

Third, higher education of Negro youth, —

and concentrate all their energies on industrial education, the accumulation of wealth, and the conciliation of the South. This policy has been courageously and insistently advocated for over fifteen years, and has been triumphant for perhaps ten years. As a result of this tender of the palm-branch, what has been the return? In these years there have occurred:

1. The disfranchisement of the Negro.
2. The legal creation of a distinct status of civil inferiority for the Negro.
3. The steady withdrawal of aid from institutions for the higher training of the Negro.

These movements are not, to be sure, direct results of Mr. Washington's teachings; but his propaganda has, without a shadow of doubt, helped their speedier accomplishment. The question then comes: Is it possible, and probable, that nine millions of men can make effective progress in economic lines if they are deprived of political rights, made a servile caste, and allowed only the most

SOURCE: W. E. B. Du Bois, *The Souls of Black Folk* (Chicago, 1903), 50–52, 57–59.

meagre chance for developing their exceptional men? If history and reason give any distinct answer to these questions, it is an emphatic *No*. And Mr. Washington thus faces the triple paradox of his career:

1. He is striving nobly to make Negro artisans business men and property-owners; but it is utterly impossible, under modern competitive methods, for workingmen and property-owners to defend their rights and exist without the right of suffrage.
2. He insists on thrift and self-respect, but at the same time counsels a silent submission to civic inferiority such as is bound to sap the manhood of any race in the long run.
3. He advocates common-school and industrial training, and depreciates institutions of higher learning; but neither the Negro common-schools, nor Tuskegee itself, could remain open a day were it not for teachers trained in Negro colleges, or trained by their graduates....

It would be unjust to Mr. Washington not to acknowledge that in several instances he has opposed movements in the South which were unjust to the Negro; he sent memorials to the Louisiana and Alabama constitutional conventions, he has spoken against lynching, and in other ways has openly or silently set his influence against sinister schemes and unfortunate happenings. Notwithstanding this, it is equally true to assert that on the whole the distinct impression left by Mr. Washington's propaganda is, first, that the South is justified in its present attitude toward the Negro because of the Negro's degradation; secondly, that the prime cause of the Negro's failure to rise more quickly is his wrong education in the past; and, thirdly, that his future rise depends primarily on his own efforts. Each of these propositions is a dangerous half-truth. The supplementary truths must never be lost sight of: first, slavery and race-prejudice are potent if not sufficient causes of the Negro's position; second, industrial and common-school training were necessarily slow in planting because they had to await the black teachers trained by higher institutions, —it being extremely doubtful if any essentially different development was possible, and certainly a Tuskegee was unthinkable before 1880; and third, while it is a great truth to say that the Negro must strive and strive mightily to help himself, it is equally true that unless his striving be not simply seconded, but rather aroused and encouraged, by the initiative of the richer and wiser environing group, he cannot hope for great success.

In his failure to realize and impress this last point, Mr. Washington is especially to be criticised. His doctrine has tended to make the whites, North and South, shift the burden of the Negro problem to the Negro's shoulders and stand aside as critical and rather pessimistic spectators; when in fact the burden belongs to the nation, and the hands of none of us are clean if we bend not our energies to righting these great wrongs.

The South ought to be led, by candid and honest criticism, to assert her better self and do her full duty to the race she has cruelly wronged and is still wronging. The North—her co-partner in guilt—cannot salve her conscience by plastering it with gold. We cannot settle this problem by diplomacy and suaveness, by "policy" alone. If worse come to worst, can the moral fibre of this country survive the slow throttling and murder of nine millions of men?

The black men of America have a duty to perform, a duty stern and delicate, —a forward movement to oppose a part of the work of their greatest leader. So far as Mr. Washington preaches Thrift, Patience, and Industrial Training for the masses, we must hold up his hands and strive with him, rejoicing in his honors and glorying in the strength of this Joshua called of God and of man to lead the headless host. But so far as Mr. Washington apologizes for injustice, North or South, does not rightly value the privilege and duty of voting, belittles the emasculating effects of caste distinctions, and opposes the higher training and ambition of our brighter minds, —so far as he, the South, or the Nation, does this, —we must unceasingly and firmly oppose them. By every civilized and peaceful method we must strive for the rights which the world accords to men, clinging unwaveringly to those great words which the sons of the Fathers would fain forget: "We hold these truths to be self-evident: That all men are created equal; that they are endowed by their Creator with certain unalienable rights; that among these are life, liberty, and the pursuit of happiness."

149

The Unwanted Immigrants: The Chinese (1878)

Fleeing political and economic hardships, Chinese immigrants came to the West Coast and settled first in California. Initially it was the California gold rush that attracted Chinese immigrants, but the western railroad companies actively recruited large numbers of Chinese immigrants to construct their tracks. Known for their willingness to work long hours for little pay, these "coolies," as whites called them, filled many manual labor jobs when railroad construction declined. White workers, who came to resent the industrious Chinese and their different customs and lifestyle, began pressuring state governments for action. Even though in 1878 the Chinese composed only 1 percent of California's population (and 0.002 percent of the nation's), the California legislature investigated the nature and impact of Chinese immigration. The committee's report, excerpted here, warned the nation about the "evils" of the Chinese and reflected the racism that had developed; four years later, Congress passed the Chinese Exclusion Act (1882) and suspended Chinese immigration for ten years.

Questions to Consider

1. According to this California state government report, in what ways do Californians oppose the Chinese immigrants?

2. For what reasons were the Chinese singled out, and not other immigrant groups?

3. Why would Congress pass the Chinese Exclusion Act, if the Chinese are identified as problems only in California?

4. How might Ida Wells Barnett ("Lynching in the South," Document 147) respond to the sentiments contained in this document?

The Chinese have now lived among us, in considerable numbers, for a quarter of a century, and yet they remain separate, distinct from, and antagonistic to our people in thinking, mode of life, in tastes and principles, and are as far from assimilation as when they first arrived.

They fail to comprehend our system of government; they perform no duties of citizenship; they are not available as jurymen; cannot be called upon as a *posse comitatus* to preserve order, nor be relied upon as soldiers.

They do not comprehend or appreciate our social ideas, and they contribute but little to the support of any of our institutions, public or private.

They bring no children with them, and there is, therefore, no possibility of influencing them by our ordinary educational appliances.

There is, indeed, no point of contact between the Chinese and our people through which we can Americanize them. The rigidity which characterizes these people forbids the hope of any essential change in their relations to our own people or our government.

We respectfully submit the admitted proposition that no nation, much less a republic, can safely permit the presence of a large and increasing element among its people which cannot be assimilated or made to comprehend the responsibilities of citizenship.

The great mass of the Chinese residents of California are not amenable to our laws. It is almost impossible to procure the conviction of Chinese criminals, and we are never sure that a conviction, even when obtained, is in accordance with justice.

This difficulty arises out of our ignorance of the Chinese language and the fact that their moral ideas are wholly distinct from our own. They do not recognize the sanctity of an oath, and utterly fail to comprehend the crime of perjury. Bribery, intimidation, and other methods of baffling judicial action, are considered by them as perfectly legitimate. It is an established fact that the administration of justice among the Chinese is almost impossible, and we are, therefore, unable to protect them against the persecutions of their own countrymen, or punish them for offenses against our own people. This anomalous condition, in

SOURCE: California Senate, Special Committee on Chinese Immigration, "An Address to the American People of the United States upon the Evils of Chinese Immigration," *Report of the Special Committee on Chinese Immigration to the California State Senate, 1878,* 8–9, 25, 35, 46–47.

which the authority of law is so generally vacated, imperils the existence of our republican institutions to a degree hitherto unknown among us....

We now come to an aspect of the question more revolting still. We would shrink from the disgusting details did not a sense of duty demand that they be presented. Their lewd women induce, by the cheapness of their offers, thousands of boys and young men to enter their dens, very many of whom are inoculated with venereal diseases of the worst type. Boys of eight and ten years of age have been found with this disease, and some of our physicians treat a half dozen cases daily. The fact that these diseases have their origin chiefly among the Chinese is well established....

But we desire to call your attention to the sanitary aspect of the subject. The Chinese herd together in one spot, whether in city or village, until they transform the vicinage into a perfect hive—there they live packed together, a hundred living in a space that would be insufficient for an average American family.

Their place of domicile is filthy in the extreme, and to a degree that cleansing is impossible except by the absolute destruction of the dwellings they occupy. But for the healthfulness of our climate, our city populations would have long since been decimated by pestilence from these causes. And we do not know how long this natural protection will suffice us.

In almost every house is found a room devoted to opium smoking, and these places are visited by white boys and women, so that the deadly opium habit is being introduced among our people....

We now call attention to an aspect of the subject of such huge proportions, and such practical and pressing importance, that we almost dread to enter upon its consideration, namely, the effect of Chinese labor upon our industrial classes. We admit that the Chinese were, in the earlier history of the State, when white labor was not attainable, very useful in the development of our peculiar industries; that they were of great service in railroad building, in mining, gardening, general agriculture, and as domestic servants.

We admit that the Chinese are exceedingly expert in all kinds of labor and manufacturing; that they are easily and inexpensively handled in large numbers.

We recognize the right of all men to better their condition when they can, and deeply sympathize with the overcrowded population of China....

Our laborers cannot be induced to live like vermin, as the Chinese and these habits of individual and family life have ever been encouraged by our statesmen as essential to good morals.

Our laborers require meat and bread, which have been considered by us as necessary to that mental and bodily strength which is thought to be important in the citizens of a Republic which depends upon the strength of its people, while the Chinese require only rice, dried fish, tea, and a few simple vegetables. The cost of sustenance to the whites is four-fold greater than that of the Chinese, and the wages of the whites must of necessity be greater than the wages required by the Chinese. The Chinese are, therefore, able to underbid the whites in every kind of labor. They can be hired in masses; they can be managed and controlled like unthinking slaves. But our laborer has an individual life, cannot be controlled as a slave by brutal masters, and this individuality has been required of him by the genius of our institutions, and upon these elements of character the State depends for defense and growth....

As a natural consequence the white laborer is out of employment, and misery and want are fast taking the places of comfort and plenty.

Now, to consider and weigh the benefits returned to us by the Chinese for these privileges and for these wrongs to our laboring classes. They buy little or nothing from our own people, but import both their food and clothing from China; they send their wages home; they have not introduced a single industry peculiar to their own country; they contribute nothing to the support of our institutions; can never be relied upon as defenders of the State; they have no intention of becoming citizens; they acquire no homes, and are a constant tax upon the public treasury....

150

"The Story of a Sweatshop Girl" (1902)

The adaptation of machines to methods of production brought changes to the workforce as well as to the way goods were made. The garment industry was among those businesses affected by the change. The development of standard clothing sizes, the use of the electrically powered sewing machine, and the availability of low-wage workers allowed for the mass production of inexpensive clothes for both men and women. In most instances, garment businesses were located in cities. Often taking over a floor or floors of a former warehouse, the owners crammed numerous workers and machines into these floors, creating crowded and dangerous workplaces that became known as sweatshops. The workforce was usually composed of young females, often recent immigrants, as the garment trades offered women one of the few sources of income outside the home. These women assembled parts of clothing, performing the same sewing task repetitiously for hours on end. In 1902, Sadie Frowne, a Polish immigrant, told her story as a sweatshop girl to a reporter from the news magazine The Independent. *Excerpts of her account follow.*

Questions to Consider

1. How does Sadie Frowne describe her work and the conditions in the sweatshop?

2. In what ways does Sadie Frowne seek to improve her life?

3. What does this document reveal about life and work for immigrant women?

4. How might Sadie Frowne respond to David A. Wells ("The Impact of
    Mechanization," Document 142)?

... Aunt Fanny had always been anxious for me to get an education, as I did not
know how to read or write, and she thought that was wrong. Schools are different in Poland from what they are in this country, and I was always too busy to
learn to read and write. So when mother died I thought I would try to learn a
trade and then I could go to school at night and learn to speak the English language well.

So I went to work in Allen street (Manhattan) in what they call a sweatshop,
making skirts by machine. I was new at the work and the foreman scolded me a
great deal.

"Now, then," he would say, "this place is not for you to be looking around
in. Attend to your work. That is what you have to do."

I did not know at first that you must not look around and talk, and I made
many mistakes with the sewing, so that I was often called a "stupid animal." But
I made $4 a week by working six days in the week. For there are two Sabbaths
here—our own Sabbath, that comes on a Saturday, and the Christian Sabbath
that comes on Sunday. It is against our law to work on our own Sabbath, so
we work on their Sabbath....

Two years ago I came to this place, Brownsville, where so many of my people are, and where I have friends. I got work in a factory making underskirts—all
sorts of cheap underskirts, like cotton and calico for the summer and woolen for
the winter, but never the silk, satin or velvet underskirts. I earned $4.50 a week
and lived on $2 a week, the same as before....

It isn't piecework in our factory, but one is paid by the amount of work
done just the same. So it is like piecework. All the hands get different amounts,
some as low as $3.50 and some of the men as high as $16 a week. The factory is
in the third story of a brick building. It is in a room twenty feet long and fourteen broad. There are fourteen machines in it. I and the daughter of the people
with whom I live work two of these machines. The other operators are all men,
some young and some old....

I get up at half-past five o'clock every morning and make myself a cup of
coffee on the oil stove. I eat a bit of bread and perhaps some fruit and then go to
work. Often I get there soon after six o'clock so as to be in good time, tho the
factory does not open till seven. I have heard that there is a sort of clock that calls
you at the very time you want to get up, but I can't believe that because I don't
see how the clock would know.

At seven o'clock we all sit down to our machines and the boss brings to each
one the pile of work that he or she is to finish during the day, what they call in
English their "stint." This pile is put down beside the machine and as soon as a
skirt is done it is laid on the other side of the machine. Sometimes the work is
not all finished by six o'clock and then the one who is behind must work

SOURCE: "The Story of a Sweatshop Girl," *The Independent* 54 (25 September 1902): 2279–82.

overtime. Sometimes one is finished ahead of time and gets away at four or five o'clock, but generally we are not done till six o'clock. The machines go like mad all day, because the faster you work the more money you get. Sometimes in my haste I get my finger caught and the needle goes right through it. It goes so quick, tho, that it does not hurt much. I bind the finger up with a piece of cotton and go on working. We all have accidents like that. Where the needle goes through the nail it makes a sore finger, or where it splinters a bone it does much harm. Sometimes a finger has to come off. Generally, tho, one can be cured by a salve.

All the time we are working the boss walks about examining the finished garments and making us do them over again if they are not just right. So we have to be careful as well as swift. But I am getting so good at the work that within a year I will be making $7 a week, and then I can save at least $3.50 a week. I have over $200 saved now.

The machines are all run by foot power, and at the end of the day one feels so weak that there is a great temptation to lie right down and sleep. But you must go out and get air, and have some pleasure. So instead of lying down I go out, generally with Henry. Sometimes we go to Coney Island, where there are good dancing places, and sometimes we go to Ulmer Park to picnics....

I am going back to night school again this winter. Plenty of my friends go there. Some of the women in my class are more than forty years of age. Like me, they did not have a chance to learn anything in the old country. It is good to have an education; it makes you feel higher. Ignorant people are all low. People say now that I am clever and fine in conversation.

We have just finished a strike in our business. It spread all over and the United Brotherhood of Garment Workers was in it. That takes in the cloakmakers, coatmakers, and all the others. We struck for shorter hours, and after being out four weeks won the fight. We only have to work nine and a half hours a day and we get the same pay as before. So the union does good after all in spite of what some people say against it—that it just takes our money and does nothing.

I pay 25 cents a month to the union, but I do not begrudge that because it is for our benefit. The next strike is going to be for a raise of wages, which we all ought to have. But tho I belong to the Union I am not a Socialist or an Anarchist. I don't know exactly what those things mean. There is a little expense for charity, too. If any worker is injured or sick we all give money to help....

151

An Italian Immigrant's Experience in America (1902)

In the Gilded Age the nature of European immigration to America changed. The number of immigrants increased dramatically, and the ethnic composition changed. Unlike earlier immigrants who came from northern and western Europe, these "New Immigrants" came from southern and eastern Europe. These Italians, Russian Jews, Poles, Slovaks, to name a few, brought languages, religions, and customs that sharply contrasted with native-born American lifestyles. The new immigrants clustered into the growing cities, often forming easily identified ethnic neighborhoods ("Little Italy," for example) as a refuge from the realities of life in America. Often uneducated and lacking job skills, many immigrants found work in low-paying, menial occupations. One example of an immigrant's experience was Rocco Corresca's. Raised as an orphan in Italy, Corresca was forced to beg and steal in the streets for a living. Corresca and his friend Francisco fled to America, where they fell victim to the exploitive padrone system. In 1902, the news magazine The Independent *published Rocco Corresca's account of life in America, which is excerpted below.*

Questions to Consider

1. What services did the padrone (Bartolo) provide to Rocco and Francisco?
2. In what ways did Rocco and Francisco adapt to life in America? Not adapt?
3. What does this account reveal about the Italian immigrant experience?
4. In what ways does the experiences of Rocco and Francisco differ from Sadie Frowne ("The Story of a Sweatshop Girl," Document 150) or from the Chinese ("The Unwanted Immigrants: The Chinese," Document 149).

Now and then I had heard things about America—that it was a far off country where everybody was rich and that Italians went there and made plenty of money, so that they could return to Italy and live in pleasure ever after. One day I met a young man who pulled out a handful of gold and told me he had made that in America in a few days.

I said I should like to go there, and he told me that if I went he would take care of me and see that I was safe. I told Francisco and he wanted to go too....

SOURCE: Rocco Corresca, "The Biography of a Bootblack," *The Independent* 54 (4 December 1902): 2863–67.

... We were all landed on an island and the bosses there said that Francisco and I must go back because we had not enough money, but a man named Bartolo came up and told them that we were brothers and he was our uncle and would take care of us. He brought two other men who swore that they knew us in Italy and that Bartolo was our uncle. I had never seen any of them before, but even then Bartolo might be my uncle, so I did not say anything. The bosses of the island let us go out with Bartolo after he had made the oath....

Most of the men in our room worked at digging the sewer. Bartolo got them the work and they paid him about one quarter of their wages. Then he charged them for board and he bought the clothes for them, too. So they got little money after all.

Bartolo was always saying that the rent of the room was so high that he could not make anything, but he was really making plenty. He was what they call a padrone and is now a very rich man. The men that were living with him had just come to the country and could not speak English. They had all been sent by the young man we met in Italy. Bartolo told us all that we must work for him and that if we did not the police would come and put us in prison....

We were with Bartolo nearly a year, but some of our countrymen who had been in the place a long time said that Bartolo had no right to us and we could get work for a dollar and a half a day, which, when you make it *lire* (reckoned in the Italian currency) is very much. So we went away one day to Newark and got work on the street. Bartolo came after us and made a great noise, but the boss said that if he did not go away soon the police would have him. Then he went, saying that there was no justice in this country.

We paid a man five dollars each for getting us the work and we were with that boss for six months. He was Irish, but a good man and he gave us our money every Saturday night. We lived much better than with Bartolo, and when the work was done we each had nearly $200 saved. Plenty of the men spoke English and they taught us, and we taught them to read and write. That was at night, for we had a lamp in our room, and there were only five other men who lived in that room with us....

When the Newark boss told us that there was no more work Francisco and I talked about what we would do and we went back to Brooklyn to a saloon near Hamilton Ferry, where we got a job cleaning it out and slept in a little room upstairs. There was a bootblack named Michael on the corner and when I had time I helped him and learned the business. Francisco cooked the lunch in the saloon and he, too, worked for the bootblack and we were soon able to make the best polish.

Then we thought we would go into business and we got a basement on Hamilton avenue, near the Ferry, and put four chairs in it. We paid $75 for the chairs and all the other things. We had tables and looking glasses there and curtains. We took the papers that have the pictures in and made the place high toned. Outside we had a big sign that said:

THE BEST SHINE FOR TEN CENTS.

Men that did not want to pay ten cents could get a good shine for five cents, but it was not an oil shine. We had two boys helping us and paid each of them fifty cents a day. The rent of the place was $20 a month, so the expenses were very great but we made money from the beginning. We slept in the basement, but got our meals in the saloon till we could put a stove in our place, and then Francisco cooked for us all. That would not do, tho, because some of our customers said that they did not like to smell garlic and onions and red herrings. I thought that was strange, but we had to do what the customers said. So we got the woman who lived upstairs to give us our meals and paid her $1.50 a week each. She gave the boys soup in the middle of the day—five cents for two plates....

We had said that when we saved $1,000 each we would go back to Italy and buy a farm, but now that the time is coming we are so busy and making so much money that we think we will stay. We have opened another parlor near South Ferry, in New York. We have to pay $30.00 a month rent, but the business is very good. The boys in this place charge sixty cents a day because there is so much work.

At first we did not know much of this country, but by and by we learned. There are here plenty of Protestants who are heretics, but they have a religion, too. Many of the finest churches are Protestant, but they have no saints and no altars, which seems strange....

I and Francisco are to be Americans in three years. The court gave us papers and said we must wait and we must be able to read some things and tell who the ruler of the country is.

There are plenty of rich Italians here, men who a few years ago had nothing and now have so much money that they could not count all their dollars in a week. The richest ones go away from the other Italians and live with the Americans....

I am nineteen years of age now and have $700. saved. Francisco is twenty-one and has about $900. We shall open some more parlors soon. I know an Italian who was a bootblack ten years ago and now bosses bootblacks all over the city, who has so much money that if it was turned into gold it would weigh more than himself....

I often think of Ciguciano and Teresa [in Italy]. He is a good man, one in a thousand, and she was very beautiful. Maybe I shall write to them about coming to this country.

152

A Woman's Perspective on Women and the Economy (1898)

Women in the Gilded Age faced considerable obstacles. Most states denied women the right to vote and often relegated women to a status secondary to men. Married women were often burdened with the responsibilities of maintaining the home; they had little opportunity for leisure or social interaction. Their days were consumed with dreary housework and raising the children, while their husband worked and enjoyed recreation outside the home. These women were placed in a separate sphere from men, and they were to accept this subordinate position. Even though the numbers of employed women increased significantly in the Gilded Age, many were domestics in other people's homes or became nurses and teachers. Despite new occupations in clerical work (such as receptionists and typists) and jobs in retail sales, women were often denied opportunities for jobs outside of traditional women's work. In the late nineteenth century, Charlotte Perkins Gilman wrote Women and Economics, *in which she challenged the conventional view of womanhood, work, marriage, domesticity, the separate sphere, and the woman's economic dependence on men. She focused on the home as limiting women. Excerpted here are Gilman's comments on the economic situation for women.*

Questions to Consider

1. How does Charlotte Perkins Gilman see the status of women?
2. In what ways does Gilman connect women to the economy?
3. What does Gilman suggest about women in Gilded Age America?
4. What does this document reveal about the lives and work of women?

Is this the condition of human motherhood? Does the human mother, by her motherhood, thereby lose control of brain and body, lose power and skill and desire for any other work? Do we see before us the human race, with all its females segregated entirely to the uses of motherhood, consecrated, set apart, specially developed, spending every power of their nature on the service of their children?

We do not. We see the human mother worked far harder than a mare, laboring her life long in the service, not of her children only, but of men;

SOURCE: Charlotte Perkins Gilman, *Women and Economics* (Boston, 1898), 19–21, 117–21.

husbands, brothers, fathers, whatever male relatives she has; for mother and sister also; for the church a little, if she is allowed; for society, if she is able; for charity and education and reform,— working in many ways that are not the ways of motherhood.

It is not motherhood that keeps the housewife on her feet from dawn till dark; it is house service, not child service. Women work longer and harder than most men, and not solely in maternal duties. The savage mother carries the burdens, and does all menial service for the tribe. The peasant mother toils in the fields, and the workingman's wife in the home. Many mothers, even now, are wage-earners for the family, as well as bearers and rearers of it. And the women who are not so occupied, the women who belong to rich men,— here perhaps is the exhaustive devotion to maternity which is supposed to justify an admitted economic dependence. But we do not find it even among these. Women of ease and wealth provide for their children better care than the poor woman can; but they do not spend more time upon it themselves, nor more care and effort. They have other occupation.

In spite of her supposed segregation to maternal duties, the human female, the world over, works at extra-maternal duties for hours enough to provide her with an independent living, and then is denied independence on the ground that motherhood prevents her working!...

The working power of the mother has always been a prominent factor in human life. She is the worker *par excellence*, but her work is not such as to affect her economic status. Her living, all that she gets,— food, clothing, ornaments, amusements, luxuries,— these bear no relation to her power to produce wealth, to her services in the house, or to her motherhood. These things bear relation only to the man she marries, the man she depends on,— to how much he has and how much he is willing to give her....

... For the woman there is, first, no free production allowed; and, second, no relation maintained between what she does produce and what she consumes. She is forbidden to make, but encouraged to take. Her industry is not the natural output of creative energy, not the work she does because she has the inner power and strength to do it; nor is her industry even the measure of her gain. She has, of course, the natural desire to consume; and to that is set no bar save the capacity or the will of her husband.

Thus we have painfully and laboriously evolved and carefully maintain among us an enormous class of non-productive consumers, — a class which is half the world, and mother of the other half. We have built into the constitution of the human race the habit and desire of taking, as divorced from its natural precursor and concomitant of making. We have made for ourselves this endless array of "horse-leech's daughters, crying, Give! give!" To consume food, to consume clothes, to consume houses and furniture and decorations and ornaments and amusements, to take and take and take forever, — from one man if they are virtuous, from many if they are vicious, but always to take and never to think of giving anything in return except their womanhood, — this is the enforced condition of the mothers of the race. What wonder that their sons go into business "for what there is in it"! What wonder that the world is full of the desire to get as much as possible and to give as little as possible! What wonder, either, that the glory and sweetness of love are but a name among us, with here and there a strange and beautiful exception, of which our admiration proves the rarity!

Between the brutal ferocity of excessive male energy struggling in the market-place as in a battlefield and the unnatural greed generated by the perverted condition of female energy, it is not remarkable that the industrial evolution of humanity has shown peculiar symptoms. One of the minor effects of this last condition — this limiting of female industry to close personal necessities, and this tendency of her over-developed sex-nature to overestimate the so-called "duties of her position" — has been to produce an elaborate devotion to individuals and their personal needs, — not to the understanding and developing of their higher natures, but to the intensification of their bodily tastes and pleasure. The wife and mother, pouring the rising tide of racial power into the same old channels that were allowed her primitive ancestors, constantly ministers to the physical needs of her family with a ceaseless and concentrated intensity. They like it, of course. But it maintains in the individuals of the race an exaggerated sense of the importance of food and clothes and ornaments to themselves, without at all including a knowledge of their right use and value to us all. It developes personal selfishness.

Again, the consuming female, debarred from any free production, unable to estimate the labor involved in the making of what she so lightly destroys, and her consumption limited mainly to those things which minister to physical pleasure, creates a market for sensuous decoration and personal ornament, for all that is luxurious and enervating, and for a false and capricious variety in such supplies, which operates as a most deadly check to true industry and true art. As the priestess of the temple of consumption, as the limitless demander of things to use up, her economic influence is reactionary and injurious. Much, very much, of the current of useless production in which our economic energies run waste—man's strength poured out like water on the sand—depends on the creation and careful maintenance of this false market, this sink into which human labor vanishes with no return. Woman, in her false economic position, reacts injuriously upon industry, upon art, upon science, discovery, and progress. The sexuo-economic relation in its effect on the constitution of the individual keeps alive in us the instincts of savage individualism which we should otherwise have well outgrown. It sexualizes our industrial relation and commercializes our sex-relation. And, in the external effect upon the market, the over-sexed woman, in her unintelligent and ceaseless demands, hinders and perverts the economic development of the world.

18

The Progressive Movement

The polarization of society into rich and poor, assimilable and unassimilable in the late nineteenth century prompted many middle-class Americans into action. The reformers who emerged to cure these ills came to be known as the Progressives. Eschewing the laissez-faire approach of the past, the movement believed that through the expansion of democracy, active government, and the regulation of business to create opportunity, a new class of well-trained professionals could solve society's problems. Although some contemporaries criticized the Progressives' efforts as radical, the leaders of the movement actually sought a more centrist approach in solving these problems. The next group of documents illustrates the problems facing, and solutions advocated by, the Progressives and the Socialists.

153

An Insider's View of Hull House

One of the initial efforts to bring about progressive reform came with individuals like Jane Addams, who helped establish the settlement house movement in America. Part of a first generation of college-educated women, Addams declined marriage and motherhood and devoted her life to the poor and to social reform. In 1889 she and a college friend, Ellen Starr, bought the Hull House mansion in a Chicago immigrant neighborhood and created a model settlement house that offered services to the poor in the neighborhood. But Addams realized that such neighborhood activities were futile unless laws were reformed to address larger problems, so she campaigned to pass state and local laws that would improve conditions in the urban neighborhoods. Addams publicized Hull House and social reform with lecture tours and writings. Hilda S. Polacheck, the author of the following excerpted selection, was a recent Polish immigrant who discovered Hull House and its offerings. Her account presents a unique insider's view of Hull House and the services it provided for immigrants in the neighborhood. Polacheck credits Hull House, and especially Jane Addams, with making her life in America better.

Questions to Consider

1. In what ways did Hull House help immigrants and urban dwellers?
2. For what reasons did Hilda Polacheck visit and then work at Hull House?
3. What did Jane Addams hope to accomplish at Hull House?
4. What do you think Jane Addams and Hilda Polacheck had in common? How were they different? From this document, what can you deduce about the differences between native and foreign-born Americans?

She took me up a flight of stairs and then down a flight and we came to the Labor Museum. The museum had been opened a short time before and it was a very special addition to the work at Hull-House and very dear to her heart. As I look back, and this may be wishful thinking, I feel that she sensed what I needed most at that time....

There were many classes connected with the Labor Museum. Here we could learn how to cook and sew and also learn about millinery and embroidery....

There was still another function that the Labor Museum filled. Miss Addams found that there was a definite feeling of superiority on the part of children of immigrants toward their parents. As soon as the children learned to speak English, they were prone to look down on those who could not speak the language. I am grateful that I never had that feeling toward my parents, but I often talked to playmates who would disdainfully say: "Aw, she can't talk English."

I recall having an argument with a girl whose mother could speak German, French, Russian, and Polish but had not yet learned to speak English. That girl did not realize that her mother was a linguist. To her, the mother was just a greenhorn.

For such children the Labor Museum was an eye-opener. When they saw crowds of well-dressed Americans standing around admiring what Italian, Irish, German, and Scandinavian mothers could do, their disdain for their mothers often vanished.

SOURCE: From Hilda Satt Polacheck, *I Came a Stranger: The Story of a Hull-House Girl*, ed. Dena J. Polacheck Epstein (Urbana, IL, 1989), 63–67, 70–73, 91–92, 102. Copyright © 1989 by the Board of Trustees of the University of Illinois. Used with permission of the University of Illinois Press.

The Labor Museum did not solve all the problems of immigrant parents and their children. There were many problems that were not easy to solve. Children, by going to school and to work, did come in contact with forces in American life and had a better chance of becoming Americanized. But I am sure the Labor Museum reduced the strained feelings on the part of immigrants and their children....

I soon branched out into other activities. I joined a reading class that was conducted by Miss Clara Landsberg....

... She opened new vistas in reading for me. In her class we would be assigned a book, which we were to read during the week and then discuss the following session of the class. The class met once a week. I not only read the assigned books but every book I could borrow. Dickens, Scott, Thackeray, Louisa May Alcott, Victor Hugo, Alexander Dumas, and many others now became my friends. The daily monotony of making cuffs was eased by thinking of these books and looking forward to evenings at Hull-House.

For ten years I spent most of my evenings at Hull-House. The first three years of that time I saw Jane Addams almost every night. As more and more people found their way to this haven of love and understanding, she began to relegate the work to other people and to seek rest at the home of friends. But her presence was always felt, whether she was there in person or in spirit....

Bad housing of the thousands of immigrants who lived near Hull-House was the concern of Jane Addams. Where there were alleys in back of the houses, these alleys were filled with large wooden boxes where garbage and horse manure were dumped. In most cases these boxes did not have covers and were breeding places for flies and rats. The city gave contracts to private scavengers to collect the garbage. Its responsibility seemed to end there. There was no alley inspection and no one checked on these collectors.

When Jane Addams called the attention of the health department to the unsanitary conditions, she was told that the city had contracted to have the garbage collected and it could do nothing else. When the time came to renew contracts for garbage collection, Miss Addams, with the backing of some businessmen, put in a bid to collect garbage. Her bid was never considered, but she was appointed garbage inspector for the ward. I have a vision of Jane Addams, honored by the great of the world, acclaimed as the first citizen of Chicago, following a filthy garbage truck down an alley in her long skirt and immaculate white blouse....

Being allowed to teach English to immigrants at Hull-House did more for me than anything that I imparted to my students. It gave me a feeling of security that I so sorely needed. What added to my confidence in the future was that my class was always crowded and the people seemed to make good progress. From time to time Jane Addams would visit the class to see what I was doing, and she always left with that rare smile on her face; she seemed to be pleased....

But to come back to the subject of textbooks, since there were none, I decided to use the Declaration of Independence as a text. It was a distinct success. The students did not find the words difficult; so in addition to learning English, we all learned the principles of Americanism.

I next introduced the manual on naturalization and the class learned English while studying how to become a citizen. It was all very exciting and stimulating.

My students were now beginning to confide in me. Classes at Hull-House were never just classes where people came to learn a specific subject. There was a human element of friendliness among us. Life was not soft or easy for any of them. They worked hard all day in shops and factories and made this valiant effort to learn the language of their adopted country. At times they needed real help, and they knew that somewhere in this wonderful house on Halsted Street they would get it....

As time went on, I discovered that Hull-House was the experimental laboratory for Jane Addams's interests and services. To create opportunities for young people of the neighborhood, to bring a little sunshine into otherwise bleak lives of older immigrants, to point out the evils of miserable housing; in short, to tell Chicago what its responsibility to the poor was, was just first aid to the problem. She traveled through America spreading the gospel of a better life than she had found on South Halsted Street. As a result, social settlements sprang up all over the country. Chicago became dotted with playgrounds. Social centers were added to these playgrounds and became the responsibility of the city government.

154

"The American Forests" (1901)

For some progressive reformers, a key issue was conservation. Many Americans had long believed that the nation's natural resources were unlimited and could be selfishly plundered. By the late nineteenth century, it became clear that the natural landscape was altered in potentially harmful ways and that limited resources were being depleted at an alarming rate. The impact of such behavior caused others to launch the conservation movement. The question of how to best approach, or even define, conservation divided Progressives. Gifford Pinchot led one camp of conservationists. A specialist in forestry management, Pinchot headed the newly created U.S. Forest Service and would advocate a program that natural resources be used efficiently. He regulated the use of government land through user fees, created a competitive bidding process for lumbering on government lands, and insisted on an efficient harvest of the forest crop that should be replenished for future generations. Taking the approach of preservation was John Muir. Born in Scotland, raised in Wisconsin, Muir was a naturalist and advocate of protecting land from human interference. In 1897, Muir published the article excerpted here in the respected Atlantic Monthly; *he would later include the article in* Our National Parks *(1901), where he outlined the preservationist approaches to conservation. He was one of the principal founders of the Sierra Club and served as its first president.*

Questions to Consider

1. In what ways does Muir characterize the activities of man in the forest?
2. According to Muir, what do forests provide humankind?
3. For what reasons does Muir argue for federal government involvement in forest lands?
4. In what ways are the two positions on conservation (Muir's and Pinchot's) relevant today?

... American forests! the glory of the world! Surveyed thus from the east to the west, from the north to the south, they are rich beyond thought, immortal, immeasurable, enough and to spare for every feeding, sheltering beast and bird, insect and son of Adam; and nobody need have cared had there been no pines in Norway, no cedars and deodars on Lebanon and the Himalayas, no vine-clad selvas in the basin of the Amazon. With such variety, harmony, and triumphant exuberance, even nature, it would seem, might have rested content with the forests of North America, and planted no more.

So they appeared a few centuries ago when they were rejoicing in wildness. The Indians with stone axes could do them no more harm than could gnawing beavers and browsing moose. Even the fires of the Indians and the fierce shattering lightning seemed to work together only for good in clearing spots here and there for smooth garden prairies, and openings for sunflowers seeking the light. But when the steel axe of the white man rang out on the startled air their doom was sealed. Every tree heard the bodeful sound, and pillars of smoke gave the sign in the sky.

I suppose we need not go mourning the buffaloes. In the nature of things they had to give place to better cattle, though the change might have been made without barbarous wickedness. Likewise many of nature's five hundred kinds of wild trees had to make way for orchards and cornfields. In the settlement and civilization of the country, bread more than timber or beauty was wanted; and in the blindness of hunger, the early settlers, claiming Heaven as their guide, regarded God's trees as only a larger kind of pernicious weeds, extremely hard to get rid of. Accordingly, with no eye to the future, these pious destroyers waged interminable forest wars; chips flew thick and fast; trees in their beauty fell crashing by millions, smashed to confusion, and the smoke of their burning has been rising to heaven more than two hundred years....

The legitimate demands on the forests that have passed into private ownership, as well as those in the hands of the government, are increasing every year with the rapid settlement and up-building of the country, but the methods of

SOURCE: John Muir, *Our National Parks* (Boston, 1901), chapter 10, "The American Forests." Originally published as John Muir, "The American Forests," *Atlantic Monthly* 80 (August 1897): 145–57.

lumbering are as yet grossly wasteful. In most mills only the best portions of the best trees are used, while the ruins are left on the ground to feed great fires, which kill much of what is left of the less desirable timber, together with the seedlings, on which the permanence of the forest depends. Thus every mill is a centre of destruction far more severe from waste and fire than from use. The same thing is true of the mines, which consume and destroy indirectly immense quantities of timber with their innumerable fires, accidental or set to make open ways, and often without regard to how far they run. The prospector deliberately sets fires to clear off the woods just where they are densest, to lay the rocks bare and make the discovery of mines easier. Sheep-owners and their shepherds also set fires everywhere through the woods in the fall to facilitate the march of their countless flocks the next summer, and perhaps in some places to improve the pasturage. The axe is not yet at the root of every tree, but the sheep is, or was before the national parks were established and guarded by the military, the only effective and reliable arm of the government free from the blight of politics....

Notwithstanding all the waste and use which have been going on unchecked like a storm for more than two centuries, it is not yet too late—though it is high time—for the government to begin a rational administration of its forests. About seventy million acres it still owns,—enough for all the country, if wisely used. These residual forests are generally on mountain slopes, just where they are doing the most good, and where their removal would be followed by the greatest number of evils; the lands they cover are too rocky and high for agriculture, and can never be made as valuable for any other crop as for present crop of trees....

In their natural condition, or under wise management, keeping out destructive sheep, preventing fires, selecting the trees that should be cut for lumber, and preserving the young ones and the shrubs and sod of herbaceous vegetation, these forests would be a never failing fountain of wealth and beauty....

... The wonderful advance made in the last few years, in creating four national parks in the West, and thirty forest reservations, embracing nearly forty million acres; and in the planting of the borders of streets and highways and spacious parks in all the great cities, to satisfy the natural taste and hunger for landscape beauty and righteousness that God has put, in some measure, into every human being and animal, shows the trend of awakening public opinion....

All sorts of local laws and regulations have been tried and found wanting, and the costly lessons of our own experience, as well as that of every civilized nation, show conclusively that the fate of the remnant of our forests is in the hands of the federal government, and that if the remnant is to be saved at all, it must be saved quickly.

Any fool can destroy trees. They cannot run away; and if they could, they would still be destroyed,—chased and hunted down as long as fun or a dollar could be got out of their bark hides, branching horns, or magnificent bole backbones. Few that fell trees plant them; nor would planting avail much towards getting back anything like the noble primeval forests. During a man's life only saplings can be grown, in the place of the old trees—tens of centuries old—that have been destroyed. It took more than three thousand years to make some of the trees in these Western woods,—trees that are still standing in perfect strength and beauty, waving and singing in the mighty forests of the Sierra. Through all the wonderful, eventful centuries since Christ's time—and long before that—God has cared for these trees, saved them from drought, disease, avalanches, and a thousand straining, leveling tempests and floods; but he cannot save them from fools,—only Uncle Sam can do that.

155

Boss Government at Work (1903)

In the early twentieth century, a group of investigative journalists began writing exposés about the social, political, and economic problems of the nation. They considered their work scientific and objective. President Theodore Roosevelt contemptuously nicknamed them "muckrakers" from a character in John Bunyan's Pilgrim's Progress *who "could look no way but downward with a muckrake in his hands" as he dug up filth rather than see more important issues by looking up. The beginning of muckraking journalism is often associated with* McClure's Magazine *when it published a series of Lincoln Steffens articles on municipal corruption in various American cities. The articles, later collected in a book,* The Shame of the Cities, *focused national attention on the problem and helped bring about reform. Steffens spent his career as a reporter and editor with New York newspapers and magazines and prided himself on objective reporting that was not self-righteous. The final article in the* McClure's *series, which is excerpted here, focused on the Democratic Party machine—Tammany Hall—in New York City and revealed how this boss government operated.*

Questions to Consider

1. According to Steffens, in what ways does Tammany Hall obtain and preserve political power?
2. For what reasons is Steffens suspicious of "municipal reform"?
3. What circumstances in urban America allowed boss governments like Tammany Hall to be blatantly dishonest and politically powerful?
4. How might Hilda Polacheck ("An Insider's View of Hull House," Document 153), have described Tammany Hall? How do you account for these differences?

Tammany is bad government; not inefficient, but dishonest; not a party, not a delusion and a snare, hardly known by its party name—Democracy; having little standing in the national councils of the party and caring little for influence outside of the city. Tammany is Tammany, the embodiment of corruption. All the world knows and all the world may know what it is and what it is after. For hypocrisy is not a Tammany vice. Tammany is for Tammany, and the Tammany men say so. Other rings proclaim lies and make pretensions; other rogues talk about the tariff and imperialism. Tammany is honestly dishonest. Time and time again, in private and in public, the leaders, big and little, have said they are out for themselves and their own; not for the public, but for "me and my friends"; not for New York, but for Tammany. Richard Croker said under oath once that he worked for his own pockets all the time, and Tom Grady, the Tammany orator, has brought his crowds to their feet cheering sentiments as primitive, stated with candor as brutal. The man from Mars would say that such an organization, so self-confessed, could not be very dangerous to an intelligent people. Foreigners marvel at it and at us, and even Americans—Pennsylvanians, for example—cannot understand why we New Yorkers regard Tammany as so formidable. I think I can explain it. Tammany is corruption with consent; it is bad government founded on the suffrages of people.... Tammany rules, when it rules, by right of the votes of the people of New York....

Tammany's democratic corruption rests upon the corruption of the people, the plain people, and there lies its great significance; its grafting system is one in which more individuals share than any I have studied. The people themselves get very little; they come cheap, but they are interested. Divided into districts, the organization subdivides them into precincts or neighborhoods, and their sovereign power, in the form of votes, is brought up by kindness and petty privileges. They are forced to a surrender, when necessary, by intimidation, but the leader and his captains have their hold because they take care of their own. They speak pleasant words, smile friendly smiles, notice the baby, give picnics up the River or the Sound, or a slap on the back; find jobs, most of them at the city's expense, but they have also news-stands, peddling privileges, railroad and other business places to dispense, they permit violations of the law, and, if a man has broken the law without permission, see him through the court. Though a blow in the face is as readily given as a shake of the hand, Tammany kindness is real kindness, and will go far, remember long, and take infinite trouble for a friend.

The power that is gathered up thus cheaply, like garbage, in the districts is concentrated in the district leader, who in turn passes it on through a general committee to the boss. This is a form of living government, extra-legal, but very actual, and, though the beginnings of it are purely democratic, it develops at each stage into an autocracy....

Tammany leaders are usually the natural leaders of the people in these districts, and they are originally good-natured, kindly men. No one has a more

SOURCE: Lincoln Steffens, *Shame of the Cities* (New York, 1904), 279–94, 302–3. Originally published as "New York: Good Government to the Test," *McClure's Magazine* 22 (November 1903): 84–92.

sincere liking than I for some of those common but generous fellows; their charity is real, at first. But they sell out their own people. They do give them coal and help them in their private troubles, but, as they grow rich and powerful, the kindness goes out of the charity and they not only collect at their saloons or in rents—cash for their "goodness"; they not only ruin fathers and sons and cause the troubles they relieve; they sacrifice the children in the schools; let the Health Department neglect the tenements, and, worst of all, plant vice in the neighborhood and in the homes of the poor.

This is not only bad; it is bad politics; it has defeated Tammany. Woe to New York when Tammany learns better. Honest fools talk of the reform of Tammany Hall. It is an old hope, this, and twice it has been disappointed, but it is not vain. That is the real danger ahead. The reform of a corrupt ring means, as I have said before, the reform of its system of grafting and a wise consideration of certain features of good government....

156

common theme journalism?

The Jungle (1906)

Early in the twentieth century, some individuals questioned the quality of food and medicine production in America. The "embalmed beef" scandal of the Spanish-American War—involving tainted provisions for troops—as well as muckraking exposés of patent medicines and the "beef trust" had alerted the American people that some problems existed. But when Upton Sinclair's novel, The Jungle, *was published in January 1906, it created an immediate furor. The novel was intended to advocate Socialism as it depicted the difficult life of Lithuanian immigrant Jurgis Rudkus and his friends in the fictitious Packingtown. Sinclair also included some descriptions of conditions in the meatpacking houses where Jurgis worked. It was these shocking descriptions, some of them excerpted here, that appalled the American people. President Theodore Roosevelt read the book and then sent two agents to investigate Chicago's meatpacking houses to learn if Sinclair's depiction was accurate—and it was. Within six months, the Pure Food and Drug Act was passed. Sinclair later wrote about his novel: "I aimed at the public's heart and by accident hit it in the stomach."*

Questions to Consider

1. What is more shocking, the work conditions or the preparation of meat for the American consumers? Why?

2. In what ways could government regulation address the situations in the meatpacking industry?

3. Compare the description of Sinclair with that found in "The Cattle Industry" (Document 141). In what ways had conditions changed?

4. How would labor and immigrants' rights advocates have responded to this selection?

… So Jurgis learned a few things about the great and only Durham canned goods, which had become a national institution. They were regular alchemists at Durham's; they advertised a mushroom catsup, and the men who made it did not know what a mushroom looked like. They advertised "potted chicken,"—and it was like the boarding-house soup of the comic papers, through which a chicken had walked with rubbers on. Perhaps they had a secret process for making chickens chemically—who knows? Said Jurgis's friends; the things that went into the mixture were tripe, and the fat of pork, and beef suet, and hearts of beef, and finally the waste ends of veal, when they had any. They put these up in several grades, and sold them at several prices; but the contents of the cans all came out of the same hopper. And then there was "potted game" and "potted grouse," "potted ham" and "devilled ham"—de-vyled, as the men called it. "De-vyled" ham was made out of the waste ends of smoked beef that were too small to be sliced by the machines; and also tripe, dyed with chemicals so that it would not show white; and trimmings of hams and corned beef; and potatoes, skins and all; and finally the hard cartilaginous ingenious mixture was ground up and flavoured with spices to make it taste like something. Anybody who could invent a new imitation had been sure of a fortune from old Durham....

There was another interesting set of statistics that a person might have gathered in Packingtown—those of the various afflictions of the workers. When Jurgis had first inspected the packing plants with Szedvilas, he had marvelled while he listened to the tale of all the things that were made out of the carcasses of animals, and of all the lesser industries that were maintained there; now he found that each one of these lesser industries was a separate little inferno, in its way as horrible as the killing beds, the source and fountain of them all. The workers in each of them had their own peculiar diseases. And the wandering visitor might be sceptical about all the swindles, but he could not be sceptical about these, for the worker bore the evidence of them about on his own person—generally he had only to hold out his hand.

There were the men in the pickle rooms, for instance, where old Antanas had gotten his death; scarce a one of these that had not some spot of horror on his person. Let a man so much as scrape his finger pushing a truck in the pickle rooms, and he might have a sore that would put him out of the world; all the joints in his fingers might be eaten by the acid, one by one. Of the butchers and floorsmen, the beef-boners and trimmers, and all those who used knives, you

SOURCE: Upton Sinclair, *The Jungle* (New York, 1906), 115–20.

could scarcely find a person who had the use of his thumb; time and time again the base of it had been slashed, till it was a mere lump of flesh against which the man pressed the knife to hold it. The hands of these men would be criss-crossed with cuts, until you could no longer pretend to count them or to trace them. They would have no nails—they had worn them off pulling hides; their knuckles were swollen so that their fingers spread out like a fan. There were men who worked in the cooking rooms, in the midst of steam and sickening odours, by artificial light; in these rooms the germs of tuberculosis might live for two years, but the supply was renewed every hour. There were the beef-luggers, who carried two-hundred-pound quarters into the refrigerator cars—a fearful kind of work, that began at four o'clock in the morning, and that wore out the most powerful men in a few years. There were those who worked in the chilling rooms, and whose special disease was rheumatism; the time limit that a man could work in the chilling rooms was said to be five years. There were the wool-pluckers, whose hands went to pieces even sooner than the hands of the pickle men; for the pelts of the sheep had to be painted with acid to loosen the wool, and then the pluckers had to pull out this wool with their bare hands, till the acid had eaten their fingers off. There were those who made the tins for the canned meat; and their hands, too, were a maze of cuts, and each cut represented a chance for blood poisoning. Some worked at the stamping machines, and it was seldom that one could work long there at the pace that was set, and not give out and forget himself, and have a part of his hand chopped off. There were the "hoisters," as they were called, whose task it was to press the lever which lifted the dead cattle off the floor. They ran along upon a rafter, peering down through the damp and the steam; and as old Durham's architects had not built the killing room for the convenience of the hoisters, at every few feet they would have to stoop under a beam, say four feet above the one they ran on; which got them into the habit of stooping, so that in a few years they would be walking like chimpanzees. Worst of any, however, were the fertilizer-men, and those who served in the cooking rooms. These people could not be shown to the visitor, for the odour of a fertilizer-man would scare any ordinary visitor at a hundred yards; and as for the other men, who worked in tank rooms full of steams, and in some of which there were open vats near the level of the floor, their peculiar trouble was that they fell into the vats; and when they were fished out, there was never enough of them left to be worth exhibiting—sometimes they would be overlooked for days, till all but the bones of them had gone out to the world as Durham's Pure Leaf Lard!

157

The Socialist Alternative (1908)

*As progressive reformers sought to cure the ills plaguing American society, increasing num-
bers of Americans came to support the Socialist Party as an alternative to mainstream progressive reform. While the Socialist Party was particularly strong in Europe and had close
links with European labor unions, the Socialist Party of America was not formed until
1901. The party gained strength by uniting disaffected Populists, western miners, intellectuals, and certain members of the labor movement. It was, however, the work of Eugene V.
Debs, who—following release from prison after the Pullman Strike of 1894—traveled
across the country spreading socialist ideas and trying to unite its diverse followers. His
presidential candidacy showed the rising popularity of the Socialist platform: In 1900 he
received over 4,000 votes; in 1904 and 1908 he received over 400,000 votes. The
Socialist Party was also successful in local elections, winning a number of local offices and
electing over thirty mayors. By 1912 the Socialist Party had reached its peak. The growth
of this political party and its reform aspirations caught the attention of the editors of the
newsmagazine* The Outlook. *Their editorial about the Socialist Party is excerpted here.*

Questions to Consider

1. According to the editorial, what were the components of the Socialist
   program?
2. For what reasons does the editorial believe the "Socialist spirit" is admirable?
3. Why would the Socialist Party be attractive to workers, disaffected Populists,
   intellectuals, and miners?
4. How might Theodore Roosevelt ("The New Nationalism of Theodore
   Roosevelt," Document 159) react to the Socialist program?

The Socialist programme, as interpreted by the platform of the Socialist party and
by the books of its most intellectual leaders, involves the collective ownership of
all producing property and the collective control of all producing industry. In
this programme, *The Outlook* does not believe. We think it would not be any
remedy for present industrial ills; that it would aggravate the evils it seeks to
cure.

But there is much in the Socialist spirit that is admirable. There are in it two
elements that are wholly admirable.

SOURCE: "The Socialist Spirit," *Outlook* 90 (12 September 1908): 61–63.

It looks at the facts of life courageously. To thousands of men and women today life is a tragedy. They live in crowded sections of a city where they are denied participation in the common gifts of God—fresh air, pure water, cheering sunshine. They watch the ebbing life of their dear ones, knowing well that the deadly disease is needless; perhaps knowing that the mortality in their homes is three times what it is in the homes of the prosperous. They see their children denied the pleasures of childhood that they may help earn the daily bread of the household, or driven to seek their playgrounds in the squalid streets and their playmates among the hoodlums. They suffer sometimes the pangs of physical hunger and always the pangs of hunger of mind and soul for leisure and the means to nourish the higher life. They are often unable to get work because no one will hire them, often compelled to take a wage barely sufficient to keep them in tolerable conditions as working machines. The conditions of their employment are often neither comfortable nor sanitary; sometimes so far unendurable that the power to endure them is exhausted by half a score of years. When their wages are adequate and their conditions favorable, both are, or seem to them to be, dependent on the good will and the business capacity of an employer in the selection of whom they have no voice. They help to elect the President who administers the affairs of the Nation, but not the boss who administers the affairs of their mine or factory. In the profits of their industry they have no share; or, if some share is accorded to them, it is in the form of increased wages, not in the form of profits. And all the while they see neighbors whose problem appears to be, not how to live on their income, but how to spend it. It is not strange that, with Frederic Harrison, who is not a Socialist, they wonder, "Are rich men likely to provide of any real social use, or will it be better for society to abolish the institution?" Nor strange that they lend eager attention to reformers who propose to abolish rich men and give to the workers the ownership and the management of the mine and the factory.

Socialism has dared to see these facts and to make society see them. Socialism is making one half the world know how the other half lives. "A prudent man," says the proverb, "seeth the evil; the simple pass on and are mulcted." ... Socialism sees, and is compelling a reluctant society to see, the evil of our present industrial system.... It is true that the Socialist pictures are sometimes exaggerated and often ill-proportioned. Nevertheless, for a vivid and even for a careful scientific account of the evils of the wages system the student must go to the Socialist literature. Too long the prosperous have been blind and deaf. Socialism sees and hears, and is compelling the prosperous to see and hear. For the courage and the persistence with which the Socialists reiterate their disagreeable revelation they deserve both honor and thanks.

With this spirit of courage goes a spirit of brotherhood. It is true that this is often marred by a distinctive and even a bitter class feeling, witnessed by the title of one Socialist publication, "The Class War"; indicated by the closing paragraph of the Socialist Political Platform, which demands for the workers the whole power of government and the sole control of industry.

Nevertheless, in the main a spirit of brotherhood inspires the great world-wide Socialist movement. It is not class ambition nor class jealousy that has drawn such men … or has won from even the conservative clergy in both continents so much sincere if not always intelligent sympathy. Even the class feeling is an advance on individual selfishness. "An injury to one is an injury to all" is as yet only a class motto, the motto of the trades union. So *Noblesse oblige* was a class motto, the motto of the feudal nobility. But either of them is better than the motto, "Every man for himself and the devil takes the hindmost," which is the motto of individualism.

The hopes of the Socialists are not class hopes. Illusive they may be, but they are certainly human. The Rev. Charles H. Vail, in his "Principles of Scientific Socialism," includes in his catalogue of the advantages of Socialism, increased production, orderly and equable distribution, prevention of waste, elevation of woman, better conditions for children, abolition of taxation, an end to enforced idleness, to business dishonesty, to divorce and to prostitution, the elimination of crime, the prevention of intemperance and insanity, and the cure of poverty. These hopes are very enticing. If they were only true or even plausible!

Socialism sees clearly social evils which have grown unendurable; it is animated by a spirit of brotherhood which is sometimes a class feeling, but is sometimes a feeling of humanity; and it prescribes a panacea from which it anticipates a millennium which will bring equal benefits to all. The antidote for Socialism is not in ignoring the evils which it portrays, but in seeing them more clearly and understanding more correctly the causes which have produced them. It is not in sneering at the spirit of brotherhood which the Socialists profess, but in a wider spirit of brotherhood which shall include the rich as well as the poor in its fellowship. It is not by simply pointing out the inadequacy of the proposed economic panacea, but in discerning and setting in operation those combined and co-operative forces—spiritual, intellectual, industrial, and political—which alone can regenerate society and so effectually reform its institutions. The Socialists would do well to ponder this sentence from Frederic Harrison: "We must regenerate domestic life, personal life, moral life, social life, political life, religious life, and not manufacturing and trading life alone." But that sentence the opponents of Socialism would also do well to ponder. For Socialism will win the opportunity to try its experiment, in spite of all opposition, unless its opponents have some better social order to offer to the world than a mere continuance of present conditions.

158

"Why Women Should Vote" (1910)

In the several decades after the Seneca Falls Convention (1848), women argued that suffrage was a natural right—a position that threatened male political dominance and was therefore denied. At the dawn of the twentieth century, the women's suffrage campaign languished, but a less-threatening expediency argument emerged to help revive the movement. Frustrated with combating state and local politicians to bring about social improvement, the settlement house women realized they needed the vote in order to challenge the politicians and to make America better. The best-known settlement house woman was Jane Addams, who published the following excerpted article in the Ladies' Home Journal *in 1910. Addams placated the middle-class female audience of this magazine by arguing that the woman's domain remained the home and cultural affairs, but that women voting could help with the larger problems of social housekeeping. With this argument (and others like it)—coupled with new publicity generated by the actions of radical suffragettes, a revitalized moderate suffragist organization, and women's good deeds in wartime—public support for women's suffrage grew rapidly. In 1920, the Nineteenth Amendment, granting women the right to vote, was ratified.*

Questions to Consider

1. In what ways does Jane Addams argue for giving women the right to vote?
2. For what reasons does Addams soften the perceived threat to male political power?
3. How radical a change in women's roles does Addams advocate?
4. How would women and men react to this article?

This paper is an attempt to show that many women today are failing to discharge their duties to their own households properly simply because they do not perceive that as society grows more complicated it is necessary that woman shall extend her sense of responsibility to many things outside of her own home if she would continue to preserve the home in its entirety. One could illustrate in many ways. A woman's simplest duty, one would say, is to keep her house clean and wholesome and to feed her children properly. Yet if she lives in a tenement house, as so many of my neighbors do, she cannot fulfill these simple obligations by her own efforts because she is utterly dependent upon the city administration for the conditions which render decent living possible.... In a crowded city

SOURCE: Jane Addams, "Why Women Should Vote," *Ladies' Home Journal* 27 (January 1910): 21–30.

quarter, however, if the street is not cleaned by the city authorities no amount of private sweeping will keep the tenement free from grime; if the garbage is not properly collected and destroyed a tenement-house mother may see her children sicken and die of diseases from which she alone is powerless to shield them, although her tenderness and devotion are unbounded.... In short, if woman would keep on with her old business of caring for her house and rearing her children she will have to have some conscience in regard to public affairs lying quite outside of her immediate household. The individual conscience and devotion are no longer effective....

If women follow only the lines of their traditional activities there are certain primary duties which belong to even the most conservative women, and which no one woman or group of women can adequately discharge unless they join the more general movements looking toward social amelioration through legal enactment.

The first of these ... is woman's responsibility for the members of her own household that they may be properly fed and clothed and surrounded by hygienic conditions. The second is a responsibility for the education of children: (a) that they may be provided with good schools; (b) that they may be kept free from vicious influences on the street; (c) that when working they may be protected by adequate child-labor legislation.

(a) The duty of a woman toward the schools which her children attend is so obvious that it is not necessary to dwell upon it. But even this simple obligation cannot be effectively carried out without some form of social organization as the mothers' school clubs and mothers' congresses testify, and to which the most conservative women belong because they feel the need of wider reading and discussion concerning the many problems of childhood. It is, therefore, perhaps natural that the public should have been more willing to accord a vote to women in school matters than in any other, and yet women have never been members of a Board of Education in sufficient numbers to influence largely actual school curriculi....

(b) But women are also beginning to realize that children need attention outside of school hours; that much of the petty vices in cities is merely the love of pleasure gone wrong, the overrestrained boy or girl seeking improper recreation and excitement. It is obvious that a little study of the needs of children, a sympathetic understanding of the conditions under which they go astray, might save hundreds of them. Women traditionally have had an opportunity to observe the plays of children and the needs of youth, and yet in Chicago, at least, they had done singularly little in this vexed problem of juvenile delinquency until they helped to inaugurate the Juvenile Court movement a dozen years ago....

(c) As the education of her children has been more and more transferred to the school, so that even children four years old go to the kindergarten, the woman has been left in a household of constantly-narrowing interests, not only because the children are away, but also because one industry after another is slipping from the household into the factory.... Because many thousands of those working in factories and shops are girls between the ages of fourteen and twenty-two there is a necessity that older women should be interested in the conditions of industry. The very fact that these girls are not going to remain in industry permanently makes it more important that some one should see to it that they shall not be incapacitated for their future family life because they work for exhausting hours and under insanitary conditions.

... If conscientious women were convinced that it was a civic duty to be informed in regard to these grave industrial affairs, and then to express the conclusions which they had reached by depositing a piece of paper in a ballot-box, one cannot imagine that they would shirk simply because the action ran counter to old traditions....

This is, perhaps, the attitude of many busy women who would be glad to use the ballot to further public measures in which they are interested and for which they have been working for years. It offends the taste of such a woman to be obliged to use indirect "influence" when she is accustomed to well-bred, open action in other affairs, and she very much resents the time spent in persuading a voter to take her point of view, and possibly to give up his own, quite as honest and valuable as hers, although different because resulting from a totally different experience. Public-spirited women who wish to use the ballot, as I know them, do not wish to do the work of men nor to take over men's affairs. They simply want an opportunity to do their own work and to take care of those affairs which naturally and historically belong to women, but which are constantly being overlooked and slighted in our political institutions....

In closing, may I recapitulate that if woman would fulfill her traditional responsibility to her own children; if she would educate and protect from danger factory children who must find their recreation on the street; if she would bring the cultural forces to bear upon our materialistic civilization; and if she would do it all with the dignity and directness fitting one who carries on her immemorial duties, then she must bring herself to the use of the ballot—that latest implement for self-government. May we not fairly say that American women need this implement in order to preserve the home?

159

The New Nationalism of Theodore Roosevelt (1912)

Disappointed with William Howard Taft's conservative nature and his unwillingness to pursue progressive policies, former President Theodore Roosevelt began challenging Taft's position while offering a new brand of Progressivism. Roosevelt gave a series of speeches throughout the country in which he gradually formulated his program—the "New Nationalism." Roosevelt called for expanding the federal government's powers to control and regulate big business, new measures of direct democracy, and a program of labor and social legislation. In February 1912, Roosevelt addressed the Ohio Constitutional Convention and offered one of the clearest explanations of the New Nationalism. The speech is excerpted here. Several days after the address, Roosevelt announced he would seek the Republican Party's presidential nomination in 1912. When the Republicans chose Taft, Roosevelt bolted the party and established the Progressive or Bull Moose Party, which used the New Nationalism as its platform.

Questions to Consider

1. What problems does Theodore Roosevelt identify in the American political process?

2. For what purposes does Roosevelt propose to expand democracy in the United States?

3. In what ways will the functions of government change because of the reforms Roosevelt offered in this speech?

4. In what ways does Roosevelt's speech reflect progressive ideals?

This is the reason why I have for so many years insisted, as regards our national government, that it is both futile and mischievous to endeavor to correct the evils of big business by an attempt to restore business conditions as they were in the middle of the last century, before railways and telegraphs rendered larger business organizations both inevitable and desirable....

All business into which the element of monopoly in any way or degree enters, and where it proves in practice impossible totally to eliminate this element of monopoly, should be carefully supervised, regulated and controlled by governmental authority; and such control should be exercised by administrative, rather than judicial officers. No effort should be made to destroy a big corporation merely because it is big, merely because it has shown itself a particularly efficient business instrument.

But we should not fear, if necessary, to bring the regulation of big corporations to the point of controlling conditions so that the wage-worker shall have a wage more than sufficient to cover the basic cost of living, and hours of labor not so excessive as to wreck his strength by the strain of unending toil and leave him unfit to do his duty as a good citizen in the community. Where regulation by competition (which is, of course, preferable), proves insufficient, we should not shrink from bringing governmental regulation to the point of control of monopoly prices if it should ever become necessary to do so, just as in exceptional cases railway rates are now regulated....

The people have nothing whatever to fear from giving any public servant power so long as they retain their own power to hold him accountable for his

SOURCE: "Roosevelt Would Give People Right to Recall Judges' Decisions: Favors Initiative and Referendum, Carefully Safeguarded," (Columbus) *Ohio State Journal*, 22 February 1912, p. 4.

use of the power they have delegated to him. You will get the best service where you elect only a few men, and where each man has his duties and responsibilities, and is obliged to work in the open, so that the people who know who he is and what he is doing, and have the information that will enable them to hold him to account for his stewardship.

I believe in providing for direct nominations by the people, including therein direct presidential primaries for the election of delegates to the national nominating conventions. Not as a matter of theory, but as a matter of plain and proved experience, we find that the convention system, while it often records the popular will, is also often used by adroit politicians as a method of thwarting the popular will. In other words, the existing machinery for nominations is cumbrous, and is not designed to secure the real expression of a majority of the people, but we do not like to acquiesce in a nomination secured by adroit political management in defeating the wish of the majority of people.

I believe in the election of United States senators by direct vote. Just as actual experience convinced our people that presidents should be elected (as they are now in practice, although not in theory) by direct vote of the people instead of by indirect vote through an untrammeled electoral college, so actual experience has convinced us that senators should be elected by direct vote of the people instead of indirectly through the various legislatures.

I believe in the initiative and the referendum, which should be used not to destroy representative government, but to correct it whenever it become misrepresentative. Here again I am concerned not with theories but with actual facts. If in any state the people are themselves satisfied with their present representative system, then it is, of course, their right to keep that system unchanged; and it is nobody's business but theirs.

But in actual practice it has been found in very many states that legislative bodies have not been responsive to the popular will. Therefore I believe that the state should provide for the possibility of direct popular action in order to make good such legislative failure.

The power to invoke such direct action, both by initiative and referendum, should be provided in such fashion as to prevent its being wantonly or too frequently used. I do not believe that it should be made the easy or ordinary way of taking action. In the great majority of cases it is far better that action on legislative matters should be taken by those specifically delegated to perform the task.... But where the men thus delegated fail to perform their duty, then it should be in the power of the people themselves to perform the duty....

I do not believe in adopting the recall save as a last resort, when it has become clearly evident that no other course will achieve the desired result. But either the recall will have to be adopted or else it will have to be made much easier than it now is to get rid, not merely of a bad judge, but of a judge who, however virtuous, has grown so out of touch with social needs and facts that he is unfit longer to render good service on the bench....

When the supreme court of the state declares a given statute unconstitutional, because in conflict with the state or the national constitution, its opinion should be subject to revision by the people themselves. Such an opinion ought always to be created with great respect by the people, and unquestionably in the majority of cases would be accepted and followed by them. But actual experience has shown the vital need of the people reserving to themselves the right to pass upon such opinion....

I do not say that the people are infallible. But I do say that the American people are more often sound in their decisions than is the case with any of the governmental bodies to whom, for their convenience, they have delegated portions of their power. If this is not so, then there is no justification for the existence of our government; and if it is so, then there is no justification for refusing to give the people the real, and not merely the nominal, ultimate decision on questions of constitutional law.... [S]o I hold that now the American people as a whole have shown themselves wiser than the courts in the way they have approached and dealt with such vital questions of our day as those concerning the proper control of the big corporations and of securing their rights to industrial workers.

160

Women and the Middle-Class Home (1913)

In the early twentieth century, the growth of middle-class families changed the lives of women. Within the home, more labor- and time-saving devices and increased access to processed and packaged foods made the maintenance of the household less difficult than ever before. Outside the home, growing numbers of middle-class women were hired in new occupations such as telephone operators, secretaries in businesses, and department store clerks as well as holding down traditional occupations in nursing and teaching. Furthermore, the woman's suffrage movement gained momentum and publicity as part of the Progressive Era reform effort. Faced with the changes taking place, many middle-class women sought ways to improve their homes by borrowing the Progressive Movement's ideal of "efficiency." Martha Bensley Bruère and Robert W. Bruère investigated this development, then wrote Increasing Home Efficiency, *which is excerpted below.*

Questions to Consider

1. According to the Bruères, what has produced the frustration for some middle-class women?

2. In what ways have the lives of women changed?

3. What do the Bruères suggest as the solutions to the problems?

4. In what ways might an early twentieth-century middle-class woman respond to the ideas of Dorothy Dunbar Bromley ("The New Woman," Document 178) or Betty Friedan ("The Problem That Has No Name," Document 208) or Phyllis Schlafly ("The Differences Between Men and Women," Document 220)?

We kept house one summer in an attractive middle-class suburb, under the ordinary conditions that make for comfort and compel circumspection among middle-class people.

One day our next door neighbor came running across the lawn and flounced—there is no other name for it—flounced down upon our veranda.

"I'm nothing but a family clearing house!" she cried distractedly. "I run up the family bills one month and pay them the next! I buy what the stores have to sell at the price they choose to set, I pay rent for a house somebody else has chosen to build,—I send the children to the sort of school the town has happened to establish,—I dress, and come, and go, and read, and see, as other people have arranged for me! What have I to do with it all? Merely to pay the bills with money I haven't earned! I don't control a single thing that goes into my housekeeping, and yet I know that unless I see to it that we have what it is best for us to have, I am not running my home efficiently."

This was considerable of a jounce to us. Was not our neighbor's house clean to whiteness? Her children literate and well mannered? Her dress in fashion? Her mind well stocked? Moreover had we not eaten happily at her board? Not efficient indeed! What problems did she find unsolvable?...

We have not found the middle-class housewife perplexed over how to cook, or clean, over how to serve her meals or how to wash her clothes. The technique of these employments has been pretty well worked out, and the general feeling seems to be that the woman who hasn't mastered them has nobody to blame but herself or her grandmother. Anyone who can measure flour in a cup and watch the clock, can cook....

Our ancestors had easier problems to solve than we have for the very simple reason that theirs were nearer at hand. Ours must be solved at long range. The tools which the middle-class housewife once used to feed and clothe and educate her children have fled from the middle-class home, and the middle-class housewife, hampered by the length of the lever she must use to control them, bound by the romantic tradition of "the Proper sphere of woman," and terrified at the indelicate possibility of appearing unwomanly, flutters ineptly on her threshold.

Part of her inefficiency would seem to grow out of the mental confusion under which the middle-class woman labors. She seems to think that her function is to preserve the home as a sort of shrine, a thing apart, an end in itself. She does not see it as a part of the great factory for the production of citizens, nor understand that her job is exactly the same as that of any other factory

SOURCE: Martha Bensley Bruère and Robert W. Bruère, *Increasing Home Efficiency* (New York 1913), 1–2, 288–92.

manager—to turn out the product. Shall she preserve the white hands of her sensibilities at the expense of the race?

The things with which the on-coming citizens are to be fed and clothed and educated and launched are no longer within the gates of the home. The industrial revolution in sweeping the loom and the distaff into the factory, in trustifying the production of cloth and food, in substituting the telephone and telegraph for the village crier and the neighborhood gossip, the railroad and trolley for the democrat and prairie schooner, the public school for the itinerant pedagogue, has dropped such a boulder into the "circle of woman's influence" as has spread waves to the ends of the earth. So long as women content themselves with fluttering about inside four walls under the delusion that these mark their proper sphere of activity, they cannot so much as grapple the problem of home efficiency. They must do their work where it is to be done if they do it at all.

Woman the idler, must become woman the worker. She must do the same work she did before the invention of steam engine and power loom left her sitting empty handed. She must do the same work her great grandmother did, but by the new and improved methods. She must follow her tools of production into the mine, the mill and the factory. It is as much her duty today to see to it that her tools are wisely used in the interest of her home and in fairness to the workers as it ever was. And since production without adequate distribution is vain, it is as much her business as it ever was to control the means of distribution. The evident fact that no woman can do any of these things single handed, is but another proof that she must fit the manner of her work to the new conditions. She must get out of the individualistic groove in which she is helpless, she must see her home as part of a greater unit to be controlled only by the greater power of many people working together. She must democratize industry as we are striving to democratize government. If the truth were known Politics and Parenthood are pretty close kin.

In a word the one answer to many questions is that the middle-class mother must stop soldiering on her job; she must follow the spinning wheel into the world; she must take up her share of the duties of citizenship. For after all what is the home but a flower pot in which to grow the family tree? What are all the family trees for but to furnish the timber for the social building? And yet today industry and the home are in a state of abnormal and immoral divorce. The health goes out of industry when it forgets that its only normal purpose is to cooperate with the home, not as equal but as servant, in the perpetuation of the race and the nurture of good citizens. So long as women do not do the work set for them to do, and men make business a gamble and a sport, our homes cannot be efficient. Business is woman's affair as much as man's. The home is man's affair as much as woman's. What we need most today is the domestication of business and the socialization of the home.

We have found that the goddess of the Home is Our Lady of Public Service,—not the hired girl. That the altar of the home isn't the cook-stove but the factory furnace, and that when God made homemakers, male and female created He them!

19

America on the World Stage

The social Darwinist attitudes that supported economic exploitation and white Anglo-Saxon superiority in the United States combined to buttress a new imperialism abroad. Though traditionally expansionistic, the United States had previously confined its ambitions to the North American continent. During the 1890s, however, the "closing" of the frontier, a search for new economic opportunities, national pride, and competition with European rivals caused many Americans to champion a more aggressive policy overseas. In the early twentieth century, the values of the Progressive movement were expressed on a wider scale when the United States entered the First World War. Government-employed professionals, using a centrist approach to solve problems, now directed their methods against the United States' foreign enemies. The ensuing crusade to save democracy set off a similar movement at home, where those who lacked this progressive sense of patriotism—particularly leftists—were subject to persecution by both the government and private citizens. The following set of documents captures the various moods and issues of the era.

161

The Sinking of the *Maine* (1898)

In 1895, the Cuban revolution against Spain flared up again. Spain sent troops under General Valeriano Weyler to quell the revolt, and he began a policy of reconcentrado—assembling peasants into camps before laying waste to the countryside. The revolt was bloody and savage on both sides. Sensationalist American newspapers, especially William Randolph Hearst's New York Journal *and Joseph Pulitzer's* New York World, *began publishing lurid—and often exaggerated—accounts and drawings of Spanish atrocities in an effort to increase circulation. This "yellow journalism" only created more American interest and sympathy in the Cuban revolt. When riots broke out in Havana, Cuba, in 1898, fears that American citizens might be endangered led the United States government to dispatch the U.S. battleship* Maine *to Havana, supposedly on a courtesy call. On 15 February 1898, the* Maine *exploded and sank with the loss of 260 sailors. Rumors circulated that Spain had sunk the battleship, and the tabloid newspapers ran blaring headlines accusing Spain while clamoring for war. The selection here is the* New York Journal's *editorial on the sinking of the* Maine.

Questions to Consider

1. According to the *New York Journal*, in what ways was the *Maine* an "object lesson" to the United States?

2. What reasons does the *New York Journal* give for U.S. intervention in Cuba?

3. In what ways did the sinking of the *Maine* move the United States closer to war with Spain?

4. How do you think William Graham Sumner ("The Forgotten Man," Document 144) would have responded to the views expressed in this editorial?

The prudent, proper and patriotic policy for the United States Government to adopt in dealing with the Cuban question is not changed by the disaster to the Maine. What the Journal said months ago is perfectly applicable to the situation today. It is the duty of the United States to intervene in Cuba, not because an American war ship has been destroyed in Havana harbor by a suspicious "accident," but because every dictate of national self-protection, every impulse of humanity compels such intervention.

The disaster to the Maine is an object lesson to the Administration rather than a present cause for war. If the inquiry which begins this week shall show

SOURCE: "Enforce Peace in Cuba," *New York Journal*, 21 February 1898, p. 10.

it to have been the result of the faulty construction of the vessel, or of care-lessness, it of course offers no reason for attack upon Spain. If it be shown to be the work of irresponsible individuals, malignant fanatics or murderous Weylerites the United States will demand full reparation and a money indemnity from Spain, the refusal of which would necessarily lead to war. If, what is almost incredible, the explosion should be shown to have been caused with connivance or by the act of responsible Spanish officers, a declaration of war would be instant and the war would be one of chastisement and revenge.

There are countless reasons to believe that the second hypothesis will be supported by the finding of the court of inquiry; but, even so, reliance upon it would defer tediously the time of American intervention in Cuba. After the time spent in investigation would come the delay attendant upon diplomatic corre-spondence with a nation which never does to-day what it can put off until tomorrow. That is why the disaster to the Maine is not to be regarded as an immediate cause for war.

But it is an object lesson which the Administration may well heed. For two years the Spaniards have carried on in Cuba a warfare which has outraged humanity and violated the laws of civilized nations. They have destroyed American property and imprisoned and murdered American citizens. The navy of the United States has been forced to do police duty on the seas that the Spaniards might prosecute their outrages the more securely. The commerce of the United States with Cuba has been destroyed. American vessels have been illegally fired upon and the United States flag insulted. To-day the revolution is no nearer suppression than it ever was. Spanish power in Cuba is a myth—it extends just far enough to give Spanish officials an opportunity to enrich them-selves by plundering their own troops.

These reasons why the United States should intervene have existed ever since the McKinley Administration came into power. Had the right course been promptly taken the Spaniards would have been driven out of Cuba at probably a [lower] cost to the United States in lives than the "accident" to the Maine entailed. Are we to wait now until the ship sent to take the place of the Maine also meets with an "accident"? Shall we give Spain time to complete her projected alliance with the Spanish-American republics against the United States?

The result of the inquiry at Havana may make instant war with Spain inevitable. But the reasons why the United States should insure peace in their hemisphere by enforcing peace in Cuba would be as forceful today if the gallant Maine and her noble crew were still floating in Havana harbor.

162

Aguinaldo's Call for Philippine Independence (1899)

The Spanish-American War began with a stunning naval victory in the Philippines. The plan was to inflict severe damage on the Spanish colony of the Philippines and coerce Spain to liberate Cuba. Commodore George Dewey and the Asiatic squadron destroyed the Spanish fleet in Manila Bay; but lacking sufficient numbers of troops, the squadron could not occupy territory until an expeditionary force arrived from America. Helping liberate the countryside was Filipino nationalist Emilio Aguinaldo. He had been leading a rebellion against the Spanish colonial government before the war broke out in 1898. Understanding that the American motive in the war was to liberate Cuba from Spanish colonial rule, Aguinaldo assumed that helping American forces remove Spanish troops might mean independence for the Philippines. Aguinaldo and his supporters even established a temporary government. When they realized that America would not leave the Philippines, Aguinaldo issued a call for independence and rebelled against the United States, touching off a war that lasted nearly three years. His declaration of independence—as presented in The Outlook, *a popular newsmagazine—follows.*

Questions to Consider

1. What are Aguinaldo's reasons for waging war against the United States?
2. In what ways does Aguinaldo use references about America to support his case for Filipino independence?
3. For what reasons does Aguinaldo dismiss "this autonomy America offers"?
4. On what issues would Aguinaldo agree with Senator George F. Hoar ("An Anti-Imperialist Perspective," Document 163)? On what issues would they disagree?

Filipinos: Beloved daughter of the ardent sun of the tropics, commended by Providence to the care of noble Spain, be not ungrateful to her salute who warmed you with the breath of her own culture and civilization. It is true she sought to crush thy aspiration for independence, as a loving mother opposes separation forever from the daughter of her bosom. This but proves the excess of affection and love Spain feels for thee, Filipinos! Delicate flower of the East,

SOURCE: "Pleas for Independence," *The Outlook* 62 (22 July 1899): 677.

scarcely eight months weaned from the breast of thy mother, thou hast dared to brave a great and powerful nation such as is the United States, after barely organizing and disciplining thy little army. Yet we reply, we will be slaves to none, nor allow ourselves to be deceived by soft words. Let us continue to defend our fatherland till independence is assured, for this is justice. We shall see at last that the great American Nation will acknowledge the right which is on our side. That doctrine of the great Monroe, that America is for Americans, is not forgotten: just as we affirm that the Philippines are for the Filipinos. Some States of the American Union have arisen in our favor. Especially is the Democratic party convinced that both victors and vanquished will lose precious lives. Thus many of the people and many statesmen censure President McKinley as inhuman for having ordered his military representatives at Manila to seek means to bring about hostilities with the Filipinos. These facts prove that they wish to try us, to see if we are able to live up to the second color of our banner, red, which signifies courage, heroism, and martyrdom. Therefore we should not resent this struggle with the Americans. In spite of their expressed desire to dominate all the Philippines, well convinced are they that we fight with justice and right on our side, and that autonomy is all a show of deceit, only serving to save certain accumulated wealth. We have never concealed our aspirations, that we aspire but to independence, that we will struggle on to obtain it, perhaps from those who are now our enemies and to-morrow will be our allies, as they were for the overthrowal of the power of Spain. We might well accept this autonomy America offers, but what can we do with it if our ambition is independence, and if we are to accept it only to later overthrow by force of arms the sovereignty of America? As I believe it is the intention of the autonomists to make use of treachery and deceit, we cannot accept such a procedure. We do not wish to be traitors afterward. We wish to show our character of frankness and sincerity, and nothing more. Let us avoid the example of those natives who, having at one time been colonists, accepted autonomy to enable them to make their work surer once everything was prepared. History has given us an example of this in recent events. Let us persist in our idea, which is only the legitimate and noble aspiration of a people which is desirous at all cost to preserve its national honor spotless and as pure as crystal. Thus, then, there will not be a single Filipino autonomist. Those who are so are in the eyes of the people but time-servers, fearful of losing their riches threatened by risks of war. Filipinos! Let us be constant! Let us strengthen the bonds of our union!...

163

An Anti-Imperialist Perspective (1899)

Congress declared war against Spain in April 1898 to establish Cuban independence; but the opening battle of the war was fought halfway around the world when Commodore George Dewey attacked the Spanish fleet in Manila, Philippines. The Spanish surrendered Manila to the Americans while Filipino insurgent leader Emilio Aguinaldo, working with the Americans, liberated the countryside and established a temporary government. The war's end left the Philippines under joint American-Filipino control, but the country's future was in the hands of Congress. The Philippine annexation issue—perhaps the most important foreign policy decision of the time—became hotly debated, with the sides sharply drawn between imperialists and anti-imperialists. Among the first to denounce annexation was George F. Hoar, an aged four-term Republican senator from Massachusetts. Hoar's political career spanned nearly fifty years: He helped form the Republican Party, he oversaw the Republican Party's shift to support business, and he denounced the popular election of senators. His speech, excerpted here, was given as the Senate considered ratifying the Treaty of Paris, which officially ended the war and made the Philippines an American possession.

Questions to Consider

1. For what reasons does George F. Hoar oppose the annexation of the Philippines?

2. Why does Hoar believe the imperialists are hypocrites?

3. On what issues would Hoar disagree with Senator Albert K. Beveridge's views ("The New Manifest Destiny," Document 164)?

4. Compare and contrast Beveridge's views with those expressed by W. E. B. Du Bois ("On Race Relations," Document 148).

Mr. President, the persons who favor the ratification of this treaty without conditions and without amendment differ among themselves certainly in their views, purposes, and opinions.... In general, the state of mind and the utterance of the lips are in accord. If you ask them what they want, you are answered with a shout: "Three cheers for the flag! Who will dare haul it down? Hold on to everything you can get. The United States is strong enough to do what it likes. The Declaration of Independence and the counsel of Washington and the Constitution of the United States have grown rusty and musty. They are for little

SOURCE: "Acquisition of Territory," *Congressional Record*, 55th Congress, 3rd Session (9 January 1899), 493–503.

countries and not for great ones. There is no moral law for strong nations. America has outgrown Americanism.".…

If you can not take down a national flag where it has once floated in time of war, we were disgraced when we took our flag down in Mexico, and in Vera Cruz, or after the invasion of Canada; England was dishonored when she took her flag down after she captured this capital; and every nation is henceforth pledged to the doctrine that where ever it puts its military foot or its naval power with the flag over it, that must be a war to the death and to extermination or the honor of the state is disgraced by the flag of that nation being withdrawn.…

Now Mr. President, there are Senators here yet hesitating as to what their action may be in the future, who will tell you that they loathe and hate this doctrine that we may buy nations at wholesale; that we may acquire imperial powers or imperial regions by conquest; that we may make vassal states and subject peoples without constitutional restraint, and against their will, and without any restraint but our own discretion.…

The Monroe Doctrine is gone. Every European nation, every European alliance, has the right to acquire dominion in this hemisphere when we acquire it in the other. The Senator's doctrine put anywhere in practice will make our beloved country a cheap-jack country, raking after the cart for the leaving of European tyranny.…

Our fathers dreaded a standing army; but the Senator's doctrine put in practice anywhere, now or hereafter, renders necessary a standing army, to be reenforced by a powerful navy. Our fathers denounced the subjection of any people whose judges were appointed or whose salaries were paid by a foreign power; but the Senator's doctrine, whenever it shall be put in practice, will entail upon us a national debt larger than any now existing on the face of the earth, larger than any ever known in history.

Our fathers dreaded the national taxgatherers; but the doctrine of the Senator from Connecticut, if it be adopted, is sure to make our national taxgatherers the most familiar visitant to every American home.…

… My proposition, summed up in a nut shell is this: I admit you have the right to acquire territory for constitutional purposes, and you may hold land and govern men on it for the constitutional purpose of a seat of government or for the constitutional purpose of admitting it as a State. I deny the right to hold land or acquire any property for any purpose not contemplated by the Constitution. The government of foreign people against their will is not a constitutional purpose, but a purpose expressly forbidden by the Constitution. Therefore I deny the right to acquire this territory and to hold it by the Government for that purpose.…

Now, I claim that under the Declaration of Independence you can not govern a foreign territory, a foreign people, another people than your own, that you can not subjugate them and govern them against their will, because you think it is for their good, when they do not: because you think you are going to give them the blessings of liberty. You have no right at the cannon's mouth to impose on an unwilling people your Declaration of Independence and your Constitution and your notions of freedom and notions of what is good....

But read the account of what is going on in Iloilo. The people there have got a government, with courts and judges, better than those of the people of Cuba, who, it was said, had a right to self-government, collecting their customs; and it is proposed to turn your guns on them, and say "We think that our notion of government is better than the notion you have got yourselves." I say that when you put that onto them against their will and say that freedom as we conceive it, not freedom as they conceive it, public interest as we conceive it, not as they conceive it, shall prevail and that if it does not we are to force it on them at the cannon's mouth—I say that the nation which undertakes that plea and says it is subduing these men for their good, will encounter the awful and terrible rebuke, "Beware of the leaven of the Pharisees, which is hypocrisy."

164

The New Manifest Destiny (1900)

In the Philippine annexation debates, one of the most forceful advocates of imperialism was Albert J. Beveridge, a first-term Republican senator from Indiana. Known for powerful political oratory and Anglo-Saxon supremacy before arriving in the Senate, Beveridge broke with tradition and gave a major speech as a freshman senator. To obtain information about the Philippine issue, Beveridge traveled to the islands and made a personal investigation. This inquiry added credibility to his annexation position. Excerpted here is Beveridge's eloquent Senate speech on the question of Philippine annexation. Beveridge served two terms in the Senate and was often considered one of the original "Progressive" Republicans. He lost a reelection bid in 1911 and became a distinguished historian. His best work was The Life of John Marshall *(four volumes), which received the Pulitzer prize for historical biography.*

Questions to Consider

1. According to Albert J. Beveridge, for what reasons should the United States annex the Philippines?

2. In what ways does Beveridge address the anti-imperialist issues of constitutional authority and intent of the Founders?

3. Compare Beveridge's argument for annexing the Philippines to the position of George F. Hoar ("An Anti-Imperialist Perspective," Document 163).

4. Why is Beveridge's speech significant to the annexation movement?

Mr. President, the times call for candor. The Philippines are ours forever, "territory belonging to the United States," as the Constitution calls them. And just beyond the Philippines are China's illimitable markets. We will not retreat from either. We will not repudiate our duty in the archipelago. We will not abandon our opportunity in the Orient. We will not renounce our part in the mission of our race, trustee, under God, of the civilization of the world. And we will move forward to our work, not howling out regrets like slaves whipped to their burdens, but with gratitude for a task worthy of our strength, and thanksgiving to Almighty God that He has marked us as His chosen people, hence forth to lead in the regeneration of the world.

This island empire is the last land left in all the oceans. If it should prove a mistake to abandon it, the blunder once made would be irretrievable. If it proves a mistake to hold it, the error can be corrected when we will. Every other progressive nation stands ready to relieve us.

But to hold it will be no mistake. Our largest trade henceforth must be with Asia. The Pacific is our ocean. More and more Europe will manufacture the most it needs, secure from its colonies the most it consumes. Where shall we turn for consumers of our surplus? Geography answers the question. China is our natural customer. She is nearer to us than to England, Germany, or Russia, the commercial powers of the present and the future. They have moved nearer to China by securing permanent bases on her borders. The Philippines give us a base at the door of all the East.

Lines of navigation from our ports to the Orient and Australia; from the Isthmian Canal to Asia; from all Oriental ports to Australia, converge at and separate from the Philippines. They are a self-supporting, dividend-paying fleet, permanently anchored at a spot selected by the strategy of Providence, commanding the Pacific. And the Pacific is the ocean of the commerce of the future. Most future wars will be conflicts for commerce. The power that rules the Pacific, therefore, is the power that rules the world. And, with the Philippines, that power is and will forever be the American Republic....

Here, then, Senators, is the situation. Two years ago there was no land in all this world which we could occupy for any purpose. Our commerce was daily turning toward the Orient, and geography and trade developments made necessary our commercial empire over the Pacific. And in that ocean we had no commercial, naval, or military base. To-day we have one of the three great ocean possessions on the globe, located at the most commanding commercial, naval, and military points in the eastern seas, within hail of India, shoulder to shoulder with China, richer in its own resources than any equal body of land on the entire globe, and peopled by a race which civilization demands shall be improved. Shall we abandon it? That man little knows the common people of the Republic, little understands the instincts of our race, who thinks we will not hold it fast and hold it forever, administering just government by simplest methods....

SOURCE: "Policy Regarding the Philippines," *Congressional Record*, 56th Congress, 1st Session (9 January 1900), 704–12.

But Senators, it would be better to abandon this combined garden and Gibraltar of the Pacific, and count our blood and treasure already spent a profitable loss, than to apply any academic arrangement of self-government to these children. They are not capable of self-government. How could they be? They are not of a self-governing race. They are Orientals, Malays, instructed by Spaniards in the latter's worst estate.

They know nothing of practical self-government except as they have witnessed the weak, corrupt, cruel, and capricious rule of Spain. What magic will anyone employ to dissolve in their minds and characters those impression of governors and governed which three centuries of misrule has created? What alchemy will change the oriental quality of their blood and set the self-government currents of the American pouring through their Malay veins? How shall they, in the twinkling of an eye, be exalted to the heights of self-governing peoples which required a thousand years, Anglo-Saxon though we are?...

No one need fear their competition with our labor. No reward could beguile, no force compel, these children of indolence to leave their trifling lives for the fierce and fervid industry of high wrought America. The very reverse is the fact. One great problem is the necessary labor to develop these islands—to build the roads, open the mines, clear the wilderness, drain the swamps, dredge the harbors. The natives will not supply it....

Senators in opposition are estopped from denying our constitutional power to govern the Philippines as circumstances may demand, for such power is admitted in the case of Florida, Louisiana, Alaska. How, then, is it denied in the Philippines? Is there a geographical interpretation to the Constitution? Do degrees of longitude fix constitutional limitations? Does a thousand miles of ocean diminish constitutional power more than a thousand miles of land?...

Mr. President, this question is deeper than any question of party politics; deeper than any question of the isolated policy of our country even; deeper even than any question of constitutional power. It is elemental. It is racial. God has not been preparing the English-speaking and Teutonic peoples for a thousand years for nothing but vain and idle self-contemplation and self-admiration. No! He has made us the master organizers of the world to establish a system where chaos reigns. He has given us the spirit of progress to overwhelm the forces of reaction throughout the earth. He has made us adept in government that we may administer government among savage and senile peoples. Were it not for such a force as this the world would relapse into barbarism and night. And of all our race He has marked the American people as His chosen nation to finally lead in the regeneration of the world. This is the divine mission of America, and it holds for us all the profit, all the glory, all the happiness possible to man. We are the trustees of the world's programs, guardians of its righteous peace. The judgment of the Master is upon us: "Ye have been faithful over a few things; I will make you ruler over many things."

What shall history say of us? Shall it say that we renounced that holy trust, left the savage to his base condition, the wilderness to the reign of waste, deserted duty, abandoned glory, forget our sordid profits even, because we feared our strength and read the charter of our powers with the doubter's eye and the quibbler's mind? Shall it say that, called by events to captain and command the proudest, ablest, purest race of history in history's noblest work, we declined that great commission? Our fathers would not have had it so. No! They founded no paralytic government, no sluggard people, passive while the world's work calls them. They established no reactionary nation. They unfurled no retreating flag....

    Mr. President and Senators, adopt the resolution offered, that peace may quickly come and that we may begin our saving, regenerating, and uplifting work.... Reject it, and the world, history, and the American people will know where to forever fix the awful responsibility for the consequences that will surely follow such failure to do our manifest duty. How dare we delay when our soldier's blood is flowing?

165

Perspectives of Overseas Expansion (1898, 1899, 1900)

The quick victory in the Spanish-American War thrust the United States into a new role as a global power. The United States declared in the Teller Amendment that Cuba would not be annexed, but other lands, either former Spanish colonies or lands not taken by European imperialistic powers, were seen as possible American possessions. The United States annexed Hawai'i (or the Sandwich Islands) prior to the war, and acquired Puerto Rico, Guam, and the Philippines from Spain. In addition, Secretary of State John Hay issued the Open Door Notes (1899), which declared that China's sovereignty be preserved and that the European spheres of influence could not deny American access to trade within China. Such dramatic changes to American foreign policy were hotly debated and prompted a number of political cartoons that attempted to capture the various perspectives on the issue. The first cartoon is from the Boston Globe *and was published just as the war with Spain began. The next two cartoons were drawn for* Puck *by J. [John] S. Pughe, an artist who continued that magazine's cartoon tradition of vivid imagery. His first cartoon below addressed the Open Door policy, while the second was a commentary on American territorial expansion.*

Questions to Consider

1. In what ways are the issues facing the United States illustrated in each of these cartoons?

2. In what ways is Uncle Sam depicted in each of these cartoons? What sentiment does the cartoonist wish to convey?

3. What is the significance to the portrayal of President William McKinley in the first and third cartoons?

WELL, I HARDLY KNOW WHICH TO TAKE FIRST!

Well, I hardly know which to take first!
SOURCE: Library of Congress Prints and Photographs Division

PUTTING HIS FOOT DOWN
Uncle Sam (to the Powers)—Gentlemen, you may cut up the map as much as you like, but remember that I'm here to stay, and that you can't divide *me* up into spheres of influence!
SOURCE: [LC-USZ62-52569]/Library of Congress Prints and Photographs Division

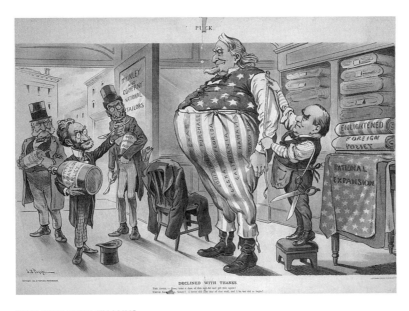

DECLINED WITH THANKS
The Antis, "Here, take a dose of this anti-fat and get thin again!"
Uncle Sam, "No, Sonny! I never did like any of that stuff, and I'm too old to begin!"
SOURCE: [LC-USZC4-2158]/Library of Congress Prints and Photographs Division

166

"A Colombian View of the Panama Canal Question" (1903)

Since the 1840s Americans had considered constructing a Central American canal to facili-tate interocean transportation, but little was done until the twentieth century. A French company—Compagnie Universelle du Canal de Panama—*obtained the rights to build a canal in the Colombian province of Panama in 1881, but the effort ended in bankruptcy. When an American commission recommended construction of a canal in Nicar-agua, representatives of the defunct French company, who held the rights to a Panama canal, lobbied Congress to adopt their route. When the group, led by Philippe Bunau-Varilla, lowered their asking price for the rights to build in Panama from $109 million to $40 million, Congress authorized construction of a Panama canal. In early 1903, Con-gress ratified the Hay-Herran Treaty and presented it to the Colombian government. The treaty authorized an American canal zone ten miles wide for $10 million and an annual payment of $250,000. As the Colombian government considered the treaty, Raul Perez, Colombia's ambassador to the United States, published an article in the* North Ameri-can Review. *While not representing Colombia's official position, the article—excerpted here—indicates apprehension over America's intervention as well as Colombia's potential loss from the canal.*

Questions to Consider

1. For what reasons does Raul Perez oppose the Hay-Herran Treaty?
2. In what ways does Perez propose a better treaty for Colombia?
3. What happened to Colombia's interest in the canal a few months after this article appeared?
4. How would Albert J. Beveridge ("The New Manifest Destiny," Document 164) respond to Perez's views?

The most important matter to be settled with regard to opening the canal is that of exactly defining the status of the party that will carry on the enterprise. It is evident at a glance that there is a wide difference between a private corporation, such as the *Compagnie Universelle du Canal de Panama*, and the powerful govern-ment to the United States of America. The Company has been doing and was to

SOURCE: Raul Perez, "A Colombian View of the Panama Canal Question," *North American Review* 177 (July 1903): 63–68.

do business under the protection of the Colombian laws, subject to those laws in every detail; being considered simply as any other "juridical person"—that is, any Colombian citizen....

If the substitution of the United States government for the *Compagnie Universelle* were once affected, and the consequent transference of rights carried out, would the United States submit to be considered merely a "juridical person," with no more rights than any other Colombian citizen carrying on business in Colombian territory, under protection of the Colombian Laws and subject to those laws in every respect? Such is not the spirit of the Herran-Hay treaty; and, even if it were, Colombians would have plausible reasons for misgivings or apprehensions on that point. No one willing to consider the situation with absolute impartiality can criticise those who desire that the status of Panama Canal builders should be most clearly defined, particularly in a case where a World Power is to be the builder....

Let it be well understood that the Colombians ... are decidedly favorable to the opening of the canal by the United States, should the negotiations be concluded in a manner that would result in real and lasting good to their country....

The ten millions of dollars that Colombia would receive as the only compensation is considered inadequate, and the same would be the case if the sum were increased to fifty millions. This may sound preposterous on first consideration, but not to those who know that the money would be distributed among the dictator's clique and the religious orders....

There is also a very erroneous impression to the effect that the canal when completed will have a great beneficial influence on our country. The conditions as they exist to-day place Colombia in the position of the owner of a bridge, over which an immense traffic is constantly passing. There are many steamship lines converging on the ports of Panama and Colon that load and unload there enormous quantities of merchandise in transit, while large numbers of passengers are compelled to stop at both ends of the trans-Isthmian railroad.... Such will not be the case when the canal is opened. Steamers will go through as rapidly as possible, the passengers dreading the unhealthy climate. There will be no loading of cargoes....

The facts stated are perfectly well known to Colombians, who from the time of Bolivar have imagined that within the narrow strip linking the two American continents, Colombia held her great trump card. It would be an unspeakable disappointment to them to see that advantage fall into other hands, with no return but a few millions of dollars to be employed not for but against their welfare and prosperity. Indeed, so strong is this sentiment that it seems more patriotic to feel that no compensation at all would be preferable. There are many who maintain that a seizure of the Isthmus by a world Power would be more satisfactory, inasmuch as Colombians would be in a position to repeat in all coming years the phrase: "*Tout est perdu, fors L'honneur*" [all is lost except honor]. The rights of Colombia in that case would hold good forever, and the day might come when they would be revindicated; but no such hope could be entertained if the dishonest band of clericals, who act as the government of Colombia, give a seemingly legal consent to the transaction.

The members of that band are in favor of the canal ... simply because they see the possibility of securing ten millions of dollars to be applied to their own purposes. They argue more or less thus: "The Isthmus is a segregated limb of the country where we have not full sway. We may just as well abandon it in exchange for ten millions of dollars with which to establish our uncontested dominion in the rest of the territory."

The other enthusiastic supporters of the canal treaty as it stands are the short-sighted inhabitants of the Isthmus, who long to kill the goose that lays the golden eggs. They see in the near future a boom for their region—excavation contracts, which they imagine will be as profitable as were those of the good old times of the *Compagnie Universelle*; an increase in the value of property; thousands of people coming to make their fortunes, and all the business opportunities attending an undertaking of this kind....

What the Colombians would like to do about the canal would be to have their country hold a permanent interest in the enterprise as a partner of the United States, deriving an income that would benefit not a few officials and one political party but all the people for generations to come. There is no reason why a partnership of that nature could not be successfully carried out, in the same way as a partnership between individuals. All details could be deliberately and safely settled between the two countries to the entire satisfaction of both, bearing in mind that a century in the life of a nation counts no more than one year in the life of a man, and that the canal must be of vast consequence for ages. The desire to cut the canal open as rapidly as possible is praiseworthy, but it is more important to lay first the solid foundations of the transaction and establish the exact limitations of the rights of those concerned, so as to avoid all possible friction in the future.

167

Roosevelt Corollary to the Monroe Doctrine (1904)

Victory in the Spanish-American War thrust the United States into a new position of world power, but it was problems in the Western Hemisphere that attracted American inter-ests. Many Caribbean countries were plagued with political instability, and violent revolu-tions often broke out. Compounding the problem was the poor financial state of these countries. Concerned with stability in the region and wary that hostile foreign powers might use military force to collect debts from these countries and establish a presence in the hemisphere, President Theodore Roosevelt intervened in the domestic affairs of neighboring countries to provide stability and order. This intervention also created investment opportunities for American bankers and businessmen. Such shortsighted activities became a pattern and helped create a legacy of distrust between Latin American nations and the United States. In his 1904 annual message to Congress, excerpted here, Roosevelt offered an explanation for intervention in his famous "corollary" to the Monroe Doctrine.

Questions to Consider

1. According to Roosevelt, for what reasons would the United States intervene in a Caribbean basin country's affairs?

2. What are the potential problems of becoming an "international police power"?

3. In what instances would the Roosevelt Corollary to the Monroe Doctrine be used?

4. How might George F. Hoar ("An Anti-Imperialist Perspective," Document 163) respond to the Roosevelt Corollary?

It is not true that the United States feels any land hunger or entertains any projects as regards the other nations of the Western Hemisphere save such as are for their welfare. All that this country desires is to see the neighboring countries stable, orderly, and prosperous. Any country whose people conduct themselves well can count upon our hearty friendship. If a nation shows that it knows how to act with reasonable efficiency and decency in social and political matters, if it keeps order and pays its obligations, it need fear no interference from the United States. Chronic wrongdoing, or an impotence which results in a general loosening of the ties of civilized society, may in America, as elsewhere, ultimately require intervention by some civilized nation, and in the Western Hemisphere the adherence of the United States to the Monroe Doctrine may force the United States, however reluctantly, in flagrant cases of such wrongdoing or impotence, to the exercise of an international police power. If every country washed by the Caribbean Sea would show the progress in stable and just civilization which with the aid of the Platt amendment Cuba has shown since our troops left the island, and which so many of the republics in both Americas are constantly and brilliantly showing, all question of interference by this Nation with their affairs would be at an end. Our interests and those of our southern neighbors are in reality identical. They have great natural riches, and if within their borders the reign of law and justice obtains, prosperity is sure to come to them. While they thus obey the primary laws of civilized society they may rest assured that they will be treated by us in a spirit of cordial and helpful sympathy. We would interfere with them only in the last resort, and then only if it became evident that their inability or unwillingness to do justice at home and abroad had violated the rights of the United States or had invited foreign aggression

SOURCE: "Theodore Roosevelt, Fourth Annual Message," *The State of the Union Messages of the Presidents, 1790–1966*, ed. Fred L. Israel, vol. 2, *1861–1904* (New York, 1967), 2134–35.

to the detriment of the entire body of American nations. It is a mere truism to say that every nation, whether in America or anywhere else, which desires to maintain its freedom, its independence, must ultimately realize that the right of such independence can not be separated from the responsibility of making good use of it.

In asserting the Monroe Doctrine, in taking such steps as we have taken in regard to Cuba, Venezuela, and Panama, and in endeavoring to circumscribe the theater of war in the Far East, and to secure the open door in China, we have acted in our own interest as well as in the interest of humanity at large. There are, however, cases in which, while our own interests are not greatly involved, strong appeal is made to our sympathies. Ordinarily it is very much wiser and more useful for us to concern ourselves with striving for our own moral and material betterment here at home than to concern ourselves with trying to better the condition of things in other nations. We have plenty of sins of our own to war against, and under ordinary circumstances we can do more for the general uplifting of humanity by striving with heart and soul to put a stop to civic corruption, to brutal lawlessness and violent race prejudices here at home than by passing resolutions about wrongdoing elsewhere. Nevertheless there are occasional crimes committed on so vast a scale and of such peculiar horror as to make us doubt whether it is not our manifest duty to endeavor at least to show our disapproval of the deed and our sympathy with those who have suffered it. The cases must be extreme in which such a course is justifiable. There must be no effort made to remove the mote from our brother's eye if we refuse to remove the beam from our own. But in extreme cases action may be justifiable and proper. What form the action shall take must depend upon the circumstances of the case; that is, upon the degree of the atrocity and upon our power to remedy it. The cases in which we could interfere by force of arms as we interfered to put a stop to intolerable conditions in Cuba are necessarily very few.

168

Woodrow Wilson's Declaration of War Message (1917)

When the First World War broke out in August 1914, President Woodrow Wilson gave the routine declaration of neutrality and urged Americans to be "impartial in thought as well as action." This stance would prove difficult to maintain. As the largest neutral nation with huge economic resources available, the United States was vulnerable to efforts to control trade from both sides in the conflict. The British, whose surface fleet controlled the Atlantic, were very successful at maintaining trade with the United States. To counter British naval supremacy and throttle trade with Great Britain, the Germans began submarine warfare. The U-boat violated traditional naval warfare by sinking merchant ships without warning. When American lives were lost, especially when the passenger liner Lusitania *was sunk in 1915, the Wilson administration protested and the Germans agreed to limit their submarine attacks. In late January 1917, in an attempt to win the war, the Germans announced unrestricted submarine warfare against any ship bound for Great Britain. Several American ships were sunk in February and March. Even though he was reelected in 1916 on the slogan "He kept us out of war," Wilson asked Congress for a declaration of war on 2 April 1917. Excerpted here is Wilson's war message.*

Questions to Consider

1. For what reasons is Woodrow Wilson asking for a declaration of war?
2. Who is the audience of this speech?
3. Why is it significant that Wilson wants war declared against the German government, but not the German people?
4. What is the purpose of America's war effort?

The present German submarine warfare against commerce is a warfare against mankind.

It is a war of all nations. American ships have been sunk, American lives taken, in ways which it has stirred us very deeply to learn of, but the ships and people of other neutral and friendly nations have been sunk and overwhelmed in the waters in the same way. There has been no discrimination. The challenge is to all mankind. Each nation must decide for itself how it will meet it. The choice we make for ourselves must be made with a moderation of counsel and a temperance of judgment befitting our character and our motives as a nation. We must put excited feeling away. Our motive will not be revenge or the victorious assertion of the physical might of the nation, but only the vindication of right, of human right, of which we are only a single champion....

With a profound sense of the solemn and even tragical character of the step I am taking and of the grave responsibilities which it involves, but in unhesitating obedience to what I deem my constitutional duty, I advise that the Congress declare the recent course of the Imperial German Government to be in fact nothing less than war against the government and people of the United States; that it formally accept the status of belligerent which has thus been thrust upon it; and that it take immediate steps, not only to put the country in a more thorough state of defense but also to exert all its power and employ all its resources to bring the Government of the German Empire to terms and end the war....

Our object now, as then, is to vindicate the principles of peace and justice in the life of the world as against selfish and autocratic power and to set up among the really free and self-governed peoples of the world such a concert of purpose

SOURCE: "Address by the President of the United States," *Congressional Record*, 65th Congress, 1st Session (2 April 1917), 102–4.

and of action as will henceforth ensure the observance of those principles. Neutrality is no longer feasible or desirable where the peace of the world is involved and the freedom of its peoples, and the menace to that peace and freedom lies in the existence of an autocratic government backed by an organized force which is controlled wholly by their will, not the will of their people. We have seen the last of neutrality in such circumstances. We are at the beginning of an age in which it will be insisted that the same standards of conduct and of responsibility for wrong done shall be observed among nations and their governments that are observed among the individual citizens of civilized states.

We have no quarrel with the German people. We have no feeling toward them but one of sympathy and friendship. It was not upon their impulse that their government acted in entering this war. It was not with their previous knowledge or approval. It was a war determined as wars used to be determined in the old, unhappy days when peoples nowhere consulted by their rulers and wars were provoked and waged in the interest of dynasties or of little groups of ambitious men who were accustomed to use their fellowmen as pawns and tools....

The world must be made safe for democracy. Its peace must be planted upon the tested foundations of political liberty. We have no selfish ends to serve. We desire no conquest, no domination. We seek no indemnities for ourselves, no material compensation for the sacrifices we shall freely make. We are but one of the champions of the rights of mankind. We shall be satisfied when those rights have been made as secure as the faith and the freedom of nations can make them....

It will be all the easier for us to conduct ourselves as belligerents in a high spirit of right and fairness because we act without animus, not in enmity toward a people or with the desire to bring any injury or disadvantage upon them, but only in armed opposition to an irresponsible government which has thrown aside all considerations of humanity and of right and is running amuck. We are, let me say again, the sincere friends of the German people, and shall desire nothing so much as the early reestablishment of intimate relations of mutual advantage between us—however hard it may be between them, for the time being, to believe that this is spoken from our hearts. We have borne with their present government through all these bitter months because of that friendship,—exercising a patience and forebearance which would otherwise have been impossible. We shall, happily, still have an opportunity to prove that friendship in our daily attitude and actions toward the millions of men and women of German birth and native sympathy who live among us and share our life, and we shall be proud to prove it toward all who are in fact loyal to their neighbors and to the Government in the hour of test. They are, most of them, as true and loyal Americans as if they had never known any other fealty or allegiance....

It is a distressing and oppressive duty, gentlemen of Congress, which I have performed in thus addressing you. There are, it may be, many months of fiery trial and sacrifice ahead of us. It is a fearful thing to lead this great peaceful nation into war, into the most terrible and disastrous of all wars, civilization itself seeming to be in the balance. But the right is more precious than peace, and we shall fight for the things which we have always carried nearest our hearts, —for democracy, for the right of those who submit to authority to have a voice in their own governments, for the rights and liberties of small nations, for a universal dominion of right by such a concert of free peoples as shall bring peace and safety to all nations and make the world itself at last free. To such a task we can dedicate our lives and our fortunes, everything that we are and everything that we have, with the pride of those who know that the day has come when America is privileged to spend her blood and her might for the principles that gave her birth and happiness and the peace which she has treasured. God helping her, she can do no other.

169

Advertising the War Effort (1920)

Just a week after Congress declared war on the German government, President Woodrow Wilson created the Committee on Public Information (CPI) to mobilize public opinion in support of the war effort. Journalist George W. Creel was chosen to head the committee. He quickly shifted the CPI from a government news agency into a powerful public relations machine designed to generate support for the war and to minimize dissent—what he called the "nation's second line." Making use of simple themes like unity, patriotism and the just cause, the CPI essentially sold the war to the American people through an extensive and sophisticated advertising campaign. The committee would employ over 100,000 people to advertise the war effort, and even Hollywood actors like Charlie Chaplin, Mary Pickford, and Douglas Fairbanks were hired to speak at huge rallies to sell war bonds. Shortly after the war concluded, Creel wrote How We Advertised America, *which described the activities of the CPI. An excerpt from the book is below.*

Questions to Consider

1. According to Creel, what was the necessity of the Committee on Public Information?

2. In what ways did the committee advertise the war?

3. What were the various audiences for the advertising campaign?

4. What is the overall tone of Creel's account?

... the war was not fought in France alone. Back of the firing-line, back of armies and navies, back of the great supply-depots, another struggle waged with the same intensity and with almost equal significance attaching to its victories and defeats. It was the fight for the *minds* of men, for the "conquest of their convictions," and the battle-line ran through every home in every country....

The Committee on Public Information was called into existence to make this fight for the "verdict of mankind," the voice created to plead the justice of America's cause before the jury of Public Opinion. The fantastic legend that associated gags and muzzles with its work may be likened only to those trees which are evolved out of the air by Hindu magicians and which rise, grow, and flourish in gay disregard of such usual necessities as roots, sap, and sustenance. *In no degree was the Committee an agency of censorship, a machinery of concealment or repression. Its emphasis throughout was on the open and the positive. At no point did it seek or exercise authorities under those war laws that limited the freedom of speech and press.* In all things, from first to last, without halt or change, it was a plain publicity proposition, a vast enterprise in salesmanship, the world's greatest adventure in advertising.

Under the pressure of tremendous necessities an organization grew that not only reached deep into every American community, but that carried to every corner of the civilized globe the full message of America's idealism, unselfishness, and indomitable purpose. We fought prejudice, indifference, and disaffection at home and we fought ignorance and falsehood abroad. We strove for the maintenance of our own morale and the Allied morale by every process of stimulation; every possible expedient was employed to break through the barrage of lies that kept the people of the Central Powers in darkness and delusion; we sought the friendship and support of the neutral nations by continuous presentation of facts. We did not call it propaganda, for that word, in German hands, had come to be associated with deceit and corruption. Our effort was educational and informative throughout, for we had such confidence in our case as to feel that no other argument was needed than the simple, straightforward presentation of facts.

There was no part of the great war machinery that we did not touch, no medium of appeal that we did not employ. The printed word, the spoken word, the motion picture, the telegraph, the cable, the wireless, the poster, the sign-board—all these were used in our campaign to make our own people and all other peoples understand the causes that compelled America to take arms. All that was fine and ardent in the civilian population came at our call until more than one hundred and fifty thousand men and women were devoting highly specialized abilities to the work of the Committee, as faithful and devoted in their service as though they wore the khaki....

Starting with the initial conviction that the war was not the war of an administration, but the war of one hundred million people, and believing that public support was a matter of public understanding, we opened up the activities

SOURCE: George Creel, *How We Advertised America* (New York, 1920), 3–9.

of government to the inspection of the citizenship. A voluntary censorship agreement safeguarded military information of obvious value to the enemy, but in all else the rights of the press were recognized and furthered. Trained men, at the center of effort in every one of the war making branches of government, reported on progress and achievement, and in no other belligerent nation was there such absolute frankness with respect to every detail of the national war endeavor.

As swiftly as might be, there were put into pamphlet form America's reasons for entering the war, the meaning of America, the nature of our free institutions, our war aims, likewise analyses of the Prussian system, the purposes of the imperial German government, and full exposure of the enemy's misrepresentations, aggressions, and barbarities. Written by the country's foremost publicists, scholars, and historians, and distinguished for their conciseness, accuracy, and simplicity, these pamphlets blew as a great wind against the clouds of confusion and misrepresentation. Money could not have purchased the volunteer aid that was given freely, the various universities lending their best men and the National Board of Historical Service placing its three thousand members at the complete disposal of the Committee. Some thirty-odd booklets, covering every phase of America's ideals, purposes, and aims, were printed in many languages other than English. Seventy-five millions reached the people of America, and other millions went to every corner of the world, carrying our defense and our attack....

The Four Minute Men, an organization that will live in history by reason of its originality and effectiveness, commanded the volunteer services of 75,000 speakers, operating in 5,200 communities, and making a total of 755,190 speeches, every one having the carry of shrapnel....

It gathered together the leading novelists, essayists, and publicists of the land, and these men and women, without payment, worked faithfully in the production of brilliant, comprehensive articles that went to the press as syndicate features....

Through the medium of the motion picture, America's war progress, as well as the meanings and purposes of democracy, were carried to every community in the United States and to every corner of the world. "Pershing's Crusaders," "America's Answer," and "Under Four Flags" were types of feature films by which we drove home America's resources and determinations, while other pictures, showing our social and industrial life, made our free institutions vivid to foreign peoples....

Turning away from the United States to the world beyond our borders, a triple task confronted us. First, there were the peoples of the Allied nations that had to be fired by the magnitude of the American effort and the certainty of speedy and effective aid in order to relieve the war-weariness of the civilian population and also to fan the enthusiasm of the firing-line to new flame. Second, we had to carry the truth to the neutral nations, poisoned by German lies; and third, we had to get the ideals of America, the determination of America, and the invincibility of America into the Central Powers.

170

Opposition to the League
of Nations (1919)

When the peace conference convened in France in 1919, President Woodrow Wilson attended and took an active role in negotiations in the hope of preserving his proposed idealistic blueprint for peacemaking, the Fourteen Points. The resulting Treaty of Versailles contained little of the original Fourteen Points except a League of Nations, which Wilson believed would correct the mistakes of the peace treaty. The heart of the new League of Nations was Article 10, which urged league members "to respect and preserve" the territory of members from external aggression. When Democrat Wilson submitted the treaty to the U.S. Senate for ratification, it came under the close scrutiny of Republican Henry Cabot Lodge, chair of the Foreign Relations Committee. Born in Massachusetts and educated at Harvard (the first PhD in political science), Lodge was known for his clear and forceful arguments in the thirty-seven years he served in Congress. In a speech on the Senate floor, which is excerpted here, Lodge offered his reasons for opposing the Treaty of Versailles (and the League of Nations). The Senate would defeat the treaty ratification in two separate votes, mainly along partisan lines.

Questions to Consider

1. For what reasons does Henry Cabot Lodge oppose the treaty?
2. What changes would he make in the treaty?
3. How does he propose to maintain world peace? Is that possible?
4. Is Lodge an isolationist? What is the significance of his opposition to the ratification of the Treaty of Versailles?

I object in the strongest possible way to having the United States agree, directly or indirectly, to be controlled by a league which may at any time, and perfectly lawfully and in accordance with the terms of the covenant, be drawn in to deal with internal conflicts in other countries, no matter what those conflicts may be. We should never permit the United States to be involved in any internal conflict in another country, except by the will of her people expressed through the Congress which represents them.

SOURCE: "League of Nations," *Congressional Record*, 66th Congress, 1st Session, part 4 (12 August 1919), 3778–84.

With regard to wars of external aggression on a member of the league, the case is perfectly clear. There can be no genuine dispute whatever about the meaning of the first clause of article 10. In the first place, it differs from every other obligation in being individual and placed upon each nation without the intervention of the league. Each nation for itself promises to respect and preserve as against external aggression the boundaries and the political independence of every member of the league....

Any analysis of the provisions of this league covenant, however, brings out in startling relief one great fact. Whatever may be said, it is not a league of peace; it is an alliance, dominated at the present moment by five great powers, really by three, and it has all the marks of an alliance. The development of international law is neglected. The court which is to decide disputes brought before it fills but a small place. The conditions for which this league really provides with the utmost care are political conditions, not judicial questions, to be reached by the executive council and the assembly, purely political bodies without any trace of a judicial character about them. Such being its machinery, the control being in the hands of political appointees whose votes will be controlled by interest and expedience it exhibits that most marked characteristic of an alliance—that its decisions are to be carried out by force. Those articles upon which the whole structure rests are articles which provide for the use of force; that is, for war. This league to enforce peace does a great deal for enforcement and very little for peace. It makes more essential provisions looking to war than to peace for the settlement of disputes....

Taken altogether, these provisions for war present what to my mind is the gravest objection to this league in its present form. We are told that of course nothing will be done in the way of warlike acts without the assent of Congress. If that is true let us say so in the covenant. But as it stands there is no doubt whatever in my mind that American troops and American ships may be ordered to any part of the world by nations other than the United States, and that is a proposition to which I for one can never assent....

Those of us, Mr. President, who are either wholly opposed to the league, or who are trying to preserve the independence and the safety of the United States by changing the terms of the league, and who are endeavoring to make the league, if we are to be a member of it, less certain to promote war instead of peace have been reproached with selfishness in our outlook and with a desire to keep our country in a state of isolation. So far as the question of isolation goes, it is impossible to isolate the United States.... But there is a wide difference between taking a suitable part and bearing a due responsibility in world affairs and plunging the United States into every controversy and conflict on the face of the globe. By meddling in all the differences which may arise among any portion or fragment of humankind we simply fritter away our influence and injure ourselves to no good purpose....

... In the prosecution of the war we gave unstintedly American lives and American treasure. When the war closed we had 3,000,000 men under arms. We were turning the country into a vast workshop for war. We advanced ten billions to our allies. We refused no assistance that we could possibly render. All the great energy and power of the Republic were put at the service of the good cause. We have not been ungenerous. We have been devoted to the cause of freedom, humanity, and civilization everywhere. Now we are asked, in the making of peace, to sacrifice our sovereignty in important respects, to involve ourselves almost without limit in the affairs of other nations and to yield up policies and rights which we have maintained throughout our history. We are asked to incur liabilities to an unlimited extent and furnish assets at the same time which no man can measure. I think it is not only our right but our duty to determine how far we shall go....

No doubt many excellent and patriotic people see a coming fulfillment of noble ideals in the words "league for peace." We all respect and share these aspirations and desires, but some of us see no hope, but rather defeat, for them in this murky covenant. For we, too have our ideals, even if we differ from those who have tried to establish a monopoly of idealism. Our first ideal is our country, and we see her in the future, as in the past, giving service to all her people and to the world. Our ideal of the future is that she should continue to render that service of her own free will. She has great problems of her own to solve, very grim and perilous problems, and a right solution, if we can attain to it, would largely benefit mankind. We would have our country strong to resist a peril from the West, as she has flung back the German menace from the East. We would not have our politics distracted and embittered by the dissensions of other lands. We would not have our country's vigor exhausted or her moral force abated, by everlasting meddling and muddling in every quarrel, great and small, which afflicts the world. Our ideal is to make her ever stronger and better and finer, because in that way alone, as we believe, can she be of the greatest service to the world's peace and to the welfare of mankind.

171

The Red Scare (1920)

A series of labor strikes convulsed the country in 1919. When the Post Office discovered nearly forty bombs addressed to various prominent officials (one was delivered, and it exploded), many Americans were further convinced of a pending communist plot. Coming on the heels of the Russian Revolution and socialist challenges to a number of European governments, these perceived communist tactics, the wartime hysteria against all things German (and foreign), the intolerance of dissenting opinions, and fervent nationalism all combined for an easy shift into the Red Scare. Recently appointed Attorney General A. Mitchell Palmer led a nationwide witch hunt to find the "Reds" and prevent the perceived revolution. The main targets of this effort were radicals, recent immigrants, and some labor union leaders and members. Under Palmer's direction, the Justice Department launched several raids that rounded up nearly 5,000 radicals and aliens, even deporting some individuals without benefit of a court hearing. Riding the crest of popular support, Palmer published the excerpted article below in the respected magazine The Forum *to justify the raids.*

Questions to Consider

1. According to Palmer, in what ways were the "Reds" so threatening to America?
2. What was in jeopardy?
3. What does he ask the American people to do?
4. In what ways might Congressman Meyer London ("A Speech Against Immigration Restriction," Document 172) respond to Palmer's article?

Like a prairie-fire, the blaze of revolution was sweeping over every American institution of law and order a year ago. It was eating its way into the homes of the American workman, its sharp tongues of revolutionary heat were licking the altars of the churches, leaping into the belfry of the school bell, crawling into the sacred corners of American homes, seeking to replace marriage vows with vows of libertine laws, burning up the foundations of society.

Robbery, not war, is the ideal of communism. This has been demonstrated in Russia, Germany, and in America. As a foe, the anarchist is fearless of his own life, for his creed is a fanaticism that admits no respect of any other creed. Obviously it is the creed of any criminal mind, which reasons always from motives impossible to clean thought. Crime is the degenerate factor in society.

Upon these two basic certainties, first that the "Reds" were criminal aliens, and secondly that the American Government must protect crime, it was decided that there could be no nice distinctions between the theoretical ideals of the radicals and their actual violations of our national laws....

My information showed that communism in this country was an organization of thousands of aliens, who were the direct allies of Trotzky. Aliens of the same misshapen cast of mind and indecencies of character, and it showed that they were making the same glittering promises of lawlessness, of criminal autocracy to Americans, that they had made to the Russian peasants. How the Department of Justice discovered upwards of 60,000 of these organized agitators of the Trotzky doctrine in the United States, is the confidential information upon which the Government is now sweeping the nation clean of such alien filth....

One the chief incentives of the present activity of the Department of Justice against the "Reds" has been the hope that American citizens will, themselves, become voluntary agents for us, in a vast organization for mutual defense against the sinister agitation of men and women aliens, who appear to be either in the pay or under the criminal spell of Trotzky and Lenine....

SOURCE: A. Mitchell Palmer, "The Case Against the 'Reds,'" *The Forum* 63 (February 1920): 173–85.

Behind, and underneath, my own determination to drive from our midst the agents of Bolshevism with increasing vigor and with greater speed, until there are no more of them left among us, so long as I have the responsible duty of that task, I have discovered the hysterical methods of these revolutionary humans with increasing amazement and suspicion. In the confused information that sometimes reaches the people, they are compelled to ask questions which involve the reasons for my acts against the "Reds." I have been asked, for instance, to what extent deportation will check radicalism in this country. Why not ask what will become of the United States Government if these alien radicals are permitted to carry out the principles of the Communist Party as embodied in its so-called laws, aims and regulations?

There wouldn't be any such thing left. In place of the United States Government we should have the horror and terrorism of Bolsheviki tyranny such as is destroying Russia now. Every scrap of radical literature demands obedience to the instincts of criminal minds, that is, to the lower appetites, material and moral. The whole purpose of communism appears to be a mass formation of the criminals of the world to overthrow the decencies of private life, to usurp property that they have not earned, to disrupt the present order of life regardless of health, sex or religious rights. By a literature that promises the wildest dreams of such low aspirations, that can occur only to the criminal minds, communism distorts our social law.

The chief appeal of communism makes is to "The Worker." If they can lure the wage-earner to join their own gang of thieves, if they can show him that he will be rich if he steals, so far they have succeeded in betraying him to their own criminal course....

It has been inferred by the "Reds" that the United States Government, by arresting and deporting them, is returning to the autocracy of Czardom, adopting the system that created the severity of Siberian banishment. My reply to such charges is, that in our determination to maintain our government we are treating our alien enemies with extreme consideration. To deny them the privilege of remaining in the country which they have openly deplored as an unenlightened community, unfit for those who prefer the privileges of Bolshevism, should be no hardship. It strikes me as an odd form of reasoning that these Russian Bolsheviks who extol the Bolshevik rule, should be so unwilling to return to Russia. The nationality of most of the alien "Reds" is Russian and German. There is almost no other nationality represented among them.

It has been impossible in so short a space to review the entire menace of the internal revolution in this country as I know it, but this may serve to arouse the American citizen to its reality, its danger, and the great need of united effort to stamp it out, under our feet, if needs be. It is being done. The Department of Justice will pursue the attack of these "Reds" upon the Government of the United States with vigilancy, and no alien, advocating the overthrow of existing law and order in this country, shall escape arrest and prompt deportation.

It is my belief that while they have stirred discontent in our midst, while they have caused irritating strikes, and while they have infected our social ideas with the disease of their own minds and their unclean morals, we can get rid of them! and not until we have done so shall we have removed the menace of Bolshevism for good.

20

The Return to "Normalcy"

During the 1920s, America withdrew from the world and attempted to return to a simpler, pre-progressive time. The decade proved to be one of paradoxes. For many Americans, the time was one of abundance; great fortunes were made, unprecedented mobility was enjoyed through the use of the automobile, and a new morality evolved. For other Americans, the decade had a far harsher reality. The reemergence of nativism in the wake of increased immigration led to persecution of ethnic, religious, and racial minorities. In the countryside, farmers who had enjoyed boom years a decade earlier stood on the brink of financial ruin. The following documents bring the decade's many inconsistencies into sharp relief.

172

A Speech Against Immigration Restriction (1921)

The First World War had slowed immigration to a trickle; but in the first year following the war nearly 800,000 people, mostly from southern and eastern Europe, entered the country. The flood of immigrants to America had resumed in earnest. Many Americans, possessing strong nativistic tendencies following the war and reacting to the labor strikes, bombings, and the Red Scare within the United States, believed these immigrants brought radical ideas and alien customs that threatened American institutions and ways of life. Some believed the recent immigrants would take jobs from Americans. In 1921 Congress considered enacting emergency immigration legislation to reduce significantly the number of immigrants. They proposed to limit by quota the number of immigrants from any country to 3 percent of the persons from that nationality who resided in the United States according to the census of 1910. The proposed legislation would limit total immigration to just over 350,000 per year. Congressman Meyer London of New York opposed this action. London came to the United States from Russia when he was twenty years old, practiced law in New York City, and for over thirty years was active in the labor movement and the Socialist Party. He was elected to Congress twice as a Socialist Party candidate. Excerpted here are London's comments about restricting immigration.

Questions to Consider

1. For what reasons does Congressman London oppose immigration restriction?
2. Why does he argue that immigration is a problem of humanity and that civilization is at risk?
3. How might the supporters of the Red Scare ("The Red Scare," Document 171) and the Ku Klux Klan ("The Ku Klux Klan's Perspective," Document 177) have responded to London's speech?

I have no hope of presenting even an outline of this subject. The world is still crazy. The war is not over. After preaching for thousands of years the fatherhood of God and the brotherhood of man, and then engaging for five years in slaughter, it is but natural that we should be in an abnormal state. While the killing of men's bodies has stopped, the poisoning of minds has just begun. This bill is a continuation of the war upon humanity. It is an assertion of that exaggerated nationalism which never appeals to reason and which has for its main source the self-conceit of accumulated prejudice.

At whom are you striking in this bill? Why, at the very people whom a short while ago you announced you were going to emancipate. We sent 2,000,000 men abroad to make the world "safe for democracy," to liberate these very people. Now you shut the doors to them. Yes. So far, we have made the world safe for hypocrisy and the United States incidentally unsafe for the Democratic Party, temporarily at least. [Laughter.]

The supporters of the bill claim that the law will keep out radicals. The idea that by restricting immigration you will prevent the influx of radical thought is altogether untenable. You can not confine an idea behind prison bars. You can not exclude it by the most drastic legislation. The field of thought recognizes no barriers. The fact that there was almost no immigration during the war did not prevent us from importing every abominable idea from Europe. We brought over the idea of deportation of radicals from France, not from the France of Rousseau, Jaurés, and Victor Hugo, but from the France of the Bourbons. We imported the idea of the censorship of the press and the passport system from Russia, not from the Russia of Kropotkin and Tolstoy, but from the Russia of Nicholas II. We have imported the idea of universal military service from Germany, not from the Germany of Heine, Boerne, and Freiligrath, but from the Germany of the Kaiser.

SOURCE: *Congressional Record*, 67th Congress, 1st Session (21 April 1921), 515.

Ideas can neither be shut in or shut out. There is only one way of contending with an idea, and that is the old and safe American rule of free and untrammeled discussion. Every attempt to use any other method has always proven disastrous.

While purporting to be a temporary measure, just for a year or so, this bill is really intended to pave the way to permanent exclusion.

To prevent immigration means to cripple the United States. Our most developed industrial States are those which have had the largest immigration. Our most backward States industrially and in the point of literacy are those which have had no immigration to speak of.

The extraordinary and unprecedented growth of the United States is as much a cause as the effect of immigration.

Defenders of this bill thoughtlessly repeat the exploded theory that there have been two periods of immigration, the good period, which the chairman of the committee fixes up to the year 1900, and the bad period since. The strange thing about it is that at no time in history has any country made such rapid progress in industry, in science, and in the sphere of social legislation as this country has shown since 1900.

The new immigration is neither different nor worse, and besides that, identically the same arguments were used against the old immigration.

By this bill we, who have escaped the horrors of the war, will refuse a place of refuge to the victims of the war.

I repeat, this is an attempt at civilization. Progress is by no means a continuous or uninterrupted process. Many a civilization has been destroyed in the tortuous course of history and has been followed by hundreds or thousands of years of darkness. It is just possible that unless strong men who love liberty will everywhere assert themselves, the world will revert to a state of savagery. Just now we hear nothing but hatred, nothing but the ravings of the exaggerated I—"I am of the best stock, I do not want to be contaminated; I have produced the greatest literature; my intellect is the biggest; my heart is the noblest"—and this is repeated in every parliament in every country, by every fool all over the world. [Applause.]....

I insist that the prosperity and growth of the United States can not be separated from the question of immigration. When the United States was formed its flag had only 13 stars, and it is due to the immigrants and their offspring that 35 stars were added to the flag. Every American problem is a problem of humanity.

173

The Role of Advertising (1922)

A by-product of industrialization was the creation of the mass consumer culture. By the 1920s increasing numbers of middle-class families had the income to purchase goods and services beyond basic necessities. Americans bought new appliances, such as the refrigerator and vacuum cleaner. They used new products, such as cigarettes, toothpaste, and mouthwash. Such consumer spending helped fuel the changing American economy. But advertising was particularly influential in promoting the consumer economy, becoming a booming business in the 1920s. Advertisers found new and creative ways to market products, placing appealing ads in newspapers and magazines, erecting billboards along the ever increasing number of highways, and using air time on the recently developed radio broadcasts to acquaint the public with consumer items. Such efforts typically identified products with a certain lifestyle and persuaded potential customers that purchasing the product would enrich their life. Below are three advertisements from the 1920s that represent this appeal to middle-class consumers.

Questions to Consider

1. In what ways do these advertisements appeal to middle-class consumers? What can you deduce about middle class values?
2. How do the companies depict their products?
3. In what ways are current print advertisements different from those in the 1920s?

Poster advertising payment plans for Ford Model T, about 1925

SOURCE: From the Collections of The Henry Ford

MRS. REGINALD VANDERBILT
gives her skin this exquisite care

"YOUTHFULNESS is the real pot of gold at the end of every woman's rainbow. Pond's Two Creams are a wonderful help to this coveted end."

Gloria M Vanderbilt

MY first glimpse of Mrs. Reginald Vanderbilt brought a little catch to my throat.

I had heard she was very lovely—this young woman, barely twenty-one, two years married to the son of one of America's oldest, wealthiest, most distinguished families, and mother of an exquisite baby girl. But I was unprepared for beauty so compelling, so unique.

"It's partly because she's so tall," I said to my companion, "and so slender. Did you *ever* see such grace?"

Sunlight breaks the shadows of her almost black hair, into shimmering bronze. In the depths of her dark eyes burn the fires of golden topazes. And in the snows of her delicate skin blooms the rose of her full-blown lips, ruby-red and strangely beautiful.

"What *a bouquet* she lends that gown," I murmured, as Mrs. Vanderbilt moved into the room. "Its black velvet is richer for contrast with arms and shoulders of such dazzling whiteness."

"But the contrast is in the color alone," said someone in our group. "When it comes to texture, there's little to choose between chiffon velvet and Mrs. Vanderbilt's skin."

"IT ought to be a good skin," Mrs. Vanderbilt spoke seriously. "I take good care of it."

"No doubt you devote hours of every day to keeping it exquisite," my friend rejoined.

"On the contrary," cried Mrs. Vanderbilt, "only a few moments—far less time than many of my friends. It's not the *time* that counts. It's the *method!*"

"Do tell us what your method is," we queried.

"Two Creams," said Mrs. Vanderbilt, "made by the Pond's Laboratories. One to cleanse the skin and keep it fresh and firm. The other to protect and give it that 'velvety' finish you've just spoken of. I've used them for a long time and have never found any better."

It is this approval given by the women of Society who *must* keep their youth and beauty—for Mrs. Vanderbilt is only one of many—that is the final proof of the sterling worth of Pond's Two Creams.

The first step in following the Pond's method of skin care is a deep, thorough cleansing with Pond's Cold Cream. Smooth it lavishly over your face, neck, arms and hands. Let it stay on a few moments so that its pure oils may soften the dust, soot, powder and rouge that choke the pores.

WIPE all the cream off and note the dirt it brings with it. Repeat the process. Now close the pores with a dash of cold water or a rub with ice.

This daily Pond's cleansing should follow any prolonged time spent out of doors. If your skin is inclined to be either very dry or oily, you should use it twice or more. And to overcome the dryness that forms lines and wrinkles, leave some of the cream on all night.

The second step is a soft finish and protection with Pond's Vanishing Cream. Fluff just a light film over your face and hands. It will vanish—for Pond's Vanishing Cream is greaseless. Notice now, how even the surface of your skin looks, how soft, bright and clear its tone.

And how well your rouge and powder blend and stay over this delicate foundation cream!

You should always use Pond's Vanishing Cream before you powder, and before going out. For it protects your skin so that wind, dust, sun and soot cannot rob it of its natural oils, its bloom of youth.

FOLLOW the lead of Mrs. Reginald Vanderbilt. Buy your own Pond's Creams. Find out for yourself that what she says is wholly true—"They constitute as simple, as effectual a method of caring for the skin as has yet been discovered." You may have the Cold Cream in extra large jars now. And, of course, both creams in the smaller jars you are familiar with. The Pond's Extract Company.

FREE OFFER—*Mail this coupon and we will send you free tubes of these two creams and an attractive little folder telling how to use them.*

The Pond's Extract Company, Dept. E
135 Hudson Street, New York City

Name ....

Street ....

City .... State............

MRS. REGINALD C. VANDERBILT
As Miss Gloria Morgan she spent her girlhood abroad. Since her marriage she has become a distinguished leader of the exclusive society of New York and Newport.

EVERY SKIN NEEDS THESE TWO CREAMS

In using advertisements see page 6   103

Pond's Extract Company, "Mrs. Reginald Vanderbilt gives her skin this exquisite care,"

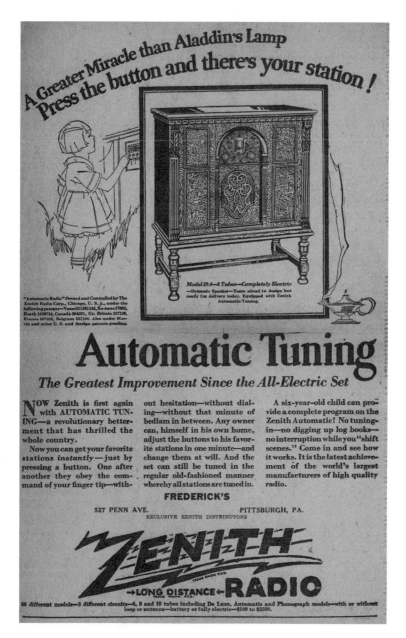

Zenith Radio, "Automatic Tuning: The Greatest Achievement Since the All-Electric Set," *Pittsburgh Press* (1928).

SOURCE: Duke University Archives

174

The Impact of the Automobile (1922)

The most significant social and economic development of the 1920s was the automobile. It speeded transportation, created a movement for improved roads, helped accelerate suburban sprawl, and gave American youths a sense of independence. The Ford Motor Company, founded by Henry Ford in 1903, revolutionized the auto industry with the assembly line and mass production techniques used to make the Model T. Before stopping production of the "tin lizzie" after twenty years, Ford manufactured over 15 million Model Ts, selling them for as little as $290 in 1927. Other automobile makers adopted the mass production techniques, but fierce price competition and the large capital outlays required to maintain production reduced the number of companies from 253 in 1908 to 44 in 1929. The "Big Three" auto manufacturers—Ford, General Motors, and Chrysler—made 80 percent of the cars in the United States in the 1920s. In 1922, Allen D. Albert published the following article on the "social influence of the automobile" in Scribner's Magazine, *a popular news periodical. His article appeared as the popularity of the automobile became increasingly widespread.*

Questions to Consider

1. According to Allen D. Albert, what changes occurred because of the automobile?
2. What does Albert believe are the less-desirable changes?
3. Why were Americans able to adjust so quickly to the automobile?
4. How might the automobile enhance democracy and individualism in American life? How might it undermine these traits?

We look along a perspective of lights dazzling in their intensity and realize wearily, any hot evening, that the procession along the boulevard will not cease till bedtime. Or we jerk ahead and wait, jerk ahead again and wait again, in a choke of purring cars after a football game. Or we look up from a hardware counter and see a farmer who has driven five miles from the harvest-field to get a ball of twine. Or we hunt for a parking space outside a Chautauqua tent. A dozen times a year, in as many situations, the newness and far reach of the motor-driven vehicle catch up our thought as does the airplane which lands in the field near our house.

SOURCE: Allen D. Albert, "The Social Influence of the Automobile," *Scribner's Magazine* 71 (1922): 685–88.

"It is so wonderfully new," we say to ourselves time and again. Still we do not appreciate how new it really is!...

Are you still shocked by reading "Auto Bandits" in the head-lines? Have you passed at the side of a country road a car with no lights and two young figures shoulder against shoulder in a corner of the rear seat? Do you know that banks are still refusing to make loans for the buying of cars? Have you observed the bootlegger in the automobile, the doctor in his little coupé, the rural carrier in his Ford, the children in the school bus?

We have in 1921 about nine million motor-cars in the United States, hardly a third as many as our horses. Yet I think there can be no serious question that the motor-car has come to be more important to us socially than the horse.

The most comprehensive change it has wrought for us has been the general widening of the circle of our life. City folk feel this in the evening and at the week-end. Farmer folk feel it from early morning till bedtime every day.

Our mail comes to our R.F.D. box usually not later than eleven in the morning, and ours is the last delivery but one on our route. Some who work, in every town, now have year-round houses in the country. There is, in fact, a tangible and powerful movement directly opposite to that of the retired farmer. He came to town to rest; city folk are going to the country to rest, and in the era of the automobile they do not lose the diversions that appealed so strongly to the retired farmer....

We have seen our architecture develop the garage in lieu of the old carriage-house and livery-barn. We have heard our speech enlivened with automobile terms, such as when our children describe a teacher of undistinguished personality as a "flat tire." We have noted the entire disappearance of the victoria before the "chummy car" or the "roadster," and some of us have sighed for an aristocracy that is never more to be.

Strange-looking driveways called "filling stations," with glowing lamps at night, long railroad-trains of tank-cars, streets painted with white lines to mark zones for safety for pedestrians and parking spaces for cars—how almost without a pause in our thinking have we adjusted our lives to these factors new since yesterday!...

We of the motor era do not bow to each other in passing on the highway as once we did. The car makes that impracticable. Sometimes we recognize the approaching machine and sometimes we make out the person who is driving. Before there can be any exchange of recognition, however, we have flown past each other....

Automobile outlawry and lawlessness are now more serious, I believe, than they are to be hereafter. It is absurd to expect a great new social agency to come into use without abuse. Almost invariably abuse is the concomitant of use.

The same machine that hurries the surgeon to the bedside of the child with a broken foot will hurry the yeggman [slang for thief or burglar] in his getaway from a hold-up. The boy who acts the pig in his home will not suddenly become considerate of others when given absolute control of a vehicle swifter and heavier than the others on the street. Traffic squads are already making his control far from absolute in the more travelled thoroughfares. Within such limits it is to be expected that he and his highwayman associates will shortly be checked by some device that will stop all vehicular movement within a fixed limit on the sounding of an alarm. The car that persists in shooting ahead will thus be brought into clear view, while if the joy-rider or the thief stopped with the others ordinarily, he would only await capture....

When the new defense is provided, as surely it will be, perhaps it may modify one of the new problems of education produced by the automobile. In an older day it was feasible for the college authorities to keep some sort of watch over their students. Now a boy at school in Connecticut can motor to New York City and back between his last lecture of one day and his first class of the next.

What are campus regulations to students who have the range of an extra-campus radius of one hundred miles? Assuredly the best answer will be the development of a motive in the life of the student that will keep him safe wherever he is. But while we wait for that approach to undergraduate perfection, there will be a value no male parent will question in the student's realization that the automobile thoroughfares around the campus are patrolled sensibly and sufficiently. Longer motor journeys will hasten the day of such control.

Bus lines are reporting to our village squares with little or no preliminary announcement. They make about the same time as accommodations trains, they travel more direct routes, they traverse a landscape unspoiled by cuts and fills and tracks, and they deliver us if not at our exact destinations into the very heart of town rather than at railway-stations away from the heart of town....

Roads are improving farther from those busy streets. Touring-cars are improving likewise. One need not move around like a farm-hand on a load of hay, almost swamped by bulgy equipment. Compact outfits, touring vehicles as ingeniously designed as yachts, hotels cleanly kept and courteously managed, all promise a freer movement of the people to every interesting section of the country. In that freer movement the automobile will justify itself most of all, I believe, as an agent of the wholesome sociability in our modern life.

175

The New Negro (1925)

The First World War created both opportunity and despair for African Americans. In the years before the war, some blacks left the segregationist South and moved to the North for economic opportunity and the hope of a better life. When the war created labor shortages, however, this "Great Migration" swelled, as several thousand African Americans moved to the North to work in war industries. Blacks were drafted into the military, and segregated units fought in Europe. The migration continued after the war as another 1 million African Americans migrated to the North, often crowding into urban ghettos such as New York's Harlem, Chicago's South Side, and Philadelphia's Seventh Ward. These ghettos became centers of African American culture; storefront churches, newspapers, jazz and blues clubs, and literary salons helped form a black cultural identity. One observer of this movement was a Howard University philosophy professor and literary critic, Alain Locke. In 1925, Locke wrote The New Negro, *an essay depicting the changes that were taking place.* The New Negro *is excerpted here.*

Questions to Consider

1. According to Locke, who is the "New Negro"?
2. What resulted from the migration of African Americans to the cities of the North?
3. What is the significance of the "new spirit"?
4. How might W. E. B. Du Bois ("W. E. B. Du Bois On Race Relations," Document 148) have responded to Locke's views on the "New Negro"?

In the last decade something beyond the watch and guard of statistics has happened in the life of the American Negro and the three norns [one of the fates—past, present, future] who have traditionally presided over the Negro problem have a changeling in their laps. The Sociologist, the Philanthropist, the Race-leader are not unaware of the New Negro, but they are at a loss to account for him. He simply cannot be swathed in their formulae. For the younger generation is vibrant with a new psychology; the new spirit is awake in the masses, and under the very eyes of the professional observers is transforming what has been a perennial problem into the progressive phases of contemporary Negro life....

Recall how suddenly the Negro spirituals revealed themselves; suppressed for generations under the stereotypes of Wesleyan hymn harmony, secretive, half-ashamed, until the courage of being natural brought them out—and behold, there was folk-music. Similarly the mind of the Negro seems suddenly to have slipped from under the tyranny of social intimidation and to be shaking off the psychology of imitation and implied inferiority. By shedding the old chrysalis of the Negro problem we are achieving something like a spiritual emancipation. Until recently, lacking self-understanding, we have been almost as much of a problem to ourselves as we still are to others. But the decade that found us with a problem has left us with only a task. The multitude perhaps feels as yet only a strange relief and a new vague urge, but the thinking few know that in the reaction the vital inner grip of prejudice has been broken.

With this renewed self-respect and self-dependence, the life of the Negro community is bound to enter a new dynamic phase, the buoyancy from within compensating for whatever pressure there may be of conditions from without.

The migrant masses, shifting from countryside to city, hurdle several generations of experience at a leap, but more important, the same thing happens spiritually in the life-attitudes and self-expression of the Young Negro, in his poetry, his art, his education and his new outlook, with the additional advantage, of course, of the poise and greater certainty of knowing what it is all about. From this comes the promise and warrant of new leadership....

First we must observe some of the changes which since the traditional lines of opinion were drawn have rendered these quite obsolete. A main change has been, of course, that shifting of the Negro population which has made the Negro problem no longer exclusively or even predominantly Southern. Why should our minds remain sectionalized, when the problem itself no longer is? Then the trend of migration has not only been toward the North and the Central Midwest, but city-ward and to the great centers of industry—the problems of adjustment are new, practical, local and not peculiarly racial. Rather they are an integral part of the large industrial and social problems of our present-day democracy. And finally, with the Negro rapidly in process of class differentiation, if it ever was warrantable to regard and treat the Negro *en masse* it is becoming with every day less possible, more unjust and more ridiculous.

In the very process of being transplanted, the Negro is becoming transformed.

The tide of Negro migration, northward and city-ward, is not to be fully explained as a blind flood started by the demands of war industry coupled with the shutting off of foreign migration, or by the pressure of poor crops coupled with increased social terrorism in certain sections of the South and Southwest. Neither labor demand, the bollweevil nor the Ku Klux Klan is a basic factor, however contributory any or all of them may have been. The wash and rush of this human tide on the beach line of the northern city centers is to be explained primarily in terms of a new vision of opportunity, of social and economic freedom, of a spirit to seize, even in the face of an extortionate and heavy toll, a chance for the improvement of conditions. With each successive wave of it, the movement of the Negro becomes more and more a mass movement toward the larger and the more democratic chance—in the Negro's case a deliberate flight not only from countryside to city, but from medieval America to modern.

Take Harlem as an instance of this. Here in Manhattan is not merely the largest Negro community in the world, but the first concentration in history of so many diverse elements of Negro life. It has attracted the African, the West Indian, the Negro American; has brought together the Negro of the North and the Negro of the South; the man from the city and the man from the town and village; the peasant, the student, the business man, the professional man, artist, poet, musician, adventurer and worker, preacher and criminal, exploiter and social outcast. Each group has come with its own separate motives and for its own special ends, but their greatest experience has been the finding of one another. Proscription and prejudice have thrown these dissimilar elements into a common area of contact and interaction. Within this area, race sympathy and unity have determined a further fusing of sentiment and experience. So what began in terms of segregation becomes more and more, as its elements mix and react, the laboratory of a great race-welding. Hitherto, it must be admitted that

American Negroes have been a race more in name than in fact, or to be exact, more in sentiment than in experience. The chief bond between them has been that of a common condition rather than a common consciousness; a problem in common rather than a life in common. In Harlem, Negro life is seizing upon its first chances for group expression and self-determination. It is—or promises at least to be—a race capital. That is why our comparison is taken with those nascent centers of folk-expression and self-determination which are playing a creative part in the world to-day. Without pretense to their political significance, Harlem has the same role to play for the New Negro as Dublin has had for the new Ireland or Prague for the New Czechoslovakia....

When the racial leaders of twenty years ago spoke of developing race-pride and stimulating race-consciousness, and of the desirability of race solidarity, they could not in any accurate degree have anticipated the abrupt feeling that has surged up and now pervades the awakened centers. Some of the recognized Negro leaders and a powerful section of white opinion identified with "race work" of the older order have indeed attempted to discount this feeling as a "passing phase," an attack of "race nerves" so to speak, an "aftermath of the war," and the like. It has not abated, however, if we are to gauge by the present tone and temper of the Negro press, or by the shift in popular support from the officially recognized and orthodox spokesmen to those of the independent, popular, and often radical type who are unmistakable symptoms of a new order. It is a social disservice to blunt the fact that the Negro of the Northern centers has reached a stage where tutelage, even of the most interested and well-intentioned sort, must give place to new relationships, where positive self-direction must be reckoned with in ever increasing measure. The American mind must reckon with a fundamentally changed Negro....

176

Religion and the Scopes Trial (1925)

The 1920s produced a cultural clash over the place of religion in America. Protestants were divided into two camps on the proper position of Christians toward modern science, evolution, and secular ideas. In one camp were the modernists, mostly middle-class people who had attempted to adapt their religion to the more scientific, modern world. In the other camp were the fundamentalists. They were mostly rural residents who sought to keep religion as the focal point in American life by reaffirming the literal interpretation of the Bible. Fundamentalists achieved a political victory when Tennessee outlawed the teaching of evolution in public schools. When biology teacher John T. Scopes was arrested for teaching evolution, it *began the Scopes trial that had religion at its core. The trial attracted widespread media attention. Defending Scopes was the recently formed American Civil Liberties Union and prominent trial lawyer Clarence Darrow. Aiding the prosecution was William Jennings Bryan, a former presidential candidate and now an important fundamentalist spokesman. The trial's high point came when Darrow cross-examined Bryan, who defended the literal interpretation of the Bible. Scopes was found guilty and fined $100. Bryan prepared a closing argument for the prosecution that he never delivered. Instead, the argument was printed in* The Memoirs of William Jennings Bryan. *It is excerpted here.*

Questions to Consider

1. According to Bryan, what are the limits of science?
2. Why is evolution a danger to Christianity?
3. Why had the Scopes trial become so significant?
4. Does prosecuting Scopes constitute a threat to freedom of expression? Do Scopes's teachings pose a threat to freedom of religion?
5. In what ways are Bryan's arguments similar to Jerry Falwell's in "The Christian Right's Call to Action" (Document 223)?

Can any Christian remain indifferent? Science needs religion to direct its energies and to inspire with lofty purpose those who employ the forces that are unloosed by science. Evolution is at war with religion because religion is supernatural; it is, therefore, the relentless foe of Christianity, which is a revealed religion.

Let us, then, hear the conclusion of the whole matter. Science is a magnificent material force, but it is not a teacher of morals. It can perfect machinery, but it adds no moral restraints to protect society from the misuse of the machine. It can also build gigantic intellectual ships, but it constructs no moral rudders for the control of storm-tossed human vessels. It not only fails to supply the spiritual element needed but some of its unproven hypotheses rob the ship of its *compass* and thus endanger its cargo.

In war, science has proven itself an evil genius; it has made war more terrible than it ever was before. Man used to be content to slaughter his fellowmen on a single plain—the earth's surface. Science has taught him to go down into the water and shoot up from below, and to go up into the clouds and shoot down from above, thus making the battlefield three times as bloody as it was before; but science does not teach brotherly love. Science has made war so hellish that civilization was about to commit suicide; and now we are told that newly discovered instruments of destruction will make the cruelties of the late war seem trivial in comparison with the cruelties of wars that may come in the future. If civilization is to be saved from the wreckage threatened by intelligence not consecrated by love, it must be saved by the moral code of the meek and

SOURCE: William Jennings Bryan and Mary Baird Bryan, The Memoirs of Williams Jennings Bryan (Chicago, 1925), 554–556. John C. Winston Company, 1925. Copyright © 1925 Henry Holt and Company. Reprinted by permission of Henry Holt and Company, LLC.

lowly Nazarene. His teachings, and His teachings alone, can solve the problems that vex the heart and perplex the world.

The world needs a Saviour more than it ever did before, and there is only one "Name under heaven given among men whereby we must be saved." It is this Name that evolution degrades, for, carried to its logical conclusion, it robs Christ of the glory of a virgin birth, of the majesty of His deity and mission, and of the triumph of His resurrection. It also disputes the doctrine of the atonement.

It is for the jury to determine whether this attack upon the Christian religion shall be permitted in the public schools of Tennessee by teachers employed by the State and paid out of the public treasury. This case is no longer local; the defendant ceases to play an important part. The case has assumed the proportions of a battle-royal between unbelief that attempts to speak through so-called science and the defenders of the Christian faith, speaking through the Legislators of Tennessee. It is again a choice between God and Baal; it is also a renewal of the issue in Pilate's court. In that historic trial—the greatest in history—force, impersonated by Pilate, occupied the throne. Behind it was the Roman Government, mistress of the world, and behind the Roman Government were the legions of Rome. Before Pilate, stood Christ, the Apostle of Love. Force triumphed; they nailed Him to the tree and those who stood around mocked and jeered and said, "He is dead." But from that day the power of Caesar waned and the power of Christ increased. In a few centuries the Roman government was gone and its legions forgotten; while the crucified and risen Lord has become the greatest fact in history and the growing figure of all time.

Again force and love meet face to face, and the question, "What shall I do with Jesus?" must be answered. A bloody, brutal doctrine—Evolution—demands, as the rabble did nineteen hundred years ago, that He be crucified. That cannot be the answer of this jury representing a Christian State and sworn to uphold the laws of Tennessee. Your answer will be heard throughout the world; it is eagerly awaited by a praying multitude. If the law is nullified, there will be rejoicing wherever God is repudiated, the Saviour scoffed at and the Bible ridiculed. Every unbeliever of every kind and degree will be happy. If, on the other hand, the law is upheld and the religion of the school children protected, millions of Christians will call you blessed and, with hearts full of gratitude to God, will sing again that grand old song of triumph:

Faith of our fathers, living still,
In spite of dungeon, fire and sword;
O how our hearts beat high with joy
Whene'er we hear that glorious word—
Faith of our fathers—holy faith;
We will be true to thee til death!

177

The Ku Klux Klan's Perspective (1926)

In 1915, William J. Simmons revived the Ku Klux Klan. Patterned after the group formed during Reconstruction, the new Klan languished until a promotional campaign, several well-publicized investigations, and America's disillusionment following the First World War combined to boost membership into the millions (estimates range from 3 to 8 million). Appealing to America's nativistic tendencies and fears, the Klan spread beyond the South and became a powerful national organization that influenced state and local politics, conducted parades of members wearing white robes and hoods, and held rallies where crosses were burned. In 1922 a revolt removed Simmons as Klan leader, and a dentist from Dallas, Texas—Hiram W. Evans—became the Klan's new Imperial Wizard. Evans oversaw much of the Klan's spectacular rise and its decline. In 1926, he published an article, excerpted here, in the respected North American Review *that explained the Klan's purpose and moral agenda for America.*

Questions to Consider

1. What is the purpose of the Ku Klux Klan? How does it plan to carry out its goals?
2. What does the Klan oppose? Who would join the Klan? Why?
3. What does this document reveal about certain segments of American society in the 1920s?
4. How would Alain Locke ("The New Negro," Document 175) or the authors of the California Senate report on the Chinese ("The Unwanted Immigrants: The Chinese," Document 149) or Congressman Gary Miller ("A Perspective on Limiting Immigration to the United States," Document 236) respond to this document?

The Ku Klux Klan, in short, is an organization which gives expression, direction and purpose to the most vital instincts, hopes and resentments of the old stock Americans, provides them with leadership, and is enlisting and preparing them for militant, constructive action toward fulfilling their racial and national destiny....

There are three of these great racial instincts, vital elements in both the historic and the present attempts to build an America which shall fulfill the

SOURCE: Hiram Wesley Evans, "The Klan's Fight for Americanism," *North American Review* 223 (March–April–May 1926): 33–61.

aspirations and justify the heroism of the men who made the nation. These are the instincts of loyalty to the white race, to the traditions of America, and to the spirit of Protestantism, which has been an essential part of Americanism ever since the days of Roanoke and Plymouth Rock. They are condensed into the Klan slogan: "Native, white, Protestant supremacy."

First in the Klansman's mind is patriotism—America for Americans. He believes religiously that a betrayal of Americanism or the American race is treason to the most sacred of trusts, a trust from his fathers and a trust from God. He believes, too, that Americanism can only be achieved if the pioneer stock is kept pure....

Americanism, to the Klansman, is a thing of the spirit, a purpose and a point of view, that can only come through instinctive racial understanding. It has, to be sure, certain defined principles, but he does not believe that many aliens understand those principles, even when they use our words in talking about them. Democracy is one, fairdealing, impartial justice, equal opportunity, religious liberty, independence, self-reliance, courage, endurance, acceptance of individual responsibility as well as individual rewards for effort, willingness to sacrifice for the good of his family, his nation and his race before anything else but God, dependence on enlightened conscience for guidance, the right to unhampered development—these are fundamental. But within the bounds they fix there must be the utmost freedom, tolerance, liberalism. In short, the Klansman believes in the greatest possible diversity and individualism within the limits of the American spirit. But he believes also that few aliens can understand that spirit, that fewer try to, and that there must be resistance, intolerance even, toward anything that threatens it, or the fundamental national unity based upon it.

The second word in the Klansman's trilogy is "white." The white race must be supreme, not only in America but in the world. This is equally undebatable, except on the ground that the races might live together, each with full regard for the rights and interests of others, and that those rights and interests would never conflict. Such an idea, of course, is absurd; the colored races today, such as Japan, are clamoring not for equality but for their supremacy.... The world has been so made that each race must fight for its life, must conquer, accept slavery or die. The Klansman believes that the whites will not become slaves, and he does not intend to die before his time.

Moreover, the future of progress and civilization depends on the continued supremacy of the white race.... Until the whites falter, or some colored civilization has a miracle of awakening, there is not a single colored stock that can claim even equality with the white; much less supremacy.

The third of the Klan principles is that Protestantism must be supreme; that Rome shall not rule America. The Klansman believes this not merely because he is a Protestant, nor even because the Colonies that are now our nation were settled for the purpose of wresting America from the control of Rome and establishing a land of free conscience. He believes it also because Protestantism is an essential part of Americanism; without it America could never have been created and without it she cannot go forward. Roman rule would kill it.

Protestantism contains more than religion. It is the expression in religion of the same spirit of independence, self-reliance and freedom which are the highest achievements of the Nordic race....

Let it be clear what is meant by "supremacy." It is nothing more than power of control, under just laws. It is not imperialism, far less is it autocracy or even aristocracy of a race or stock of men. What it does mean is that we insist on our inherited right to insure our own safety, individually and as a race, to secure the future of our children, to maintain and develop our racial heritage in our own, white, Protestant, American way, without interference....

And we deny that either bigotry or prejudice enters into our intolerance or our narrowness. We are intolerant of everything that strikes at the foundations of our race, our country or our freedom of worship. We are narrowly opposed to the use of anything alien—race, loyalty to any foreign power or to any religion whatever—as a means to win political power.... This is our intolerance; based on the sound instincts which have saved us many times from the follies of the intellectuals. We admit it. More and worse, we are proud of it....

The Negro, the Klan considers a special duty and problem of the white American. He is among us through no wish of his; we owe it him and to ourselves to give him full protection and opportunity. But his limitations are evident; we will not permit him to gain sufficient power to control our civilization. Neither will we delude him with promises of social equality which we know can never be realized. The Klan looks forward to the day when the Negro problem will have been saved on some much saner basis than miscegenation, and when every State will enforce laws making any sex relations between a white and a colored person a crime.

For the alien in general we have sympathy, opportunity, justice, but no permanent welcome unless he becomes truly American. It is our duty to see that he has every chance for this, and we shall be glad to accept him if he does. We hold no rancor against him; his race, instincts, training, mentality and whole outlook of life are usually widely different from ours. We cannot blame him if he adheres to them and attempts to convert us to them, even by force. But we must see that he can never succeed....

178

The New Woman (1927)

The 1920s witnessed the emergence of the "new woman." Having achieved suffrage with the Nineteenth Amendment, some women turned their attention to other feminine issues— such as political equality, economic independence, and improved relations between the sexes—to broaden their reform efforts, but this movement lacked cohesion. Some feminists advocated an equal rights amendment, individualism, female solidarity, and equality with men while retaining differences from men. Other women pursued reforms in the workplace and acceptance from men. Some young women—the "flappers"—received considerable press coverage for their revolution in morals: They wore lipstick, cut their hair short, smoked, drank alcohol, dressed in short skirts, attended wild parties, and were obsessed with sex. Meanwhile other women, stagnating in male-dominated marriages that relegated them to care for the household and children, hoped to improve relations in the home. The new woman, then, worked for different agendas and with contrasting methods to challenge the prevailing convention. In an article published in Harper's Monthly Magazine, *Dorothy Dunbar Bromley promoted the "Feminist—New Style," a woman who understood the roots of feminism and was willing to make changes in her life.*

Questions to Consider

1. What is the purpose of Dorothy Dunbar Bromley's article?
2. What is the new style of feminist, and how does she differ from the old feminists and the new feminists?
3. How would men react to Bromley's article?
4. What can be deduced from this document about gender relations in the 1920s?

"Feminism" has become a term of opprobrium to the modern young woman. For the word suggests either the old school of fighting feminists who wore flat heels and had very little feminine charm, or the current species who antagonize men with their constant clamor about maiden names, equal rights, woman's place in the world, and many another cause ... *ad infinitum*....

But what of the constantly increasing group of young women in their twenties and thirties who are truly modern ones, those who admit that a full life calls for marriage and children as well as a career? These women if they launch upon marriage are keen to make a success of it and an art of child-rearing. But *at the same time* they are moved by an inescapable inner compulsion to be individuals in their own right. And in this era of simplified housekeeping they see their opportunity, for it is obvious that a woman who plans intelligently can salvage some time for her own pursuits. Furthermore, they are convinced that they will be better wives and mothers for the breadth they gain from functioning outside the home. In short, they are highly conscious creatures who feel obliged to plumb their own resources to the very depths, despite the fact that they are under no delusions as to the present inferior status of their sex in most fields of endeavor.

Numbers of these honest, spirited young women have made themselves heard in article and story. But since men must have things pointed out to them

SOURCE: Dorothy Dunbar Bromley, "Feminist—New Style," Harper's Monthly Magazine 155 (October 1927): 552–560. Copyright © 1927 by Harper's Magazine. All rights reserved. Reproduced from the October issue by special permission.

in black and white, we beg leave to enunciate the tenets of the modern woman's credo. Let us call her "Feminist—New Style."

First Tenet. Our modern young woman freely admits that American women have so far achieved but little in the arts, sciences, and professions as compared with men....

But it remains true that a small percentage of women have proved the capacity, even the creative power of the feminine mind. Or have they not rather proved the fallacy of drawing a hard and fast distinction between the quality of men's minds and the quality of women's minds?...

Second Tenet. Why, then, does the modern woman care about a career or a job if she doubts the quality and scope of women's achievement to date? There are three good reasons why she cares immensely: first, she may be of that rare and fortunate breed of persons who find a certain art, science, or profession as inevitable a part of their lives as breathing; second, she may feel the need of a satisfying outlet for her energy whether or not she possesses creative ability; third, she may have no other means of securing her economic independence. And the latter she prizes above all else, for it spells her freedom as an individual, enabling her to marry or not marry, as she chooses, to terminate a marriage that has become unbearable, and to support and educate her children if necessary....

Third Tenet. She will not, however, live for her job alone, for she considers that a woman who talks and thinks only shop has just as narrow a horizon as the housewife who talks and thinks only husband and children—perhaps more so, for the latter may have a deeper understanding of human nature. She will there-fore refuse to give up all of her personal interests, year in and year out, for the sake of her work....

Fourth Tenet. Nor has she become hostile to the other sex in the course of her struggle to orient herself. On the contrary, she frankly likes men and is grate-ful to more than a few for the encouragement and help they have given her.

In the business and professional world, for instance, Feminist—New Style has observed that more and more men are coming to accord women as much responsibility as they show themselves able to carry. She and her generation have never found it necessary to bludgeon their way, and she is inclined to think that certain of the pioneers would have got farther if they had relied on their ability rather than on their militant methods....

Fifth Tenet. By the same corollary, Feminist—New Style professes no loyalty to women *en masse*, although she staunchly believes in individual women. Surveying her sex as a whole, she finds their actions petty, their range of interests narrow, their talk trivial and repetitious. As for those who set themselves up as leaders of the sex, they are either strident creatures of so little ability and balance that they have won no chance to "express themselves" (to use their own hack-neyed phrase) in a man-made world; or they are brilliant, restless individuals who too often battle for women's rights for the sake of personal glory....

Sixth Tenet. There is, however, one thing which Feminist—New Style envies Frenchwomen, and that is their sense of "chic." Indeed, she is so far removed from the early feminists that she is altogether baffled by the psychology which led some of them to abjure men in the same voice with which they aped them. Certainly their vanity must have been anaesthetized, she tells herself, as she pictures them with their short hair, so different from her own shingle, and dressed in their unflattering mannish clothes—quite the antithesis of her own boyish effects which are subtly designed to set off feminine charms....

Seventh Tenet. Empty slogans seem to Feminist—New Style just as bad taste as masculine dress and manners. They serve only to prolong the war between the sexes and to prevent women from learning to think straight. Take these, for instance, "Keep your maiden name." "Come out of the kitchen." "Never darn a sock.",...

Eighth Tenet. As for "free love," she thinks that it is impractical rather than immoral. With society organized as it is, the average man and woman cannot carry on a free union with any degree of tranquillity.

Incidentally, she is sick of hearing that modern young women are cheapening themselves by their laxity of morals. As a matter of fact, all those who have done any thinking, and who have any innate refinement, live by an aesthetic standard of morals which would make promiscuity inconceivable....

Ninth Tenet. She readily concedes that a husband and children are necessary to the average woman's fullest development, although she knows well enough that women are endowed with varying degrees of passion and of maternal instinct....

But no matter how much she may desire the sanction of marriage for the sake of having children, she will not take any man who offers. First of all a man must satisfy her as a lover and a companion. And second, he must have the mental and physical traits which she would like her children to inherit....

This business of combining two careers presents its grave difficulties. In fact, it is a bigger job than any man has ever attempted. But because it *is* a big job, and because she has seen a few women succeed at it, Feminist—New Style will rise to the challenge....

Tenth Tenet. But even while she admits that a home and children may be necessary to her complete happiness, she will insist upon *more freedom and honesty within the marriage relation....*

Finally, Feminist—New Style proclaims that men and children shall no longer circumscribe her world, although they may constitute a large part of it. She is intensely self-conscious whereas the feminists were intensely sex-conscious. Aware of possessing a mind, she takes a keen pleasure in using that mind for some definite purpose; and also in learning to think clearly and cogently against a background of historical and scientific knowledge.... She knows that it is her American, her twentieth-century birth right to emerge from a creature of instinct into a full-fledged individual who is capable of molding her own life. And in this respect she holds that she is becoming man's equal.

If this be treason, gentlemen, make the most of it.

179

American Individualism (1928)

Herbert Hoover had a long and distinguished career as a government worker before seeking the presidency in 1928. Born in Iowa and raised a Quaker, Hoover became a wealthy engineer-businessman before age forty. He headed the Food Administration during the First World War, using voluntary methods and a propaganda campaign to raise food production while reducing civilian consumption. Hoover served as secretary of commerce under Presidents Warren G. Harding and Calvin Coolidge, and he transformed the insignificant department into one of the most dynamic agencies of the federal government. He helped promote new markets for business, developed industrial standardization, and established regulations for the infant radio and aviation industries. Hoover was well known to Americans, had established a reputation as a brilliant administrator, and was a successful businessman when he ran for president against Democratic candidate Al Smith in 1928. Many argued Hoover would "engineer" the country to continued prosperity. Hoover concluded his presidential campaign in New York with the speech excerpted here. It embodied Herbert Hoover's belief in American individualism as well as the Republican Party's philosophy in the 1920s.

Questions to Consider

1. According to Herbert Hoover, why did America have a strong economy in the 1920s?
2. What is Hoover's "American system"?
3. Why does Hoover fear government involvement in the economy? Is his argument valid?
4. How would the families discussed in "Urban Families in the Great Depression" (Document 180) or Meridel Le Sueur ("Women on the Breadlines," Document 181) have responded to Hoover's concept of "rugged individualism"?

When the war closed, the most vital of all issues both in our own country and throughout the world was whether governments should continue their wartime ownership and operation of many instrumentalities of production and distribution. We were challenged with a peace-time choice between the American system of rugged individualism and a European philosophy of diametrically opposed doctrines—doctrines of paternalism and state socialism. The acceptance of these ideas would have meant the destruction of self-government through

SOURCE: "Text of Hoover's Speech on Relation of Government to Industry," *New York Times*, 23 October 1928, p. 2.

centralization of government. It would have meant the undermining of the individual initiative and enterprise through which our people have grown to unparalleled greatness.

The Republican Party from the beginning resolutely turned its face away from these ideas and these war practices.... When the Republican Party came into full power it went at once back to our fundamental conception of the state and the rights and responsibilities of the individual. Thereby it restored confidence and hope in the American people, it freed and stimulated enterprise, it restored the government to its position as an umpire instead of a player in the economic game. For these reasons the American people have gone forward in progress while the rest of the world has halted, and some of the countries have even gone backwards....

There has been revived in this campaign, however, a series of proposals which, if adopted, would be a long step toward the abandonment of our American system and a surrender to the destructive operation of governmental conduct of commercial business. Because the country is faced with difficulty and doubt over certain national problems—that is prohibition, farm relief, and electrical power—our opponents propose that we must thrust government a long way into the businesses which give rise to these problems. In effect, they abandon the tenets of their own party and turn to state socialism as a solution for the difficulties presented by all three. It is proposed that we shall change from prohibition to the state purchase and sale of liquor. If their agricultural relief program means anything, it means that the Government shall directly or indirectly buy and sell and fix prices of agricultural products. And we are to go into the hydroelectric power business. In other words, we are confronted with a huge program of government in business.

There is, therefore, submitted to the American people a question of fundamental principle. That is: shall we depart from the principles of our American political and economic system, upon which we have advanced beyond all the rest of the world, in order to adopt methods based on principles destructive of its very foundations? And I wish to emphasize the seriousness of these proposals. I wish to make my position clear; for this goes to the very roots of American life and progress....

Let us first see the effect upon self-government. When the Federal Government undertakes to go into commercial business it must at once set up the organization and administration of that business, and it immediately finds itself in a labyrinth, every alley of which leads to the destruction of self-government....

Bureaucracy is ever desirous of spreading its influence and its power. You cannot extend the mastery of the Government over the daily working life of a people without at the same time making it the master of the people's souls and thoughts. Every expansion of Government in business means that Government in order to protect itself from the political consequences of its errors and wrongs is driven irresistibly without peace to greater and greater control of the nation's press and platform. Free speech does not live many hours after free industry and free commerce die.

It is a false liberalism that interprets itself into the government operation of commercial business. Every step of bureaucratizing the business of our country poisons the very roots of liberalism—that is, political equality, free speech, free assembly, free press, and equality of opportunity. It is the road not to more liberty, but to less liberty. Liberalism should be found not striving to spread bureaucracy but striving to set bounds to it. True liberalism seeks all legitimate freedom first in the confident belief that without such freedom the pursuit of all other blessings and benefits is vain. That belief is the foundation of all American progress, political as well as economic.

Liberalism is a force truly of the spirit, a force proceeding from the deep realization that economic freedom cannot be sacrificed if political freedom is to be preserved. Even if Governmental conduct of business could give us more efficiency instead of less efficiency, the fundamental objection to it would remain unaltered and unabated. It would destroy political equality. It would increase rather than decrease abuse and corruption. It would stifle initiative and invention. It would undermine the development of leadership. It would cramp and cripple the mental and spiritual energies of our people. It would extinguish equality and opportunity. It would dry up the spirit of liberty and progress. For these reasons primarily it must be resisted. For a hundred and fifty years liberalism has found its true spirit in the American system, not in the European systems....

By adherence to the principles of decentralized self-government, ordered liberty, equal opportunity, and freedom to the individual, our American experiment in human welfare has yielded a degree of well-being unparalleled in all the world. It has come nearer to the abolition of poverty, to the abolition of fear of want, than humanity has ever reached before. Progress of the past seven years is the proof of it. This alone furnishes the answer to our opponents, who ask us to introduce destructive elements into the system by which this has been accomplished....

I have endeavored to present to you that the greatness of America has grown out of a political and social system and a method of control of economic forces distinctly its own—our American system—which has carried this great experiment in human welfare farther than ever before in all history. We are nearer today to the ideal of the abolition of poverty and fear from the lives of men and women than ever before in any land. And I again repeat that the departure from our American system by injecting principles destructive to it which our opponents propose, will jeopardize the very liberty and freedom of our people, and will destroy equality of opportunity not alone to ourselves but to our children....

✳

FDR and the New Deal

The uneven prosperity of the 1920s vanished with the onset of the Great Depression. As America's leaders searched for a solution to the crisis, large numbers of Americans sank into poverty. Thousands of Americans imbued with the values of rugged individualism begged for food, while many others wandered in search of opportunity. The Great Depression gave the Democrats political control of the country. Behind the leadership of President Franklin D. Roosevelt, the government energetically sought a variety of means to revive the economy and restore hope to the American people. Despite these efforts, political opposition hampered these attempts. The following documents depict the despair of many Americans and the varying efforts undertaken to alleviate these conditions.

180

Urban Families in the Great Depression (1931)

The economic boom of the 1920s vanished with the stock market crash in October 1929, and the country slid into the Great Depression. While it did not cause the Great Depression, the crash revealed the unsound nature of business and helped trigger the economic collapse. Millions of workers lost their jobs as companies retrenched; prices dropped dramatically, and consumer spending virtually ceased. Thousands of businesses failed, and the banking system neared disintegration under the financial strain. At the nadir of the Great Depression the standard of living had dropped by 50 percent, and over one-third of the workforce was fully unemployed (some received shorter work hours but were considered employed). Among the people hardest hit were the urban poor and those living on the margin of poverty. As the depression worsened, Congress heard testimony from many individuals operating private relief agencies about conditions for urban residents. Dorothy Kahn, executive director of the Jewish Welfare Society of Philadelphia, Pennsylvania, testified before the Senate Subcommittee on Unemployment Relief in December 1931. Her excerpted statement here reveals the plight of the urban family in the midst of the Great Depression.

Questions to Consider

1. What happened to urban families in Philadelphia in the Great Depression? How did they react to these circumstances?

2. According to Dorothy Kahn, what was the attitude of the unemployed?

3. Why does she explain this attitude to the congressional committee?

4. How would these families respond to "The Socialist Alternative" (Document 157)? How might they respond to the views contained in William Graham Sumner's "The Forgotten Man" (Document 144)?

THE CHAIRMAN: What happens to these families when they are evicted?

MISS KAHN: The families in Philadelphia are doing a number of things. The dependence of families upon the landlords, who seem to have a remarkable willingness to allow people to live in their quarters, rent free, is something that has not been measured. I think the only indication of it is the mounting list of sheriff's sales where property owners are simply unable to maintain their small pieces of property because rents are not being paid. Probably most of you saw in the newspapers the account of the "organized" representation of the taxpayers recently, where they vigorously and successfully opposed a rise in local taxes, largely because of the fact that they are under a tremendous burden through nonpayment of rents. That, of course, is the least of the difficulties, although I think this is the point at which we ought to stress one of the factors that Mr. West and other speakers have brought out in their testimony, that is the effect on families of the insecurity of living rent free, and in addition to that, the effect on their attitude toward meeting their obligations. Some of us would not be surprised if rent paying became an obsolete custom in our community. There are also, of course, evictions and the evictions in Philadelphia are frequently accompanied not only by the ghastly placing of a family's furniture on

SOURCE: U.S. Congress, Senate, Subcommittee on Unemployment Relief, "Statement of Miss Dorothy Kahn," *Hearings before the Senate Subcommittee on Unemployment Relief, Senate Committee on Manufacturers*, 72nd Congress, 1st Session (28 December 1931), 73–77.

the street, but the actual sale of the family's household goods by the constable. These families are, in common Philadelphia parlance, "sold out."

One of the factors that is never counted in all of the estimates of relief in this country is the factor of neighborliness. That factor of neighborliness is a point that I would like to stress here, because it seems to us who are close to this problem that this factor has been stretched not only beyond its capacity but beyond the limits of human endurance. We have no measure in Philadelphia to-day of the overcrowding that is a direct or indirect result of our inability to pay rent for families. Only the other day a case came to my attention in which a family of 10 had just moved in with a family of 6 in a 3-room apartment. However shocking that may be to the members of this committee, it is almost an every-day occurrence in our midst. Neighbors do take people in. They sleep on chairs, they sleep on the floor. There are conditions in Philadelphia that beggar description. There is scarcely a day that calls do not come to all of our offices to find somehow a bed or a chair. The demand for boxes on which people can sit or stretch themselves is hardly to be believed....

Only the other day a man came to our office, as hundreds do day after day, applying for a job, in order not to have to apply for relief. I think we have already stressed the reluctance of individuals to accept relief, regardless of the source from which it comes. This man said to our worker: "I know you haven't any money to give us. I know there isn't enough money in the city to take care of the needs of everybody, but I want you to give me a job." Now, we have so many applications of that kind during the day that it has gotten to the point where we can scarcely take their names as they come in, because we have no facilities for giving jobs. In this particular case this individual interested me because when he heard that we had no jobs to give him, he said: "Have you anybody you can send around to my family to tell my wife you have no job to give me! Because she doesn't believe that a man who walks the street from morning till night, day after day, actually can't get a job in this town. She thinks I don't want to work." I think it is not necessary to dramatize the results of a situation like that. And there are thousands of them. It is only one illustration.

Another thing, it seems to me to be important to stress is the effect of this situation on the work habits of the next generation. I think it has not been brought out that in the early period of this so-called "depression" one of the most outstanding features of it was the fact that young people could get jobs even when old people of 40 years and over could not get jobs, and it has become quite customary for families to expect that their young members who are just coming of working age can replace the usual breadwinner, the father of the family. It is easy to forget about these young boys and girls reaching 14, 15, 16, 17, 18 years of age, who have had no work experience, and if we think of work not as merely a means of livelihood but as an aspect of our life and a part of our life, it has a good deal of significance that these young people are having their first work experience, and experience not with employment but with unemployment; that in addition to that they are looked to as potential breadwin-ners in the family; that they are under the same strain, the same onus that the father of the family is under, suspected of malingering, suspected of not wanting to work—all of these things which the average individual sees not as clearly as we see them in terms of millions of unemployed....

181

Women on the Breadlines (1932)

The economic collapse of the Great Depression caused thousands of businesses to fail and millions to lose their jobs. The widespread unemployment also strained numerous families, as many lined up to receive bread or found a free or inexpensive meal in soup kitchens. Numerous men left their wives and children to find work in other cities, and women remained behind to maintain the family and fend for themselves while their husbands roamed the country looking for a job. Journalist Meridel Le Sueur observed the unemployed as she traveled the country reporting for The New Masses, *a left-wing newspaper. Raised in a socially and politically radical family, Le Sueur was interested in those who were less fortunate, and she was particularly sympathetic toward the plight of women. Below is an excerpt from Le Sueur's article in* The New Masses *about women in the Great Depression.*

Questions to Consider

1.   In what ways does Le Sueur characterize the unemployed?
2.   What are Le Sueur's comments about married couples?
3.   What does Le Sueur observe about women in the Great Depression?
4.   What is the purpose of Le Sueur's comments about Mrs. Grey's life?

I am sitting in the city free employment bureau. It's the woman's section. We have been sitting here now for four hours. We sit here every day, waiting for a job. There are no jobs. Most of us have had no breakfast. Some have had scant rations for over a year. Hunger makes a human being lapse into a state of lethargy, especially city hunger. Is there any place else in the world where a human being is supposed to go hungry amidst plenty without an outcry, without protest, where only the boldest steal or kill for bread, and the timid crawl the streets, hunger like the beak of a terrible bird at the vitals? We sit looking at the floor. No one dares think of the coming winter. There are only a few more days of

SOURCE: Meridel Le Sueur, "Women on the Breadlines," from Harvest: Collected Stories. Reprinted with the permission of West End Press, Albuquerque, New Mexico.

summer. Everyone is anxious to get work to lay up something for that long siege of bitter cold. But there is no work. Sitting in the room we all know it. That is why we don't talk much. We look at the floor dreading to see that knowledge in each other's eyes. There is a kind of humiliation in it. We look away from each other. We look at the floor. It's too terrible to see this animal terror in each other's eyes....

This is a domestic employment bureau. Most of the women who come here are middle-aged, some have families, some have raised their families and are now alone, some have men who are out of work. Hard times and the man leaves to hunt for work. He doesn't find it. He drifts on. The woman probably doesn't hear from him for a long time. She expects it. She isn't surprised. She struggles alone to feed the many mouths. Sometimes she gets help from the charities. If she's clever she can get herself a good living from the charities, if she's naturally a lick-spittle, naturally a little docile and cunning. If she's proud then she starves silently, leaving her children to find work, coming home after a day's searching to wrestle with her house, her children....

It's one of the great mysteries of the city where women go when they are out of work and hungry. There are not many women in the bread line. There are no flop houses for women as there are for men, where a bed can be had for a quarter or less. You don't see women lying on the floor at the mission in the free flops. They obviously don't sleep in the jungle or under newspapers in the park. There is no law I suppose against their being in these places but the fact is they rarely are.

Yet there must be as many women out of jobs in cities and suffering extreme poverty as there are men. What happens to them? Where do they go? Try to get into the Y. W. without any money or looking down at heel. Charities take care of very few and only those that are called "deserving." The lone girl is under suspicion by the virgin women who dispense charity.

I've lived in cities for many months broke, without help, too timid to get in bread lines. I've known many women to live like this until they simply faint on the street from privations, without saying a word to anyone. A woman will shut herself up in a room until it is taken away from her, and eat a cracker a day and be as quiet as a mouse so there are no social statistics concerning her....

Sometimes a girl facing the night without shelter will approach a man for lodging. A woman always asks a man for help. Rarely another woman. I have known girls to sleep in men's rooms for the night, on a pallet without molestation, and given breakfast in the morning....

Mrs. Grey, sitting across from me is a living spokesman for the futility of labour. She is a warning. Her hands are scarred with labour. Her body is a great puckered scar. She has given birth to six children, buried three, supported them all alive and dead, bearing them, burying them, feeding them. Bred in hunger they have been spare, susceptible to disease. For seven years she tried to save her boy's arm from amputation, diseased from tuberculosis of the bone. It is almost too suffocating to think of that long close horror of years of child bearing, child feeding, rearing, with the bare suffering of providing a meal and shelter.

Now she is fifty. Her children, economically insecure, are drifters. She never hears of them. She doesn't know if they are alive. She doesn't know if she is alive. Such subtleties of suffering are not for her. For her the brutality of hunger and cold, the bare bone of life. That is enough. These will occupy a life. Not until these are done away with can those subtle feelings that make a human being be indulged....

The young ones know though. I don't want to marry. I don't want any children. So they all say. No children. No marriage. They arm themselves alone, keep up alone. The man is helpless now. He cannot provide. If he propagates he cannot take care of his young. The means are not in his hands. So they live alone. Get what fun they can. The life risk is too horrible now. Defeat is too clearly written on it.

It is appalling to think that these women sitting so listless in the room may work as hard as it is possible for a human being to work, may labour night and day, like Mrs. Grey wash street cars from midnight to dawn and offices in the early evening, scrubbing for fourteen and fifteen hours a day, sleeping only five hours or so, doing this their whole lives, and never earn one day of security, having always before them the pit of the future. The endless labour, the bending back, the water soaked hands, earning never more than a week's wages never having in their hands more life than that.

182

Franklin D. Roosevelt's First Inaugural Address (1933)

The dominant issue in the presidential election in 1932 was the Great Depression. The Republicans renominated Herbert Hoover, who campaigned defensively on his record, while the Democrats selected New York Governor Franklin Delano Roosevelt, who offered few specific proposals to end the Depression but radiated confidence as he pledged a New Deal for the American people. Roosevelt won the presidency in a landslide (472 electoral votes to 59) and the Democrats gained control of both houses of Congress. But in the four long months between the election and inauguration—later remedied when the Twentieth Amendment moved the inauguration from 4 March to 20 January—the Great Depression worsened: unemployment increased, more businesses failed, and there were numerous "runs" on banks, as panicked depositors withdrew life savings, an act that forced some banks to close their doors. On inauguration day 80 percent of America's banks were closed (either by declared state holiday or by failure), and the country was near economic ruin. Roosevelt's inaugural address, excerpted here, exuded a sense of vigor and action at a time when Americans suffered a crisis of confidence.

Questions to Consider

1. In what ways does Franklin Roosevelt seek to build the American people's confidence?

2. What does Roosevelt believe are the significant problems facing the nation? How does he propose to solve them?

3. For what purposes does Roosevelt refer to the crisis as similar to war?

4. In what ways does Roosevelt differ from William Lloyd Garrison Jr. ("A Businessman's View of the New Deal," Document 183) in his approach to America's economic problems?

I am certain that my fellow Americans expect that on my induction into the Presidency I will address them with a candor and a decision which the present situation of our Nation impels. This is preeminently the time to speak the truth, the whole truth, frankly and boldly. Nor need we shrink from honestly facing conditions in our country today. This great Nation will endure as it has endured, will revive and will prosper. So, first of all, let me assert my firm belief that the only thing we have to fear is fear itself—nameless, unreasoning, unjustified terror which paralyzes needed efforts to convert retreat into advance. In every dark hour of our national life a leadership of frankness and vigor has met with that understanding and support of the people themselves which is essential to victory. I am convinced that you will again give that support to leadership in these critical days.

In such a spirit on my part and on yours we face our common difficulties. They concern, thank God, only material things. Values have shrunken to fantastic levels; taxes have risen; our ability to pay has fallen; government of all kinds is faced by serious curtailment of income; the means of exchange are frozen in the currents of trade; the withered leaves of industrial enterprise lie on every side; farmers find no markets for their produce; the savings of many years in thousands of families are gone.

More important, a host of unemployed citizens face the grim problem of existence, and an equally great number toil with little return. Only a foolish optimist can deny the dark realities of the moment.

Yet our distress comes from no failure of substance. We are stricken by no plague of locusts. Compared with the perils which our forefathers conquered because they believed and were not afraid, we have still much to be thankful for. Nature still offers her bounty and human efforts have multiplied it. Plenty is at our doorstep, but a generous use of it languishes in the very sight of the supply....

Our greatest primary task is to put people to work. This is no unsolvable problem if we face it wisely and courageously. It can be accomplished in part by direct recruiting by the Government itself, treating the task as we would treat the emergency of a war, but at the same time, through this employment,

SOURCE: "Inaugural Address, March 4, 1933," *The Public Papers and Addresses of Franklin D. Roosevelt*, Vol. 2: *The Year of Crisis, 1933*, comp. Samuel I. Rosenman (New York, 1938), 11–16.

accomplishing greatly needed projects to stimulate and reorganize the use of our natural resources.

Hand in hand with this we must frankly recognize the overbalance of population in our industrial centers and, by engaging on a national scale in a redistribution, endeavor to provide a better use of the land for those best fitted for the land. The task can be helped by definite efforts to raise the values of agricultural products and with this the power to purchase the output of our cities. It can be helped by preventing realistically the tragedy of the growing loss through foreclosure of our small homes and our farms. It can be helped by insistence that the Federal, State, and local governments act forthwith on the demand that their cost be drastically reduced. It can be helped by the unifying of relief activities which today are often scattered, uneconomical, and unequal. It can be helped by national planning for and supervision of all forms of transportation and of communications and other utilities which have a definitely public character. There are many ways in which it can be helped, but it can never be helped by merely talking about it. We must act and act quickly.

Finally, in our progress toward a resumption of work we require two safeguards against a return of the evils of the old order; there must be a strict supervision of all banking and credits and investments, so that there will be an end to speculation with other people's money; and there must be provision for an adequate but sound currency.

These are the lines of attack. I shall presently urge upon a new Congress, in special session, detailed measures for their fulfillment, and I shall seek the immediate assistance of the several States....

I am prepared under my constitutional duty to recommend the measures that a stricken Nation in the midst of a stricken world may require. These measures, or such other measures as the Congress may build out of its experience and wisdom, I shall seek, within my constitutional authority, to bring to speedy adoption.

But in the event that the Congress shall fail to take one of these two courses, and in the event that the national emergency is still critical, I shall not evade the clear course of duty that will then confront me. I shall ask the Congress for the one remaining instrument to meet the crises—broad Executive power to wage a war against the emergency, as great as the power that would be given to me if we were in fact invaded by a foreign foe.

For the trust reposed in me I will return the courage and the devotion that befit the time. I can do no less.

We face the arduous days that lie before us in the warm courage of national unity; with the clear consciousness of seeking old and precious moral values; with the clean satisfaction that comes from the stern performance of duty by old and young alike. We aim at the assurance of a rounded and permanent national life.

We do not distrust the future of essential democracy. The people of the United States have not failed. In their need they have registered a mandate that they want direct, vigorous action. They have asked for discipline and direction under leadership.

They have made me the present instrument of their wishes. In the spirit of the gift I take it.

In this dedication of a Nation we humbly ask the blessing of God. May He protect each and every one of us. May He guide me in the days to come.

183

A Businessman's View of the New Deal (1934)

The flood of legislation that produced the first New Deal sought to solve the economic problems created by the Great Depression. Although it enjoyed widespread public support, the program brought only modest economic recovery. The New Deal program, however, did change the role of government, especially the federal government. The National Recovery Administration, for example, had labor, business, and government officials draw up "codes of fair practices" to establish prices, wages, and hours in the workday. Participating businesses displayed the Blue Eagle crest to show "We Do Our Part." Congress also passed legislation and created bureaucracies to regulate the activities of banks and the stock exchange to prevent another economic collapse and to restore confidence in financial activities. In addition, Roosevelt dropped the gold standard and experimented with the value of the dollar to boost prices. Such activities enlarged the size of the federal government, broadened its scope, and greatly increased the debt. In 1934, The Nation *magazine published a series of articles by businessmen discussing various issues of the New Deal. Recently retired Boston investment banker William Lloyd Garrison, Jr., grandson of the famed abolitionist, offered the following commentary on the New Deal.*

Questions to Consider

1. What are Garrison's views on the New Deal?
2. According to Garrison, what New Deal programs seem to be working?
3. What does he believe are the problems of the New Deal?
4. What does Garrison hope to accomplish with this article?

... What he [Roosevelt] chose to call the New Deal was, in part, his concept for coping with an acute and threatening emergency. Without delay he displayed his courage and vigor of action by his affirmative handling of the demoralized

SOURCE: William Lloyd Garrison, Jr., "The Hand of Improvidence: What Businessmen Think," The Nation 139 (14 November 1934): 562–563. Reprinted with permission from the November 14, 1934, issue of The Nation. For subscription information, call 1-800-333-8536. Portions of each week's nation magazine can be accessed at http://www.thenation.com.

banking situation, then on the verge of collapse. His steady and confident temper generated a new hope which was immediately reflected in national sentiment and duly recorded in the quotations of the market-place. But that episode was merely a beginning. The New Deal, being both a philosophy and a mode of action, began to find expression in diverse forms which were often contradictory. Some assisted and some retarded the recovery of industrial activity. Bold and novel experiments on the part of the New Dealers soon began to startle the conservative element. An enormous outpouring of federal money for human relief and immense sums for public-works projects started to flow to all points of the compass. The nation began to think in terms of nine ciphers. Six billion dollars was added to the national debt, thereby offsetting in an incredibly short time the farsighted post-war reduction of that debt by the Coolidge Administration in the years of plenty. A bureaucracy in Washington grew by leaps and bounds, led and manned by the faithful, eager to make history. And finally, to lend the picture the heightened academic touch, John Maynard Keynes, of Cambridge, England, appeared in Washington and again commended the plan of buying Utopia for cash.

Meanwhile the old freedoms, or, if you prefer, the old anarchies, of the business world are in process of restraint. New statutes hedge about the activities of bankers, brokers, industrialists, and all those who direct the use of capital. Even the rights of sovereign States and their individual citizens seem to be somewhat dimmed. The lines of separation of governmental functions have become decidedly hazy. The President is almost a legislator. A bureau chief becomes the judicial interpreter of administrative law. A Supreme Court justice lends his wisdom to the administrative arm. Controls, restrictions, prohibitions, and warning become the order of the day. The American business man, once the symbol of free initiative, awakens to find himself "cribbed, cabined, and confined," shorn of much of his former prestige. If he possesses a sense of humor he must recognize, of course, that the old hand of the old dealers was obviously overplayed. The aberrations of the war markets, the dizzy height of commodity prices just prior to Armistice Day, the fantastic and frantic happenings from 1922 to 1929 explain for him the political earthquake of 1932. He is busy adjusting himself to the new circumstances as he gazed upon a situation where a huge unemployment dominates the necessities of political action, as poverty and distress on the grand scale have to be dealt with daily by the masters of the state.

Yet he finds the practical problem of producing profits at this juncture to be extremely difficult, save where government spending has happily flowed out in his direction. As matters stand today, an industrial or mercantile concern can only find its foreign markets sharply restricted but sees its home market adversely affected by serious drought and by widespread and militant strikes. It must reckon with higher taxes, higher material costs, and higher wages. It must carry on its business in terms of a dollar that is subject to further possible devaluation. It finds the government establishing or fostering competing agencies of business, and it fears further legislation hostile to its interests. On the other hand, the talons of the Blue Eagle look less terrifying since the bluff General Johnson relinquished his efforts to do the impossible. The voluntary cooperation of business developed under the NRA should stand as a permanent national benefit. The attempt at price-fixing will presumably go to the error side of the trial-and-error column. Likewise the attempt to advance wages ahead of the effective demand for goods has revealed its futility, to say nothing of its economic unorthodoxy.

The morale of the business man is, however, shaken as he observes increasingly in the government service, and in command of vastly powerful bureaus, men who are frankly Socialists in their economic faith. For the New Deal turned out to be a tripartite adventure which looked to results far beyond national recovery. It sought a recasting of our social scheme and embodied what is termed a "planned economy."…

What could be done to save us from such a calamity? The President alone has the power to give effective encouragement to business at this time. The business and banking community awaits some sincere assurance that there will be less interference by government agencies with the law of supply and demand. It wants to hear that an immediate effort will be made to check the flood of expenditures, thereby insuring an honest purpose to balance the budget.

A more hopeful and even more significant move would be the early inclusion among the President's advisers of more men of high reputation and long experience in the realm of practical affairs. The responsible man of affairs, with capital at risk in enterprise, who has known the alternations of hope and fear and has come to comprehend the significance of those consequences which tie together the periods of peak prosperity and panic decline, has procured an education through experience that has in it the beginnings of wisdom. To a man of such training, much of the hasty and emotional legislation of the New Deal is not only absurd but hopelessly obstructive to the government's own program of recovery.…

The democratic plan of government is not fool proof. It works very badly—panic succeeding prosperity.… But a mere transfer from individual monopoly to state monopoly, with its consequent regimentation and fettering of essential freedoms, can effect no cure of the malady. A democracy can be wrecked by bureaucrats, however high-sounding their ideals, who fail to conserve the nation's credit and thereby open wide the door, even if unintentionally, to the destructive forces of anarchy. When the history of our times is written, it is probable that the demoralization of the voters of the country by the distribution of floods of money from the public treasury, coupled with a false philosophy which declares that every man is entitled to be maintained out of the public funds, will be regarded as the most glaring of the political errors of our generation.

Even so, is there not some effective and hopeful means for dealing with our immediate national problems? As affairs now stand, specific recommendations seem well-nigh futile. So general has been the flouting of economic law that "confusion now hath made its masterpiece." The false price and wages levels decreed by the NRA; the disruptive and punitive character of the Securities Act and the Stock Exchange Act, with the consequent starving of the heavy industries; the prentice work of the New Deal surgeons upon the corpus of the public utilities—all suggest that time and reflection must first be permitted to color the thought and action of the Congress, the Cabinet and the Chief Executive.

We may be grateful, however, that some measure of recovery from the depths of depression is evident throughout the world. This tendency should help to carry us gradually, if haltingly, forward.

184

Editorial Cartoons On the New Deal (1934, 1935)

The New Deal sought to end the Great Depression and reform the American economy through a variety of means. The first few years of the Franklin Roosevelt administration saw the creation of numerous government agencies designed to support the banking system, regulate stock market activities, extend aid to the unemployed, and promote economic recovery—the so-called "alphabet agencies." Such actions were a significant departure from traditional laissez-faire policies as they expanded the size and role of the federal government in American life. Some believed these actions were unconstitutional. Furthermore, some new government agencies, most notably the Works Progress Administration (WPA), poured millions of dollars into public works programs hoping to stimulate the economy. Playing a key role in advising Roosevelt on New Deal policies were a diverse group of academics nicknamed the "brains trust" who were often depicted in cartoons as individuals wearing academic robes and mortar boards. Below are two Clifford Berryman cartoons published in a Washington DC newspaper that criticized New Deal policies.

Questions to Consider

1. What themes does Berryman address in these cartoons?
2. In what ways was Berryman critical of the New Deal?
3. What does Berryman want viewers to consider in the second cartoon, with FDR as the physician and Congress as the nurse?
4. How might the following react to these cartoons: William Lloyd Garrison, Jr. ("A Businessman's View of the New Deal," Document 183), Meridel Le Sueur ("Women on the Breadlines," Document 181), and Eleanor Roosevelt ("Eleanor Roosevelt on Social Welfare," Document 186)?

Clifford Berryman, "It is evolution, not revolution, gentlemen!," *Washington Evening Star*
(Washington, DC), April 26, 1934.

SOURCE: http://www.loc.gov/pictures/item/acd1996001037/PP/

Clifford Berryman, "Of course we may have to change remedies if we don't get results,"
Washington Evening Star (Washington, DC), January 5, 1934.

SOURCE: http://www.loc.gov/pictures/item/acd1996000384/PP/

185

The "Dust Bowl" (1935)

The Great Plains region including Oklahoma, the Texas panhandle, Kansas, Colorado, and New Mexico is known for its sparse rainfall, thin soil, high winds, and expanse of natural prairie grasses. During the late nineteenth and early twentieth century, the prairie grasses adequately supported the ranching industry; but during the First World War, farmers, enticed by high grain prices and using tractors, plowed up millions of acres of the grass cover to plant wheat. They helped create an environmental tragedy. In the mid-1930s a drought struck the region, and without the natural root system to keep the soil in place, high winds loosened the topsoil and swirled it into great dust clouds that people called black blizzards. As the article in Literary Digest *made clear to its readers, the continued winds wreaked havoc in what became known as the Dust Bowl. Nearly 60 percent of the area's population was driven out; many, called Okies, moved to cities on the West Coast.*

Questions to Consider

1. What are the short-term effects of the Dust Bowl? The long-term effects?
2. What helped create this environmental tragedy? What would drought relief programs do?
3. What does this document reveal about agriculture in the Great Plains in the 1930s?
4. Compare and contrast the description of the Great Plains found here and in "A Native American Remembers Life on the Great Plains" (Document 132). Which approach to land use seems more ecologically sound?

Recurrent dry winds continued last week to spread a suffocating pall over more than a dozen States. AAA [Agricultural Adjustment Administration] officials said continuation of the great siege from the air would mean a new drought-relief grant. The Independent Kansas City *Star,* however, minimized the extent of the dust storms and their effect. Kansas City, it said, "sits in a vast empire of green, extending in every direction."

Others reported the sun hidden in several localities. Lands laid bare by the plow in the old cow-country to grow wheat during the War were surrendering top-soil to every breeze. People and animals were finding it difficult to breathe. Housewives were taping their windows to keep out the wind-blown soil, made so fine that it could sift in. Cow-country families were reported fighting their

SOURCE: "Dust and the Nation's 'Bread-Basket,'" *Literary Digest* 119 (20 April 1935): 10.

way eastward through the choking pall. Trains, struggling through, were several hours late.

"Noon was like night," said Walter Knudsen, Conductor of the Santa Fe Navajo, when the train reached Chicago six hours behind time. "There was no sun, and, at times, it was impossible to see a yard. The engineer could not see the signal-lights."

R. G. Goetze, Conductor of the Rock Island Colorado Express, which arrived in Chicago two and a half hours late, said, according to the Associated Press, which also had quoted Conductor Knudsen: "There was a heavy coating of dust on the streets when we left Denver. Then it snowed. The mixture put a plaster on the sides of the train."

In several places schools closed, and business was at a standstill. In Memphis, people covered their faces with handkerchiefs. Arkansas was covered by haze of dust. In Texas, birds feared to take wing. Texas State Senators put on surgical-masks. "Point of order," shouted Senator Ben G. Oneal of Wichita Falls, "the Governor is trying to gag the Senate."

The brunt of the storm, reports indicate, fell on Western Kansas, East Colorado and Wyoming, Western Oklahoma, virtually all of Texas, and parts of New Mexico. Dust swirled over Missouri, Iowa, and Arkansas, crossed the Mississippi, and sifted down on Illinois, Indiana, Kentucky, Tennessee, and Louisiana.

Kenneth Welch, relief-administrator in Baca County, Colorado, reported that "dust-pneumonia is rapidly increasing among children." Scores of women and children had been sent out of the country.

Report had it, too, that some live stock had suffocated in Kansas. There was said to be a staggering crop-damage.

Walter Barlow of Amarillo, Texas, a grain-elevator operator, estimated that the wheat-crop damage in the Texas Panhandle was between $18,000,000 and $20,000,000. Harry B. Cordell, President of the Oklahoma State Board of Agriculture, said the last of that State's wheat-planting had virtually been destroyed by dust-storms of the last forty-eight hours. Government reports showed that much land in the nation's "bread-basket" was being abandoned.

Meanwhile, the Government was moving to expand its drought-relief program. Officials were planning to use $150,000,000 of work-relief money. Ten years, said Secretary of Agriculture Henry A. Wallace, would be required to make the program effective. Grass and other cover-crops, and tree-belts, will have to be planted; dams and terraces be constructed.

186

Eleanor Roosevelt on Social Welfare (1936)

Eleanor Roosevelt revolutionized the role of First Lady. She transformed a position that had no duties or responsibilities into a platform to advocate New Deal policies and other reforms. Roosevelt became the eyes and ears of her husband, as she traveled throughout the country on behalf of President Franklin Roosevelt giving speeches and meeting people in the midst of the Great Depression. She also wrote numerous newspaper and magazine articles that advanced particular causes. She supported civil rights for African Americans, the youth, equality for women, and was a steadfast believer that the federal government was a positive force in improving people's lives. Roosevelt's actions were controversial, but she earned the respect of many because of her willingness to voice her convictions. Below is an excerpted article published in Parent's Magazine *that represents Roosevelt's support of children, the family, and the role of the federal government.*

Questions to Consider

1.   What are Roosevelt's concerns for the family, especially the youth?
2.   What areas of expanded federal government powers does Roosevelt advocate?
3.   According to Roosevelt, in what ways would the Social Security Act benefit families?
4.   What does Roosevelt want the arts and education to provide Americans?
5.   Can government programs assist in the pursuit of happiness?
6.   How might Eleanor Roosevelt have responded to the *Chicago Tribune* cartoons ("Editorial Cartoons on the New Deal," Document 184)?

With a committee actually appointed in Congress to consider the efficiency and reorganization of the government's business in Washington, I suppose we may expect a careful survey of all the functions of the federal government departments, and a reclassification to bring into a better grouping such things as are related to each other.

With this in mind, it has long seemed to me that fathers and mothers in this country would be deeply interested in the creation of a department in the

SOURCE: Eleanor Roosevelt, "Are We Overlooking the Pursuit of Happiness?" *Parent's Magazine* 11 (September 1936): 21, 67.

Federal Government which dealt directly with the problems touching most closely the homes and the children of the nation.

All government departments touch our homes and our general welfare in one way or another, but certain things very obviously touch more closely than others the daily life of the home. Health, for instance. The Public Health Service does much to cooperate with the various state departments of health and now through the new Social Security Act, we shall be able to do much more than ever before for our handicapped and crippled children, our blind children and for dependent children either living at home with a widowed or deserted mother, or orphaned and living in foster homes or in institutions.

All social welfare measures touch the home very closely. Take the question of old age pensions. This has direct bearing on the employment of youth, for if we take out of the labor market the older people there naturally will be more opportunity for the young. Added to that, many and many a home where young people love their parents has become embittered by the fact that so much had to be given up in order to take care of the old people. I remember a story my mother-in-law used to tell me of an old Scotch farmer who remarked to her that one father and mother could take care of any number of children but any number of children never could take care of one old father and mother!

It is all very well to think that young people are selfish. I have seen them struggle many a time to do what they felt was right for parents, and as their children grew up they wanted to give them opportunities for education or recreation or even provide them with proper food for building healthy bodies for the future, and the drag of the responsibility for the older people became almost more than human nature could stand.

For the old people who have lived so long a life of independence, how bitter it must be to come for everything they need to the youngsters who once turned to them!

From every point of view, it seems to me that the old age pension for people who so obviously could not lay aside enough during their working years to live on adequately through their old age is a national responsibility and one that must be faced when we are planning for a better future.

Unemployment insurance in many homes is all that stands between many a family and starvation. Given a breathing spell, a man or woman may be able to get another job or to re-educate himself in some new line of work, but few people live with such a wide margin that they have enough laid aside to face several months of idleness.

Next comes education and we are certainly coming to realize that education is of vital importance. Many of us who have completely accepted the idea that our system of education is perfect in this country have made a mistake in not realizing that nothing in the world is ever perfect and that we should watch and constantly study public education to make it more responsive to the needs of our day.

We must equalize educational opportunities throughout the country. We must see that rural children have as good a general education as city children can acquire, and the advantages of both groups must if possible be made interchangeable. No city child should grow up without knowing the beauty of spring in the country or where milk comes from, how vegetables grow and what it is like to play in a field instead of on a city street. No country child who knows these things should be deprived, however, of museums, books, music and better teachers because it is easier to find them and to pay for them in big cities than it is in rural districts.

With more leisure time, we are discovering that the arts are a necessity in our lives, not only as a method of self-expression, but because of the need for enjoyment and occupation which requires appreciation of many things which we could never hope to understand when we toiled from dawn till dark and had no time for any aspirations.

The arts are no longer a luxury but a necessity to the average human being and they should be included in any department which includes health, social security and education. It seems to me also that crafts and recreation should come under this department.

All these things belong together, they deal with the daily lives of the people.

We are entering a period when there are vast possibilities for the creation of a new way of living. It only requires sufficient imagination and sufficient actual knowledge on the part of all those who are considering this reorganization of government to bring into the government picture today one of the objectives laid down by our forefathers for government, but which seemed in the past too impossible of achievement to receive consideration.

The attainment of life and liberty required most of our energy in the past, so the pursuit of happiness and the consideration of the lives of human beings remained in the background. Now is the time to recognize the possibilities which lie before us in the taking up and developing of this part of our forefathers' vision. Therefore, I hope that the parents in this country will take enough interest in the new reorganization plans to realize that the interests of youth which lie close to their hearts can best be served by a federal department which will include such things as I have suggested and which touch primarily the homes and the youth of America.

187

The Tennessee Valley Authority (1937)

Since the mid-1920s regional planners had advocated a series of dams along the Tennessee River Valley to prevent flooding, enhance river navigation, and generate electrical power in the seven-state region. It was also hoped that the valley's economy, one of the poorest in the country, would improve. Progress on this regional plan was slow until Franklin Roosevelt took office. The Tennessee Valley Authority (TVA) was part of the first New Deal, and it was intended as a massive public works project and experiment in regional planning. Perhaps the TVA's most controversial aspect was this government agency's production and sale of electrical power to customers in the region. Dutch novelist and travel account author Odette Keun visited the Tennessee Valley in 1935 to observe the work of the TVA first-hand. Excerpted here are comments from her book, A Foreigner Looks at the TVA.

Questions to Consider

1. According to Odette Keun, what did the TVA hope to accomplish?
2. Why did she support the generation and sale of electrical power?
3. Why was she so enthusiastic about the TVA? Was the TVA successful?
4. What do her observations reveal about tensions between government and private enterprise in the New Deal?
5. How might a Socialist ("The Socialist Alternative," Document 157) or Theodore Roosevelt in 1912 ("The New Nationalism of Theodore Roosevelt," Document 159) react to Odette Keun's evaluation of the TVA?

Since, according to its constitutional functions with respect to navigation and flood control, the TVA has constructed dams, it has almost limitless falling water at its disposal. Where there is falling water, there is power. Two things can be done with power: let it go to waste, or harness it and utilize it in the form of electricity by putting the water through turbines and generators. It is stupid to the point of being unthinkable that power should be allowed to go to waste when with an often relatively small additional equipment it can be harnessed and put into work in the form of electricity. Besides, it was imperative that the TVA should have some source of revenue. It has received, up to date, about 140 million dollars from the Federal government. But it must become more or less self-supporting, and to a large extent meet the expenses incurred by its activities. Neither its dams, nor its navigation scheme, nor its agricultural program, nor anything else, will bring in money. Quite the opposite: they all represent money that flows out. Only the sale of power is a financial asset. So, spurred on by common sense, economy and the spirit of the times, one of the aspects of which is electrification, Congress, by the Act of 1933 and successive amendments, gave the TVA the following powers:

Authority to dispose of all surplus electricity.

Authority directly to give preference to States, counties, municipalities, co-operative nonprofit organizations of citizens or farmers, and to domestic and rural customers rather than to commercial and industrial consumers.

Authority to construct transmission lines.

Authority to construct and operate rural distribution where farms and small villages are not already served at reasonable rates.

SOURCE: Odette Keun, *A Foreigner Looks at the TVA* (New York, 1937), 25–30, 44–45, 88–89.

Authority to prescribe, in the power contracts, terms and conditions of resale including resale rates.

Authority to acquire existing electric facilities used in serving farms and small villages.

Authority to make loans to public agencies for the acquisition of existing distribution systems.

Authority to cancel the contracts made with public customers if these public customers practice discrimination against their own customers.

... The TVA stands upright for many noble and magnificent things, but for nothing more fervently than the abundant life and the happier social destiny which plentiful and cheap electricity can bring about. The fundamental mechanism for this electrical life is already here, in the dams, the turbines, the generators, the transmission lines, the motors. It is only partially utilized. The TVA holds that it must be fully utilized, and after it has been utilized to the full extent of its present capacity, it must be further developed. It must be perpetually developed. And as it develops it has to be introduced, on a national scale, by appropriate social and political techniques, into the system of democracy which America represents. This system does not correspond today to the basic American faith in equality and liberty, nor to the natural and technical sciences and the social necessities of our times. To satisfy these imperatives, existing institutions must be adapted to a socialized organization of production and distribution, capable of maintaining secure abundance and of raising the material and cultural welfare of the people. It is important to make this transition as quickly as possible....

As I see it, the main points of the TVA's power policy are five. To make America electricity-conscious. To stimulate the electrification of industry. To put electricity and electricity-using appliances in every available home and farm. To reduce the costs of operation and the rates applied to the consumer. To create a market for as wide and cheap a consumption of electricity as possible. These points lend themselves to a lot of considerations....

... Enough has been said already ... to prove that the TVA is a modern expression and practice of the *conservation movement*. The assumptions which form the basis of that movement are that the national resources of a country—minerals, soil, forests, waters—are not the possession of one generation alone but the inheritance of all the future generations of the people to whom that country belongs. Such a conception has just begun to dawn upon Americans, fascinated too long by the epic of the settler, the pioneer and the frontiersman who bequeathed to their descendants, together with heroic qualities of courage and self-reliance, a great deal of the philosophy of the brigand. The body of this land has been racked and torn and plundered, and in parts murdered by its children as mercilessly as by any foreign invader. It is a matter of vital national importance to preserve what is left, to heal it if possible, and to develop it wisely: quite as vital as to defend America against any enemy from overseas. The freedom of a nation is founded just as much upon its economy, which includes natural resources, as upon its armies. The TVA is doing invaluable work for the United States in checking floods and soil-erosion, promoting irrigation, planning the systematic use of rivers, husbanding the water-table. I hope I've shown that. But there is still another aspect of its water program which I want to mention. America has been pillaged by a lot of brutal and rapacious Americans, certainly, but she is also being depleted of the natural resources which are the origin of energy, by time itself. The whole world is being depleted in this manner, and a running-down process is perceptible everywhere. Everywhere, the products of the earth which are the origin of energy, coal, wood, oil, minerals, phosphates, are being exhausted. These materials are either non-replenishable or replenishable only over a period of so many centuries that it is essential to employ them with great foresight, prudence, and care. Only one source of energy is very easily replenishable, and that is falling water, for water is being ceaselessly restored to the world by the hydrologic cycle—the action of the sun which draws it up from the surface and lets it fall abundantly again....

The Tennessee Valley Authority is laying it down. Handicapped and restricted though it is in all sorts of ways, it is the noblest, the most intelligent, and the best attempt made in this country or in any other democratic country, to economize, marshal and integrate the actual assets of a region, plan its development and future, ameliorate its standards of living, establish it in a more enduring security, and render available to the people the benefits of the wealth of their district, and the results of science, discovery, invention, and disinterested forethought. In its inspiration and its goal there is goodness, for goodness is that which makes for unity of purpose with love, compassion and respect for every life and every pattern of living. The economic machine, bad though it is, has not been smashed in the Tennessee Watershed; it is being very gradually, very carefully, very equitably reviewed and amended, and the citizens are being taught and directed, but not bullied, not coerced, not regimented, not frightened, within the constitutional frame the nation itself elected to build.

188

An African American Evaluation of the New Deal (1940)

African Americans and other minorities were particularly hard hit during the Great Depression. Franklin Roosevelt's New Deal programs often only partially included minorities, or in some cases discriminated against them. For example, the Federal Housing Administration (FHA) was to help families purchase houses, but it refused to guarantee mortgages of homes purchased by blacks in white neighborhoods. On the other hand, the Civilian

Conservation Corps (CCC), the Tennessee Valley Authority (TVA), and the National Youth Administration (NYA) included African Americans but placed them in segregated camps because the Roosevelt administration did not wish to antagonize powerful southern Democrats by challenging existing patterns of segregation. Despite modest gains from the New Deal, many African Americans left the Republican Party in the election of 1936 and voted for Democrats, hoping a new era in race relations was dawning. As the 1940 election approached, The Crisis, *the publication of the National Association for the Advancement of Colored People (NAACP), offered the following assessment of the Roosevelt administration and the New Deal.*

Questions to Consider

1. On what issues is *The Crisis* critical? On what issues is *The Crisis* supportive?
2. What is the overall assessment of the Roosevelt administration and New Deal for African Americans?
3. According to *The Crisis*, what is the function of government?
4. Based on this editorial, how should African Americans vote in the election of 1940?
5. How might Alain Locke ("The New Negro," Document 175) and Martin Luther King, Jr. ("Letter from Birmingham Jail," Document 210) respond to this editorial?

On the subject of the Negro, the Roosevelt record is spotty, as might be expected in an administration where so much power is in the hands of the southern wing of the Democratic party. And yet Mr. Roosevelt, hobbled as he has been by the Dixie die-hards, has managed to include Negro citizens in practically every phase of the administration program. In this respect, no matter how far behind the ideal he may be, he is far ahead of any other Democratic president, and of recent Republican ones.

The best proof that Mr. Roosevelt has not catered always to the South and has insisted on carrying the Negro along with his program is to be found in the smearing, race-hating propaganda used against him in the 1936 campaign by southern white groups. Both he and Mrs. Roosevelt were targets of filthy mud-slinging simply because they did not see eye to eye with the South on the Negro.

This does not mean that the Roosevelt administration has done all that it could have done for the race. Its policies in many instances have done Negroes great injustice, and have helped to build more secure walls of segregation.

On the anti-lynching bill Mr. Roosevelt has said not a mumbling word. His failure to endorse this legislation, to bring pressure to break the filibuster, is a black mark against him. It does no good to say that the White House could

SOURCE: "The Roosevelt Record," *The Crisis* 47 (November 1940): 343. The publisher wishes to thank the Crisis Publishing Co., Inc., the publisher of the magazine of the National Association for the Advancement of Colored People, for the use of this material first contained in the November, 1940 issue of *The Crisis*.

not pass down some word on this bill. The White House spoke on many bills. Mr. Roosevelt might have pressed the anti-lynching bill to a vote, especially during January and February, 1938, when there was tremendous public opinion supporting the bill. His failure to act, or even speak, on the anti-lynching bill was the more glaring because, while mobs in America were visiting inhumanities upon Negroes, Mr. Roosevelt periodically was rebuking some foreign government for inhumanity, and enunciating high sentiments of liberty, tolerance, justice, etc.

To declare that the Roosevelt administration has tried to include the Negro in nearly every phase of its program for the people of the nation is not to ignore the instances where government policies have harmed the race.

At Boulder dam, for example, the administration continued the shameful policy begun by Hoover of forbidding Negroes to live in Boulder City, the government-built town. And in its own pet project, the TVA, the administration forbid Negroes to live in Norris, another government-built town at Norris dam.

Full credit must go to the administration for its program of low-cost housing, so sorely needed by low-income families. No one pretends that the American housing program is more than a beginning, but Negroes have shared in it in the most equitable manner. However, there were, outside the slum-clearance program, some damaging practices. The FHA, which insures mortgages for home buyers, has enforced a regulation which puts the power and approval of the government on ghetto life. No Negro family which sought a home outside the so-called "Negro" neighborhood could get a FHA-insured loan.

The vast program for youth, the CCC and the NYA, has included our young people, but in the CCC, a justifiable complaint has been that Negro instructors, advisers, and reserve army officers were not appointed in any but the tiniest proportion.

There is little need to mention relief and the WPA. Mr. Roosevelt's critics concede what his administration has done in these two branches of his program by concentrating their attack upon the relief that the New Deal has given Negroes. In relief the government set the tone. That tone was so much higher than the city, county and state standards for Negroes in certain areas that, even though differentials existed, the net result was more than it would have been without government supervision. Collective bargaining and the Wages and Hours act have aided Negro workers in private industry.

The farm program has not been ideally administered, but colored people have shared in the benefits. More than 50,000 families have been assisted by the Farm Security administration.

Mr. Roosevelt had the courage to appoint a Negro to a federal judgeship, the first in the history of the country. His nominee was confirmed by a Democratic senate without a murmur. Complaint has been made that in naming about a score of colored administrative assistants and advisers, Mr. Roosevelt has kept Negroes out of any real posts in the government. If it be true that Mr. Roosevelt has created Negro appendages to various bureaus, it cannot be denied that colored people know more about their government and have penetrated nearer to policy-making desks than ever before.

Heavily on the debit side is Mr. Roosevelt's approval of the War department's notorious jim crow in the armed services. Most important contribution of the Roosevelt administration to the age-old color line problem in America has been its doctrine that Negroes are a part of the country and must be considered in any program for the country as a whole. The inevitable discrimination not-withstanding, this thought has been driven home in thousands of communities by a thousand specific acts. For the first time in their lives, government has taken on meaning and substance for the Negro masses.

It is foolish to deny the imperfections and shortcomings of the New Deal. But the trend always has been toward a kind of government which has meaning for the people. The New Deal could not perform miracles. It could not overrun intrenched prejudices. The poor and the underprivileged, among whom are to be found most Negroes, need not look for comparison to the days of Herbert Hoover. They need only glance about them to see who is against the present administration. We are all Americans. We all seek security, justice, liberty, peace. But by what methods? And for whom? For *all*, or for certain groups?

Negro voters are posed a question on November 5. Do they believe that in spite of admitted mistakes and failures (both as to them and to government generally) the Roosevelt administration is tending toward the kind of government that is best for the majority of the people; or has the Roosevelt record on the Negro specifically and on the government generally been such that a new administration should be voted into power?

189

"The New Deal in Review" (1940)

Franklin D. Roosevelt's administration developed the New Deal to address the many problems caused by the Great Depression. Some New Deal programs were innovative and to an extent revolutionary, while other efforts revitalized Progressive era proposals or expanded existing programs. Roosevelt experimented with a variety of New Deal programs, advancing some initiatives while abandoning those that did not stimulate the economy. The New Deal changed the role of the federal government, as new legislation and agencies enlarged the size and regulatory scope of the government. In 1940, as the New Deal initiative seemed to have stalled, The New Republic, *a journal that examined current issues, offered the following commentary on the economic and social conditions of the country in the depths of the Great Depression in 1932 and what the New Deal had done in eight years.*

Questions to Consider

1. According to *The New Republic*, what were some of the problems facing the nation in 1932?

2. What were some of the accomplishments of the New Deal?

3. What "permanent" changes, benefits, or improvements were made by the New Deal? Why would it be "improbable" that these will not be removed or destroyed by future administrations?

4. What problems has the New Deal not solved?

5. How might William Lloyd Garrison, Jr. ("A Businessman's View of the New Deal," Document 183) and Herbert Hoover ("American Individualism," Document 179) react to this commentary?

Collectively we have a short memory. The American people face the present, with a slight glance ahead; they are little interested in history, even that of their own yesterday. Only eight years later it is hard for us to recall what life was like in the last year under Hoover.

Banks were closing in 1932—not a dozen a day, as they were a little later, but one every dozen days. People nervously broke up their accounts and divided their money among three banks, or four or five. Without government guarantee of any sort, no institution was wholly safe from the fetid breath of rumor.

As the business index kept going down, the number of the unemployed steadily mounted. Nobody knew how many there were; government statistics on this point were even more inadequate than they are today. People knew, however, that on every street corner there were beggars who showed by face and manner that they were not the glib professionals of happier days. Poor people knew, because families had to double up until tenements were unendurably overcrowded and the money for food got more and more scanty. Charitable organizations, swamped with new needs, appealed desperately for donations but met a steadily dwindling response; before long they were meeting only 10 percent of the burden. On hundreds of city streets appeared apple-sellers who managed to take away a few cents' worth of business from the grocery stores and just barely keep soul and body contiguous. In every city there sprang up those ironically named Hoovervilles, settlements made of old packing boxes where homeless men lived by thousands, doing odd jobs when they could, or if not, begging at back doors, or rummaging through garbage pails and trash boxes. In New York, the lucky ones with a nickel rode the subway all night in cold weather, or put down newspapers over a grating where exhaust heat came from a building. In Chicago, they slept on the ground under double-decked Wacker Drive. Thousands and thousands of people took to the road including large numbers of young men and boys and some young women.

In the farm regions, misery was universal. Thousands of farmers who had worked hard and lived frugally all their lives but had made the mistake of buying

SOURCE: "The New Deal in Review," *The New Republic* 102 (20 May 1940): 687–708.

land on mortgage, lost their property. When they could, they went to work as hired hands or sought odd jobs from door to door in nearby small towns. In more than one area, spontaneous action of neighborhood men prevented auctioning off property; a menacing crowd would surround the sheriff and his few deputies, bid $1 for the property and give it back to the owner.

The depression was cruelly hard on boys and girls of high-school and college age who were met by blank refusals whenever they sought employment. If there was money enough for decent clothing and books and supplies, some of them went on in school because there was nothing else to do; but in thousands of cases their families could not afford these slight expenses and the young people stayed home in complete idleness. Family morale deteriorated when the unemployed father, sitting around the house all day, could no longer maintain any authority.

In the White House in Washington a grim-lipped President paced his study in desperation. When he appeared in public or spoke over the radio, his panic and despair were so evident that they invariably sent the stock market down.... He did, however, yield on one point confronted by the indisputable evidence that people were starving throughout the country in communities that had spent their last dollar, he began making limited, inadequate loans through the Reconstruction Finance Corporation to eke out curtailed local resources....

One need only recall what conditions were in 1932 to realize the amazing change in our national thinking that has taken place in the last eight years. While there is still complaint about paternalism and centralized government (from Republicans who were the great exponents of these ideas, applied under special circumstances, for the first seventy-five years of their party's life) it is obvious that even the critics are only half hearted in what they say.

As a nation we have agreed, once and forever, that the individual must not bear the sole responsibility for his failure to cope with economic problems of unemployment or old age which are, quite obviously, beyond his powers, and that society as a whole must take over a substantial part of the burden.

We have at last learned that laissez-faire has been dead for years; that the unguided lust of the businessman for profit does not infallibly produce Utopia.

And finally, we have reaffirmed in these past eight years an early American doctrine that had been all but forgotten in preceding decades: that the country exists for the welfare and happiness of its inhabitants; and that when this condition is not met, reformation is in order no matter how drastic it may be or how much it may be disliked by existing privileged minorities.

The New Deal, even in its second term, has clearly done far more for the general welfare of the country and its citizens than any administration in the previous history of the nation. Its relief for the underprivileged producers in city and country, though inadequate to the need, has been indispensable. Without this relief an appalling amount of misery would have resulted, and a dangerous political upheaval might have occurred. Since the expenditure of money for relief—even the insufficient amounts recently appropriated—has been the principal target of the administration's conservative enemies, this accomplishment alone would be sufficient reason for support of the New Deal. The assertion of the reactionaries that if the federal budget balanced by cutting expenses, business would revive sharply enough to absorb the unemployed and make relief expenditures unnecessary, is incapable of proof and seems highly improbable.

In addition, the New Deal in this second period has accomplished much of permanent benefit to the nation. Perhaps its most important achievement was the National Labor Relations Act, the result of which was to inhibit employers' opposition to union organizations and true collective bargaining, so that trade union membership was more than doubled.... Second only to the strengthening of unions is the establishment of minimum labor standards. The fury with which reactionaries have attacked these two labor measures is an index of their importance.

Other permanent improvements are the impetus given to conservation of soil and forests, the many-sided TVA, a great road building program, flood control, a good beginning at slum clearance and adequate housing for those not provided for by private construction, great hydro-electric projects, extension of electricity at reasonable rates through the Rural Electricity Administration, and the inauguration of insurance against unemployment and the other forms of social security....

It is improbable that these more permanent changes will be or even can be destroyed by any new administration.

All these extraordinary accomplishments must be remembered when we speak of the points at which the New Deal has been disappointing in its second phase. The most important of these is of course its failure to discover or apply a genuine remedy for the stagnation of our economy, and for unemployment....

The President's failure to make more progress in tackling the central problem of our economy is probably due mainly to two things—the strengthening of conservative opposition, especially since the 1938 election, and concentration on the European situation. The country is weaker, whether for war or for peace, because of this slackening of pace in the New Deal. If our foreign policy can avoid involvement in the war, we shall be fortunate. But in any case we should not rely on war, whether we are in it or not, to do for us the domestic job that remains. If the New Deal is to deserve our support in the future, it must not rest on what it has already done, great as that is, but tell how it is going to finish the task.

22

Isolationism and World War II

By the late 1930s, the attention of the United States increasingly turned overseas. In both Europe and Eastern Asia, states eager to seize territory and add
to national glory had threatened the peace. America remained divided over
whether it should become involved—until being pulled into both European
and Pacific theaters late in 1941 with the Japanese surprise attack at Pearl Harbor,
Hawaii. The war forever changed American society. On the home front,
women replaced men in many occupations; on the battlefront, the skills of modern science were applied to create tools of massive destruction. The overwhelming majority of Americans heartily supported the war effort, even though
thousands of their fellow citizens were deprived of their civil liberties. The following descriptions reveal some of the major issues and events of the war years.

190

The Four Freedoms (1941)

*When the Second World War began in Europe, most Americans believed that a German
victory would not threaten the United States; thus, many supported the continued practice
of diplomatic isolation. By mid-1940 German forces had swept across the continent,
quickly conquering most of Europe and leaving Great Britain as the only country fighting
the Nazis. It became evident that the United States was the only industrial power capable
of producing enough war matériel to stop the Nazi war machine. When British officials*

requested ships, munitions, and other assistance to fight the Germans, the Roosevelt administration provided some war matériel under the strict cash-and-carry terms of the Neutrality Acts. But it was not enough. Shortly after Franklin Roosevelt won an unprecedented third election in 1940, Great Britain informed the president they were nearly bankrupt and could not afford to purchase supplies to fight Germany. While some Americans opposed providing any direct assistance to Great Britain, public opinion was shifting away from strict isolation. Roosevelt used his State of the Union address in early January 1941 to suggest a new American policy. His speech is excerpted here.

Questions to Consider

1.   What does Roosevelt propose that America should do?
2.   Why does he suggest this commitment?
3.   What does Roosevelt hope to accomplish?
4.   What is threatened by American inaction? Why?

… The need of the moment is that our actions and our policy should be devoted primarily—almost exclusively—to meeting this foreign peril. For all our domestic problems are now a part of the great emergency.

Just as our national policy in internal affairs has been based upon a decent respect for the rights and the dignity of all our fellow men within our gates, so our national policy in foreign affairs has been based on a decent respect for the rights and dignity of all nations, large and small. And the justice of morality must and will win in the end….

I also ask this Congress for authority and for funds sufficient to manufacture additional munitions and war supplies of many kinds, to be turned over to those nations which are now in actual war with aggressor nations.

Our most useful and immediate role is to act as an arsenal for them as well as for ourselves. They do not need man power, but they do need billions of dollars worth of the weapons of defense….

Let us say to the democracies: "We Americans are vitally concerned in your defense of freedom. We are putting forth our energies, our resources and our organizing powers to give you the strength to regain and maintain a free world. We shall send you, in ever-increasing numbers, ships, planes, tanks, guns. This is our purpose and our pledge."…

The happiness of future generations of Americans may well depend upon how effective and how immediate we can make our aid felt. No one can tell the exact character of the emergency situations that we may be called upon to meet. The Nation's hands must not be tied when the Nation's life is in danger.

We must all prepare to make the sacrifices that the emergency—almost as serious as war itself—demands. Whatever stands in the way of speed and efficiency in defense preparations must give way to the national need….

SOURCE: Franklin D. Roosevelt, "State of the Union Address, January 1941," *Public Papers and Addresses of Franklin D. Roosevelt*, comp. Samuel I. Rosenman (London, 1941), 663–72.

For there is nothing mysterious about the foundations of a healthy and strong democracy. The basic things expected by our people of their political and economic systems are simple. They are:

Equality of opportunity for youth and for others.

Jobs for those who can work.

Security for those who need it.

The ending of special privilege for the few.

The preservation of civil liberties for all.

The enjoyment of the fruits of scientific progress in a wider and constantly rising standard of living.

These are the simple, basic things that must never be lost sight of in the turmoil and unbelievable complexity of our modern world. The inner and abiding strength of our economic and political systems is dependent upon the degree to which they fulfill these expectations.

Many subjects connected with our social economy call for immediate improvement.

As examples:

We should bring more citizens under the coverage of old-age pensions and unemployment insurance.

We should widen the opportunities for adequate medical care.

We should plan a better system by which persons deserving or needing gainful employment may obtain it.

I have called for personal sacrifice. I am assured of the willingness of almost all Americans to respond to that call....

In the future days, which we seek to make secure, we look forward to a world founded upon four essential human freedoms.

The first is freedom of speech and expression—everywhere in the world.

The second is freedom of every person to worship God in his own way—everywhere in the world.

The third is freedom from want—which, translated into world terms, means economic understandings which will secure to every nation a healthy peacetime life for its inhabitants—everywhere in the world.

The fourth is freedom from fear—which, translated into world terms, means a world-wide reduction of armaments to such a point and in such a thorough fashion that no nation will be in a position to commit an act of physical aggression against any neighbor—anywhere in the world.

That is no vision of a distant millennium. It is a definite basis for a kind of world attainable in our own time and generation. That kind of world is the very antithesis of the so-called new order of tyranny which the dictators seek to create with the crash of a bomb.

To that new order we oppose the greater conception—the moral order. A good society is able to face schemes of world domination and foreign revolutions alike without fear.

Since the beginning of our American history, we have been engaged in change—in a perpetual peaceful revolution—a revolution which goes on steadily, quietly adjusting itself to changing conditions—without the concentration camp or the quick-lime in the ditch. The world order which we seek is the cooperation of free countries, working together in a friendly, civilized society.

This nation has placed its destiny in the hands and heads and hearts of its millions of free men and women; and its faith in freedom under the guidance of God. Freedom means the supremacy of human rights everywhere. Our support goes to those who struggle to gain those rights or keep them. Our strength is our unity of purpose.

To that high concept there can be no end save victory.

191

Isolation from the European War (1941)

When Europe erupted in war with Germany's invasion of Poland in September 1939, America, fearfully isolationist since the previous war, proclaimed neutrality. Despite powerful isolationists sentiments, a growing number of Americans came to believe the United States should support Britain's battle, provided America did not wage war. Capitalizing on this shifting mood, President Franklin Roosevelt described the country as "the great arsenal of democracy" and proposed that Great Britain have unlimited access to American supplies. Congress complied with the Lend-Lease Act (1941), providing aid to Great Britain and drawing America closer to war. Opposed to the possible American intervention into the war, the America First Committee, comprising some prominent midwestern businessmen and politicians, was organized in July 1940. Within one year, the organization claimed 450 chapters nationwide and a membership of several hundred thousand. National hero and aviator Charles A. Lindbergh was America First's most famous spokesman. One month after passage of the Lend-Lease Act, Lindbergh addressed the New York chapter of the America First Committee. His speech, explaining the committee's position, was broadcast over the radio to a national audience.

Questions to Consider

1. What were Charles Lindbergh's reasons to oppose American intervention in this war?
2. What does Lindbergh hope to accomplish?
3. Is military preparedness a deterrent to war?
4. How might Henry Cabot Lodge ("Opposition to the League of Nations," Document 170) react to this speech?

I know I will be severely criticized by the interventionists in America when I say we should not enter a war unless we have a reasonable chance of winning. That, they will claim, is far too materialistic a standpoint.... But I do not believe that our American ideals, and our way of life, will gain through an unsuccessful war. And I know that the United States is not prepared to wage war in Europe successfully at this time....

I have said before, and I will say again, that I believe it will be a tragedy to the entire world if the British Empire collapses. That is one of the main reasons why I opposed this war before it was declared, and why I have constantly advocated a negotiated peace. I did not feel that England and France had a reasonable chance of winning. France has now been defeated; and ... it is now obvious that England is losing a war. I believe this is realized even by the British Government. But they have one last desperate plan remaining. They hope that they may be able to persuade us to send another American Expeditionary Force to Europe and to share with England militarily, as well as financially, the fiasco of this war.

I do not blame England for this hope, or for asking for our assistance....

... But we in this country have a right to think of the welfare of America first, just as the people in England thought first of their own country when they encouraged the smaller nations of Europe to fight against hopeless odds. When England asks us to enter this war, she is considering her own future, and that of her empire. In making our reply, I believe we should consider the future of the United States and that of the Western Hemisphere.

It is not only our right, but it is our obligation as American citizens to look at this war objectively and to weigh our chances for success if we should enter it. I have attempted to do this, especially from the standpoint of aviation; and I have been forced to the conclusion that we cannot win this war for England, regardless of how much assistance we send....

... There is a policy open to this nation that will lead to success—a policy that leaves us free to allow our own way of life, and to develop our own civilization. It is not a new and untried idea. It was advocated by Washington. It was incorporated in the Monroe Doctrine. Under its guidance, the United States has become the greatest nation in the world.

SOURCE: Charles Lindbergh, "We Cannot Win This War for England," *Vital Speeches of the Day* 7 (May 1941): 424–26.

It is based upon the belief that the security of a nation lies in the strength and character of its own people. It recommends the maintenance of armed forces sufficient to defend this hemisphere from attack by any combination of foreign powers. It demands faith in an independent American destiny. This is the policy of the America First Committee today. It is a policy not of isolation, but of independence; not of defeat, but of courage. It is policy that led this nation to success during the most trying years of our history, and it is a policy that will lead us to success again.

We have weakened ourselves for many months, and still worse, we have divided our own people by this dabbling in Europe's wars. While we should have been concentrating on American defense we have been forced to argue over foreign quarrels. We must turn our eyes and our faith back to our own country before it is too late....

The United States is better situated from a military standpoint than any other nation in the world. Even in our present condition of unpreparedness no foreign power is in a position to invade us today. If we concentrate on our own defenses and build the strength that this nation should maintain, no foreign army will ever attempt to land on American shores.

War is not inevitable for this country. Such a claim is defeatism in the true sense. No one can make us fight abroad unless we ourselves are willing to do so. No one will attempt to fight us here if we arm ourselves as a great nation should be armed. Over a hundred million people in this nation are opposed to entering the war. If the principles of democracy mean anything at all, that is reason enough for us to stay out. If we are forced into a war against the wishes of an overwhelming majority of our people, we will have proved democracy such a failure at home that there will be little use fighting for it abroad.

The time has come when those of us who believe in an independent American destiny must band together and organize for strength....

... These people—the majority of hardworking American citizens, are with us. They are the true strength of our country. And they are beginning to realize as you and I, that there are times when we must sacrifice our normal interests in life in order to insure the safety and the welfare of our nation....

If you believe in an independent destiny for America, if you believe that this country should not enter the war in Europe, we ask you to join the America First Committee in its stand. We ask you to share our faith in the ability of this nation to defend itself, to develop its own civilization, and to contribute to the progress of mankind in a more constructive and intelligent way than has yet been found by the warring nations of Europe. We need your support, and we need it now. The time to act is here. I thank you.

192

Roosevelt's Declaration of War Message (1941)

For nearly a decade, the Japanese had been expanding into China while the United States worked to thwart the encroachment. Tensions between the two countries remained high, as negotiations either failed or were dismissed. When Japan sought to consolidate much of Eastern Asia under its domain in 1941, the United States responded with diplomatic pressure and economic embargoes on goods vital to the Japanese economy. Japanese leaders concluded that to preserve their empire, they must fight the United States soon; so preparations were made to attack Pearl Harbor, Hawaii, and expand farther in Asia. The United States had broken Japan's diplomatic secret code and knew that some attack was imminent, but the location was not known. American leaders guessed the attack would come in Southeast Asia (possibly Malaya), so only general warnings were sent to forces at Pearl Harbor. On Sunday morning, 7 December 1941, Japanese planes struck American forces at Pearl Harbor in two separate waves, crippling the Pacific Fleet and killing over two thousand Americans. The next day, President Franklin Roosevelt gave the following speech to a joint session of Congress.

Questions to Consider

1. In what manner does Roosevelt characterize the actions of the Japanese?

2. Why does he offer a listing of locations where the Japanese have attacked?

3. How will the United States make "certain that this form of treachery shall never again endanger us"?

4. To what extent does Roosevelt's war message reflect the values expressed in "The Four Freedoms" (Document 190)?

Mr. Vice President, Mr. Speaker, members of the Senate and the House of Representatives:

Yesterday, Dec. 7, 1941—a date which will live in infamy—the United States of America was suddenly and deliberately attacked by naval and air forces of the empire of Japan.

SOURCE: "The President's Message," *New York Times*, 9 December 1941, pp. 1, 6.

The United States was at peace with that nation, and, at the solicitation of Japan, was still in conversation with its government and its Emperor looking toward the maintenance of peace in the Pacific.

Indeed, one hour after Japanese air squadrons had commenced bombing in the American island of Oahu the Japanese Ambassador to the United States and his colleague delivered to our Secretary of State a formal reply to a recent American message. And, while this reply stated that it seemed useless to continue the existing diplomatic negotiations, it contained no threat or hint of war or of armed attack.

It will be recorded that the distance of Hawaii from Japan makes it obvious that the attack was deliberately planned many days or even weeks ago. During the intervening time the Japanese Government has deliberately sought to deceive the United States by false statements and expressions of hope for continued peace.

The attack yesterday on the Hawaiian Islands has caused severe damage to American naval and military forces. I regret to tell you that very many American lives have been lost. In addition, American ships have been reported torpedoed on the high seas between San Francisco and Honolulu.

Yesterday the Japanese Government also launched an attack against Malaya.

Last night Japanese forces attacked Hong Kong.

Last night Japanese forces attacked Guam.

Last night Japanese forces attacked the Philippine Islands.

Last night Japanese attacked Wake Island.

And this morning the Japanese attacked Midway Island.

Japan has therefore undertaken a surprise offensive extending throughout the Pacific area. The facts of yesterday and today speak for themselves. The people of the United States have already formed their opinions and well understand the implications to the very life and safety of our nation.

As Commander in Chief of the Army and Navy, I have directed that all measures be taken for our defense, that always will our whole nation remember the character of the onslaught against us.

No matter how long it may take us to overcome this premeditated invasion, the American people, in their righteous might, will win through to absolute victory.

I believe that I interpret the will of the Congress and of the people when I assert that we will not only defend ourselves to the uttermost but will make it very certain that this form of treachery shall never again endanger us.

Hostilities exist. There is no blinking at the fact that our people, our territory and our interests are in grave danger.

With confidence in our armed forces, with the unbounding determination of our people, we will gain the inevitable triumph. So help us God.

I ask that the Congress declare that since the unprovoked and dastardly attack by Japan on Sunday, Dec. 7, 1941, a state of war has existed between the United States and the Japanese Empire.

193

Life in a Japanese
Internment Camp (1942)

As World War II began, more than 100,000 people of Japanese descent were living in the United States, mainly along the West Coast. After the surprise attack on Pearl Harbor, rumors spread that Japanese in America would hinder the war effort in "fifth column" (espionage or sabotage) actions. Reacting to old suspicions, ignorant fears, and racial prejudice toward all Asians, the federal government ordered Japanese Americans—regardless of loyalty or American citizenship—to abandon their homes and businesses and be placed in "relocation centers." Nearly 110,000 people were incarcerated in centers that resembled concentration camps or prisons. Among those relocated were Ted Nakashima and his family. Shortly after being interned, Nakashima wrote the following article for The New Republic, *a journal that published commentaries on political and social issues. Nakashima revealed his frustrations with the sweeping "relocation," the label placed on his family, and the camp conditions they endured.*

Questions to Consider

1. In what ways is Ted Nakashima frustrated with being "relocated"?
2. According to Nakashima's account, is his "relocation center" better than a penitentiary?
3. What does Nakashima's article reveal about the situation of Japanese Americans during World War II?
4. Were the relocation centers necessary?
5. In this war-time situation, what did the American people believe were good Americans?

Unfortunately in this land of liberty, I was born of Japanese parents; born in Seattle of a mother and father who have been in this country since 1901. Fine parents, who brought up their children in the best American way of life. My mother served with the Volunteer Red Cross Service in the last war—my father, an editor, has spoken and written Americanism for forty years.

Our family is almost typical of the other unfortunates here at the camp. The oldest son, a licensed architect, was educated at the University of Washington,

SOURCE: Ted Nakashima, "Concentration Camp: U.S. Style," *The New Republic* 106 (15 June 1942): 822–23.

has a master's degree from the Massachusetts Institute of Technology and is a scholarship graduate of the American School of Fine Arts in Fontainebleau, France. He is now in camp in Oregon with his wife and three-months-old child. He had just completed designing a much needed defense housing project at Vancouver, Washington.

The second son is an M.D. He served his internship in a New York hospital, is married and has two fine sons. The folks banked on him, because he was the smartest of us three boys. The army took him a month after he opened his office. He is now a lieutenant in the Medical Corps, somewhere in the South.

I am the third son, the dumbest of the lot, but still smart enough to hold down a job as an architectural draftsman. I have just finished building a new home and had lived in it three weeks. My desk was just cleared of work done for the Army Engineers, another stack of 391 defense houses was waiting (a rush job), when the order came to pack up and leave for this resettlement center called "Camp Harmony."

Mary, the only girl in the family, and her year-old son, "Butch," are with our parents—interned in the stables of the Livestock Exposition Buildings in Portland.

Now that you can picture our thoroughly American background, let me describe our new home.

The resettlement center is actually a penitentiary—armed guards in towers with spotlights and deadly tommy guns, fifteen feet of barbed wire fences, everyone confined to quarters at nine, lights out at ten o'clock. The guards are ordered to shoot anyone who approaches within twenty feet of the fences. No one is allowed to take the two-block-long hike to the latrines after nine, under any circumstances.

The apartments, as the army calls them, are two-block-long stables, with windows on one side. Floors are shiplaps on two-by-fours laid directly on the mud, which is everywhere. The stalls are about eighteen by twenty-one feet; some contain families of six or seven persons. Partitions are seven feet high, leaving a four foot opening above. The rooms aren't too bad, almost fit to live in for a short while.

The food and sanitation problems are the worst. We have had absolutely no fresh meat, vegetables or butter since we came here. Mealtime queues extend for blocks; standing in a rainswept line, feet in the mud, waiting for the scant portions of canned wieners and boiled potatoes, hash for breakfast or canned wieners and beans for dinner. Milk only for the kids. Coffee or tea dosed with saltpeter and stale bread are the adults' staples. Dirty, unwiped dishes, greasy silver, a starchy diet, no butter, no milk, bawling kids, mud, wet mud that stinks when it dries, no vegetables—a sad thing for the people who raised them in such abundance. Memories of a crisp head of lettuce with our special olive oil, vinegar, garlic and cheese dressing.

Today one of the surface sewage-disposal pipes broke and the sewage flowed down the streets. Kids play in the water. Shower baths without hot water. Stinking mud and slops everywhere.

Can this be the same America we left a few weeks ago?

As I write, I can remember our little bathroom—light coral walls. My wife painting them, and the spilled paint in her hair. The open towel shelving and the pretty shower curtains which we put up the day before we left. How sanitary and clean we left it for the airlines pilot and his young wife who are now enjoying the fruits of our labor.

It all seems so futile, struggling, trying to live our old lives under this useless, regimented life. The senselessness of all the inactive manpower. Electricians, plumbers, draftsmen, mechanics, carpenters, painters, farmers—every trade—men who are able and willing do all they can to lick the Axis. Thousands of men and women in these camps, energetic, quick, alert, eager for hard, constructive work, waiting for the army to do something for us, an army that won't give us butter.

I can't take it! I have 391 defense houses to be drawn. I left a fine American home which we built with our own hands. I left a life, highballs with our American friends on week-ends, a carpenter, laundry-truck driver, architect, airlines pilot—good friends, friends who would swear by us. I don't have enough of that Japanese heritage "*ga-man*"—a code of silent suffering and ability to stand pain.

Oddly enough I still have a bit of faith in army promises of good treatment and Mrs. Roosevelt's pledge of a future worthy of good American citizens. I'm banking another $67 of income tax to the future. Sometimes I want to spend the money I have set aside for income tax on a bit of butter or ice cream or something good that I might have smuggled though the gates, but I can't do it when I think that every dollar I can put into "the fight to lick the Japs," the sooner I will be home again. I must forget my stomach.

What really hurts most is the constant reference to us evacuees as "Japs." "Japs" are the guys we are fighting. We're on this side and we want to help. Why won't America let us? Ted Nakashima

194

Women in the Home-Front War Effort (1942)

World War II altered the economic status for many American women. As millions of men entered military service and the demand for labor increased dramatically, old stereotypes and barriers preventing women from entering the industrial workplace and the military were relaxed. Several hundred thousand women enlisted in the female versions of the military

(Army's WACS, Navy's WAVES, Women Marines, Coast Guard's SPARS), but the most significant change came when over 6 million women joined the workforce. Most women found work in the defense industries, mainly building ships and airplanes; but some accepted employment in arduous occupations—toolmaker, blacksmith, machinist, lumberjack—often reserved for men. A government campaign to encourage hiring women made "Rosie the Riveter" a symbol for those in war work. By 1945 over 50 percent of all employed workers in America were women. Excerpted here is a 1942 Ladies' Home Journal *article describing the new world of work for four women.*

Questions to Consider

1. According to the article, are the work opportunities for women limited because of gender?

2. What is the attitude of the women toward their work?

3. In what ways does the article suggest that the women retain their femininity even though they work on the assembly line?

4. How do you think Betty Friedan ("The Problem That Has No Name," Document 208) would respond to this selection?

Marjory Kurtz, just 20, was a $15-a-week secretary in Absecon, N.J. Now she works in the Martin plant stock rooms.

Virginia Drummond, 30, ran a beauty shop in Punxsutawney, Pa. Today she wields an electric drill on the bomber assembly line.

Tommy Joseph, 24, of Clanton, Ala., wife of a young Army lieutenant in the Pacific, now drills bulkhead webs for Army planes.

Margaret Kennedy, 22, a Lancaster, Pa., schoolteacher till January, now works the midnight shift at the Glenn Martin plant.

When brisk Ginny Drummond and her covergirl roommate of the silky black hair and gentian-blue eyes, Tommy Joseph, sink dog-tired into bed these evenings, often as not a lively jive party is just starting in the adjoining room. Getting eight hours' sleep a night to bolster aching arms and feet for another eight hours' stand on the Glenn Martin aircraft-assembly line is practically impossible when four girls, sharing the same cramped one-bedroom apartment on Baltimore's sweltering Mt. Royal Avenue, keep working hours that stretch right around the clock.

Ginny and Tommy work six days in seven from 8:45 A.M. to 4:15 P.M. Their two other roommates, twenty-year-old Marge, daughter of a small-town mayor, and ex-schoolteacher Margaret Kennedy, are on the midnight shift, from 12:30 to 8:15 A.M. While waiting until it's time to leave for the plant, they try to subdue their chatter for the benefit of the two-day shift girls sharing the same lumpy bed in the next room. But long before the doorbell starts its nerve-shattering jangle over the bedroom door, and friends crash upstairs to drive Marge and Kennedy to work, the two sleepers are thoroughly awake.

SOURCE: Written by Ruth Matthews and Betty Hannah, "This Changing World for Women". Originally published in the August 1942 issue of *Ladies Home Journal* (r) magazine, pp. 27–30. © Copyright 1942, Meredith Corporation. All rights reserved. Used with the permission of *Ladies' Home Journal*.

"Daylight" nights pose even a greater problem for Marge and Kennedy. By the time these two are back, at 9:30 the following morning, the double bed is invitingly made up again, albeit with the same sheets. But by then the sun is warm and bright, and dawdling on the white front stoop is an irresistible temptation. All too often it's late afternoon before Marge and Kennedy drop into bed. By seven the apartment is filled with the rich odors of Ginny's cooking, and by the time everyone has eaten and the dishes are washed, a hoard of swains has arrived to keep them chattering and jiving way past the day shift's ten-o'clock bedtime....

"You'll do a man's job and you'll get a man's paycheck," Glenn L. Martin tells his 4000 women employees, "but you'll be treated as the men are treated."

This means a full six-day week, taking the night shift when so assigned and, in the case of Tommy and Ginny, spending the forthcoming Thanksgiving, Christmas and New Year's holidays amid the terrific hubbub of hammers, cranes and electric drills.

Eighty per cent of the women at Martin are on the "small parts" assembly line, with a handful skilled enough to do the highly paid final installation jobs. From 3 to 5 per cent are engineers and inspectors. In aircraft manufacture for the United States as a whole, fewer than 2 per cent of the workers are women, compared with 40 to 80 per cent in some aircraft plants in Great Britain. But as more and more men are being taken into the armed forces, opportunities for women are booming. At least 2,000,000 women who have never drawn any kind of pay check in their lives—schoolgirls and housewives—will be in factories within the next year or two. They must be, if the war of production is to go forward.

Most Martin workers are between eighteen and twenty-four, although a few are over forty. Tommy, Ginny, Marge and Kennedy started off at the usual beginner's pay of 60 cents an hour with a guarantee of 75 cents an hour within three months. Already the older girls are doing skilled work such as drilling on bulkhead webs—part of the frame of a plane—and, with two raises, now net $32.67 a week. Marge and Kennedy are in the stock rooms. Although they both proudly wear bright nail polish, their hands are red and sore from handing out countless nuts, screws and bolts. (A Martin bomber has nearly 50,000 small parts, and each is nearly as important as a wing or propeller when a bomber goes into action.) They are now earning around $28 a week: "when we think what we used to make, that sure isn't hay."

An assembly-line worker has to buy her own tools, including electric hand drills, an investment that runs to about $30 cash if she's properly equipped. Tommy and Ginny say there are tools in their work kit they still don't know how to use—but they will before they're through at Martin: "There's no chance to get fed up with any particular job. The minute you've mastered one, they switch you to something harder."

Nobody at Martin has any doubt about the outcome of this war. When they watch those sleek-winged bombers line up, row on row, they feel they're helping to win it right now....

And when the war is over? Some of the girls, and certainly the men they work beside, wonder just what all these women are going to do when the boys come home. Some, of course, will quit to get married. But not all of them will have husbands, because some of these boys aren't coming back. Tommy has faced that stark possibility with grim and self-searching courage. She, like many other of the women workers, may go on to a big supervisory job in aircraft production. As for the younger girls, "When the war's over we'll probably go home again and wash dishes."

"We'd better," Ginny advises with a wry smile. "It's the only way we'll ever get our hands clean again."

195

The Second World War Homefront (1941–1945)

With America's entrance into World War II, there was a need to mobilize the economy for war-time production, train men and women for military duty, and maintain homefront support for the war effort. As in the First World War, the federal government began a media campaign to encourage women to take jobs in industry, to encourage a relaxation of racial tensions, and to call for patriotic support and personal sacrifice. Part of this publicity effort was the use of posters. Listed below are three posters that sought to muster public support for the war effort.

Questions to Consider

1. What can you deduce from the first image about gender roles during the 1940s?

2. What is the intent of the second image? How accurate is its portrayal of race relations?

3. Why is the third image comparing home front sacrifice with that experienced by soldiers at the front?

4. What can you deduce from these images about public support for the Second World War?

"We Can Do It!," National Archives

SOURCE: National Archives and Records Administration, NWDNS-179-WP-1563.

"United We Win," National Archives

SOURCE: National Archives and Records Administration, NWDNS-44-PA-370.

"You Talk of Sacrifice: He Knew the Meaning of Sacrifice!," National Archives

SOURCE: National Archives and Records Administration, NWDNS-179-WP-1386

196

African Americans
in the Military (1944)

For millions of African Americans, World War II confirmed the patterns of segregation and discrimination while also offering hope for future improvements. With the war being fought to safeguard liberty and democracy, African American leaders pointed to the hypocrisy of the effort and demanded full civil rights in the military and on the home front. During the war, membership in the NAACP skyrocketed. The African American newspaper the Pittsburgh Courier *advanced the "double V" campaign—victory over Germany and Japan and victory over segregation at home. Large numbers of African Americans moved to the West and North to take jobs in wartime production. Over 1 million African Americans served in the armed forces, though most were placed in segregated units that often performed noncombat tasks. And for the first time, some military branches included African Americans. A number of servicemen wrote letters home or to branch offices of the NAACP depicting their military experiences and expressing their frustrations. Journalist Lucille B. Milner used many of these letters to write the excerpted article here for* The New Republic, *a journal that addressed social and political issues.*

Questions to Consider

1. What were the conditions and the attitudes that African Americans faced in the military?

2. According to Milner, what were the experiences of African American soldiers outside the military camps?

3. In what ways were African American servicemen frustrated? What did they hope to accomplish?

4. How might W. E. B. Du Bois ("W. E. B. Du Bois on Race Relations," Document 148) or Alain Locke ("The New Negro," Document 175) react to the sentiments in this article?

I am a Negro soldier 22 years old. I won't fight or die in vain. If I fight, suffer or die it will be for the freedom of every black, any black man to live equally with other races.... If the life of the Negro in the United States is right as it is lived today, then I would rather be dead.

SOURCE: Lucille B. Milner, "Jim Crow in the Army," *The New Republic* 110 (13 March 1944): 339–42.

Any Negro would rather give his life at home fighting for a cause he can understand than against any enemy whose principles are the same as our so-called democracy.

A new Negro will return from the war—a bitter Negro if he is disappointed again. He will have been taught to kill, to suffer, to die for something he believes in, and he will live by these rules to gain his personal rights.

Statements like these are found over and over in the hundreds of soldiers' letters received by organizations defending the rights of the colored people. It is impossible to read a dozen of these letters picked at random without feeling their tragic significance. The war attitude of the Negro reflects today's dilemma of his race, in an intensified and critical form. The Negro soldier is deeply patriotic, vividly conscious of our aims in this war, eager to get into the fighting areas. That seems an ideal attitude for a soldier to have, but the truth is that the morale of the colored men in our armed forces is far from ideal. For they are not allowed to express their patriotism, their democracy and their militancy freely. They have fought bravely in every war, from the Revolution on, but still they are not treated like Americans.

The sense of being excluded from the mainstream of military service is expressed in their letters in phrases like these: "We really have nothing to soldier for."... "It is not like being in a soldier camp. It is more like being in prison." A soldier at an air base wrote: "Segregation in the Army is making enemies of the Negro soldier, demoralizing him. You may wonder why they don't rebel. They do, but individually, and as a result, they are either transferred to Southern parts, placed in the guardhouse or given a dishonorable discharge from the army.... We keep constantly in mind that army law is WHITE man's law."

The racial attitude of the military is a curious anachronism. Despite the gains made on the civilian front in race relations during the last two decades, actual conditions in our camps, most of which are unfortunately in the South, show a reversion to dark and ignorant prejudice. A corporal writes from the Deep South: "... It is no secret that the Negro soldier in the South is as much persecuted as is his civilian brother; the conditions existing in this Godforsaken hole which is Camp ... are intolerable, and may be considered on a par with the worst conditions throughout the South since 1865."...

From a colored officer in the Deep South:

The only desire the Negro officers could possibly have is to get completely out of the South. Many of us have never been below the Mason-Dixon Line, and are now being subjected to chain-gang practices and disgraceful and embarrassing verbal abuse.... No nursing or recreational facilities have been organized for us.... To go to a nearby city is to invite trouble, not only from civilian police but more often from the military police, who are upheld in any discourtesy, breach of discipline, arrogance and bodily assault they render the Negro officers.

Another young white officer, born in the North, made it a point to discuss race relations with hundreds of men, white and black, gathered from every part of the country at a Southern camp. He reports some reactions:

A white private from Virginia: "Gosh, I just had to salute a damn nigger lieutenant. Boy, that burns me up."

A professedly progressive school-teacher from North Carolina: "Give the Negroes equality of opportunity by all means—by themselves."

A technical sergeant from Texas: "You people up North want to change things overnight. You are heading for a revolution."...

This makes it lawful, if somewhat grotesque, for incidents like the following to happen. On a crowded troop train going through Texas, the colored soldiers were fed behind a Jim Crow curtain at one end of the dining car. In the main section, along with the white folks, a group of German war prisoners dined—and no doubt fed their illusions of race superiority on that Jim Crow curtain.

The assignment of Negro units in the Army to menial jobs is a widespread practice. Colored inductees go to camp for military training and find themselves assigned to service units—cooking, shoveling coal, waiting on the white officers. Entering service, they may find themselves building the Burma Road, or African bases, or encountering winter temperatures of 50 degrees below zero hacking the Alaska Highway or the Canal pipeline out of the Canadian wastes. Meanwhile white units trained at the same time are in the fighting war, where the Negro longs to be. "The sight of masses of Negro soldiers constantly blocked off into separate groups and assigned to menial jobs," a white officer writes, "generates in the mind of the average soldier a powerful feeling of superiority and of being 'different'."...

Buses and trains mean even more to the Negro soldier than to the white in parts of the country where there is no local Negro population, and he must travel far, or else hope for a visit from his family, in order to mingle with his own kind. The soldiers' letters describe endless troubles with buses and trains. Even when they are being transferred as troops, they are often refused service in the railway restaurants and go hungry for twenty-four hours. The wife and two babies of a Negro chaplain traveled three days to join him without being able to buy anything but cold milk and sandwiches. One gentle little Negro woman, whose soldier-husband was refused coffee at a bus terminal delivered a sermon to the snappish counter-girl. "Our boys can fight for you," she said. "They are spilling their blood for you on the battlefield, yet you can't serve them a cup of coffee." But the management still refused the coffee. "May the Lord forgive them, for they know not what they do," she said in a quiet tone as they turned and left.

From 1770, when the colored boy Crispus Attucks fell in the Boston Massacre, down through the Battle of San Juan Hill and the Meuse-Argonne offensive, the colored Americans have been collecting their traditions of war and their flags and decorations and trophies. As far as we will let them, they are fighting as Americans today, and yet they are fighting with a difference. This, from a soldier's letter, expresses what is in their hearts: "Those of us who are in the armed services are offering our lives and fortunes, not for the America we know today, but for the America we hope will be created after the war."

197

Truman's Decision to Drop the Bomb (1945)

At the behest of several refugee physicists from Europe who feared Germany might develop an atomic bomb, President Franklin Roosevelt established the ultrasecret Manhattan Project to build a nuclear weapon for the United States. Racing against time, a team of physicists under the direction of J. Robert Oppenheimer produced a working bomb in the summer of 1945. But Germany had already surrendered, and Roosevelt had died three months earlier. The new, inexperienced president, Harry S Truman, was completely uninformed about the bomb until he entered the White House; he then faced the decision of approving its use against Japan to both end the war and arrange the peace. Excerpted here is Truman's account of how he determined to use the atomic weapon.

Questions to Consider

1. According to Harry Truman, what did the advisory committee recommend?
2. What were Truman's alternatives to dropping the atomic bomb?
3. Was dropping the bomb needed to end the war? How did the bomb affect foreign relations after the war?
4. How do you think Ted Nakashima ("Life in a Japanese Internment Camp," Document 193), reacted to President Truman's decision?

Stimson was one of the very few men responsible for the setting up of the atomic bomb project. He had taken a keen and active interest in every stage of its development. He said he wanted specifically to talk to me today about the effect the atomic bomb might likely have on our future foreign relations.

He explained that he thought it necessary for him to share his thoughts with me about the revolutionary changes in warfare that might result from the atomic bomb and the possible effects of such a weapon on our civilization.

I listened with absorbed interest, for Stimson was a man of great wisdom and foresight. He went into considerable detail in describing the nature and the power of the projected weapon. If expectations were to be realized, he told me, the atomic bomb would be certain to have a decisive influence on our

SOURCE: Harry S Truman, *Memoirs, Vol. 1: Year of Decisions* (Garden City, NY, 1955), 10–11, 86–87, 418–21. Reprinted by permission of Clifton Truman Daniel.

relations with other countries. And if it worked, the bomb, in all probability, would shorten the war....

My own knowledge of these developments had come about only after I became president, when Secretary Stimson had given me the full story. He had told me at that time that the project was nearing completion and that a bomb could be expected within another four months. It was at his suggestion, too, that I had then set up a committee of top men and had asked them to study with great care the implications the new weapon might have for us....

It was their recommendation that the bomb be used against the enemy as soon at it could be done. They recommended further that it should be used without specific warning and against a target that would clearly show its devastating strength. I had realized, of course, that an atomic bomb explosion would inflict damage and casualties beyond imagination. On the other hand, the scientific advisers of the committee reported, "We can propose no technical demonstration likely to bring an end to the war; we see no acceptable alternative to direct military use." It was their conclusion that no technical demonstration they might propose, such as over a deserted island, would be likely to bring the war to an end. It had to be used against an enemy target.

The final decision of where and when to use the atomic bomb was up to me. Let there be no mistake about it. I regarded the bomb as a military weapon and never had any doubt that it should be used. The top military advisers to the President recommended its use, and when I talked to Churchill he unhesitatingly told me that he favored the use of the atomic bomb if it might aid to end the war....

In deciding to use this bomb I wanted to make sure that it would be used as a weapon of war in the manner prescribed by the laws of war. That meant that I wanted it dropped on a military target. I had told Stimson that the bomb should be dropped as nearly as possibly upon a war production center of prime military importance....

Four cities were finally recommended as targets; Hiroshima, Kokura, Nigata, and Nagasaki. They were listed in that order as targets for the importance of these cities, but allowance would be given for weather conditions at the time of the bombing....

On August 6, the fourth day of the journey home from Potsdam, came the historic news that shook the world. I was eating lunch with members of the *Augusta*'s crew when Captain Frank Graham, White House Map Room watch officer, handed me the following message:

TO THE PRESIDENT

FROM THE SECRETARY OF WAR

Big bomb dropped on Hiroshima August 5 at 7:15 P.M. Washington time. First reports indicate complete success which was even more conspicuous than earlier test.

I was greatly moved. I telephoned Byrnes aboard ship to give him the news and then said to the group of sailors around me, "This is the greatest thing in history. It's time for us to get home."

198

Remembering the Hiroshima Atomic Blast (1945)

On 6 August 1945, a B-29 Superfortress, the Enola Gay, *dropped a single atomic bomb on Hiroshima, Japan. The bomb emitted a sudden flash that demolished four square miles of the city, immediately killing nearly 80,000 people and setting fire to remaining structures. Among the survivors of this blast was Hiroko Nakamoto, a young, happy girl who came from a privileged family. Her powerful recollection of that day is excerpted here.*

Questions to Consider

1. What was most shocking to Hiroko Nakamoto about the atomic blast?
2. According to Nakamoto, was the bombing racially motivated?
3. Did American officials realize the destructiveness of the bomb? Was it necessary?
4. What can be deduced about Japanese views of the bombing of Hiroshima from Nakamoto's account?

Whenever I see strong sunshine, I remember the day very clearly, the day I will never forget as long as I live. That day, in one quick second, my world was destroyed. The day was August 6, 1945.

It was 8:15 in the morning, and I was on my way to work. I was walking. The night before, as usual, there had been alerts all night. I was groggy from lack of sleep. The all clear had sounded just as I left home. Now all seemed calm and quiet. I did not hear any sounds of airplanes overhead.

Suddenly, from nowhere, came a blinding flash. It was as if someone had taken a flashbulb picture a few inches from my eyes. There was no pain then. Only a stinging sensation, as if I had been slapped hard in the face.

I tried to open my eyes. But I could not. Then I lost consciousness.

I do not know how I got there or how long it was before I awoke. But when I opened my eyes, I was lying inside a shattered house. I was dazed and in shock, and all I knew was that I wanted to go home. I pulled myself up and started stumbling down the street. The air was heavy with a sickening odor. It was a smell different from anything I had ever known before.

SOURCE: Hiroko Nakamoto, as told to Mildred Mastin Pace, *My Japan, 1930–1951* (New York, 1970), 56–61, 64–66. Copyright © Hiroko Nakamoto. Reprinted by permission.

Now I saw dead bodies all about me. The buildings were in ruins, and from the ruins I could hear people crying for help. But I could not help them. Some people were trying, as I was, to walk, to get away, to find their homes. I passed a streetcar that was stalled. It was filled with dead people.

I stumbled on. But now a great fire came rolling toward us, and I knew it was impossible to get home.

I passed a woman on the street. She looked at me, then turned away with a gasp of horror. I wondered why. I felt as if one side of my face was detached, did not belong to me. I was afraid to touch it with my hand.

There was a river nearby, and the people who could walk began walking toward the river—burned people with clothes in shreds or no clothes at all, men and women covered with blood, crying children. I followed them....

When I reached the river, I saw that the wooden bridge which I had crossed each day on my way to the factory was on fire. I stopped. And for the first time I looked at my body. My arms, legs and ankles were burned. And I realized that the left side of my face must be burned, too. There were strange burns. Not pink, but yellow. The flesh was hanging loose. I went down to the water's edge and tried to pat the skin back with salt water from the river, as I saw others doing.

But we could not stay by the river. The fire was coming closer, and the heat was more intense. Everyone started moving again, away from the fire, moving silently, painfully....

I found myself on a wide street. I saw a number of burned people standing around a policeman. He had a small bottle of iodine, and some cotton he was dabbing it on the badly burned back of a man. I stared too dazed to realize how futile and pathetic it was....

When I awoke again, I asked a man sitting next to me what had happened.

He said a bomb had destroyed almost the entire city. For the first time, my heart was filled with hate, bitter hate, for a people who could do this. I remembered a propaganda picture we had been shown of Americans laughing as they looked at corpses of Japanese soldiers. At the time I did not believe it. But I believed it now....

By the time we reached the doctor's, his house, his office, even his yard were filled with people lying waiting for help. I lay in the yard and waited a long time. When at last he saw me, he did not even know what to do. These were burns such as no man had ever seen before. A nurse hastily put some oil on my burns, then hurried on to the next person. People were screaming; many were begging for water. And so few hands to help!

Some people were burned so black you could not tell whether they were lying face down or on their backs. It was hard to tell they were human beings.

But they were still alive.

More and more burned and injured kept arriving....

Hiroshima was burning. The sky was red. Pine Street, its trees where I spent my childhood hours, the rice warehouse, the hotel, all were destroyed.

Friends and neighbors were dead. Everything we owned was gone. The rivers where we had enjoyed boating on summer evenings were filled with dead bodies floating in the water. People were screaming as they lay along the banks of the rivers. The dead and the half dead were lying among the wreckage in the streets.

The sky was red. Hiroshima was burning. My aunt, Teruko, and all the Kaitaichi relatives sat that night, in the darkened room, watching my face in silence.

23

Postwar America

The Second World War transformed the United States in a way that few events in its history did. The war years had boosted the economy, leaving the United States the world's most prosperous and powerful nation. Unlike in the 1920s, the nation did not withdraw from the world but instead confronted its former wartime ally and new adversary, the Soviet Union, in the Cold War. Ideological differences (capitalism versus Communism), a tradition of suspicion and mistrust, and the perceived threat from this rival contributed to political maneuverings and initiated a massive arms and technology race. The Second World War also helped bring about important social changes, the most significant of which was the expansion of civil rights for African Americans. The following excerpts examine differing aspects of these major issues.

199

"Containment" (1946)

The conclusion of World War II left the United States and the Soviet Union as the two predominant world powers. But the former allies had ideological differences (capitalism and Communism) and conflicting views of the postwar world that made them adversaries in the Cold War, a conflict conducted on various levels though short of direct military clashes. Based in part on Soviet words and actions early in the Cold War, American leaders determined the Soviet Union was bent on destroying capitalism and conquering the world.

In 1946, George F. Kennan, a scholar of Russian history and an official in the American Embassy in Moscow, sent a "long telegram" to the State Department explaining the historic basis of Soviet foreign policy and warning of the Soviet threat to the United States. He also suggested how the United States could counter Soviet actions. Kennan's long telegram—and an article he published in Foreign Affairs *in 1947 under the pseudonym "X"—became the foundation of America's new foreign policy of "containment"; and Kennan, best known as "the father of containment," took a leading role in shaping many of the early Cold War policies. Excerpted here is his long telegram of February 1946.*

Questions to Consider

1. According to George Kennan, what is the political ideology of the Soviet leaders, and how does this affect postwar relations with the United States?

2. What does Kennan believe are the purposes of Soviet foreign activities?

3. Why is containment significant to understanding Cold War activities?

4. To what extent does Kennan's policy reflect a desire to preserve Roosevelt's "Four Freedoms" (Document 190)?

At bottom of Kremlin's neurotic view of world affairs is traditional and instinctive Russian sense of insecurity. Originally, this was insecurity of a peaceful agricultural people trying to live on vast exposed plain in neighborhood of fierce nomadic peoples. To this was added, as Russia came into contact with economically advanced West, fear of more competent, more powerful, more highly organized societies in that area. But this latter type of insecurity was one which afflicted rather Russian rulers than Russian people; for Russian rulers have invariably sensed that their rule was relatively archaic in form, fragile and artificial in its psychological foundation, unable to stand comparison on contact with political system of Western countries. For this reason they have always feared foreign penetration, feared direct contact between Western world and their own, feared what would happen if Russians learned truth about world without or if foreigners learned truth about world within. And they have learned to seek security only in patient but deadly struggle for total destruction of rival power, never in compacts and compromises with it.

It was no coincidence that Marxism, which had smouldered ineffectively for half a century in Western Europe, caught hold and blazed for first time in Russia. Only in this land which had never known a friendly neighbor or indeed any tolerant equilibrium of separate powers, either internal or international, could a doctrine thrive which viewed economic conflicts of society as insoluble by peaceful means. After establishment of Bolshevist regime, Marxist dogma, rendered even more truculent and intolerant by Lenin's interpretation, became a perfect vehicle for sense of insecurity with which Bolsheviks, even more than previous Russian rulers, were afflicted. In this dogma, with its basic altruism of purpose, they found justification for their instinctive fear of outside world, for

SOURCE: Department of State, *Foreign Relations of the United States, 1946*, vol. 6 (Washington, DC, 1969): 696–709.

the dictatorship without which they did not know how to rule, for cruelties they did not dare not to inflict, for sacrifices they felt bound to demand.... This thesis provides justification for that increase of military and police power of Russian state, for that isolation of Russian population from outside world, and for that fluid and constant pressure to extend limits of Russian police power which are together the natural and instinctive urges of Russian rulers. Basically this is only the steady advance of uneasy Russian nationalism, a centuries old movement in which conceptions of offense and defense are inextricably confused. But in new guise of international Marxism, with its honeyed promises to a desperate and war torn outside world, it is more dangerous and insidious than ever before....

On official plane we must look for following:

(a) Internal policy devoted to increasing in every way strength and prestige of Soviet state: intensive military-industrialization; maximum development of armed forces; great displays to impress outsiders; continued secretiveness about internal matters, designed to conceal weaknesses and to keep opponents in dark.

(b) Wherever it is considered timely and promising efforts will be made to advance official limits of Soviet power. For the moment, these efforts are restricted to certain neighboring points conceived of here as being of immediate strategic necessity, such as Northern Iran, Turkey, possibly Bornholm. However, other points may at any time come into question, if and as concealed Soviet political power is extended to new areas....

(c) Russians will participate officially in international organizations where they see opportunity of extending Soviet power or of inhibiting or diluting power of others. Moscow sees in UNO not the mechanism for a permanent and stable world society founded on mutual interest and aims of all nations, but an arena in which aims just mentioned can be favorably pursued....

(d) Toward colonial areas and backward or dependent peoples, Soviet policy, even on official plane, will be directed toward weakening of power and influence and contacts of advanced Western nations, on theory that in so far as this policy is successful, there will be created a vacuum which will favor Communist-Soviet penetration. Soviet pressure for participation in trusteeship arrangements thus represents, in my opinion, a desire to be in a position to complicate and inhibit exertion of Western influence at such points rather than to provide major channel for exerting of Soviet power....

(e) Russians will strive energetically to develop Soviet representation in, and official ties with, countries in which they sense strong possibilities of opposition to Western centers of power. This applies to such widely separated points as Germany, Argentina, Middle Eastern countries, etc.

(f) In international economic matters, Soviet policy will really be dominated by pursuit of autarchy for Soviet Union and Soviet-dominated adjacent areas taken together.... Soviet foreign trade may be restricted largely to Soviet's own security sphere, including occupied areas in Germany, and that a cold official shoulder may be turned to principle of general economic collaboration among nations.

(g) With respect to cultural collaboration, lip service will likewise be rendered to desirability of deepening cultural contacts between peoples, but this will not in practice be interpreted in any way which could weaken security position of Soviet peoples....

(h) Beyond this, Soviet official relations will take what might be called "correct" course with individual foreign governments, with great stress being laid on prestige of Soviet Union and its representatives and with punctilious attention to protocol, as distinct from good manners....

PART 5: [Practical Deductions From Standpoint of US Policy]   In summary, we have here a political force committed fanatically to the belief that with US there can be no permanent modus vivendi, that it is desirable and necessary that the internal harmony of our society be disrupted, our traditional way of life be destroyed, the international authority of our state be broken, if Soviet power is to be secure. This political force has complete power of disposition over energies of one of world's greatest people and resources of world's richest national territory, and is borne along by deep and powerful currents of Russian nationalism. In addition, it has an elaborate and far flung apparatus for exertion of its influence in other countries, an apparatus of amazing flexibility and versatility, managed by people whose experience and skill in underground methods are presumably without parallel in history. Finally, it is seemingly inaccessible to considerations of reality in its basic reactions. For it, the vast fund of objective fact about human society is not, as with us, the measure against which outlook is constantly being tested and reformed, but a grab bag from which individual items are selected arbitrarily and tendentiously to bolster an outlook already preconceived. This is admittedly not a pleasant picture. Problem of how to cope with this force [is] undoubtedly greatest task our diplomacy has ever faced and probably greatest it will ever have to face. It should be point of departure from which our political general staff work at present juncture should proceed. It should be approached with same thoroughness and care as solution of major strategic problem in war and if necessary, with no smaller outlay in planning effort. I cannot attempt to suggest all answers here. But I would like to record my conviction there are certain observations of a more encouraging nature I should like to make:

(1) Soviet power, unlike that of Hitlerite Germany, is neither schematic nor adventuristic. It does not work by fixed plans. It does not take unnecessary risks. Impervious to logic of reason, and it is highly sensitive to logic of force. For this reason it can easily withdraw—and usually does—when strong resistance is encountered at any point. Thus, if the adversary has sufficient force and makes clear his readiness to use it, he rarely has to do so. If situations are properly handled there need be no prestige-engaging showdowns.

(2) Gauged against Western World as a whole, Soviets are still by far the weaker force. Thus, their success will really depend on degree of cohesion, firmness and vigor which Western World can muster. And this is factor which it is within our power to influence.

(3) Success of Soviet system, as form of internal power, is not yet finally proven. It has yet to be demonstrated that it can survive supreme test of successive transfer of power from one individual or group to another.... In Russia, party has now become a great and—for the moment—highly successful apparatus of dictatorial administration, but it has ceased to be a source of emotional inspiration. Thus, internal soundness and permanence of movement need not yet be regarded as assured.

(4) All Soviet propaganda beyond Soviet security sphere is basically negative and destructive. It should therefore be relatively easy to combat it by any intelligent and really constructive program. For these reasons I think we may approach calmly and with good heart problem of how to deal with Russia. As to how this approach should be made, I only wish to advance, by way of conclusion, following comments:

(1) Our first step must be to apprehend, and recognize for what it is, the nature of the movement with which we are dealing. We must study it with same courage, detachment, objectivity, and same determination not to be emotionally provoked or unseated by it, with which doctor studies unruly and unreasonable individual.

(2) We must see that our public is educated to realities of Russian situation. I cannot over-emphasize importance of this. Press cannot do this alone. It must be done mainly by Government, which is necessarily more experienced and better informed on practical problems involved....

(3) Much depends on health and vigor of our own society. World communism is like malignant parasite which feeds only on diseased tissue. This is point at which domestic and foreign policies meet. Every courageous and incisive measure to solve internal problems of our own society, to improve self-confidence, discipline, morale, and community spirit of our own people, is a diplomatic victory over Moscow worth a thousand diplomatic notes and joint communiques....

(4) We must formulate and put forward for other nations a much more positive and constructive picture of sort of world we would like to see than we have put forward in past. It is not enough to urge people to develop political processes similar to our own. Many foreign peoples, in Europe at least, are tired and frightened by experiences of past, and are less interested in abstract freedom than in security. They are seeking guidance rather than responsibilities. We should be better able than Russians to give them this. And unless we do, Russians certainly will.

(5) Finally we must have courage and self-confidence to cling to our own methods and conceptions of human society. After all, the greatest danger that can befall us in coping with this problem of Soviet communism, is that we shall allow ourselves to become like those with whom we are coping.

200

NSC-68, A Blueprint for the Cold War (1950)

The Cold War between the United States and the Soviet Union had become a global confrontation by 1950. Using the "containment" policy to block communist expansion, the United States implemented the Truman Doctrine in the eastern Mediterranean, sent economic aid to Europe in the Marshall Plan, formed the North Atlantic Treaty Organization (NATO), and worked to prevent the communist takeover of China. In 1949, when it exploded its first atomic bomb, the Soviet Union joined the United States as the only nations to possess nuclear weapons. Also in 1949, the communists won control of China. Startled by these dramatic events, the National Security Council (NSC), formed early in the Cold War to provide the president with foreign policy information, drafted the secret report, Paper Number 68. NSC-68 depicted the Cold War in stark terms, arguing that the United States and the Soviet Union were polar opposites with little hope for compromise or peaceful resolution of differences. The paper also called for a shift in the policy of containment. The breakout of the Korean War and the influence of NSC-68 led to dramatic increases in military spending, a nuclear weapons buildup, and construction of the hydrogen bomb. Excerpted here is NSC-68.

Questions to Consider

1. In what ways does NSC-68 depict the Soviet Union and its activities in the post–World War II world?
2. What does NSC-68 ask the United States to do?
3. In what ways does NSC-68 want to change the policy of "containment"?
4. How might George Kennan ("Containment," Document 199) and Joseph McCarthy ("Communists in the Government," Document 201) respond to NSC-68?

Within the past thirty-five years the world has experienced two global wars of tremendous violence. It has witnessed two revolutions—the Russian and the Chinese—of extreme scope and intensity. It has also seen the collapse of five empires—the Ottoman, the Austro-Hungarian, German, Italian, and Japanese—and the drastic decline of two major imperial systems, the British and the French.

SOURCE: Department of State, *Foreign Relations of the United States, 1950, National Security Affairs; Foreign Economic Policy*, vol. 1 (Washington, DC, 1977): 237, 239, 241, 244, 252–53, 291–92.

During the span of one generation, the international distribution of power has been fundamentally altered. For several centuries it had proved impossible for any one nation to gain such preponderant strength that a coalition of other nations could not in time face it with greater strength. The international scene was marked by recurring periods of violence and war, but a system of sovereign and independent states was maintained, over which no state was able to achieve hegemony.

Two complex sets of factors have now basically altered this historic distribution of power. First, the defeat of Germany and Japan and the decline of the British and French Empires have interacted with the development of the United States and the Soviet Union in such a way that power increasingly gravitated to these two centers. Second, the Soviet Union, unlike previous aspirants to hegemony, is animated by a new fanatic faith, anti-thetical to our own, and seeks to impose its absolute authority over the rest of the world. Conflict has, therefore, become endemic and is waged, on the part of the Soviet Union, by violent or non-violent methods in accordance with the dictates of expediency. With the development of increasingly terrifying weapons of mass destruction, every individual faces the ever-present possibility of annihilation should the conflict enter the phase of total war....

The Kremlin regards the United States as the only major threat to the achievement of its fundamental design. There is a basic conflict between the idea of freedom under a government of laws, and the idea of slavery under the grim oligarchy of the Kremlin, which has come to a crisis with the polarization of power described [earlier], and the exclusive possession of atomic weapons by the two protagonists. The idea of freedom, moreover, is peculiarly and intolerably subversive of the idea of slavery. But the converse is not true. The implacable purpose of the slave state to eliminate the challenge of freedom has placed the two great powers at opposite poles. It is this fact which gives the present polarization of power the quality of crisis....

The objectives of a free society are determined by its fundamental values and by the necessity for maintaining the material environment in which they flourish. Logically and in fact, therefore, the Kremlin's challenge to the United States is directed not only to our values but to our physical capacity to protect their environment. It is a challenge which encompasses both peace and war and our objectives in peace and war must take account of it.

Thus we must make ourselves strong, both in the way in which we affirm our values in the conduct of our national life, and in the development of our military and economic strength.

We must lead in building a successfully functioning political and economic system in the free world. It is only by practical affirmation, abroad as well as at home, of our essential values, that we can preserve our own integrity, in which lies the real frustration of the Kremlin design.

But beyond thus affirming our values our policy and actions must be such as to foster a fundamental change in the nature of the Soviet system, a change toward which the frustration of the design is the first and perhaps the most important step. Clearly it will not only be less costly but more effective if this change occurs to a maximum extent as a result of internal forces in Soviet society....

Practical and ideological considerations therefore both impel us to the conclusion that we have no choice but to demonstrate the superiority of the idea of freedom by its constructive application, and to attempt to change the world situation by means short of war in such a way as to frustrate the Kremlin design and hasten the decay of the Soviet system.

For us the role of military power is to serve the national purpose by deterring an attack upon us while we seek by other means to create an environment in which our free society can flourish, and by fighting, if necessary, to defend the integrity and vitality of our free society and to defeat any aggressor. The Kremlin uses Soviet military power to back up and serve the Kremlin design. It does not hesitate to use military force aggressively if that course is expedient in the achievement of its design. The differences between our fundamental purpose and the Kremlin design, therefore, are reflected in our respective attitudes toward and use of military force....

As for the policy of "containment," it is one which seeks by all means short of war to (1) block further expansion of Soviet power, (2) expose the falsities of Soviet pretensions, (3) induce a retraction of the Kremlin's control and influence, and (4) in general, so foster the seeds of destruction within the Soviet system that the Kremlin is brought at least to the point of modifying its behavior to conform to generally accepted international standards.

It was and continues to be cardinal in this policy that we possess superior overall power in ourselves or in dependable combination with other likeminded nations. One of the most important ingredients of power is military strength. In the concept of "containment," the maintenance of a strong military posture is deemed to be essential for two reasons: (1) as an ultimate guarantee of our national security and (2) as an indispensable backdrop to the conduct of the policy of "containment." Without superior aggregate military strength, in being and readily mobilizable, a policy of "containment"—which is in effect a policy of calculated and gradual coercion—is no more than a policy of bluff....

In summary, we must, by means of a rapid and sustained build-up of the political, economic, and military strength of the free world, and by means of an affirmative program intended to wrest the initiative from the Soviet Union, confront it with convincing evidence of the determination and ability of the free world to frustrate the Kremlin design of a world dominated by its will. Such evidence is the only means short of war which eventually may force the Kremlin to abandon its present course of action and to negotiate acceptable agreements on issues of major importance.

The whole success of the proposed program hangs ultimately on recognition by this Government, the American people, and all free peoples, that the cold war is in fact a real war in which the survival of the free world is at stake....

201

Communists in the Government (1950)

The fight against Communism in the Cold War abroad spread to domestic affairs in the second Red Scare. Losing Eastern Europe and China to Communism and witnessing the Soviets develop an atomic bomb with alarming quickness convinced many Americans that secret information had been leaked. Adding to this situation were the relentless accusations from the House Committee on Un-American Activities that subversives were in the government, as well as several sensational "spy trials" involving secret documents allegedly sent to the Soviets. Early in 1950 an obscure Republican senator from Wisconsin, Joseph McCarthy, exploited this growing public fear. He launched an anticommunism campaign with a speech in Wheeling, West Virginia; he later repeated the speech in Congress due to some discrepancy over the exact number of names of communists McCarthy possessed. The speech, excerpted here, launched a four-year witch hunt during which outrageous accusations and fear of communist subversives in the government obscured evidence and substance.

Questions to Consider

1. To what does Joseph McCarthy attribute America's postwar problems?
2. Does McCarthy make a convincing argument that John S. Service should not work in the government?
3. What does this speech reveal about American fears in the early Cold War period?
4. Was Joseph McCarthy's influence on the United States positive or negative?
5. In what ways is McCarthy's views similar to those expressed by A. Mitchell Palmer after World War I ("The Red Scare," Document 171)?

Five years after a world war has been won, men's hearts should anticipate a long peace and men's minds should be free from the heavy weight that comes with war. But this is not such a period—for this is not a period of peace. This is a time of the "cold war." This is a time when all the world is split into two vast, increasingly hostile armed camps—a time of great armaments race.

Today we can almost physically hear the mutterings and rumblings of an invigorated god of war. You can see it, feel it, and hear it all the way from the hills of Indochina, from the shores of Formosa, right over into the very heart of Europe itself.

SOURCE: "Communists in Government Service," *Congressional Record*, 81st Congress, 2nd Session, part 2 (20 February 1950): 1952–54.

The one encouraging thing is that the "mad moment" has not yet arrived for the firing of the gun or the exploding of the bomb which will set civilization about the final task of destroying itself. There is still a hope for peace if we finally decide that no longer can we safely blind our eyes and close our ears to those facts which are shaping up more and more clearly. And that is that we are now engaged in a show-down fight—not the usual war between nations for land areas or other material gains, but a war between two diametrically opposed ideologies....

At war's end we were physically the strongest nation on earth and, at least potentially, the most powerfully intellectually and morally. Ours could have been the honor of being a beacon in the desert of destruction, a shining living proof that civilization was not yet ready to destroy itself. Unfortunately, we have failed miserably and tragically to arise to the opportunity.

The reason why we find ourselves in a position of impotency is not because our only powerful potential enemy has sent men to invade our shores, but rather because of the traitorous actions of those who have been treated so well by this Nation. It has not been the less fortunate or members of minority groups who have been selling this Nation out, but rather those who have had all the benefits that the wealthiest nation on earth has had to offer—the finest homes, the finest college education, and the finest jobs in Government we can give.

This is glaringly true in the State Department. There the bright young men who are born with silver spoons in their mouths are the ones who have been the worst.

Now I know it is very easy for anyone to condemn a particular bureau or department in general terms. Therefore, I would like to cite one rather unusual case—the case of a man who has done much to shape our foreign policy.

When Chiang Kai-shek was fighting our war, the State Department had in China a young man named John S. Service. His task, obviously, was not to work for the communization of China. Strangely, however, he sent official reports back to the State Department urging that we torpedo our ally Chiang Kai-shek and stating, in effect, that communism was the best hope of China.

Later, this man—John Service—was picked up by the Federal Bureau of Investigation for turning over to the Communists secret State Department information. Strangely, however, he was never prosecuted. However, Joseph Grew, the Under Secretary of State, who insisted on his prosecution, was forced to resign. Two days after Grew's successor, Dean Acheson, took over as Under Secretary of State, this man—John Service—who had been picked up by the FBI and who had previously urged that communism was the best hope of China, was not only reinstated in the State Department but promoted. And finally, under Acheson, placed in charge of all placements and promotions.

Today, ladies and gentlemen, this man Service is on his way to represent the State Department and Acheson in Calcutta—by far and away the most important listening post in the Far East.

Now, let's see what happens when individuals with Communist connections are forced out of the State Department. Gustave Duran, who was labeled as (I quote) "a notorious international Communist" was made assistant to the Assistant

Secretary of State in charge of Latin American affairs. He was taken into the State Department from his job as lieutenant colonel in the Communist International Brigade. Finally, after intense congressional pressure and criticism, he resigned in 1946 from the State Department—and, ladies and gentlemen, where do you think he is now? He took over a high-salaried job as Chief of Cultural Activities Section in the office of the Assistant Secretary General of the United Nations....

This, ladies and gentlemen, gives you somewhat of a picture of the type of individuals who have been helping to shape our foreign policy. In my opinion the State Department, which is one of the most important government departments, is thoroughly infested with Communists.

I have in my hand 57 cases of individuals who would appear to be either card carrying members or certainly loyal to the Communist Party, but who nevertheless are still helping to shape our foreign policy....

As you hear this story of high treason, I know what you are saying to yourself, "Well, why doesn't the Congress do something about it?" Actually, ladies and gentlemen, one of the most important reasons for the graft, the corruption, the dishonesty, the disloyalty, the treason in high Government positions—one of the most important reasons why this continues is a lack of moral uprising on the part of the 140,000,000 American people. In the light of history, however, this is not hard to explain.

It is the result of an emotional hang-over and a temporary moral lapse which follows every war. It is the apathy to evil which people who have been subjected to the tremendous evils of war feel. As the people of the world see mass murder, the destruction of defenseless and innocent people, and all of the crime and lack of morals which go with war, they become numb and apathetic. It has always been thus after war.

However, the morals of our people have not been destroyed. They still exist. This cloak of numbness and apathy has only needed a spark to rekindle them. Happily, this spark has finally been supplied....

202

Life in the Suburbs (1953)

Following World War II many young couples found a housing shortage in and near cities. Responding to the growing demand for new housing, William Levitt and his sons began construction of what some considered the first modern suburb—Levittown, New York—on a former potato farm. Introducing mass production techniques to the housing industry by building inexpensive, nearly identical "cookie-cutter" homes, the Levitts, and other large-scale builders who followed their practice, helped promote a white, middle-class suburban revolution in the 1950s. Because these neighborhoods were so different from previous communities, Harper's Magazine *reporter Harry Henderson was curious about the people who chose to live in these new suburbs and how this suburbanization phenomenon affected their lives. Over the course of three years, Henderson visited a number of suburbs and interviewed many residents, then wrote the article excerpted here, which offered his observations on life in these new communities.*

Questions to Consider

1. In what ways were the suburbs different from previous communities?
2. How was a suburban mentality shaped in this community?
3. In what ways did suburban living affect the lives of women?
4. According to the article, what were some of the positive attributes of suburban living? Negative aspects?

Since World War II, whole new towns and small cities, consisting of acres of near-identical Cape Cod and ranch-type houses, have been bulldozed into existence on the outskirts of America's major cities.

Begun as "veterans' housing," and still commonly called "projects," these new communities differ radically from the older urban areas whose slow, cumulative growth depended on rivers and railroads, raw materials or markets, industries and available labor. They also differ from the older suburbs which were built around existing villages. These new communities are of necessity built on open farmland—to house people quickly, cheaply, and profitably. They reflect not only the increased number of young American families, but an enormous expansion of the middle class via the easy credit extended to veterans.

The best known of these communities, Levittown, Long Island, is also the largest; its population is now estimated at 70,000. Lakewood, near Long Beach in the Los Angeles area, is a close second. Park Forest, some thirty miles south of Chicago—which has significant qualitative differences from the others, in that its social character was as conscientiously planned as its physical layout....

Socially, these communities have neither history, tradition, nor established structure—no inherited customs, institutions, "socially important" families, or "big houses." Everybody lives in a good "neighborhood": there is, to use that classic American euphemism, no "wrong side of the tracks." Outwardly, there are neither rich nor poor, and initially there were no older people, teen-agers, in-laws, family doctors, "big shots," churches, organizations, schools, or local governments. Since the builder required a large cheap site, the mass-produced suburbs are usually located at the extreme edge of the commuting radius. This means they are economically dependent on the big city, without local industry to provide employment and share tax burdens....

SOURCE: Harry Henderson, "The Mass-Produced Suburbs: How People Live in America's Newest Towns," *Harper's Magazine* 207 (November 1953): 25–32. Copyright © 1953 by Harry B. Henderson, Jr. Reproduced by permission.

At first glance, regardless of variations in trim, color, position of the houses, they seem monotonous; nothing rises above two stories, there are no full-grown trees, and the horizon is an endless picket fence of telephone poles and television aerials. (The mass builder seeks flat land because it cuts his construction costs.)

However one may feel about it aesthetically, this puts the emphasis on people and their activities. One rarely hears complaints about the identical character of the houses. "You don't feel it when you live here," most people say. One mother, a Midwestern college graduate with two children, told me: "We're not peas in a pod. I thought it would be like that, especially because incomes are nearly the same. But it's amazing how different and varied people are, likes and dislikes, attitudes and wants. I never really knew what people were like until I came here."

Since no one can acquire prestige through an imposing house, or inherited position, activity—the participation in community or group affairs—becomes the basis of prestige. In addition, it is the quickest way to meet people and make friends. In communities of strangers, where everybody realizes his need for companionship, the first year is apt to witness almost frantic participation in all kinds of activities. Later, as friends are made, this tapers off somewhat....

The populations differ strikingly from those of the older towns. The men's ages average 31 years; the women's about 26. Incomes fall somewhere between $4,000 and $7,000 yearly, although incomes in excess of this can be found everywhere. Their homes cost between $7,000 and $12,000. Roughly 90 per cent of the men are veterans. Their major occupational classifications are managers, professionals, salesmen, skilled workers, and small business men. Most communities also have sizable numbers of transient army families.

Buying or renting a home in one of these communities is, of course, a form of economic personal screening. As a result, there are no poor, no Negroes; and, as communities, these contain the best educated people in America. In Park Forest, where the screening was intensive, more than 5 per cent of the men and 25 per cent of the women are college graduates; the local movie theater survives by showing Westerns for the kids in the afternoon and foreign "art films" for the adults in the evening....

The daily pattern of household life is governed by the husband's commuting schedule. It is entirely a woman's day because virtually every male commutes. Usually the men must leave between 7:00 and 8:00 A.M. In most cases the wife rises with her husband, makes his breakfast while he shaves, and has a cup of coffee with him. Then she often returns to bed until the children get up. The husband is not likely to be back before 7:00 or 7:30 P.M.

This leaves the woman alone all day to cope with the needs of the children, her housekeeping, and shopping. (Servants, needless to say, are unknown). When the husband returns, he is generally tired, both from his work and his traveling. (Three hours a day is not uncommon; perhaps the most widespread dream of the men is a job nearer the community, and they often make earnest efforts to find it.) Often by the time the husband returns the children are ready for bed. The husband helps put them to bed; as they grow older, they are allowed to stay up later. Then he and his wife eat their supper and wash the dishes. By 10:00 P.M. most lights are out.

For the women this is a long, monotonous daily proposition. Generally the men, once home, do not want to leave. They want to "relax" or "improve the property"—putter around the lawn or shrubbery. However, the women want a "change." Thus, groups of women often go to movies together....

Many couples credit television, which simultaneously eased baby-sitting, entertainment and financial problems with having brought them closer. Their favorites are comedy shows, especially those about young couples, such as "I Love Lucy." Though often contemptuous of many programs, they speak of TV gratefully as "something we can share," as "bringing romance back." Some even credit it with having "saved our marriage." One wife said: "Until we got that TV set, I thought my husband had forgotten how to neck."

These are the first towns in America where the impact of TV is so concentrated that it literally affects everyone's life. Organizations dare not hold meetings at hours when popular shows are on. In addition, it tends to bind people together, giving the whole community a common experience....

Socially, the outstanding characteristic of these people is their friendliness, warmth, and lack of pretentious snobbery. Outgoing and buoyant, they are quick to recognize common problems and the need for co-operation; one does not find the indifference, coldness, and "closed doors" of a long-established community. There is much casual "dropping in" and visiting from house to house which results in the sharing of many problems and pleasures....

This is the big cushion which, while making life more enjoyable, protects the inhabitants of the new suburbs and solves their minor problems. It absorbs innumerable small transportation needs, puts up TV aerials, repairs cars, finishes attics, and carries the load of sudden emergencies. Nothing in these communities, to me, is more impressive than this uniform pattern of casual but warm friendliness and co-operation.

203

Governor Herman Talmadge's Statement on the *Brown* Decision (1954)

In the mid-1930s, the National Association for the Advancement of Colored People (NAACP) began to challenge school segregation in the hopes of ending the Jim Crow laws of the South. Their efforts culminated in the unanimous Supreme Court decision, Brown v. Board of Education of Topeka, Kansas (1954), which ended the "separate but equal" doctrine of racial segregation in public schools. Positive and negative responses to this decision were immediate. Georgia Governor Herman E. Talmadge, Jr. was among the first southern politicians to issue a public statement, which came the day after the Brown *decision. Talmadge had deep political roots in Georgia: His father was elected governor three times; the son filled the remainder of his father's last term and then was elected governor. Talmadge was proud that in his six years as governor, he spent more on public education for blacks and whites than had all previous administrations combined. In 1956, he was elected to the Senate and became a prominent opponent of the Civil Rights Act of 1957. His* Brown *decision statement, offered here, reflected the sentiments of many whites in the lower South.*

Questions to Consider

1. On what basis did Herman Talmadge attack the Supreme Court's decision?
2. What is Georgia's "accepted pattern of life"?
3. Why did the NAACP choose public education to challenge existing segregation laws?
4. In what ways will the South resist the *Brown* decision?

The U.S. Supreme Court by its decision today has reduced our Constitution to a mere scrap of paper. It has blatantly ignored all law and precedent and usurped from the Congress and the people the power to amend the Constitution and from the Congress the authority to make the laws of the land. Its action confirms the worst fears of the motives of the men who sit on its bench and raises a grave question as to the future course of the nation.

There is no constitutional provision, statute or precedent to support the position the court has taken. It has swept aside 88 years of sound judicial precedent, repudiated the greatest legal minds of our age and lowered itself to the level of common politics.

It has attempted in one stroke to strike the 10th Amendment from the Constitution and to set the stage for the development of an all-powerful federal bureaucracy in Washington which can regulate the lives of all the citizens in the minutest detail.

The people of Georgia believe in, adhere to and will fight for their rights under the United States and Georgia constitutions to manage their own affairs. They cannot and they will not accept a bald political decree without basis in law or practicality which overturns their accepted pattern of life.

The court has thrown down the gauntlet before those who believe the Constitution means what it says when it reserves to the individual states the right to regulate their own internal affairs. Georgians accept the challenge and will not tolerate the mixing of the races in the public schools or any of its public tax-supported institutions. The fact that the high tribunal has seen fit to proclaim its views on sociology as law will not make any difference.

If adjustments in our laws and procedures are necessary, they will be made. In the meantime all Georgians will follow their pursuits by separate paths and in accepted fashion. The U.S. and Georgia Constitutions have not been changed. The Georgia Constitution provides for separation of the races. It will be upheld.

As governor and chairman of the State Commission on Education I am summoning that body into immediate session to map a program to insure continued and permanent segregation of the races....

I urge all Georgians to remain calm and resist any attempt to arouse fear or hysteria. The full powers of my office are ready to see that the laws of our state are enforced impartially and without violence.

I was elected governor of Georgia on the solemn promise to maintain our accepted way of life. So long as I hold this office it shall be done.

204

Viewpoint on the Emmitt Till Murder Trial (1955)

The Supreme Court's unanimous decision in the Brown v. Board of Education of Topeka, Kansas *(1954) generated cautious hope among African Americans that public facilities would be integrated. Meanwhile, there was a strong undercurrent of white resistance to integration. During the summer of 1955, fourteen-year old Emmitt Till left Chicago, Illinois to visit family in Mississippi. While visiting the country store owned by Roy Bryant and his wife, Till was accused of whistling at Mrs. Bryant or making advances on the white woman. Within a few hours, Emmitt Till disappeared. His body was found a few days later in the Tallahatchie River, affixed to a cotton gin fan. His body was returned to Chicago for burial, and his mother insisted on an open-casket ceremony. Thousands came to pay their respects, and many African Americans found his funeral and the subsequent murder trial to be a galvanizing moment in the civil rights movement. The murder trial took place in September 1955. One of the leading African American newspapers in the country, the* Pittsburgh Courier, *sent reporter James Boyack to cover the trial. Below are Boyack's comments on the outcome of the trial.*

Questions to Consider

1. In what ways does Boyack express his anger about "Black Friday"?
2. What were the key moments in the trial for Boyack?

3. How does Boyack characterize Mississippi?

4. In what ways does the "miscarriage of justice" reveal the situation for African Americans in Mississippi?

SUMNER, Miss.—Tonight (Sept: 23) I'm sick ... in heart ... in soul ... in body!

This is "Black Friday" in Mississippi ... in America ... throughout the entire civilized world!

I've just witnessed the most revolting, the most disgusting, the most callous miscarriage of justice that has been my lot ... in more than twenty years of crime reporting.

I'm a hardened newspaperman ... a white reporter sent down here by my newspaper to cover the trial ... and tonight (Black Friday) I'm hanging my head in shame.

For five damnable days and nights, I've walked through this purgatory of racial tension ... this vale of hate, violence, fear ... this "hell hole" of American democracy, 1955 style!

Emmitt Till ... 14-year-old Chicago youth ... is DEAD!

But Mississippi's "unwritten law" that no all-white jury will convict ANY white man in the murder of a Negro has been upheld.

Tonight (Sept. 23), I can understand the full meaning of the quotation made by Westbrook Pegler years ago, when he wrote:

"If I were a Negro I would live in constant fury...."

★ ★ ★

I'll NEVER FORGET some of the mental pictures which are indelibly inscribed on my mind.

The picture of two white defendants ... balding, hairy-armed J. W. Milam and squint-eyed Roy Bryant ... greedily puffing their big black, fat cigars in the court room.

The "appeal to sentiment" spectacle of young "kids" ... children of the two defendants ... sitting through the trial. In Mississippi this is "routine," but I'd never want my son to witness such a spectacle.

The "phony" sad faces of the wives, who sat with their husbands throughout the trial, in an "obvious" attempt to drum up more sympathy.

The quavering voice of 64-year-old Moses Wright, uncle of the lynch victim, whose courage overcame his "fear," as he dramatically arose in the witness chair and pointed out Bryant and Milam as the "midnight visitors" to his home.

"There they are," he said ... and as he said it, some inner well of courage steadied his voice and stilled the shaking of his accusing finger.

It was a dramatic moment ... and Moses Wright was a courageous figure!

The tragic figure of Mrs. Mamie Bradley, as she told her story from the witness stand!

SOURCE: James Edmund Boyack, "Courier's James Boyack Hangs Head in Shame," *Pittsburgh Courier*, 1 October 1955, p. 1, 4.

The incredible speed with which the jury acted. The trial took five full days, with the exception of a few minutes ... the verdict was reached in SIXTY-SEVEN MINUTES!

★ ★ ★

AMERICANS WHO have never visited Mississippi ... who have never been subjected to the "fear complex" ... can't possibly understand what happens to a Negro in this state.

The Civil War was fought to make ALL AMERICANS free!

But Mississippi is still living in a civilization 100 years removed from 1955.

Sure ... Negroes outnumber the whites in this state.

But the whites have the law ... the guns ... the power!

They are a nation unto themselves, and the verdict today (Sept. 23) was a brazen attempt to "tell the world" that "nobody can run our business."

In an earlier story I told of interviewing a dozen whites here. I told *Courier* readers, then, that every white man I talked to, told me that Bryant and Milam would not be found guilty.

Mississippi was out to show up the NAACP!

Mississippi was out to show up Congressman Charles C. Diggs Jr., the "Nigra" Congressman from "up Nawth," that he couldn't intimidate them!

Mississippi was out to show them "damn Yankee" newspapermen just how "justice" is administered in our state.

Mississippi was out to show America that we can run our own business without outside interference.

And so ... a jury of their peers ... twelve white good men and true, made a mockery of justice in SIXTY-SEVEN MINUTES, and gave this nation a black eye in the court of world opinion which we'll never live down.

★ ★ ★

I LISTENED TO the wife of Roy Bryant. I heard her testimony and wondered if "God in His heaven" approved the things she said.

What she said couldn't be disputed ... because Emmett Till's story will never be told!

The prosecution says he's DEAD. But the defense has contended that the swollen, distorted, head-battered, bullet-pierced, victim dragged from the Tallahatchie River was NOT Emmett Till.

Who he was, they didn't say ... and didn't give a damn. Just another "nigra!" And a "nigra's" life is not important ... not in Mississippi!

The jury had what it needed to return a verdict.

"We, the jury, find the defendants NOT GUILTY."

I honestly believe that Judge Curtis M. Swango Jr. conducted a fair and impartial trial.

I honestly believe that District Attorney Chatham prosecuted sincerely.

★ ★ ★

WHAT IS THE meaning of the phrase: "Tried by a jury of his peers" …
when no Negro can serve on a jury in this state, because they are denied the
right to vote!

The trial itself had a regular Hollywood setting.

When the verdict was returned the defendants were mobbed by friendly
whites, whose very attitude seemed to say: "See, we took care of you. You
had nothing to worry about. You're at home in Mississippi boys, and we know
how to take care of our own."

Even the skies wept today as Mississippi meted out "justice" as they too well
know how!

The rains made it impossible to work … so the 180-seat courtroom was
jammed with almost 500, who shouted approval when the full impact of the
jury's verdict struck them.

Negroes were conspicuous by their absence … as the jury filed in!

Chatham and his assistant, former FBI lawyer Robert Smith, seemed
stunned.

Against local prejudice and heavy odds, they had lost a case, which they felt
they should have won.

Asked for a statement, Chatham turned a tired face towards me.

"The trial by jury is one of the sacred guarantees of our Constitution. I
accept the verdict and abide by it."

Thus ends "Black Friday" in Mississippi.

205

The Impact of Television (1955)

*Experimentation with broadcast television began in the late 1920s, but a host of difficulties
delayed its introduction to the public until after World War II. By the 1940s the existing
radio networks implemented their innovations in the fledgling broadcast television industry
(programming, "prime time shows," commercials), while wartime electronics assembly lines
shifted to begin mass production of television sets. After years of spending restraint in the
Great Depression and World War II, the post-war prosperity and the growing consumer
culture helped fuel the dramatic growth of the television industry. Businesses found television a convenient vehicle to market their products, while millions of Americans discovered
that it was an inexpensive form of entertainment. Shows appealing to women audiences,
children's programs, and family shows were developed. In 1947, the opening of Congress
was broadcast live on television, and some sporting events, such as baseball games, were
televised. By 1949, about one million households owned a television, and ownership was*

growing dramatically. Intrigued by the growing popularity of television and its influence on American society, the popular news magazine, U.S. News and World Report *produced a special report on the phenomenon. Excerpted below is the article that seeks to explain television's attraction and influence.*

Questions to Consider

1. According to the article, in what ways has television affected Americans?
2. How did Americans influence television?
3. Which of the three theories described in this selection seems most accurate?
4. To what extent is the commentary about television in this 1955 article relevant today?

The biggest of the new forces in American life today is television.

There has been nothing like it in the postwar decade, or in many decades before that—perhaps not since the invention of the printing press. Even radio, by contrast, was a placid experience.

The impact of TV on this country has been so massive that Americans are still wondering what hit them....

Two out of three U.S. families now own their own sets, or are paying for them. In 32 million homes, TV dials are flicked on and off, from channel to channel, at least 100 million times between 8 a.m. and midnight.

Everywhere, children sit with eyes glued to screens—for three to four hours a day on average. Their parents use up even more time mesmerized by this new marvel—or monster. They have spent 15 billion dollars to look since 1946.

Now, after nearly 10 years of TV, people are asking: "What hath TV wrought? What is this thing doing to us?"...

People have strong views. Here are some widely held convictions, both against and for television:

-   That TV has kept people from going places and doing things, from reading, from thinking for themselves. Yet it is said also that TV has taken viewers vicariously into strange and fascinating spots and situations, brought distinguished and enchanting people into their living rooms, given them a new perspective.

-   That TV has interfered with schooling, kept children from learning to read and write, weakened their eyesight and softened their muscles. But there are those who hold that TV has made America's youngsters more "knowing" about life, more curious, given them a bigger vocabulary. Teaching by TV, educators say, is going to be a big thing in the future.

-   That TV arouses morbid emotions in children, glorifies violence, causes juvenile crime—that it starts domestic quarrels, tend to loosen morals and make people lazy and sodden. However, it keeps families together at home,

SOURCE: "What TV Is Doing to America," *U.S. News and World Report* 39 (2 September 1955): 36–39. Copyright © 1955, U.S. News & World Report, L.P. Reprinted with permission.

provides a realm of cheap entertainment never before available, stimulates new lines of conversation.

- That TV is giving the U.S. an almost primitive language, made up of grunts, whistles, standardized wisecracks and clichés—that it is turning the average American into a stereotype. Yet it is breaking down regional barriers and prejudices, ironing out accents, giving people in one part of the country a better understanding of people in other parts.

- That TV is making politics "a rich man's game," turning statesmanship into a circus, handing demagogues a new weapon. But it is giving Americans their first good look at the inside of their Government, letting them judge the people they elect by sight as well as by sound and fury.

- That TV has distorted and debased salesmanship, haunting people with singing "commercials" and slogans. However, because or in spite of TV, people are buying more and more things they never before thought they needed or wanted....

On an average evening, twice as many set owners will be watching TV as are engaged in any other form of entertainment or leisure activity, such as movie-going, card playing, or reading. Seven out of 10 American children watch TV between 6 and 8 o'clock most evenings.

Analysts are intrigued by the evidence that adults, not children, are the real television fans. The newest trend in viewing habits is a rise in the number of housewives who watch TV in the morning. One out of five with a set now watches a morning show with regularity....

What does TV do to people? What do people do with TV? The researchers are digging into these questions all the time. In general, they come to theories, rather than conclusions. There are three main theories:

THEORY "A": This is widely held by people whose professions bring them into close contact with juveniles—judges, district attorneys, police officers, ministers. It assumes that TV is bound to be affecting the American mind and character because it soaks up one to five hours per day or more that used to be spent in outdoor play, in games requiring reasoning and imagination, or in reading, talking, radio listening, or movie-going.

Even the more passive of these pursuits, the theory runs, required more exercise of brain power than does TV watching. Then, too, many TV programs, the theorists say, are violent or in questionable taste.

Net effect, according to these people, is a wasting away or steady decline in certain basic skills among American youngsters. Children lose the ability to read, forfeit their physical dexterity, strength and initiative....

THEORY "B": Mainly held by sociologists, communication economists, pollsters. This is that television is changing the American mind and character, although nobody knows for sure just how. The evidence is too fragmentary.

The analysts are disturbed by some aspects of TV's effect on viewers. Some think TV is conditioning Americans to be "other directed," that is, getting their ideas from someone else....

A fancy name for this suspected effect of TV is "narcotic disfunction." This means that more and more men come home in the evening, drop into a chair in front of the TV set after supper and slip into a dream world of unreality....

THEORY "C": This is what the TV people themselves like to think. It is that television is rapidly becoming "one more service" to the U.S. public, another medium such as newspapers, magazines, radio. Some people watch TV a lot, others very little. Most people want a set around, but some don't lean on it....

Three out of every four TV programs are entertainment shows. If anything, the trend is toward a higher content of entertainment and a lower slice of information.

In a typical week of the peak TV season, in January of last year, crime, comedy, variety and Western shows accounted for 42.7 per cent of all TV program time on New York City screens. News accounted for 6.1 per cent of TV time—about the same share of time as was taken by quiz, stunt and contest shows. Other informational types of TV shows, such as interviews, weather reports, travelogues, children's instructional program and cooking classes, got 16.2 per cent of the time....

... In a two-week period last June, when two comedy programs, the "George Gobel Show" and "I Love Lucy," were at the top of the list, each reaching more than 13 million homes, the top-ranking informational programs were way down the line. The "March of Medicine," for example, was No. 62, "Meet the Press" was No. 150....

The public is fickle. Top rating is hard to hold. The viewers tire rapidly of a particular show unless the producers manage to come up with fresh material, new appeals.

206

Dwight D. Eisenhower's Farewell Address (1961)

Dwight D. Eisenhower served two consecutive terms as president in the 1950s. He brought to his job a wealth of military experience, but virtually no political seasoning. Born in Denison, Texas, but raised in Abilene, Kansas, Eisenhower finished West Point in 1915 and remained a part of the military for most of his life, serving as supreme commander of Allied forces in Europe during World War II. Pressured to seek the presidency in 1952, the popular war hero won easily on the Republican ticket. Eisenhower's presidency was often nonpartisan and conservative; he displayed the resourceful ability to stem domestic political and social forces, legitimatized many New Deal programs, and maintained many Cold War policies. Three days before leaving office, Eisenhower gave his "farewell address," which was broadcast live over radio and television. Drawing upon his knowledge of the military and changes that had taken place within the country, Eisenhower warned against dangers to American values and individual rights. His speech is excerpted here.

Questions to Consider

1. What changes have taken place regarding the military to prompt Eisenhower's warning?
2. What does he fear?
3. What does he ask Americans to do?
4. Do Eisenhower's concerns seem accurate today?

My fellow Americans:

Three days from now, after half a century in the service of our country, I shall lay down the responsibilities of office as, in traditional and solemn ceremony, the authority of the Presidency is vested in my successor....

We now stand ten years past the midpoint of a century that has witnessed four major wars among great nations. Three of them involved our own country. Despite these holocausts America is today the strongest, the most influential and most productive nation in the world. Understandably proud of this pre-eminence, we yet realize that America's leadership and prestige depend, not merely upon our unmatched material progress, riches and military strength, but on how we use our power in the interests of world peace and human betterment.

Throughout America's adventure in free government, our basic purposes have been to keep the peace; to foster progress in human achievement, and to enhance liberty, dignity and integrity among people and among nations. To strive for less would be unworthy of a free and religious people. Any failure traceable to arrogance, or our lack of comprehension or readiness to sacrifice would inflict upon us grievous hurt both at home and abroad.

Progress toward these noble goals is persistently threatened by the conflict now engulfing the world. It commands our whole attention, absorbs our very beings. We face a hostile ideology—global in scope, atheistic in character, ruthless in purpose, and insidious in method. Unhappily the danger it poses promises to be of indefinite duration. To meet it successfully, there is called for, not so much the emotional and transitory sacrifices of crisis, but rather those which enable us to carry forward steadily, surely, and without complaint the burdens

SOURCE: "Farewell Radio and Television Address to the American People," *Public Papers of the Presidents of the United States: Dwight D. Eisenhower, 1960–61* (Washington, DC, 1961), 1035–40.

of a prolonged and complex struggle—with liberty the stake. Only thus shall we remain, despite every provocation, on our charted course toward permanent peace and human betterment....

A vital element in keeping the peace is our military establishment. Our arms must be mighty, ready for instant action, so that no potential aggressor may be tempted to risk his own destruction.

Our military organization today bears little relation to that known by any of my predecessors in peacetime, or indeed by the fighting men of World War II or Korea.

Until the latest of our world conflicts, the United States had no armaments industry. American makers of plowshares could, with time and as required, make swords as well. But now we can no longer risk emergency improvisation of national defense; we have been compelled to create a permanent armaments industry of vast proportions. Added to this, three and a half million men and women are directly engaged in the defense establishment. We annually spend on military security more than the net income of all United States corporations.

This conjunction of an immense military establishment and a large arms industry is new in the American experience. The total influence—economic, political, even spiritual—is felt in every city, every statehouse, every office of the federal government. We recognize the imperative need for this development. Yet we must not fail to comprehend its grave implications. Our toil, resources, and livelihood are all involved; so is the very structure of our society.

In the councils of government, we must guard against the acquisition of unwarranted influence, whether sought or unsought, by the military-industrial complex. The potential for the disastrous rise of misplaced power exists and will persist.

We must never let the weight of this combination endanger our liberties or democratic processes. We should take nothing for granted. Only an alert and knowledgeable citizenry can compel the proper meshing of the huge industrial and military machinery of defense with our peaceful methods and goals, so that security and liberty may prosper together.

Akin to, and largely responsible for the sweeping changes in our industrial-military posture, has been the technological revolution during recent decades.

In this revolution, research has become central; it also becomes more formalized, complex, and costly. A steadily increasing share is conducted for, by, or at the direction of, the federal government....

It is the task of statesmanship to mold, to balance, and to integrate these and other forces, new and old, within the principles of our democratic system—ever aiming toward the supreme goals of our free society.

Another factor in maintaining balance involves the element of time. As we peer into society's future, we—you and I, and our government—must avoid the impulse to live only for today, plundering, for our own ease and convenience, the precious resources of tomorrow. We cannot mortgage the material assets of our grandchildren without risking the loss also of their political and spiritual heritage. We want democracy to survive for all generations to come, not to become the insolvent phantom of tomorrow.

Down the long lane of history yet to be written America knows that this world of ours, ever growing smaller, must avoid becoming a community of dreadful fear and hate, and be, instead, a proud confederation of mutual trust and respect.

Such a confederation must be one of equals. The weakest must come to the conference table with the same confidence as do we, protected as we are by our moral, economic, and military strength. That table, though scarred by many past frustrations, cannot be abandoned for the certain agony of the battlefield.

Disarmament, with mutual honor and confidence, is a continuing imperative. Together we must learn how to compose differences, not with arms, but with intellect and decent purpose. Because this need is so sharp and apparent I confess that I lay down my official responsibilities in this field with a definite sense of disappointment. As one who has witnessed the horror and the lingering sadness of war—as one who knows that another war could utterly destroy this civilization which has been so slowly and painfully built over thousands of years—I wish I could say tonight that a lasting peace is in sight.

Happily, I can say that war has been avoided. Steady progress toward our ultimate goal has been made. But, so much remains to be done. As a private citizen, I shall never cease to do what little I can to help the world advance along that road....

207

Poverty in the Age of Affluence (1962)

America in the 1950s and early 1960s was, as economist John Kenneth Galbraith labeled it, "the affluent society." Millions of Americans participated in steady economic growth as they experienced rising wages and enjoyed stable prices. Widespread use of electricity, indoor plumbing, and central heat as well as the introduction of television and automatic dishwashers in homes meant that many lived more conveniently than previous generations. However, not all Americans enjoyed this prosperity. In 1962 Michael Harrington published a powerful exposé about poverty amid plenty. In The Other America, he argued that over 40 million Americans—about 25 percent of the population—lived in poverty and were part of an "economic underworld" of unemployment, low-wage jobs, and despair. Harrington's landmark book influenced the Kennedy and Johnson administrations and helped launch the "war on poverty," a component of the "Great Society." Excerpted here is Harrington's depiction of poverty in America.

Questions to Consider

1. According to Michael Harrington, in what ways are those in poverty "invisible"?
2. Why is this invisibility important to Harrington?
3. Why does Harrington believe that poverty in this time period is new?
4. Why does Harrington believe "the other America" is trapped in a cycle of poverty?
5. In what ways are Harrington's ideas found in Johnson's speech on the "Great Society" ("Lyndon Johnson on the Great Society," Document 212)?

… The other America, the America of poverty, is hidden today in a way that it never was before. Its millions are socially invisible to the rest of us. No wonder that so many misinterpreted Galbraith's title and assumed that "the affluent society" meant that everyone had a decent standard of life. The misinterpretation was true as far as the actual day-to-day lives of two-thirds of the nation were concerned. Thus, one must begin a description of the other America by understanding why we do not see it.

There are perennial reasons that make the other America an invisible land.

Poverty is often off the beaten track. It always has been. The ordinary tourist never left the main highway, and today he rides interstate turnpikes. He does not go into the valleys of Pennsylvania where the towns look like movie sets of Wales in the thirties. He does not see the company houses in rows, the rutted roads (the poor always have bad roads whether they live in the city, in towns, or on farms), and everything is black and dirty. And even if he were to pass through such a place by accident, the tourist would not meet the unemployed men in the bar or the women coming home from a runaway sweatshop….

These are normal and obvious causes of the invisibility of the poor. They operated a generation ago; they will be functioning a generation hence. It is more important to understand that the very development of American society is creating a new kind of blindness about poverty. The poor are increasingly slipping out of the very experience and consciousness of the nation….

Now the American city has been transformed. The poor still inhabit the miserable housing in the central area, but they are increasingly isolated from contact with, or sight of, anybody else. Middle-class women coming in from Suburbia on a rare trip may catch the merest glimpse of the other America on the way to an evening at the theater, but their children are segregated in suburban schools. The business or professional man may drive along the fringes of slums in a car or bus, but it is not an important experience to him. The failures, the unskilled, the disabled, the aged, and the minorities are right there, across the tracks, where they have always been. But hardly anybody else is.

In short, the very development of the American city has removed poverty from the living, emotional experience of millions upon millions of middle-class Americans. Living out in the suburbs, it is easy to assume that ours is, indeed, an affluent society.

This new segregation of poverty is compounded by a well-meaning ignorance. A good many concerned and sympathetic Americans are aware that there is much discussion of urban renewal. Suddenly, driving through the city, they notice that a familiar slum has been torn down and that there are towering, modern buildings where once there had been tenements or hovels. There is a warm feeling of satisfaction, of pride in the way things are working out: the poor, it is obvious, are being taken care of....

Clothes make the poor invisible too: America has the best-dressed poverty the world has ever known. For a variety of reasons, the benefits of mass production have been spread much more evenly in this area than in many others. It is much easier in the United States to be decently dressed than it is to be decently housed, fed, or doctored. Even people with terribly depressed incomes can look prosperous....

Then, many of the poor are the wrong age to be seen. A good number of them (over 8,000,000) are sixty-five years of age or better; an even larger number are under eighteen. The aged members of the other America are often sick, and they cannot move. Another group of them live out their lives in loneliness and frustration: they sit in rented rooms, or else they stay close to a house in a neighborhood that has completely changed from the old days. Indeed, one of the worst aspects of poverty among the aged is that these people are out of sight and out of mind, and alone.

The young are somewhat more visible, yet they too stay close to their neighborhoods. Sometimes they advertise their poverty through a lurid tabloid story about a gang killing. But generally they do not disturb the quiet streets of the middle class.

And finally, the poor are politically invisible. It is one of the cruelest ironies of social life in advanced countries that the dispossessed at the bottom of society are unable to speak for themselves. The people of the other America do not, by far and large, belong to unions, to fraternal organizations, or to political parties. They are without lobbies of their own; they put forward no legislative program. As a group, they are atomized. They have no face; they have no voice.

Thus, there is not even a cynical political motive for caring about the poor, as in the old days. Because the slums are no longer centers of powerful political organizations, the politicians need not really care about their inhabitants. The slums are no longer visible to the middle class, so much of the idealistic urge to fight for those who need help is gone. Only the social agencies have a really direct involvement with the other America, and they are without any great political power....

As the society became more technological, more skilled, those who learn to work the machines, who get the expanding education, move up. Those who miss out at the very start find themselves at a new disadvantage. A generation ago in American life, the majority of the working people did not have high-school educations. But at that time industry was organized on a lower level of skill and competence. And there was a sort of continuum in the shop: the youth who left school at sixteen could begin as a laborer, and gradually pick up skill as he went along.

Today the situation is quite different. The good jobs require much more academic preparation, much more skill from the very outset. Those who lack a high-school education tend to be condemned to the economic underworld—to low-paying service industries, to backward factories, to sweeping and janitorial duties. If the fathers and mothers of the contemporary poor were penalized a generation ago for their lack of schooling, their children will suffer all the more. The very rise in productivity that created more money and better working conditions for the rest of the society can be a menace to the poor....

Poverty in the 1960's is invisible and it is new, and both these factors make it more tenacious. It is more isolated and politically powerless than ever before. It is laced with ironies, not the least of which is that many of the poor view progress upside-down, as a menace and a threat to their lives. And if the nation does not measure up to the challenge of automation, poverty in the 1960's might be on the increase.

208

"The Problem That Has No Name" (1963)

The two decades following World War II marked the nadir of the feminist movement, as returning veterans and mass culture influenced women to assume domestic roles of mother and housewife and to forsake independent careers (even working mothers were criticized). Despite the prevailing attitude, significant changes were taking place. The number of women who received a college education increased rapidly, and more women, especially married women, joined the workforce. The feminist movement was revived in 1963 with Betty Friedan's best seller, The Feminine Mystique, *which is excerpted here. Friedan, a Smith College graduate, mother of three, and freelance writer, based her book partly on a questionnaire she sent to former classmates asking about their lives after school and partly on some further research. The book challenged the happy suburban housewife myth and found a receptive audience among many middle-class women who identified with its thesis. Friedan became an instant celebrity and spearheaded an active woman's rights campaign; in 1966 she helped found the National Organization for Women (NOW).*

Questions to Consider

1. According to Betty Friedan, how were women pressured into accepting the role of "housewife" in the post–World War II years?

2. What is the "problem that has no name"? What caused the problem?

3. What solutions does Friedan suggest? Who was the audience?

4. In what ways are Friedan's ideas similar to those expressed by Jane Addams ("Why Women Should Vote," Document 158) and Dorothy Dunbar Bromley ("The New Woman," Document 178)? How are they different? In comparing these documents, what conclusions might you draw about the changing status of women?

The problem lay buried, unspoken, for many years in the minds of American women. It was a strange stirring, a sense of dissatisfaction, a yearning that women suffered in the middle of the twentieth century in the United States. Each suburban wife struggled with it alone. As she made the beds, shopped for groceries, matched slipcover material, ate peanut butter sandwiches with her children, chauffeured Cub Scouts and Brownies, lay beside her husband at night—she was afraid to ask even of herself the silent question—"Is this all?"

For over fifteen years there was no word of this yearning in the millions of words written about women, for women, in all the columns, books and articles by experts telling women their role was to seek fulfillment as wives and mothers. Over and over women heard in voices of tradition and of Freudian sophistication that they could desire no greater destiny than to glory in their own femininity. Experts told them how to catch a man and keep him, how to breastfeed children and handle their toilet training, how to cope with sibling rivalry and adolescent rebellion; how to buy a dishwasher, bake bread, cook gourmet snails, and build a swimming pool with their own hands; how to dress, look, and act more feminine and make marriage more exciting; how to keep their husbands from dying young and their sons from growing into delinquents. They were taught to pity the neurotic, unfeminine, unhappy women who wanted to be poets or physicists or presidents. They learned that truly feminine women do not want careers, higher education, political rights—the independence and the opportunities that the old-fashioned feminists fought for. Some women, in their forties and fifties, still remembered painfully giving up those dreams, but most of the younger women no longer even thought about them. A thousand expert voices applauded their femininity, their adjustment, their new maturity. All they had to do was devote their lives from earliest girlhood to finding a husband and bearing children....

In the fifteen years after World War II, this mystique of feminine fulfillment became the cherished and self-perpetuating core of contemporary American culture. Millions of women lived their lives in the image of those pretty pictures of the American suburban housewife, kissing their husbands goodbye in front of the picture window, depositing their stationwagonsful of children at school, and smiling as they ran the new electric waxer over the spotless kitchen floor. They baked their own bread, sewed their own and their children's clothes, kept their new washing machines and dryers running all day. They changed the sheets on the beds twice a week instead of once, took the rug-hooking class in adult education, and pitied their poor frustrated mothers, who had dreamed of having a career. Their only dream was to be perfect wives and mothers; their highest ambition to have five children and a beautiful house, their only fight to get and keep their husbands. They had no thought for the unfeminine problems of the world outside the home; they wanted the men to make the major decisions. They gloried in their role as women, and wrote proudly to make the major decisions. They gloried in their role as women, and wrote proudly on the census blank: "Occupation: housewife."...

If a woman had a problem in the 1950's and 1960's, she knew that something must be wrong with her marriage, or with herself. Other women were satisfied with their lives, she thought. What kind of a woman was she if she did not feel this mysterious fulfillment waxing the kitchen floor? She was so ashamed to admit her dissatisfaction that she never knew how many other women shared it. If she tried to tell her husband, he didn't understand what she was talking about. She did not really understand it herself. For over fifteen years women in America found it harder to talk about this problem than about sex. Even the psychoanalysts had no name for it. When a woman did, she would say, "I'm so ashamed," or "I must be hopelessly neurotic."...

Gradually I came to realize that the problem that has no name was shared by countless women in America.... The groping words I heard from other women, on quiet afternoons when children were at school or on quiet evenings when husbands worked late, I think I understood first as a woman long before I understood their larger social and psychological implications.

Just what was this problem that has no name? What were the words women used when they tried to express it? Sometimes a woman would say "I feel empty somehow ... incomplete." Or she would say, "I feel as if I don't exist." Sometimes she blotted out the feeling with a tranquilizer. Sometimes she thought the problem was with her husband, or her children, or that what she really needed was to redecorate her house, or move to a better neighborhood, or have an affair, or another baby. Sometimes, she went to a doctor with symptoms she could hardly describe: "A tired feeling ... I get so angry with the children it scares me ... I feel like crying without any reason." (A Cleveland doctor called it "the housewife's syndrome.") ...

It is no longer possible to ignore that voice, to dismiss the desperation of so many American women. This is not what being a woman means, no matter what the experts say. For human suffering there is a reason; perhaps the reason has not been found because the right questions have not been asked, or pressed far enough. I do not accept the answer that there is no problem because American women have luxuries that women in other times and lands never dreamed of; part of the strange newness of the problem is that it cannot be understood in terms of the age-old material problems of man: poverty, sickness, hunger, cold....

It is no longer possible today to blame the problem on loss of femininity: to say that education and independence and equality with men have made American women unfeminine. I have heard so many women try to deny this dissatisfied voice within themselves because it does not fit the pretty-picture of femininity the experts have given them. I think, in fact, that this is the first clue to the mystery: the problem cannot be understood in the generally accepted terms by which scientists have studied women, doctors have treated them, counselors have advised them, and writers have written them. Women who suffer this problem in whom this voice is tiring, have lived their whole lives in the pursuit of feminine fulfillment. They are not career women (although career women may have other problems); they are women whose greatest ambition has been marriage and children. For the oldest of these women, these daughters of the American middle class, no other dream was possible. The ones in their forties and fifties who once had other dreams gave them up and threw themselves joyously into life as housewives. For the youngest, the new wives and mothers, this was the only dream. They are the ones who quit high school and college to marry, or marked time in some job in which they had no real interest until they married. These women are very "feminine" in the usual sense, and yet they still suffer the problem....

If I am right, the problem that has no name stirring in the midst of so many American women today is not a matter of loss of femininity or too much education, or demands of domesticity. It is far more important than anyone recognizes. It is the key to women and their husbands and children, and puzzling their doctors and educators for years. It may well be the key to our future as a nation and a culture. We can no longer ignore that voice within women that says: "I want something more than my husband and my children and my home."

24

The Turbulent Sixties

M any Americans believed they stood at the beginning of a new era as the 1960s began. An exuberant belief that government could solve virtually any problem seemed to assure that the nation would enjoy continued peace and prosperity. The events of the decade quickly shattered these hopes. America's effort to check the spread of Communism led it into Vietnam, an issue that ultimately divided the nation. On the domestic front, the fight for civil rights continued, despite an increase in violence. Many of the children who had grown up in prosperous surroundings of the 1950s entered colleges in record numbers and soon questioned many of the most cherished beliefs of their parents' generation. The following documents illustrate the idealism, disillusion, and turmoil that characterized the period.

209

Silent Spring (1962)

After the initial surge of public awareness about conservation in the early twentieth century, the movement to conserve natural resources and preserve natural lands lost momentum. However, in the post–World War II period, the desire to improve the quality of life contributed to the emergence of a powerful environmental movement. The increased use of automobiles and some businesses polluted the air; many major cities, Los Angeles especially, experienced poor air quality. Certain industrial processes and the growing use of household washing machines dumped alarming amounts of chemicals into rivers and streams, contributing to water pollution. Nuclear weapons testing and the growth of atomic power plants generated alarms about radiation. And the use and disposal of some toxic chemicals was haphazard. In 1962, naturalist Rachel Carson sounded an alarm about the environment when she published Silent Spring, *one of the most influential books of the last half of the twentieth century. Trained as a biologist and equipped with gifted writing skills, she eloquently explained that the uncontrolled use of chemical pesticides—especially DDT—to improve crop yields or to eradicate harmful insects had disastrous environmental consequences. Her best-selling book helped spark the environmental movement in the 1960s. The excerpt here is from* Silent Spring.

Questions to Consider

1. According to Carson, in what ways was the pesticide aldrin most alarming?
2. Does Carson suggest alternatives to limiting harmful insects such as the Japanese beetle?
3. What does Carson hope to accomplish with her depiction?
4. How do you think Carson might respond to the growth of suburbia? Why?

During the fall of 1959 some 27,000 acres in southeastern Michigan, including numerous suburbs of Detroit, were heavily dusted from the air with pellets of aldrin, one of the most dangerous of all the chlorinated hydrocarbons. The program was conducted by the Michigan Department of Agriculture with the cooperation of the United States Department of Agriculture; its announced purpose was control of the Japanese beetle....

From its original point of entrance the Japanese beetle has spread rather widely throughout many of the states east of the Mississippi, where conditions of temperature and rainfall are suitable for it. Each year some outward movement beyond the existing boundaries of its distribution usually takes place. In the eastern areas where the beetles have been longest established, attempts have been made to set up natural controls. Where this has been done, the beetle populations have been kept at relatively low levels, as many records attest.

Despite the record of reasonable control in eastern areas, the midwestern states now on the fringe of the beetle's range have launched an attack worthy of the most deadly enemy instead of only a moderately destructive insect, employing the most dangerous chemicals distributed in a manner that exposes large numbers of people, their domestic animals, and all wildlife to the poison intended for the beetle. As a result these Japanese beetle programs have caused shocking destruction of animal life and have exposed human beings to undeniable hazard. Sections of Michigan, Kentucky, Iowa, Indiana, Illinois, and Missouri are all experiencing a rain of chemicals in the name of beetle control.

The Michigan spraying was one of the first large-scale attacks on the Japanese beetle from the air. The choice of aldrin, one of the deadliest of all chemicals, was not determined by any peculiar suitability for Japanese beetle control, but simply by the wish to save money—aldrin was the cheapest of the compounds available. While the state in its official release to the press acknowledged that aldrin is a "poison," it implied that no harm could come to human beings in the heavily populated areas to which the chemical was applied. (The official answer to the query "What precautions should I take?" was "For you, none.") An official of the Federal Aviation Agency was later quoted in the local press to the effect that "this is a safe operation" and a representative to the Detroit Department of Parks and Recreation added his assurance that "the dust is harmless to humans and will not hurt plants or pets." One must assume that none of these officials had consulted the published and readily available reports of the United States Public Health Service, the Fish and Wildlife Service, and other evidence of the extremely poisonous nature of aldrin.

Acting under the Michigan pest control law which allows the state to spray indiscriminately without notifying or gaining permission of individual land-owners, the low-lying planes began to fly over the Detroit area. The city authorities and the Federal Aviation Agency were immediately besieged by calls from worried citizens. After receiving nearly 800 calls in a single hour, the police begged radio and television stations and newspapers to "tell the watchers what they were seeing and advise them it was safe," according to the Detroit *News*.... as the planes went about their work the pellets of insecticide fell on beetles and humans alike, showers of "harmless" poison descending on people shopping or going to work and on children out from school for the lunch hour. Housewives swept the granules from porches and sidewalks, where they are said to have "looked like snow." As pointed out later by the Michigan Audubon Society, "In the spaces between shingles on roofs, in eaves-troughs, in the cracks in bark and twigs, the little white pellets of aldrin-and-clay, no bigger than a pin head, were lodged by the millions.... When the snow and rain came, every puddle became a possible death potion."

Within a few days after the dusting operation, the Detroit Audubon Society began receiving calls about the birds. According to the Society's secretary, Mrs. Ann Boyes, "The first indication that the people were concerned about the spray was a call I received on Sunday morning from a woman who reported that coming home from church she saw an alarming number of dead and dying birds. The spraying there had been done on Thursday. She said there were no birds at all flying in the area, that she had found at least a dozen [dead] in her backyard and that the neighbors had found dead squirrels." All other calls received by Mrs. Boyes that day reported "a great many dead birds and no live ones.... People who had maintained bird feeders said there were no birds at all at their feeders." Birds picked up in a dying condition showed the typical symptoms of insecticide poisoning—tremoring, loss of ability to fly, paralysis, convulsions.

Nor were birds the only forms of life immediately affected. A local veterinarian reported that his office was full of clients with dogs and cats that had suddenly sickened. Cats, who so meticulously groom their coats and lick their paws, seemed to be most affected. Their illness took the form of severe diarrhea, vomiting, and convulsions. The only advice the veterinarian could give his clients was not to let the animals out unnecessarily, or to wash the paws promptly if they did so. (But the chlorinated hydrocarbons cannot be washed even from fruits or vegetables, so little protection could be expected from this measure.)

Despite the insistence of the City-County Health Commissioner that the birds must have been killed by "some other kind of spraying" and that the outbreak of throat and chest irritations that followed the exposure to aldrin must have been due to "something else," the local Health Department received a constant stream of complaints. A prominent Detroit internist was called upon to treat four of his patients within an hour after they had been exposed while watching the planes at work. All had similar symptoms: nausea, vomiting, chills, fever, extreme fatigue, and coughing.

The Detroit experience has been repeated in many other communities as pressure has mounted to combat the Japanese beetle with chemicals. At Blue Island, Illinois, hundreds of dead and dying birds were picked up. Data collected by birdbanders here suggest that 80 per cent of the songbirds were sacrificed. In Joliet, Illinois, some 3000 acres were treated with heptachlor in 1959. According to reports from a local sportsmen's club, the bird population within the treated area was "virtually wiped out." Dead rabbits, muskrats, opossums, and fish were also found in numbers, and one of the local schools made the collection of insecticide-poisoned birds a science project....

210

Letter from Birmingham Jail (1963)

The Civil Rights Movement made sporadic gains in the decade following the Brown *decision, but not enough to please many Americans. Civil rights activism took the form of isolated local protests, which ultimately culminated in a massive social movement. The most famous incident was Rosa Parks's refusal to abandon her bus seat to a white rider (violating a city law) and the subsequent Montgomery bus boycott. One of the boycott's leaders was Martin Luther King, Jr. An eloquent Georgian who had recently received his PhD in theology from Boston University, he served as a Baptist minister in Montgomery. King adopted the nonviolent resistance tactics of India's Mahatma Gandhi to the Civil Rights Movement with great success. He helped form and led the clergy-based Southern Christian Leadership Conference (SCLC), and he emerged as the most prominent spokesman for African Americans. SCLC organized nonviolent direct action campaigns in cities throughout the South. When King was arrested for leading a Birmingham, Alabama, demonstration, several white clergymen wrote to King criticizing his tactics. King's response was his famous "Letter from Birmingham Jail," which is excerpted here.*

Questions to Consider

1. What are the central issues that King addresses in his letter?
2. Why was King disappointed in moderate whites in the South?
3. What social changes does King hope to accomplish?
4. What does this document reveal about the King-led Civil Rights Movement?
5. Compare King's proposal to that presented in "Malcolm X on Race Relations" (Document 211).

You deplore the demonstrations taking place in Birmingham. But your statement, I am sorry to say, fails to express a similar concern for the conditions that brought about the demonstrations. I am sure that none of you would want to rest content with the superficial kind of social analysis that deals merely with effects and does not grapple with underlying causes. It is unfortunate that demonstrations are taking place in Birmingham, but it is even more unfortunate that the city's white power structure left the Negro community with no alternative.

In any nonviolent campaign there are four basic steps: collection of the facts to determine whether injustices exist; negotiation; self-purification; and direct action. We have gone through all these steps in Birmingham. There can be no gainsaying the fact that racial injustice engulfs this community. Birmingham is probably the most thoroughly segregated city in the United States. Its ugly record of brutality is widely known. Negroes have experienced grossly unjust treatment in the courts. There have been more unsolved bombings of Negro homes and churches in Birmingham than in any other city in the nation. These are the hard, brutal facts of the case. On the basis of these conditions, Negro leaders sought to negotiate with the city fathers. But the latter consistently refused to engage in good-faith negotiation....

We have waited for more than 340 years for our constitutional and God-given rights. The nations of Asia and Africa are moving with jetlike speed toward gaining political independence, but we still creep at horse-and-buggy pace toward gaining a cup of coffee at a lunch counter. Perhaps it is easy for those who have never felt the stinging darts of segregation to say, "Wait." But when you have seen vicious mobs lynch your mothers and fathers at will and drown your sisters and brothers at whim; when you have seen hate-filled policemen curse, kick and even kill your black brothers and sisters; when you see the vast majority of your twenty million Negro brothers smothering in an airtight cage of poverty in the midst of an affluent society; when you suddenly find your tongue

SOURCE: Martin Luther King, Jr., *Why We Can't Wait* (New York: Harper & Row, 1964), 77–100. Reprinted by arrangement with The Heirs to the Estate of Martin Luther King, Jr., c/o Writers House, Inc., as agent for the proprietor New York, NY. *Copyright 1963 by Martin Luther King, Jr., copyright renewed 1991 by Coretta Scott King.*

twisted and your speech stammering as you seek to explain to your six-year-old daughter why she can't go to the public amusement park that has just been advertised on television, and see tears welling up in her eyes when she is told that Funtown is closed to colored children, and see ominous clouds of inferiority beginning to form in her little mental sky, and see her beginning to distort her personality by developing an unconscious bitterness toward white people; when you have to concoct an answer for a five-year-old son who is asking: "Daddy, why do white people treat colored people so mean?"; when you take a cross-country drive and find it necessary to sleep night after night in the uncomfortable corners of your automobile because no motel will accept you; when you are humiliated day in and day out by nagging signs reading "white" and "colored"; when your first name becomes "nigger," your middle name becomes "boy" (however old you are) and your last name becomes "John," and your wife and mother are never given the respected title "Mrs."; when you are harried by day and haunted by night by the fact that you are a Negro, living constantly at tiptoe stance, never quite knowing what to expect next, and are plagued with inner fears and outer resentments; when you are forever fighting a degenerating sense of "nobodiness"—then you will understand why we find it difficult to wait. There comes a time when the cup of endurance runs over, and men are no longer willing to be plunged into the abyss of despair. I hope, sirs, you can understand our legitimate and unavoidable impatience.

You express a great deal of anxiety over our willingness to break laws. This is certainly a legitimate concern. Since we so diligently urge people to obey the Supreme Court's decision of 1954 outlawing segregation in the public schools, at first glance it may seem rather paradoxical for us consciously to break laws. One may well ask: "How can you advocate breaking some laws and obeying others?" The answer lies in the fact that there are two types of laws: just and unjust. I would be the first to advocate obeying just laws. One has not only a legal but a moral responsibility to obey just laws. Conversely, one has a moral responsibility to disobey unjust laws. I would agree with St. Augustine that "an unjust law is no law at all."...

I hope you are able to see the distinction I am trying to point out. In no sense do I advocate evading or defying the law, as would the rabid segregationist. That would lead to anarchy. One who breaks an unjust law must do so openly, lovingly, and with a willingness to accept the penalty. I submit that an individual who breaks a law that conscience tells him is unjust, and who willingly accepts the penalty of imprisonment in order to arouse the conscience of the community over its injustice, is in reality expressing the highest respect for law....

I must make two honest confessions to you, my Christian and Jewish brothers. First, I must confess that over the past few years I have been gravely disappointed with the white moderate. I have almost reached the regrettable conclusion that the Negro's great stumbling block in his stride toward freedom is not the White Citizen's Counciler or the Ku Klux Klanner, but the white moderate, who is more devoted to "order" than to justice; who prefers a negative peace which is the absence of tension to a positive peace which is the presence of justice; who constantly says: "I agree with you in the goal you seek, but

I cannot agree with your methods of direct action"; who paternalistically believes he can set the timetable for another man's freedom; who lives by a mythical concept of time and who constantly advises the Negro to wait for a "more convenient season."...

You speak of our activity in Birmingham as extreme. At first I was rather disappointed that fellow clergymen would see my nonviolent efforts as those of an extremist. I began thinking about the fact that I stand in the middle of two opposing forces in the Negro community. One is a force of complacency, made up in part of Negroes who, as a result of long years of oppression, are so drained of self-respect and a sense of "somebodiness" that they have adjusted to segregation; and in part of a few middle-class Negroes who, because of a degree of academic and economic security and because in some ways they profit by segregation, have become insensitive to the problems of the masses. The other force is one of bitterness and hatred, and it comes perilously close to advocating violence. It is expressed in the various black nationalist groups that are springing up across the nation, the largest and best-known being Elijah Muhammad's Muslim movement. Nourished by the Negro's frustration over the continued existence of racial discrimination, this movement is made up of people who have lost faith in America, who have absolutely repudiated Christianity, and who have concluded that the white man is an incorrigible "devil."

I have tried to stand between these two forces, saying that we need emulate neither the "do-nothingism" of the complacent nor the hatred and despair of the black nationalist. For there is the more excellent way of love and nonviolent protest. I am grateful to God that, through the influence of the Negro church, the way of nonviolence became an integral part of our struggle....

211

Malcolm X on Race Relations (1964)

Not all African Americans supported the nonviolent, direct action campaigns of the mainstream Civil Rights Movement. Frustrated at the slow progress of change, some wanted a more demanding, more militant approach. Many of these advocates of Black Nationalism, or "Black Power" as it came to be called, were inspired by Malcolm X. Born Malcolm Little, he was a high school dropout and was jailed for an attempted burglary. While serving a ten-year prison term, he was converted to the separatist doctrine of Elijah Muhammad and the Nation of Islam. He adopted "X" to replace "the white slave-master name which had been imposed upon my paternal forebears by some blue-eyed devil." Released from prison, Malcolm X became a popular and controversial Black Muslim spokesman, who attracted large audiences—both black and white—because of his fiery rhetoric, charisma, and militancy on such topics as Black Nationalism, self-help, and white racism. After a 1964 pilgrimage to Mecca, where he witnessed white Muslims who were free of prejudice, Malcolm X softened his attacks on whites, rejected black separatism, and considered political power as essential for black advances. He would break from the Nation of Islam and form his own organization. In April 1964, just before leaving on his pilgrimage to Mecca, Malcolm X spoke to a New York audience, where he addressed issues of Black Nationalism and revolution. The speech is excerpted here.

Questions to Consider

1. What is the "black revolution" that Malcolm X discussed?
2. In what ways was he critical of the Civil Rights Movement?
3. How does Malcolm X believe the black revolution will come about?
4. How does this speech reveal both the militancy of Malcolm X as well as his moderating views toward whites?
5. Compare Malcolm X's message to that presented in King's "Letter from Birmingham Jail" (Document 210).

1964 will be America's hottest year; her hottest year yet; a year of much racial violence and much racial bloodshed. But it won't be blood that's going to flow only on one side. The new generation of black people that have grown up in this country during recent years are already forming the opinion, and it's a just opinion, that if there is to be bleeding, it should be reciprocal—bleeding on both sides....

So today, when the black man starts reaching out for what America says are his rights, the black man feels that he is within his rights—when he becomes the victim of brutality by those who are depriving him of his rights—to do whatever is necessary to protect himself. An example of this was taking place last night at this same time in Cleveland, where the police were putting water hoses on our people there and also throwing tear gas at them—and they met a hail of stones, a hail of rocks, a hail of bricks. A couple of weeks ago in Jacksonville, Florida, a young teen-age Negro was throwing Molotov cocktails.

Well, Negroes didn't do this ten years ago. But what you should learn from this is that they are waking up. It was stones yesterday, Molotov cocktails today; it will be hand grenades tomorrow and whatever else is available the next day. The seriousness of this situation must be faced up to. You should not feel that I am inciting someone to violence. I'm only warning of a powder-keg situation. You can take it or leave it. If you take the warning, perhaps you can still save yourself. But if you ignore it or ridicule it, well, death is already at your door-step. There are 22 million African-Americans who are ready to fight for independence right here. When I say fight for independence right here, I don't

SOURCE: "The Black Revolution," George Breitman and Betty Shabazz, eds., *Malcolm X Speaks* (New York: Pathfinder Press, 1989), 48–59. Copyright 1965, 1989 by Betty Shabazz and Pathfinder Press. Reprinted by permission.

means any nonviolent fight, or turn-the-other-cheek fight. Those days are gone. Those days are over....

This is a real revolution. Revolution is always based on land. Revolution is never based on begging somebody for an integrated cup of coffee. Revolutions are never fought by turning the other cheek. Revolutions are never based upon love-your-enemy and pray-for-those-who-spitefully-use-you. And revolutions are never waged singing "We Shall Overcome." Revolutions are based upon bloodshed. Revolutions are never compromising. Revolutions are never based upon negotiations. Revolutions are never based upon any kind of tokenism whatsoever. Revolutions are never even based upon that which is begging a corrupt society or a corrupt system to accept us into it. Revolutions overturn systems. And there is no system on this earth which has proven itself more corrupt, more criminal, than this system that in 1964 still colonizes 22 million African-Americans, still enslaves 22 million Afro-Americans.

There is no system more corrupt than a system that represents itself as the example of freedom, the example of democracy, and can go all over this earth telling other people how to straighten out their house, when you have citizens of this country who have to use bullets if they want to cast a ballot.

The greatest weapon the colonial powers have used in the past against our people has always been divide-and-conquer. America is a colonial power. She has colonized 22 million Afro-Americans by depriving us a first-class citizenship, by depriving us of civil rights, actually by depriving us of human rights. She has not only deprived us of the right to be a citizen, she has deprived us of the right to be human beings, the right to be recognized and respected as men and women. In this country the black can be fifty years old and he is still a "boy."...

All of our people have the same goals, the same objective. That objective is freedom, justice, equality. All of us want recognition and respect as human beings. We don't want to be integrationists. Nor do we want to be separationists. We want to be human beings. Integration is only a method that is used by some groups to obtain freedom, justice, equality and respect as human beings. Separation is only a method that is used by other groups to obtain freedom, justice, equality or human dignity....

We have to keep in mind at all times that we are not fighting for integration, nor are we fighting for separation. We are fighting for recognition as human beings. We are fighting for the right to live as free humans in this society. In fact, we are actually fighting for rights that are even greater than civil rights and that is human rights....

And today you have a new generation of black people who have come on the scene, who have become disenchanted with the entire system, who have become disillusioned over the system, and who are ready now and willing to do something about it.

So, in my conclusion, in speaking about the black revolution, America today is at a time or in a day or at an hour where she is the first country on this earth that can actually have a bloodless revolution. In the past, revolutions have been bloody. Historically you just don't have a peaceful revolution. Revolutions are bloody, revolutions are violent, revolutions cause bloodshed and death follows in their paths. America is the only country in history in a position to bring about a revolution without violence and bloodshed. But America is not morally equipped to do so....

And the only way without bloodshed that this can be brought about is that the black man has to be given full use of the ballot in every one of the fifty states. But if the black man doesn't get the ballot, then you are going to be faced with another man who forgets the ballot and starts using the bullet....

So you have a people today who not only know what they want, but also know what they are supposed to have. And they themselves are creating another generation that is coming up that not only will know what it wants and know what it should have, but also will be ready and willing to do whatever is necessary to see that what they should have materializes immediately. Thank you.

212

Lyndon Johnson on the Great Society (1964)

By the early 1960s, some paradoxes had developed in American society. Amid the prosperous times were growing numbers of people who lived in poverty; as the urban population increased, the infrastructure of roads and housing deteriorated; some public schools provided excellent educational opportunities while others, often in poor areas, lagged behind. In race relations, the contrast between whites and blacks was increasingly apparent. The Kennedy administration believed that the federal government should become more active in resolving problems to create a better society and had conceived of some programs to effect change. When Lyndon B. Johnson became president following Kennedy's assassination, he was able to win support for many of Kennedy's proposals. He also began creating his own program, which he called the "Great Society." In May 1964, Johnson spoke to students at the University of Michigan. The speech, excerpted here, provided a framework of the Great Society and its goals.

Questions to Consider

1. What is the Great Society that Johnson proposes?
2. Why does he target cities, rural areas, and education as the starting places for the Great Society?

3. How does he hope to accomplish the Great Society?

4. In what ways is the Great Society similar to the "New Nationalism" of Theodore Roosevelt (Document 159)? How is it different?

5. In what ways is the Great Society similar to Franklin Roosevelt's New Deal ("Franklin D. Roosevelt's First Inaugural Address," Document 182)? How is it different?

The challenge of the next half century is whether we have the wisdom to use that wealth to enrich and elevate our national life, and to advance the quality of our American civilization.

Your imagination, your initiative, and your indignation will determine whether we build a society where progress is the servant of our needs, or a society where old values and new visions are buried under unbridled growth. For in your time we have the opportunity to move not only toward the rich society and the powerful society, but upward to the Great Society.

The Great Society rests on abundance and liberty for all. It demands an end to poverty and racial injustice, to which we are totally committed in our time. But that is just the beginning.

The Great Society is a place where every child can find knowledge to enrich his mind and to enlarge his talents. It is a place where leisure is a welcome chance to build and reflect, not a feared cause of boredom and restlessness. It is a place where the city of man serves not only the needs of the body and the demands of commerce but the desire for beauty and the hunger for community.

It is a place where man can renew contact with nature. It is a place which honors creation for its own sake and for what it adds to the understanding of the race. It is a place where men are more concerned with the quality of their goals than the quantity of their goods.

But most of all, the Great Society is not a safe harbor, a resting place, a final objective, a finished work. It is a challenge constantly renewed, beckoning us toward a destiny where the meaning of our lives matches the marvelous products of our labor.

So I want to talk to you today about three places where we begin to build the Great Society—in our cities, in our countryside, and in our classrooms.

Many of you will live to see the day, perhaps 50 years from now, when there will be 400 million Americans—four-fifths of them in urban areas. In the remainder of this century urban population will double, city land will double, and we will have to build homes, highways, and facilities equal to all those built since this country was first settled. So in the next 40 years we must rebuild the entire urban United States....

The catalog of ills is long: there is the decay of the centers and the despoiling of the suburbs. There is not enough housing for our people or transportation for our traffic. Open land is vanishing and old landmarks are violated.

SOURCE: "Remarks at the University of Michigan, May 22, 1964," *Public Papers of the Presidents of the United States, Lyndon B. Johnson, 1963–64* (Washington, DC, 1965): 704–7.

Worst of all expansion is eroding the precious and time honored values of community with neighbors and communion with nature. The loss of these values breeds loneliness and boredom and indifference.

Our society will never be great until our cities are great. Today the frontier of imagination and innovation is inside those cities and not beyond their borders....

A second place where we begin to build the Great Society is in our countryside. We have always prided ourselves on being not only America the strong and America the free, but America the beautiful. Today that beauty is in danger. The water we drink, the food we eat, the very air that we breathe, are threatened with pollution. Our parks are overcrowded, our seashores overburdened. Green fields and dense forests are disappearing.

A few years ago we were greatly concerned about the "Ugly American." Today we must act to prevent an ugly America.

For once the battle is lost, once our natural splendor is destroyed, it can never be recaptured. And once man can no longer walk with beauty or wonder at nature his spirit will wither and his sustenance be wasted.

A third place to build the Great Society is in the classroom of America. There your children's lives will be shaped. Our society will not be great until every young mind is set free to scan the farthest reaches of thought and imagination. We are still far from that goal.

Today, 8 million adult Americans, more than the entire population of Michigan, have not finished 5 years of school. Nearly 20 million have not finished 8 years of school. Nearly 54 million—more than one-quarter of all America—have not even finished high school....

In many places, classrooms are overcrowded and curricula are outdated. Most of our qualified teachers are underpaid, and many of our paid teachers are unqualified. So we must give every child a place to sit and a teacher to learn from. Poverty must not be a bar to learning, and learning must offer an escape from poverty.

But more classrooms and more teachers are not enough. We must seek an educational system which grows in excellence as it grows in size. This means better training for our teachers. It means preparing youth to enjoy their hours of leisure as well as their hours of labor. It means exploring new techniques of teaching, to find new ways to stimulate the love of learning and the capacity for creation.

These are three of the central issues of the Great Society. While our Government has many programs directed at those issues, I do not pretend that we have the full answer to those problems....

The solution to these problems does not rest on a massive program in Washington, nor can it rely solely on the strained resources of local authority. They require us to create new concepts of cooperation, a creative federalism, between the national Capital and the leaders of local communities....

For better or for worse, your generation has been appointed by history to deal with those problems and to lead America toward a new age. You have the chance never before afforded to any people in any age. You can help build a society where the demands of morality, and the needs of the spirit, can be realized in the life of the Nation....

213

SDS Call for a March
on Washington (1965)

Since the end of World War II, presidential administrations sought to "contain" communist efforts to overthrow South Vietnam by providing military aid and advisors. In August 1964 two U.S. naval ships engaged North Vietnamese gunboats in the Gulf of Tonkin, off the coast of North Vietnam. President Lyndon Johnson asked Congress for permission to "take all necessary measures" to prevent further aggression, and the resulting Gulf of Tonkin Resolution gave Johnson the authority to escalate the war in Vietnam. Following an attack at Pleiku in February 1965 that left 8 Americans dead and more than 100 wounded, Johnson ordered sustained bombings of North Vietnam; in March, the first combat troops arrived in South Vietnam. By the end of the year, there were over 180,000 American troops in Vietnam; by the end of 1966, there were more than 380,000; and by 1969, there were over 500,000. The escalation of the war divided the nation. Among those who protested the war were college students, particularly members of the Students for a Democratic Society (SDS). In April 1965, the SDS sponsored the first major antiwar rally in Washington. But with the Johnson administration continuing to send more combat troops to Vietnam, the SDS announced another antiwar rally in Washington in November 1965. Following is an SDS leaflet that called for this protest outside the White House.

Questions to Consider

1. For what reasons does the SDS oppose the war in Vietnam?

2. How does the SDS propose to end the war?

3. Besides its opposition to the war, what does the SDS also hope to accomplish in Vietnam and in the United States?

4. How might Martin Luther King, Jr. ("Letter from Birmingham Jail," Document 210) or Malcolm X ("Malcolm X on Race Relations," Document 211) have responded to the call of the SDS?

SDS Call for a March on Washington

In the name of freedom, America is mutilating Vietnam. In the name of peace, America turns that fertile country into a wasteland. And in the name of democracy, America is burying its own dreams and suffocating its own potential.

SOURCE: TAKIN' IT TO THE STREETS: SIXTIES READER edited by Alexander Bloom and Wini Breines (1995) Chp. "SDS Call for a March on Washington" pp. 226–27. Copyright © 1995 by Alexander Bloom and Wini Breines. By permission of Oxford University Press, Inc.

Americans who can understand why the Negroes of Watts can rebel should understand too why Vietnamese can rebel. And those who know the American South and the grinding poverty of our Northern cities should understand that our real problems lie not in Vietnam but at home—that the fight we seek is not with Communism but with the social desperation that makes good men violent, both here and abroad.

THE WAR MUST BE STOPPED

Our aim in Vietnam is the same as our aim in the United States: that oligarchic rule and privileged power be replaced by popular democracy where the people make the decisions which affect their lives and share in the abundance and opportunity that modern technology makes possible. This is the only solution for Vietnam in which Americans can find honor and take pride. Perhaps the war has already so embittered and devastated the Vietnamese that that ideal will require years of rebuilding. But the war cannot achieve it, nor can American military presence, nor our support of repressive unrepresentative governments.

The war must be stopped. There must be an immediate cease fire and demobilization in South Vietnam. There must be a withdrawal of American troops. Political amnesty must be guaranteed. All agreements must be ratified by the partisans of the "other side"—the National Liberation Front and North Vietnam.

We must not deceive ourselves: a negotiated agreement cannot guarantee democracy. Only the Vietnamese have the right of nationhood to make their government democratic or not, free or not, neutral or not. It is not America's role to deny them the chance to be what they will make of themselves. That chance grows more remote with every American bomb that explodes in a Vietnamese village.

But our hopes extend not only to Vietnam. Our chance is the first in a generation to organize the powerless and the voiceless at home to confront America with its racial injustice, its apathy, and its poverty, and with that same vision we dream for Vietnam: a vision of a society in which all can control their own destinies.

We are convinced that the only way to stop this and future wars is to organize a domestic social movement which challenges the very legitimacy of our foreign policy; this movement must also fight to end racism, to end the paternalism of our welfare system, to guarantee decent incomes for all, and to supplant the authoritarian control of our universities with a community of scholars.

This movement showed its potential when 25,000 people—students, the poverty-stricken, ministers, faculty, unionists, and others—marched on Washington last April. This movement must now show its force. SDS urges everyone who believes that our warmaking must be ended and our democracy-building must begin, to join in a March on Washington on November 27, at 11 A.M. in front of the White House.

214

Views of the War in Vietnam (1967)

The United States' effort to prevent the spread of communism into South Vietnam led to a massive commitment of American blood and treasure. By 1967 over 400,000 troops were deployed in South Vietnam to prevent communists under the leadership of North Vietnam leader Ho Chi Minh from taking over the country. The United States claimed to be winning the war with its superior manpower and technology, often laying waste to villages and hamlets, bombing key cities and destroying the countryside with defoliants like Agent Orange and napalm, a jellied gasoline. The conflict also produced anti-war protests in the United States as well as tensions within the federal government over the rising costs of both the war effort overseas and the domestic programs of the Great Society. Below are three cartoons that make use of imagery to comment on some issues of the war in Vietnam in 1967.

Questions to Consider

1. What issues does "The Train Robbery" suggest?
2. In what ways does the second cartoon reveal the problems with the war effort?
3. What does the third cartoon imply about the war in Vietnam?
4. Compare these images with those depicting American participation in World War II ("The Second World War Homefront," Document 195)? What is similar? Different?

The Train Robbery

Norman Mansbridge, "The Train Robbery," *Punch*, 18 January 1967

SOURCE: Punch Cartoon Library and Archive

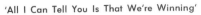

Paul Szep, "All I can tell you is we're winning," *Boston Globe* (1967)

SOURCE: Cartoon by Paul Szep.

**"THERE'S MONEY ENOUGH TO SUPPORT BOTH OF YOU ----
NOW, DOESN'T THAT MAKE YOU FEEL BETTER?"**

Herb Block, "There's Money Enough to Support Both of You," *The Washington Post*, 1 August 1967, p. A12

SOURCE: Library of Congress, Prints & Photographs Division, [LC-USZ62-132512]

215

"I Made Promises to Dead People" (1967–1968)

The Domino Theory, which warned that Communism must be halted before it spread, led U.S. policymakers to begin sending large numbers of U.S. troops to Vietnam in 1965. To many Americans, the Vietnam conflict seemed part of America's altruistic effort to make the world a better place. But increasingly, the war in Vietnam frustrated America. By 1968, over 500,000 Americans were deployed in Southeast Asia, and the United States' efforts to use its colossal military firepower and resources to defeat the communist Vietcong were ineffective. The war soon came to represent a hopeless cause that led to personal alienation and deep distrust of American institutions among many young Americans. The ensuing document records the insights of Jack McCloskey, an Army medic who served in Vietnam in 1967–1968.

Questions to Consider

1. Why do you suppose that nonwhites and poor whites seem to account for most of the soldiers in Vietnam?
2. According to Jack McCloskey, why did Vietnam veterans become so alienated?
3. How did returning veterans cope with this alienation?
4. What is the difference between McCloskey's perception of the war in Vietnam and his father's and uncles's perception of World War II?
5. After reading this document, how would you define patriotism?

What were your first impressions in Vietnam?

There was a lot of racial shit in Vietnam—in the rear especially. We'd go into Danang, and we'd see rebel flags and this bullshit. In the field, at least in my company, there was no racial tension whatsoever. I'd say 60 percent of my company was third world, Hispanic or black, and Native American. The rest were poor whites....

What was that experience like? How did it affect you?

SOURCE: Jack McCloskey, "I Made Promises to Dead People," in *Winter Soldiers: An Oral History of the Vietnam Veterans Against the War*, ed. Richard Stacewicz (New York, 1997), 96–100.

I remember the first guy I treated [voice cracks; tears in eyes]—a nineteen-year-old Marine who stepped on a bouncing betty [a mine that explodes at groin level]. I remember running up and him saying, "Doc, doc, I'm going to live, ain't I?" I said, "Sure, babe," and he died. I remember crying, holding his hand, and crying. I cried at the next one, I cried at the next one, and I cried at the next one, until I got to a point where I wanted to either jump up and shoot myself or shut down.

Inevitably you get close to people in Vietnam. I got close to people, and they got killed. At that point, Vietnam had robbed me of one of the greatest human dignities a person can have—that's the ability to cry; that's the ability to feel. It got to a point where I didn't want to know where guys were from in the company. I didn't want to know their backgrounds. If they get hurt, I'll treat them; just don't talk to me.

There was also, though, in Vietnam.... [Breaks down.] I have never, ever, in my life, had a family like that, and that family was destroyed. When you're on the line like that, sharing like that, when your life depends on the other person and his life depends on you, you become so close. If I could gain that feeling now, that tightness that I had in Vietnam, I would do anything for that; but I can't get it anymore back here, and that's where the love-hate relationship comes in....

Why?

This had become my family. By the time I returned to Vietnam, I was the senior medic in the company. There was a part of you that was God in Vietnam. You had to choose who would live and who would die. I went back because I thought I could make a better choice. I sometimes feel that was arrogance on my part. I felt that I was a very good medic. I did everything from tracheotomies to suturing people.

My last six months in Nam were with a helicopter assault battalion. We never had a base camp. We were aboard this ship called the *USS Tripoli*, and we would go all over, from Danang up to the DMZ [Demilitarized Zone], from three days to 30 days. We never knew where the fuck we were going. I remember being back on ship, never in the field that much. I'd start thinking of Casey and Allen [friends killed in action], remembering the good times, and I'd start shaking. I started using morphine. As a medic, I had an unlimited supply. I never mainlined; it was always in the asscheek or arm. Under that medication, I was able to remember the good times we had. I could get away from the horror. I could get away from their deaths....

I'd say from July of 1969, when I got out of the service, to September 1969, I never talked to anybody. Nobody. I then went to school at City College here [New York City], getting my A.A. degree [an associate's degree]. I never mentioned to anybody in school that I was a Vietnam veteran. Until I got involved, all I would do was go to school and get drunk, go to school and get drunk. I was not involved in anything. It wasn't until Kent State and Cambodia that I started getting active again. When they turned the guns against their own people here at Kent State, when I saw American people believing the lies about Cambodia, that was it.

What compelled you to speak out? Why not just go on with your life?

When you're in Vietnam, you dream—dream about your girlfriend, dream about your wife—but you're dreaming of what it was before you left. When we came back to the world, it wasn't the world we left: your girlfriend's changed, you've changed—even though you don't think you've changed—so you go through this psychological "Hey, what the fuck is this back here in the world? This is the world I fought for?" I come back. I don't understand it; it doesn't understand me.

In Vietnam you came back as an individual. Seventy-two hours before, you're in combat. Seventy-two hours later, you're here in the world. What you learned for survival in Vietnam are not the norms for survival back here in the world. The Vietnam vet came back to a society, most especially to those among our own peer group, that in a lot places in a lot of ways rejected them.

What do you do if you're eighteen or nineteen and you're from Harlem, you're a good machine gunner, you're a good medic, you're a good squad leader, you're a good mine-detector person, you're a good this, you're a good that? What do you do? For the first time in your life, you've been given responsibility, and you do a good job—and even if that good job means killing people, you've done a good job. [Then] you come back home, and you're just another nigger again?

You have to remember [that] the anger, the frustration, the alienation, that a lot of veterans came back with, to me are signs of sanity, not insanity. How else could you react to that situation?

This is why I'm very very proud that a lot of vets didn't fucking go off, didn't come back and start killing people, even as hurt and as painful as it was for them, they came back and didn't take their revenge out on the American public. In fact, they came back trying to change it.

You've got to remember that we were promised that if we go fight this war, we've got all this shit – we've got education, all these jobs waiting for us when we come home. What did it turn out to be? Bullshit. So I think it was a combination of seeing the war itself and understanding what that was about, and the other part of it, I think, for most white veterans that joined VVAW, was the shattering of the American dream. "I was given all these promises. I come home and they're not there."

I remember, when I first came back from Vietnam, trying to talk to my father, who had served in the Second World War; trying to talk to my uncles who had all served—but when I questioned my war, they thought I was questioning their war. They didn't want to hear it. I'm saying to them, "I'm not questioning your war. What you taught me, believing in America, believing in the Bill of Rights, I still believe in. The difference is [that] now I know my country can be wrong, and because I love my country, I want my country to start looking at that Bill of Rights." We did what we did because we loved our country and wanted our country to realize that it made mistakes. I am just as patriotic as my father or my uncle or anybody.

216

A Report on Racial Violence in the Cities (1968)

In the mid-1960s a series of race riots convulsed America. Frustrated with the slow gains of the mainstream, nonviolent Civil Rights Movement and the raised hopes of President Lyndon Johnson's Great Society, urban African Americans took matters into their own hands. Beginning with the Watts riot in Los Angeles in August 1965, each of the next three summers witnessed the eruption of widespread violence, property destruction, and looting within the black neighborhoods of cities like Detroit, Cleveland, Chicago, and Newark, New Jersey. Several hundred people died, thousands were injured, and millions of dollars worth of property was destroyed. President Johnson selected Otto Kerner, governor of Illinois and a strong civil rights advocate, as chair of a federal commission to investigate the "civil disorders." The commission's published findings, often called the Kerner Report, *offered the following explanation for the race riots of the 1960s.*

Questions to Consider

1. According to the *Kerner Report*, what has helped shape white racial attitudes?
2. According to the report, who were the rioters and why did they riot?
3. What solutions does the report offer?
4. How might Herman Talmadge ("Statement on the *Brown* Decision," Document 203), have responded to this report?

The record before this Commission reveals that the causes of recent racial disorders are imbedded in a massive tangle of issues and circumstances—social, economic, political, and psychological—which arise out of the historical pattern of Negro-white relations in America....

Despite these complexities, certain fundamental matters are clear. Of these, the most fundamental is the racial attitude and behavior of white Americans toward black Americans. Race prejudice has shaped our history decisively in the past; it now threatens to do so again. White racism is essentially accumulating in our cities since the end of World War II. At the base of this mixture are three of the most bitter fruits of white racial attitudes:

SOURCE: National Advisory Commission on Civil Disorders, *Report of the National Advisory Commission on Civil Disorders* (New York, 1968), 203–6.

Pervasive Discrimination and Segregation   The first is surely the continuing exclusion of great numbers of Negroes from the benefits of economic progress through discrimination in employment and education, and their enforced confinement in segregated housing and schools. The corrosive and degrading effects of this condition and the attitudes that underlie it are the source of the deepest bitterness and at the center of the problem of racial disorder.

Black Migration and White Exodus   The second is the massive and growing concentration of impoverished Negroes in our major cities resulting from Negro migration from the rural South, rapid population growth and the continuing movement of the white middle-class to the suburbs. The consequence is a greatly increased burden on the already depleted resources of cities, creating a growing crisis of deteriorating facilities and services and unmet human needs.

Black Ghettos   Third, in the teeming racial ghettos, segregation and poverty have intersected to destroy opportunity and hope and to enforce failure. The ghettos too often mean men and women without jobs, families without men, and schools where children are processed instead of educated, until they return to the street—to crime, to narcotics, to dependency on welfare, and to bitterness and resentment against society in general and white society in particular.

These three forces have converged on the inner city in recent years and on the people who inhabit it. At the same time, most whites and many Negroes outside the ghetto have prospered to a degree unparalleled in the history of civilization. Through television—the universal appliance in the ghetto—and the other media of mass communications, this affluence has been endlessly flaunted before the eyes of the negro poor and the jobless ghetto youth.

As Americans, most Negro citizens carry within themselves two basic aspirations of our society. They seek to share in both the material resources of our system and its intangible benefits—dignity, respect and acceptance....

Yet these facts alone—fundamental as they are—cannot be said to have caused the disorders. Other and more immediate factors help explain why these events happened now.

Recently, three powerful ingredients have begun to catalyze the mixture.

Frustrated Hopes   The expectations aroused by the great judicial and legislative victories of the civil rights movement have led to frustration, hostility and cynicism in the face of the persistent gap between promise and fulfillment. The dramatic struggle for equal rights in the South has sensitized Northern Negroes to the economic inequalities reflected in the deprivations of ghetto life.

Legitimation of Violence   A climate that tends toward the approval and encouragement of violence as a form of protest has been created by white terrorism directed against nonviolent protest, including instances of abuse and even murder of some civil rights workers in the South; but the open defiance of law and federal authority by state and local officials resisting desegregation; and by some protest groups engaging in civil disobedience who turn their backs on nonviolence, go beyond the Constitutionally protected rights of petition and free assembly, and resort to violence to attempt to compel alteration of laws and policies with which they disagree....

Powerlessness   Finally, many negroes have come to believe that they are being exploited politically and economically by the white "power structure." Negroes, like people in poverty everywhere, in fact lack the channels of communication, influence and appeal that traditionally have been available to ethnic minorities within the city and which enabled them—unburdened by color—to scale the walls of the white ghettos in an earlier era. The frustrations of powerlessness have led some to the conviction that there is no effective alternative to violence as a means of expression and redress, as a way of "moving the system." More generally, the result is alienation and the white society which controls them. This is reflected in the reach toward racial consciousness and solidarity reflected in the slogan "Black Power."

These facts have combined to inspire a new mood among Negroes, particularly among the young. Self-esteem and enhanced racial pride are replacing apathy and submission to "the system." Moreover, Negro youth, who make up over half of the ghetto population, share the growing sense of alienation felt by many white youth in our country. Thus, their role in recent civil disorders reflects not only a shared sense of deprivation and victimization by white society but also the rising youth throughout the society.

Incitement and Encouragement of Violence   These conditions have created a volatile mixture of attitudes and beliefs which needs only a spark to ignite mass violence. Strident appeals to violence, first heard from white racists, were echoed and reinforced last summer in the inflammatory rhetoric of black racists and militants. Throughout the year, extremists crisscrossed the country preaching a doctrine of black power and violence. Their rhetoric was widely reported in the mass media; it was echoed by local "militants" and organizations; it became the ugly background noise of the violent summer....

The Police   It is the convergence of all these factors that makes the role of the police so difficult and so significant. Almost invariably the incident that ignites disorder arises from police action. Harlem, Watts, Newark and Detroit—all the major outbursts of recent years—were precipitated by routine arrests of Negroes for minor offenses by white police.

But the police are not merely the spark. In discharge of their obligation to maintain order and insure public safety in the disruptive conditions of ghetto life, they are inevitably involved in sharper and more frequent conflicts with ghetto residents than with the residents of other areas. Thus, to many Negroes police have come to symbolize white power, white racism and white repression. And the fact is that many police do reflect and express these white attitudes. The atmosphere of hostility and cynicism is reinforced by a widespread perception among Negroes of the existence of police brutality and corruption, and of a "double standard" of justice and protection—one for Negroes and one for whites.

217

César Chávez and La Causa (1975)

For the thousands of migrant workers who toiled in the fields and orchards of California, life was difficult and demoralizing. Most of the migrants were Mexican Americans who received meager wages for backbreaking work, were forced to live in wretched migrant camps, and faced bitter racism that often excluded them from the democratic process or access to formal education. César Chávez sought to correct this situation. He was born in Arizona on his parents' farm, which they lost during the Great Depression; in 1939, when Chávez was twelve, his family became migrant workers. Chávez knew firsthand the hardships of Mexican American workers. Leaving the fields, he worked as an organizer for the Community Service Organization; but he resigned his position as director in 1962 to create a union for migrant farmworkers. He founded the Farm Workers Association (later called the United Farm Workers) that was known as La Causa. Chávez borrowed the tactics of nonviolent, direct action campaigns from India's Mahatma Gandhi and merged them with traditional labor strategies of prolonged strikes to gain recognition of the union. He also relied on volunteers from universities and religious organizations to help organize national boycotts (grapes, then lettuce) to bring growers to the bargaining table. Chávez was able to negotiate better wages and contracts for workers. In 1970 growers of California's table grapes signed contracts with the United Farm Workers. In 1975, Chávez described his accomplishments as well as the future of the union in his autobiography. It is excerpted here.

Questions to Consider

1. What were some obstacles that Chávez had to overcome to build a farmworkers' union?

2. Why does Chávez want the union to address the issues of political and economic power? How will this be done?

3. What does Chávez hope the union will accomplish?

4. In what ways is Chávez's description of the plight of immigrant labor similar to conditions described in "The Story of a Sweatshop Girl" (Document 150)? What conclusions can you draw from these similarities? What can you deduce about how American nationality is defined based on this document?

SOURCE: Jacques E. Levy, ed., *César Chávez: Autobiography of La Causa* (New York, 1975), 536–39. Reprinted by permission of Jacques E. Levy.

Once we have reached our goal and have farm workers protected by contracts, we must continue to keep our members involved. The only way is to continue struggling. It's just like plateaus. We get a Union, then we want to struggle for something else. The moment we sit down and rest on our laurels, we're in trouble.

Once we get contracts and good wages, we know the tendency will be for the majority to lose interest unless the Union is threatened or a contract is being renegotiated. The tendency will be for just a few to remain active and involved, while everybody else just holds out until something very big happens. That's true of other unions that we've seen; that's true of other institutions; that's true of our country.

To avoid that, to keep people's attention and continuing interest, we've got to expand and get them involved in other things. The Union must touch them daily.

Our best education, the most lasting, has been out on the picket line. But when the initial membership gets old and dies off, the new people coming in won't have had the same experience of building a Union. So we must get them involved in other necessary struggles.

Poor people are going to be poor for a long time to come, even though we have contracts, and economic action is an exciting thing for them. If they see an alternative, they will follow it. And we've probably got now the best organization of any poor people in all the country. That's why we can go any place in California where there are farm workers and get a whole group of people together and in action. We are hitting at the real core problems.

After we've got contracts, we have to build more clinics and co-ops, and we've got to resolve the whole question of mechanization. That can become a great issue, not fighting the machines, but working out a program ahead of time so the workers benefit.

Then there's the whole question of political action, so much political work to be done taking care of all the grievances that people have, such as the discrimination their kids face in school, and the whole problem of the police. I don't see why we can't exchange those cops who treat us the way they do for good, decent human beings like farm workers. Or why there couldn't be any farm worker judges.

We have to participate in the governing of towns and school boards. We have to make our influence felt everywhere and anywhere. It's a long struggle that we're just beginning, but it can be done because the people want it.

To get it done, there's a lot of construction work needed with our members. Many are not citizens, and others are not registered to vote. We must work toward the day when the majority of them are citizens with a vote.

But political power alone is not enough. Although I've been at it for some twenty years, all the time and the money and effort haven't brought about any significant change whatsoever. Effective political power is never going to come, particularly to minority groups, unless they have economic power. And however poor they are, even the poor people can organize economic power.

Political power by itself, as we've tried to fathom it and to fashion it, is like having a car that doesn't have any motor in it. It's like striking a match that goes out. Economic power is like having a generator to keep that bulb burning all the time. So we have to develop economic power to assure a continuation of political power.

I'm not advocating black capitalism or brown capitalism. At the worst it gets a black to exploit other blacks, or a brown to exploit others. At the best, it only helps the lives of a few. What I'm suggesting is a cooperative movement.

Power can come from credit in a capitalistic society, and credit in a society like ours means people. As soon as you're born, you're worth so much—not in money, but in the privilege to get in debt.

And I think that's a powerful weapon. If you have a lot of people, then you have a lot of credit. The idea is to organize that power and transfer it into something real....

As a continuation of our struggle, I think that we can develop economic power and put it into the hands of the people so they can have more control of their own lives, and then begin to change the system. We want radical change. Nothing short of radical change is going to have any impact on our lives or our problems. We want sufficient power to control our own destinies. This is our struggle. It's a lifetime job. The work for social change and against social injustice is never ended.

I know we're not going to see the change, but if we can get an idea and put legs under it, that's all we want. Let it go. Let it start, like the Union....

Actually, I can't see where the poor have fared that well under any political or economic system. But I think some power has to come to them so they can manage their lives. I don't care what system it is, it's not going to work if they don't have the power.

That's why if we make democracy work, I'm convinced that's by far the best system. And it will work if people want it to. But to make it work for the poor, we have to work at it full time. And we have to be willing to just give up everything and risk it all.

In the last twenty years, the farm workers' outlook has radically changed, just like day and night. Twenty years ago, to get one person to talk to me about the Union was an effort. They were afraid. Now, we've overcome that.

And the idea of serving without pay—they had never heard about that. Right now we need a good education program, a meaningful education, not just about the Union, but about the whole idea of the Cause, the whole idea of sacrificing for other people.

Fighting for social justice, it seems to me, is one of the profoundest ways in which man can say yes to man's dignity, and that really means sacrifice. There is no way on this earth in which you can say yes to man's dignity and know that you're going to be spared some sacrifice.

25

The Rising Conservative Tide

M any of the leading issues from the 1960s continued to divide the United States during the ensuing decades. In addition to the lingering turmoil from the 1960s, political corruption, a decline in the standard of living, and the failure of technology combined to erode the faith that many Americans had shared previously. Efforts to heal many of the divisions failed; indeed, new issues emerged and soon proved as divisive as the old. Reacting to what they called moral decay, conservatives became more active in politics and society— promoting a return to basic values, a more pro-business domestic stance, and a strongly anticommunist foreign policy in the hopes of reviving the nation's optimism. The ensuing selections reveal the issues that characterized this era.

218

Perspectives on Soaring Oil Prices (1973, 1974, 1976)

Since World War II the American standard of living rose continuously, in part because of inexpensive oil. Americans, long accustomed to plentiful abundance in most material goods, naively believed that natural resources, especially petroleum, were boundless. As domestic oil production declined in the 1960s, demand skyrocketed as more and more Americans drove automobiles and the economy became increasingly dependent on oil. The United States began importing increasing amounts of foreign oil, especially from the Middle East, to produce gasoline. In October 1973, this dependency was made shockingly apparent to the American public when several Arab nations imposed an oil embargo on countries that supported Israel in the "Yom Kippur War." After several months the embargo was lifted, but the Organization of the Petroleum Exporting Nations (OPEC) increased the price of crude oil and significantly cut production, which resulted in dramatically higher gasoline prices. Below are three cartoons that offer commentary on the rising costs of oil.

Questions to Consider

1. What issues about the oil embargo does the first cartoon convey?
2. In what ways does the second cartoon comment on America's increasing dependence on oil?
3. The third cartoon suggests what about OPEC?
4. What were the long-term implications of OPEC's actions?
5. How has America altered its "energy-hoggish ways"? With what success?

THE SUMMER OF 73

Paul Szep, "The Summer of '73," *Boston Globe*
SOURCE: Paul Szep

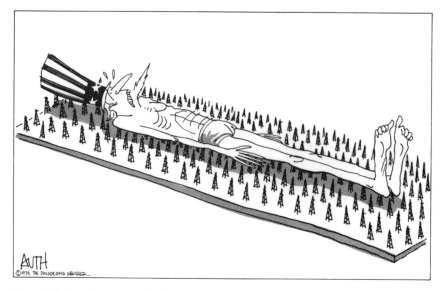

Tony Auth, "Uncle Sam's Bed of Nails," *Philadelphia Inquirer, 4* October 1974
SOURCE: Tony Auth

Don Wright, *Miami News*, 1976

SOURCE: Tribune Media Services

219

Sam Ervin on the Watergate Crisis (1974)

Due to the upheaval and paranoia of the times, the Nixon administration employed vindictive actions against those individuals who were critical of its policies. As the presidential election campaign of 1972 approached, several burglars were arrested after breaking into the Democratic Party's national headquarters in the Watergate complex in Washington, D.C. The burglars, it turned out, were employees of Nixon's reelection committee who planned to sabotage the Democratic Party's campaign. When Nixon learned of these arrests, he ordered a cover-up to thwart investigations that could link these men to his White House. Through intrepid reporting by Washington Post *journalists Carl Bernstein and Bob Woodward and their unnamed source, "Deep Throat" (later revealed to be FBI agent Mark Felt), the American public learned of these activities, prompting a congressional investigation chaired by Senator Sam Ervin (D-NC). At the end of the lengthy investigation, Sam Ervin commented on the activities of those within the Nixon administration in what was called the Watergate scandal. His views are excerpted here.*

Questions to Consider

1. According to the Sam Ervin, what had the Nixon administration done?
2. In what ways does Ervin characterize Nixon administration officials?
3. What are the limits of presidential power and prerogative?

Watergate was a conglomerate of various illegal and unethical activities in which various officers and employees of the Nixon re-election committees and various White House aides of President Nixon participated in varying ways and degrees to accomplish these successive objectives:

1. To destroy, insofar as the Presidential election of 1972 was concerned, the integrity of the process by which the President of the United States is nominated and elected.

2. To hide from law enforcement officers, prosecutors, grand jurors, courts, the news media, and the American people the identities and wrongdoing of those officers and employees of the Nixon reelection committees, and

SOURCE: U.S. Congress, Senate, *The Final Report of the Select Committee on Presidential Campaign Activities* (Washington, DC, 1974), 1098–102.

those White House aides who had undertaken to destroy the integrity of the process by which the President of the United States is nominated and elected.

To accomplish the first of these objectives, the participating officers and employees of the reelection committees, and the participating White House aides of President Nixon engaged in one or more of these things:

1. They exacted enormous contributions—usually in cash—from corporate executives by impliedly implanting in their minds the impressions that the making of the contributions was necessary to insure that the corporations would receive governmental favors, or avoid governmental disfavors, while President Nixon remained in the White House. A substantial portion of the contributions were made out of corporate funds in violation of a law enacted by Congress a generation ago.

2. They hid substantial parts of these contributions in cash in safes and secret deposits to conceal their sources and the identities of those who had made them.

3. They disbursed substantial portions of these hidden contributions in a surreptitious manner to finance the bugging and the burglary of the offices of the Democratic National Committee in the Watergate complex in Washington for the purpose of obtaining political intelligence; and to sabotage by dirty tricks, espionage, and scurrilous and false libels and slanders the campaigns and the reputations of honorable men, whose only offences were that they sought the nomination of the Democratic Party for President and the opportunity to run against President Nixon for that office in the Presidential election of 1972.

4. They deemed the departments and agencies of the Federal Government to be the political playthings for the Nixon administration rather than impartial instruments for serving the people, and undertook to induce them to channel Federal contracts, grants, and loans to areas, groups, or individuals so as to promote the reelection of the President rather than to further the welfare of the people.

5. They branded as enemies of the President individuals and members of the news media, who dissented from the President's policies and opposed his reelection, and conspired to urge the Department of Justice, the Federal Bureau of Investigation, the Internal Revenue Service, and the Federal Communications Commission to pervert the use of their legal powers to harass them for so doing.

6. They borrowed from the Central Intelligence Agency disguises which E. Howard Hunt used in political espionage operations, and photographic equipment which White House employees known as the "Plumbers" and their hired confederates used in connection with burglarizing the office of a psychiatrist which they believed contained information concerning Daniel Ellsberg which the White House was anxious to secure.

7. They assigned to E. Howard Hunt, who was at the time a White House consultant occupying an office in the Executive Office Building, the gruesome task of falsifying State Department documents which they contemplated using in their altered state to discredit the Democratic Party by defaming the memory of former President John Fitzgerald Kennedy, who as the helpless victim of an assassin's bullet had been sleeping in the tongueless silence of the dreamless dust for 9 years.

8. They used campaign funds to hire saboteurs to forge and disseminate false and scurrilous libels of honorable men running for the Democratic Presidential nomination in Democratic Party primaries.

During the darkness of the early morning of June 17, 1972, James W. McCord, security chief of the John Mitchell committee, and four residents of Miami, Fla., were arrested by Washington police while they were burglarizing the offices of the Democratic National Committee in the Watergate complex to obtain political intelligence. At the same time, the four residents of Miami had in their possession more than fifty $100 dollar bills which were subsequently shown to be a part of campaign contributions made to the Nixon reelection committees....

The arrest of McCord and the four residents of Miami created consternation in the Nixon reelection committees and the White House. Thereupon, various officers and employees of the Nixon reelection committees and various White House aides undertook to conceal from law-enforcement officers, prosecutors, grand jurors, courts, the news media, and the American people the identities and activities for the those officers and employees of the Nixon reelection committees and those White House aids who had participated in any way in the Watergate affair....

One shudders to think that the Watergate conspiracies might have been effectively concealed and their most dramatic episode might have been dismissed as a "third-rate" burglary conceived and committed for the courage and penetrating understanding of Judge Sirica, the thoroughness of the investigative reporting of Carl Bernstein, Bob Woodward, and other representatives of a free press, the labors of the Senate Select Committee and its excellent staff, and the dedication and diligence of Special Prosecutors Archibald Cox and Leon Jaworski and their associates.

Unlike the men who were responsible for Teapot Dome, the Presidential aides who perpetrated Watergate were not seduced by the love of money, which is sometimes thought to be the root of all evil. On the contrary, they were instigated by a lust for political power, which is at least as corrupting as political power itself.

They gave their allegiance to the President and his policies. They had stood for a time near to him, and had been entrusted by him with such great power, and longed for its continuance.

They knew that the power they enjoyed would be lost and the policies to which they adhered would be frustrated if the President should be defeated.

As a consequence of these things, they believed the President's reelection to be a most worthy objective, and succumbed to age-old temptations. They resorted to evil means to promote what they conceived to be a good end.

Their lust for political power blinded them to ethical considerations and legal requirements; to Aristotle's aphorism that the good of the man must be the end of politics; and to Grover Cleveland's conviction that a public office is a public trust.

They had forgotten, if they ever knew, that the Constitution is designed to be a law for rulers and people alike at all times and under all circumstances; and that no doctrine involving more pernicious consequences to the commonwealth has ever been invented by the wit of man that the notion that any of its provisions can be suspended by the President for any reason whatsoever.

On the contrary, they apparently believed that the President is above the Constitution, and has the autocratic power to suspend its provisions if he decides in his own unreviewable judgment that his action in so doing promotes his own political interests or the welfare of the Nation. As one of them testified before the Senate Select Committee, they believed that the President has the autocratic power to suspend the fourth amendment whenever he imagines that some indefinable aspect of national security is involved....

220

The Differences Between Men and Women (1977)

By the early 1970s the women's movement, led by the National Organization for Women (NOW), made gains in equality in education and employment. Some traditionally all-male schools—Yale, Princeton, University of Virginia, and the military academies—began admitting women, and female graduates from law and medical schools increased dramatically by 1980. In the workplace, however, women made more modest gains. Although some women were elected to political office and some were promoted to middle management positions, wages for women remained below those for men. In 1972 Congress sent an Equal Rights Amendment to the states for ratification. Despite these gains for women, disputes over abortion issues and equal rights splintered the women's movement. At the same time, a powerful backlash was developing. Helping this countermovement was Phyllis Schlafly, who organized opposition to the Equal Rights Amendment. Here is an excerpt from Schlafly's book, The Power of the Positive Woman, *in which she rebukes the feminists.*

Questions to Consider

1.   In what ways does Schlafly characterize the "women's liberationist"?
2.   In what ways does Schlafly compare the feminists to the "Positive Woman"?
3.   According to Schlafly, what are the differences between men and women?
4.   How might Betty Friedan ("The Problem That Has No Name," Document 208) and Dorothy Dunbar Bromley ("The New Woman," Document 178) have responded to Phyllis Schlafly's argument?

The first requirement for the acquisition of power by the Positive Woman is to understand the differences between men and women. Your outlook on life, your faith, your behavior, your potential for fulfillment, are all determined by the parameters of your original premise. The Positive Woman starts with the assumption that the world is her oyster. She rejoices in the creative capability within her body and the power potential of her mind and spirit. She understands that men and women are different, and that those very differences provide the key to her success as a person and fulfillment as a woman.

The women's liberationist, on the other hand, is imprisoned by her own negative view of herself and of her place in the world around her. This view of women was most succinctly expressed in an advertisement designed by the principal women's liberationist organization, the National Organization for Women (NOW), and run in many magazines and newspapers and as spot announcements on many television stations. The advertisement showed a darling curlyheaded girl with the caption: "This healthy, normal baby has a handicap. She was born female."

This is the self-articulated dog-in-the-manger, chip-on-the-shoulder, fundamental dogma of the women's liberation movement. Someone—it is not clear who, perhaps God, perhaps the "Establishment," perhaps a conspiracy of male chauvinist pigs—dealt women a foul blow by making them female. It becomes necessary, therefore, for women to agitate and demonstrate and hurl demands on society in order to wrest from an oppressive male-dominated social structure the status that has been wrongfully denied to women through the centuries.

By its very nature, therefore, the women's liberation movement precipitates a series of conflict situations—in the legislatures, in the courts, in the schools, in industry—with man targeted as the enemy. Confrontation replaces cooperation as the watchword of all relationships. Women and men become adversaries instead of partners.

The second dogma of the women's liberationists is that, of all the injustices perpetuated upon women through the centuries, the most oppressive is the cruel fact that women have babies and men do not. Within the confines of the women's liberationist ideology, therefore, the abolition of this overriding inequality of women becomes the primary goal. This goal must be achieved at

SOURCE: Phyllis Schlafly, *The Power of the Positive Woman* (New Rochelle, NY, 1977), 11–19. Reprinted by permission.

any and all costs—to the woman herself, to the baby, to the family, and to society. Women must be made equal to men in their ability *not* to become pregnant and *not* to be expected to care for babies they may bring into this world.

This is why women's liberationists are compulsively involved in the drive to make abortion and child-care centers for all women, regardless of religion or income, both socially acceptable and government-financed. Former Congresswoman Bella Abzug has defined the goal: "to enforce the constitutional right of females to terminate pregnancies that they do not wish to continue."

If man is targeted as the enemy, and the ultimate goal of women's liberation is independence from men and the avoidance of pregnancy and its consequences, then lesbianism is logically the highest form in the ritual of women's liberation. Many, such as Kate Millett, come to this conclusion, although many others do not.

The Positive Woman will never travel that dead-end road. It is self-evident to the Positive Woman that the female body with its baby-producing organs was not designed by a conspiracy of men but the Divine Architect of the human race. Those who think it is unfair that women have babies, whereas men cannot, will have to take up their complaint with God because no other power is capable of changing that fundamental fact....

The third basic dogma of the women's liberation movement is that there is no difference between male and female except the sex organs, and that all those physical, cognitive, and emotional differences you *think* are there, are merely the result of centuries of restraints imposed by a male-dominated society and sex-stereotyped schooling. The role imposed on women is, by definition, inferior, according to the women's liberationists....

Does the physical advantage of men doom women to a life of servility and subservience? The Positive Woman knows that she has complementary advantage which is at least as great—and, in the hands of a skillful woman, far greater. The Divine Architect who gave men a superior strength to lift weights also gave women a different kind of superior strength.

The women's liberationists and their dupes who try to tell each other that the sexual drive of men and women is really the same, and that it is only societal restraints that inhibit women from an equal desire, and equal enjoyment, and an equal freedom from the consequences, are doomed to frustration forever. It just isn't so, and pretending cannot make it so. The differences are not a woman's weakness but her strength....

The new generation can brag all it wants about the new liberation of the new morality, but it is still the woman who is hurt the most. The new morality isn't just a "fad"—it is a cheat and a thief. It robs the woman of her virtue, her youth, her beauty, and her love—for nothing, just nothing. It has produced a generation of young women searching for their identity, bored with sexual freedom, and despondent from the loneliness of living a life without commitment. They have abandoned the old commandments, but they can't find any new rules that work.

The Positive Woman recognized the fact that, when it comes to sex, women are simply not the equal of men. The sexual drive of men is much stronger than that of women. That is how the human race was designed in order that it might perpetuate itself. The other side of the coin is that it is easier for women to control their sexual appetites. A Positive Woman cannot defeat a man in a wrestling or boxing match, but she can motivate him, inspire him, encourage him, teach him, restrain him, reward him, and have power over him that he can never achieve over her with all his muscle. How or whether a Positive Woman uses her power is determined solely by the way she alone defines her goals and develops her skills.

The differences between men and women are also emotional and psychological. Without woman's innate maternal instinct, the human race would have died out centuries ago. There is nothing so helpless in all earthly life as a newborn infant. It will die within hours if not cared for. Even in the most primitive, uneducated societies, women have always cared for their newborn babies. They didn't need any schooling to teach them how. They didn't need any welfare workers to tell them it is their social obligation. Even in societies to whom such concepts as "ought," "social responsibility," and "compassion for the helpless" were unknown, mothers cared for their new babies....

The overriding psychological need of a woman is to love something alive. A baby fulfills this need in the lives of most women. If a baby is not available to fill that need, women search for a baby-substitute. This is the reason why women have traditionally gone into teaching and nursing careers. They are doing what comes naturally to the female psyche. The schoolchild or the patient of any age provokes an outlet for a woman to express her natural maternal need....

Finally, women are different from men in dealing with the fundamentals of life itself. Men are philosophers, women are practical, and 'twas ever thus. Men may philosophize about how life began and where we are heading; women are concerned about feeding the kids today. No woman would ever, as Karl Marx did, spend years reading political philosophy in the British Museum while her child starved to death. Women don't take naturally to a search for the intangible and the abstract. The Positive Woman knows who she is and where she is going, and she will reach her goal because the longest journey starts with a very practical first step.

221

The Question
of Affirmative Action (1978)

During the early 1970s, efforts were made to bring about a more integrated society. The Supreme Court ordered an end to segregation in public schools and ordered that students be bused out of their neighborhoods to achieve integration. Protests, especially from northern white families, led ultimately to a reversal on the busing issue. Also implemented in this period were affirmative action programs, which were designed to achieve racial equality in both the public and private sectors. Quotas—hiring a specific number of minorities—often were adopted to fulfill the mandates. In 1973 and 1974, Allan Bakke, a white in his late 20s, applied for admission to the Medical School of the University of California at Davis. He was denied both times, even though his admission rating was higher than that of minorities who were accepted. Bakke claimed the medical school's "special admissions program" for 16 minority students each year (out of an incoming class of 100) was illegal, and he sued for admission. The Supreme Court reached a decision in Regents of the University of California v. Bakke *in 1978. Excerpted here is the* Chicago Tribune's *editorial on the verdict and its significance.*

Questions to Consider

1. Why was the Supreme Court so divided on this issue?
2. Did the decision affect affirmative action programs?
3. Is it ever legitimate to use affirmative action to redress racial inequality? Gender inequality? Income inequality?
4. Does this case represent a backlash against gains made by the Civil Rights Movement?

The Supreme Court's long awaited, delicately balanced ruling in the Bakke "reverse discrimination" case can be welcomed by the whole spectrum of public opinion except for the extremities. The ruling's impact on existing affirmative action programs is minimal. Though many university admissions offices show some discretionary favor to "disadvantaged" individuals, few use the explicit racial quotas that the medical school of the University of California at Davis has used. This Supreme Court decision, sharply focused on university admissions, means little for other "affirmative action" contexts.

Of course the ruling is disappointing both to those who hoped the court would legitimize racial quotas and to those who hoped the court would outlaw any consideration of race in allocation of scarce opportunities. But everyone else can welcome it.

The court was anything but united. The decision itself was 5 to 4, with six opinions written. In a sense, Justice Powell determined the court's position. He agreed with four colleagues that Mr. Bakke should be admitted and that explicit racial quotas are invalid, and with his other four colleagues that race may properly be a factor in university admissions. The first four held that the Civil Rights Act of 1964 precluded race as a legal factor in admissions. The other four found no constitutional or statutory obstacle to explicit racial quotas. Because of Justice Powell, neither bloc of four altogether prevailed or was altogether outvoted.

Justice Thurgood Marshall, the only black on the court, wrote a separate opinion eloquently reciting the history of blacks' victimization by invidious racism. His reproaches of the Supreme Court's behavior in the decades following the Civil War are well justified. But his contention that court-countenanced discrimination then justifies court-countenanced reverse discrimination now is unconvincing. Two wrongs do not make a right. The objective of the courts and of society, when most faithful to our national aspirations, is justice. It is individuals who experience justice and injustice. Explicit racial quotas for admission to a medical school with no record of discriminating against a race are rightly held unfair to individual applicants [and all applicants are individuals] who had nothing to do with past discrimination against blacks.

But the bloc of four for which Justice Paul Stevens spoke is also unconvincing in its claim that Title VI of the Civil Rights Act of 1961 provides a sufficient basis for upholding Mr. Bakke and the California Supreme Court, and that no constitutional interpretation is necessary. The implication here is that, by definition, affirmative action is illegal. This would be intolerable. Congress has found no inconsistency in both enacting the Civil Rights Act and supporting affirmative action programs. For the court to have found some pervasive flaw in affirmative action programs, as many feared it might, would have a disastrous impact on current practice.

In a rather mysterious way, which resulted in the lonely position of a single justice becoming the decision of the court, the Supreme Court has rendered a balanced, judicious decision. As Atty. Gen. Griffin P. Bell, speaking for both himself and President Carter, said, the result is "a great gain for affirmative action"—as reasonably defined. It is a great gain, too, for academic freedom to exercise discretion. As Justice Powell affirmed, "The freedom of a university to make its own judgments as to education includes the selection of its student body"—as long as that selection is itself free from deliberate injustice and arbitrary quotas.

Because the Supreme Court's decision in the Bakke case was narrow rather than sweeping, it leaves numerous questions for later decision. It does not itself, one must hope, invite multiplied litigation. Academic admissions practices that comply with the Bakke decision can be so subjective, so plainly discretionary as to offer few handles for successful lawsuits. That may be frustrating to some of the losers, but any alternative would be damaging to many an individual and to both institutions and abstract justice.

222

Iranian Hostage Crisis (1979–1981)

Since the early 1950s, the United States had supported the shah of Iran's government, mainly as a supplier of oil and as a check on the Soviet Union's influence in the Middle East. By the late 1970s, the shah had become increasingly unpopular in Iran because of his repressive control and his efforts to westernize the country. When public demonstrations broke out in early 1979, the shah fled Iran; a powerful fundamentalist Islamic revolution, led by exiled religious leader Ayatollah Khomeini, swept the country. Days after President Jimmy Carter permitted the shah to enter the United States for medical treatment, militant Iranian students stormed the U.S. Embassy and took Americans hostage. The students demanded the return of the shah to Iran in exchange for the hostages' freedom. To complicate matters, the Soviet Union invaded neighboring Afghanistan just a few weeks after the hostages were seized. President Carter tried unsuccessfully to negotiate the release of the hostages and even ordered a secret military rescue mission that failed. Finally, the hostages were released after 444 days in captivity. The selection here comes from a congressional hearing on the Iranian crisis, where former Secretary of State Edmund Muskie and deputy Secretary of State Warren Christopher testified on behalf of the Carter administration.

Questions to Consider

1. What are the central issues of this hearing?
2. What was the impact of the hostage crisis on the United States?
3. How does Secretary of State Muskie defend the American position?
4. Why was the hostage crisis significant?

> **MR. WINN.**   … What if President Carter had said that within 48 hours after the hostages were seized on November 4, 1979, that we would bomb Qum [a religious center] if they were not released? What if we had threatened the power that we have?

SOURCE: "Iran's Seizure of the United States Embassy," *Hearings before the Committee on Foreign Affairs, February 17, 19, 25, and March 11, 1981* (Washington, DC, 1981): 171–77.

MR. MUSKIE. Well, then we would have been playing that old familiar game of chicken. If we made the threat and they did not respond to the threat we would have had to do it or we would not have had any credibility thereafter.

MR. WINN. Is it true the Russians told us within a week after that at the United Nations, "Do not have a military attack on Iran because of the hostages being seized, or we will have to retaliate."?

MR. MUSKIE. I am not aware of that, Congressman. I do not know about that. Chris?

MR. CHRISTOPHER. Nor am I.

MR. WINN. I was up there. The statement was not made but the rumors were pretty good. I do not know if they were throwing out smokescreens or not.

MR. MUSKIE. I may say this—and I am not sure I should say this much—but with respect to the situation in Iran following the invasion of Afghanistan, Iran became a very sensitive piece of real estate from our point of view in terms of Russian intentions, independent of the hostage situation—and I am sure it may have, from their point of view. The combination of the two has raised the visibility of Iran in terms of each country's perception of its security interests, I am sure. But I am not aware of any such exchange as you describe.

MR. CHRISTOPHER. Whether it was Monday morning or Tuesday morning or Wednesday morning or any day of the week I think it would have been a mistake to have given a 48-hour deadline with the consequences of our bombing Qum. My own judgment is Iran did not have the capacity at that time to bring itself to a decision to release the hostages and we would have been left in a situation where if we bombed the country, probably it would have cost the lives of all 53 hostages. I think it was a bad idea then and I think it is a bad idea now....

MR. MICA. Thank you, Mr. Chairman. Up to this point we have focused mainly on the status quo financial situation with the United States, what the United States has gained or lost financially. The comment essentially, is "Iran has learned a lesson. We have not lost anything financially and we achieved our goal of getting the hostages released." The thought that has been going through my mind is what have we done to deter terrorism in the future and, in fact, could you make a list of what the terrorists, those students, have gained or what may have been gained through Iranian eyes, what may be perceived throughout the world, and maybe raise this question simply for the purpose of raising it. I say to you very respectfully, I have no answers to these but these are some of the thoughts that I just jotted down. The terrorists had an opportunity to air their grievances to the world. They paraded the so-called victims of the Shah and propagandized the Shah's regime very heavily for 444 days before the world. They forced nations around the world, like Mexico, to heed to their demand not to accept the Shah. They did indeed rally their countrymen for 444 days behind a very nebulous and questionable cause in leadership. And as you said, Mr. Secretary, they even put into place their political institutions. They—encouraged I think by the atmosphere—created assaults on at least two other embassies during the period the hostages were taken, and in one case a life was lost, a U.S. Marine. I think more importantly—and you alluded to this in your opening comments—they impacted the future of the United States. They altered the future of the United States by impacting a U.S. Presidential election, numerous House races and Senate races throughout this country. I think they probably created a better situation for the Russians to look at Afghanistan with their aggressive intentions and, not to mention the lives lost in the rescue attempt, created havoc and a very poor feeling about the United States throughout the world for a long time. Something that may take years to correct. So as Mr. Solarz indicated, when we talk about no negotiation versus extended or protracted negotiation, would these possible benefits to terrorists lead us to seek a new approach that may be some-what other than bombing, but certainly not the type of public negotiation that would lead to the kind of situation we had?

MR. MUSKIE. You mentioned effects of the hostage crisis. Of course it had effects. It had effects on our political situation here in the United States. It resulted in a rescue attempt which cost some lives. It had effects. But none of those effects were included in the goals of those who seized the hostages. Their goals were to get the Shah back, to extract an apology from the United States, to achieve a condemnation of the United States worldwide on the basis of the years of the Shah's rule and our alleged involvement in his misrule. They did not achieve any of those goals that I can see. With respect to whether or not we have been diminished, that is a judgment call. I do not think we have. I think we might have been diminished if we had bombed Qum 48 hours later because they were in a position to respond to the threat. That might well have been perceived as misuse of power by one of the world's two superpowers.... So whatever means you use there are effects, but whether or not these militants achieved their goal is a different question. Of course they achieved some effect. They preoccupied our country for 14 months with an agonizing, frustrating situation that we would have preferred not to have lived through. But I do not see that as a benefit that offsets the costs which their country paid. Maybe they do. I would doubt it.

MR. MICA.   The statement is that the terrorists have learned a lesson. Their goals, as you stated, were very finite; apology, return of some wealth, but instead they have achieved a stability that may not have ever been. It may fall tomorrow. Have they come out better, and have they really learned a lesson because we protracted these negotiations to the extent we did?

MR. MUSKIE.   You speak of the incident and possible repetition of it as involving the same people. I do not know whether the same militants would try the same thing if we should reestablish diplomatic relations with Iran but with respect to acts of irrationality surely we live in a world in which we have seen it possible for people to create disruption, to threaten the peace, to disrupt communities. We have said it here in Washington. I saw nobody arguing we should not negotiate their release and the release was negotiated, as you can remember very well.... But the fact is Iran now is busy seeking to repair the rend in its relations, economic, diplomatic and otherwise with the rest of the world because it has come to learn it cannot live in a world alone. It lives in an interdependent world and if it fails to recognize that fact, Iran's real interests are seriously impacted. I think that is the lesson. Whether it would be a lesson terrorist minded people will absorb in the future I surely would not guarantee....

223

The Christian Right's Call to Action (1980)

In the late 1970s, as an evangelical movement swept the country, some people believed the United States was experiencing a religious revival comparable to the earlier Great Awakenings. Membership in churches rose, and large numbers of Americans considered themselves to be "born again." Evangelical ministers established their own radio and television stations and created their own religious programming, such as Pat Robertson's 700 Club or Jim Bakker's PTL (Praise the Lord), to reach an audience beyond the church pulpit. Many evangelicals broadened their message to a crusade against the evils of modern society. The Reverend Jerry Falwell of Virginia was among the most active in waging a "war against sin." In 1979 he founded the Moral Majority to provide political clout for the so-called Religious or Christian Right in their efforts to remove what they perceived as sinful portions of modern culture. Excerpted here is Falwell's call for a Bible-based, moral America and a justification for the Moral Majority.

Questions to Consider

1. According to Jerry Falwell, what are the major problems facing American society?
2. According to Jerry Falwell, what are the purposes of Moral Majority?
3. For what reasons is Falwell so pessimistic about the future of America?
4. What is the significance of this evangelical movement?
5. How is Reverend Falwell's message similar to that found in "Religion and the Scopes Trial" (Document 176)?

I believe that Americans want to see this country come back to basics, back to values, back to biblical morality, back to sensibility, and back to patriotism. Americans are looking for leadership and guidance. It is fair to ask the question, "If 84 per cent of the American people still believe in morality, why is America having such internal problems?" We must look for the answer to the highest places in every level of government. We have a lack of leadership in America. But Americans have been lax in voting in and out of office the right and the wrong people.

My responsibility as a preacher of the Gospel is one of influence, not of control, and that is the responsibility of each individual citizen. Through the ballot box Americans must provide for strong moral leadership at every level. If our country will get back on the track in sensibility and moral sanity, the crises that I have herein mentioned will work out in the course of time and with God's blessings....

While sins of America are certainly many, let us summarize the five major problems that have political consequences, political implications that moral Americans need to be ready to face.

1. ABORTION—Nine men, by majority vote, said it was okay to kill unborn children. In 1973, two hundred million Americans and four hundred thousand pastors stood by and did little to stop it. Every year millions of babies are murdered in America, and most of us want to forget that it is happening....

SOURCE: From Listen America! by Jerry Falwell, Copyright © 1980 by Jerry Falwell. Used by permission of Doubleday, a division of Random House, Inc.

2.   HOMOSEXUALITY—In spite of the fact that the Bible clearly designates this sin as an act of a "reprobate mind" for which God "gave them up" (Rm. 1:26–28), our government seems determined to legalize homosexuals as a legitimate "minority." The National Civil Rights Act of 1979 (popularly referred to as the Gay Rights Bill) would give homosexuals the same benefits as the 1964 Civil Rights Act, meaning they could not be discriminated against by any employing body because of "sexual preference."...

3.   PORNOGRAPHY—The four-billion-dollar-per-year pornographic industry is probably the most devastating moral influence of all upon our young people. Sex magazines deliberately increase the problem of immoral lust and thus provoke increased adultery, prostitution, and sexual child abuse....

4.   HUMANISM—The contemporary philosophy that glorifies man as man, apart from God, is the ultimate outgrowth of evolutionary science and secular education. In his new book *The Battle for the Mind*, Dr. Tim LaHaye argues that the full admission of humanism as the religion of secular education came after prayer and Bible reading were excluded from our public schools. Ultimately, humanism rests upon the philosophy of existentialism, which emphasizes that one's present existence is the true meaning and purpose of life. Existentialism has become the religion of the public schools. Applied to psychology, it postulates a kind of moral neutrality that is detrimental to Christian ethics. In popular terminology it explains, "Do your own thing," and "If it feels good, do it!" It is an approach to life that has no room for God and makes man the measure of all things.

5.   THE FRACTURED FAMILY—With a skyrocketing divorce rate, the American family may well be on the verge of extinction in the next twenty years. Even the recent White House Conference on Families has called for an emphasis on diverse family forums (common-law, communal, homosexual, and transsexual "marriages"). The Bible pattern of the family has been virtually discarded by modern American society. Our movies and magazines have glorified the physical and emotional experience of sex without love to the point that most Americans do not even consider love to be important at all anymore. Bent on self-gratification, we have reinterpreted our moral values in light of our immoral life styles. Since the family is the basic unit of society, and since the family is desperately in trouble today, we can conclude that our society itself is in danger of total collapse....

To change America we must be involved, and this includes three areas of political action:

1. REGISTRATION

A recent national poll indicated that eight million American evangelicals are not registered to vote. I am convinced that this is one of the major sins of the church today. Until concerned Christian citizens become registered voters there is very little that we can do to change the tide of political influence on the social issues in our nation. Those who object to Christians being involved in the political process are ultimately objecting to Christians being involved in the social process....

2. INFORMATION

Many moral Americans are unaware of the real issues affecting them today. Many people do not know the voting record of their congressman and have no idea how he is representing them on political issues that have moral implications. This is one of the major reasons why we have established the Moral Majority organization. We want to keep the public informed on the vital moral issues. The Moral Majority, Inc., is a nonprofit organization, with headquarters in Washington, D.C. Our goal is to exert a significant influence on the spiritual and moral direction of our nation by: (a) mobilizing the grassroots of moral Americans in one clear and effective voice; (b) informing the moral majority what is going on behind their backs in Washington and in state legislatures across the country; (c) lobbying intensely in Congress to defeat left-wing, social-welfare bills that will further erode our precious freedom; (d) pushing for positive legislation such as that to establish the Family Protection Agency, which will ensure a strong, enduring America; and (e) helping the moral majority in local communities to fight pornography, homosexuality, the advocacy of immorality in school textbooks, and other issues facing each and every one of us....

3. MOBILIZATION

The history of the church includes the history of Christians' involvement in social issues....

I am convinced that we need a spiritual and moral revival in America if America is to survive the twentieth century. The time for action is now; we dare not wait for someone else to take up the banner of righteousness in our generation. We have already waited too long....

Right living must be re-established as an American way of life. We as American citizens must recommit ourselves to the faith of our fathers and to the premises and moral foundations upon which this country was established. Now is the time to begin calling America back to God, back to the Bible, back to morality! We must be willing to live by the moral convictions that we claim to believe. There is no way that we will ever be willing to die for something for which we are not willing to live. The authority of Bible morality must once again be recognized as the legitimate guiding principle of our nation. Our love for our fellow man must ever be grounded in the truth and never be allowed to blind us from the truth that is the basis of our love for our fellow man.

224

The Reagan Revolution (1981)

As the decade of the 1980s began, a conservative mood pervaded the country; Ronald Reagan both symbolized and galvanized this atmosphere. Reagan, born in Illinois and a devoted New Deal Democrat, began his career as a radio broadcaster and then became a Hollywood actor until he moved into television as an actor and program host. In the early 1960s he switched to the Republican Party and was elected to two terms as governor of California by appealing to middle-class resentments—taxes and big government. Using these issues again in 1980, Reagan won the Republican Party nomination with the support of a powerful conservative coalition, and in the campaign against Democrat Jimmy Carter, he benefited from double-digit inflation and the Iranian hostage crisis associated with Carter. He won the election easily, beginning the "Reagan Revolution." Reagan's inaugural address, excerpted here, established the initial broad themes of his administration.

Questions to Consider

1. According to Reagan, what are the problems facing the nation as he takes office?
2. What does Reagan propose for the nation?
3. Who voted for Reagan in 1980? Why?
4. How might Lyndon Johnson ("Lyndon Johnson on the Great Society," Document 212) have responded to this address?

To a few of us here today this is a solemn and most momentous occasion, and yet in the history of our nation it is a commonplace occurrence. The orderly transfer of authority as called for in the Constitution routinely takes place, as it has for almost two centuries, and few of us stop to think how unique we really are. In the eyes of many in the world, this every-4-year ceremony we accept as normal is nothing less than a miracle.

Mr. President, I want our fellow citizens to know how much you did to carry on this tradition. By your gracious cooperation in the transition process, you have shown a watching world that we are a united people pledged to maintaining a political system which guarantees individual liberty to a greater degree than any other, and I thank you and your people for all your help in maintaining the continuity which is the bulwark of our Republic.

SOURCE: "Inaugural Address," *Public Papers of the Presidents of the United States: Ronald Reagan, 1981* (Washington, DC, 1982), 1–4.

The business of our nation goes forward. The United States are confronted with an economic affliction of great proportions. We suffer from the longest and one of the worst sustained inflations in our national history. It distorts our economic decisions, penalizes thrift, and crushes the struggling young and the fixed-income elderly alike. It threatens to shatter the lives of millions of our people.

Idle industries have cast workers into unemployment, human misery, and personal indignity. Those who do work are denied a fair return for their labor by a tax system which penalizes successful achievement and keeps us from maintaining full productivity.

But great as our tax burden is, it has not kept pace with public spending. For decades we have piled deficit upon deficit, mortgaging our future and our children's future for the temporary convenience of the present. To continue this long trend is to guarantee tremendous social, cultural, political, and economic upheavals.

In this present crisis, government is not the solution to our problem; government is the problem. From time to time we've been tempted to believe that society has become too complex to be managed by self-rule, that government by an elite group is superior to government for, by, and of the people. Well, if no one among us is capable of governing himself, then who among us has the capacity to govern someone else? All of us together, in and out of government, must bear the burden. The solutions we seek must be equitable, with no one group singled out to pay a higher price.

Well, this administration's objective will be a healthy, vigorous, growing economy that provides equal opportunity for all Americans, with no barriers born of bigotry or discrimination. Putting America back to work means putting all Americans back to work. Ending inflation means freeing all Americans from the terror of runaway living costs. All must share in the productive work of this "new beginning," and all must share in the bounty of a revived economy. With the idealism and fair play which are the core of our system and our strength, we can have a strong and prosperous America, at peace with itself and the world.

So, as we begin, let us take inventory. We are a nation that has a government—not the other way around. And this makes us special among the nations of the Earth. Our government has no power except that granted it by the people. It is time to check and reverse the growth of government, which shows signs of having grown beyond the consent of the governed.

It is my intention to curb the size and influence of the Federal establishment and to demand recognition of the distinction between the powers granted to the Federal Government and those reserved to the States or to the people. All of us need to be reminded that the Federal Government did not create the States; the States created the Federal Government.

Now, so there will be no misunderstanding, it's not my intention to do away with government. It is rather to make it work—work with us, not over us; to stand by our side, not ride on our back. Government can and must provide opportunity, not smother it; foster productivity, not stifle it.

It is no coincidence that our present troubles parallel and are proportionate to the intervention and intrusion in our lives that result from unnecessary and excessive growth of government. It is time for us to realize that we are too great a nation to limit ourselves to small dreams. We're not, as some would have us believe, doomed to an inevitable decline. I do not believe in a fate that will fall on us no matter what we do. I do believe in a fate that will fall on us if we do nothing. So, with all the creative energy at our command, let us begin an era of national renewal. Let us renew our determination, our courage, and our strength. And let us renew our faith and our hope.

We have every right to dream heroic dreams. Those who say that we're in a time when there are no heroes, they just don't know where to look. You can see heroes every day going in and out of factory gates. Others, a handful in number, produce enough food to feed all of us and then the world beyond. You meet heroes across a counter, and they're on both sides of that counter. There are entrepreneurs with faith in themselves and faith in an idea who create new jobs, new wealth and opportunity. They're individuals and families whose taxes support the government and whose voluntary gifts support church, charity, culture, art, and education. Their patriotism is quiet, but deep. Their values sustain our national life.

To those neighbors and allies who share our freedom, we will strengthen our historic ties and assure them of our support and firm commitment. We will match loyalty with loyalty. We will strive for mutually beneficial relations. We will not use our friendship to impose on their sovereignty, for our own sovereignty is not for sale.

As for the enemies of freedom, those who are potential adversaries, they will be reminded that peace is the highest aspiration of the American people. We will negotiate for it, sacrifice for it; we will not surrender for it, now or ever.

Our forbearance should never be misunderstood. Our reluctance for conflict should not be misjudged as a failure of will. When action is required to preserve our national security, we will act. We will maintain sufficient strength to prevail if need be, knowing that if we do so we have the best chance of never having to use that strength.

Above all, we must realize that no arsenal or no weapon in the arsenals of the world is so formidable as the will and moral courage of free men and women. It is a weapon our adversaries in today's world do not have. It is a weapon that we as Americans do have. Let that be understood by those who practice terrorism and prey upon other neighbors.

225

Reagan's Evil Empire Speech (1983)

In the late 1970s, the Cold War between the Soviet Union and the United States ended a period of détente and entered a more confrontational phase. The Soviet invasion of Afghanistan and the subsequent arms race alarmed many Americans. President Ronald Reagan held strong convictions about the Soviet Union, seeing it as a source of trouble throughout the world. He advocated a military buildup, in part because he believed the United States could outspend the Soviet Union in an arms race. In 1983 Reagan spoke before a national meeting of evangelical Christians, hoping to affirm the support of the Christian Right and their devout anticommunist stance. Excerpted here is Reagan's address, which came to be called the "Evil Empire" speech.

Questions to Consider

1. In what ways does President Reagan depict the leaders of the Soviet Union and their ideology?

2. What does Reagan ask his audience to do?

3. To what extent does Reagan use religious imagery in this address?

4. In what ways is this speech similar to NSC-68 ("NSC-68, A Blueprint for the Cold War," Document 200)? Different?

I want you to know that this administration is motivated by a political philosophy that sees the greatness of America in you, her people, and in your families, churches, neighborhoods, communities—the institutions that foster and nourish values like concern for others and respect for the rule of law under God....

Now, obviously, much of this new political and social consensus I've talked about is based on a positive view of American history, one that takes pride in our country's accomplishments and record. But we must never forget that no government schemes are going to perfect man. We know that living in this world means dealing with what philosophers would call the phenomenology of evil or, as theologians would put it, the doctrine of sin.

There is sin and evil in the world, and we're enjoined by Scripture and the Lord Jesus to oppose it with all our might. Our nation, too, has a legacy of evil with which it must deal. The glory of this land has been its capacity for transcending the moral evils of our past. For example, the long struggle of minority

SOURCE: "Remarks at the Annual Convention of the National Association of Evangelicals in Orlando, Florida," *Public Papers of the Presidents of the United States: Ronald Reagan, 1983*, vol. 1 (Washington, DC, 1984): 359–64.

citizens for equal rights, once a source of disunity and civil war, is now a point of pride for all Americans. We must never go back. There is no room for racism, anti-Semitism, or other forms of ethnic and racial hatred in the country....

And this brings me to my final point today. During my press conference as President, in answer to a direct question, I pointed out that, as good Marxist-Leninists, the Soviet leaders have openly and publicly declared that the only morality they recognize is that which will further their cause, which is world revolution. I think I should point out I was only quoting Lenin, their guiding spirit, who said in 1920 that they repudiate all morality that proceeds from supernatural ideas—that's their name for religion—or ideas that are outside class conceptions. Morality is entirely subordinate to the interests of class war. And everything is moral that is necessary for the annihilation of the old, exploiting social order and for uniting the proletariat....

This doesn't mean we should isolate ourselves and refuse to seek an understanding with them. I intend to do everything I can to persuade them of our peaceful intent, to remind them that it was the West that refused to use its nuclear monopoly in the forties and fifties for territorial gain and which now proposes 50-percent cut in strategic ballistic missiles and the elimination of an entire class of land-based, intermediate-range nuclear missiles.

At the same time, however, they must be made to understand we will never compromise our principles and standards. We will never give away our freedom. We will never abandon our belief in God....

Yes, let us pray for the salvation of all of those who live in that totalitarian darkness—pray they will discover the joy of knowing God. But until they do, let us be aware that while they preach the supremacy of the state, declare its omnipotence over individual man, and predict its eventual domination of all peoples on the Earth, they are the focus of evil in the modern world....

Because [communist leaders] sometimes speak in soothing tones of brotherhood and peace, because, like other dictators before them, they're always making "their final territorial demand," some would have us accept them at their word and accommodate ourselves to their aggressive impulses. But if history teaches anything, it teaches that simple-minded appeasement or wishful thinking about our adversaries is folly. It means the betrayal of our past, the squandering of our freedom.

So, I urge you to speak out against those who would place the United States in a position of military and moral inferiority.... [I]n your discussion of the nuclear freeze proposals, I urge you to beware the temptation of pride—the temptation of blithely declaring yourselves above it all and label both sides equally at fault, to ignore the facts of history and the aggressive impulses of an evil empire, to simply call the arms race a giant misunderstanding and thereby remove yourself from the struggle between right and wrong and good and evil....

While America's military strength is important, let me add here that I've always maintained that the struggle now going on for the world will never be decided by bombs or rockets, by armies or military might. The real crisis we face today is a spiritual one; at root, it is a test of moral will and faith....

I believe we shall rise to the challenge. I believe that communism is another sad, bizarre chapter in human history whose last pages even now are being written. I believe this because the source of our strength in the quest for human freedom is not material, but spiritual. And because it knows no limitation, it must terrify and ultimately triumph over those who would enslave their fellow man....

Yes, change your world. One of our Founding Fathers, Thomas Paine, said, "We have it within our power to begin the world over again." We can do it, doing together what no one church could do by itself.

226

An Editorial on the Removal of the Berlin Wall (1989)

For over forty years the Cold War had divided much of the world into two opposing camps. In Europe the division was along the "iron curtain" boundary separating the communist East, under Soviet influence, from the capitalistic West, under American influence. Even Germany and its old capital of Berlin were divided along these lines. In 1985, Soviet leader Mikhail Gorbachev began policies called "perestroika" (economic restructuring) and "glasnost" (openness) to revitalize the Soviet Union's sagging economy and to achieve better relations—especially trade—with the West. These policies triggered dissent, then growing demands for more rapid reforms both within the Soviet Union and in eastern Europe. When Gorbachev agreed not to intervene in the affairs of East-bloc countries in 1989, popular uprisings ended Communist party rule and new governments were formed. Perhaps the most sensational incident of this collapse came in November 1989, when the Berlin Wall—the symbol of the Cold War since its erection in 1961—was removed and the borders between the two Germanies opened. Excerpted below is the New York Times *editorial, which places the removal of the Berlin Wall in a historical perspective.*

Questions to Consider

1. The *New York Times* editorial argues that the destruction of the Berlin Wall ended seventy-five years of European catastrophes. Is this true?
2. What else did destruction of the Berlin Wall signify?

3. How did the United States react to creation of "a European house"?

4. What is the significance of this event?

Crowds of young Germans danced on top of the hated Berlin wall Thursday night. They danced for joy, they danced for history. They danced because the tragic cycle of catastrophes that first convulsed Europe 75 years ago, embracing two world wars, a Holocaust and a cold war, seems at long last to be nearing an end.

November 11, now named Veterans Day, is the day of the armistice that ended World War I. But that war to end wars was lost when the victors bungled the peace. They exacted heavy reparations from Germany, paving the way to chaos and the rise of National Socialism. The years between the two wars turned out to be merely a truce. Hitler in 1940 received the surrender of the French forces in the same railroad car in which Germany's delegates surrendered in 1918, and Europe was again plunged into strife.

Some 20 million people died in World War I, perhaps 50 million in World War II, but even these two appalling acts of miscalculation and bloodletting did not bring Europe's torments to an end. The tragedy had a third act: the cold war divided a Europe freed from Hitler's tyranny from a Europe bowed under Stalin's. The Berlin wall, erected by Erich Honecker in 1961, stood as the foremost symbol of that division and the Continent's continuing stasis.

The reveling crowds of Berliners mingling from East and West could scarcely believe that the hated wall had at last been breached. Those watching them around the world could only share their delight—and their wonder at the meaning of it all.

If the horrifying cycle that began in 1914 is at last completed, what new wheels have begun to turn? Instability in Eastern Europe has seldom brought good news. But this dissolution may lead to settlement, even if the settlement's shape remains unclear.

Armistice is only the laying down of arms, not peace. And for as long as it has stood, the Berlin wall has symbolized a Europe not at peace, and a world polarized by Soviet-American rivalry.

Mikhail Gorbachev has spoken of a European house. No one, not even he, can yet be sure how the rooms might fit together. Still, no house has a wall through its middle, and for the first time in a generation, neither does Europe.

26

Society and Culture
At Century's End

In the last thirty-five years, American society and culture have changed dramatically. The 1970s witnessed an economic malaise, caused in part by the rising price of petroleum; the 1990s experienced an economic boom that prompted some consumer excesses. Many of the nation's baby boomers (those born between 1945–1964) were central in bringing about the economic and social changes. The country also experienced the impact of growing numbers of immigrants as well as an adjustment to the internal migration of people to the Sunbelt. In many areas, new arrangements involving immigration, class structure, gender roles, homosexuality, race relations, and health care were formed. The documents that follow reveal some aspects of American culture and society at century's end.

227

Catholic Bishops Call
for "Economic Justice" (1986)

In the late 1970s and early 1980s the American economy was in a weakened state. A combination of rising prices and increasing inflation as well as growing numbers of unemployed left the economy sluggish, and this helped produce societal inequalities. The richest Americans owned more of the nation's wealth than ever before, while income for the middle class remained stagnant and those of the poor were in decline. Growing numbers of homeless persons were seen on city streets. The economic doldrums helped fuel a growing appeal of lower taxes, reduced government regulation and cuts in social services as ways to stimulate business activity. Meanwhile, Roman Catholic bishops in the United States offered a different approach in a lengthy "pastoral letter" entitled "Economic Justice for All." The bishops castigated the American economy for its failure to provide for large numbers of citizens who languished in poverty despite the nation's obvious wealth. Below are the principal themes from this letter, which calls for changes in the U.S. economy to guarantee "minimum conditions of human dignity in the economic sphere for every person."

Questions to Consider

1. What are the six principal themes advanced in this letter?
2. To what extent is community an essential component of the bishops' call for change?
3. What are the challenges to individual Americans?
4. How realistic are the changes that the bishops propose?
5. How might Ronald Reagan ("The Reagan Revolution," Document 224) or Lyndon Johnson ("Lyndon Johnson on the Great Society," Document 212) have responded to this document?

12. The pastoral letter is not a blueprint for the American economy. It does not embrace any particular theory of how the economy works, nor does it attempt to resolve disputes between different schools of economic thought. Instead, our letter turns to Scripture and to the social teaching of the Church. There, we

discover what our economic life must serve, what standards it must meet. Let us examine some of these basic moral principles.

13. Every economic decision and institution must be judged in light of whether it protects or undermines the dignity of the human person. The pastoral letter begins with the human person. We believe the person is sacred—the clearest reflection of God among us. Human dignity comes from God, not from nationality, race, sex, economic status, or any human accomplishment. We judge any economic system by what it does *for* and *to* people and by how it permits all to *participate* in it. The economy should serve people, not the other way around.

14. Human dignity can be realized and protected only in community. In our teaching, the human person is not only sacred but social. How we organize our society—in economics and politics, in law and policy—directly affects human dignity and the capacity of individuals to grow in community. The obligation to "love our neighbor" has an individual dimension, but it also requires a broader social commitment to the common good. We have many partial ways to measure and debate the health of our economy: Gross National Product, per capita income, stock market prices, and so forth. The Christian vision of economic life looks beyond them all and asks, Does economic life enhance or threaten our life together as a community?

15. All people have a right to participate in the economic life of society. Basic justice demands that people be assured a minimum level of participation in the economy. It is wrong for a person or a group to be excluded unfairly or to be unable to participate or contribute to the economy. For example, people who are both able and willing, but cannot get a job are deprived of the participation that is so vital to human development. For, it is through employment that most individuals and families meet their material needs, exercise their talents, and have an opportunity to contribute to the larger community. Such participation has a special significance in our tradition because we believe that it is a means by which we join in carrying forward God's creative activity.

16. All members of society have a special obligation to the poor and vulnerable. From the Scriptures and church teaching, we learn that the justice of a society is tested by the treatment of the poor. The justice that was the sign of God's covenant with Israel was measured by how the poor and unprotected— the widow, the orphan, and the stranger—were treated. The kingdom that Jesus proclaimed in his word and ministry excludes no one. Throughout Israel's history and in early Christianity, the poor are agents of God's transforming power. "The Spirit of the Lord is upon me, therefore he has anointed me. He has sent me to bring glad tidings to the poor" (Lk. 4:18). This was Jesus' first public utterance. Jesus takes the side of those most in need. In the Last Judgment, so dramatically described in St. Matthew's Gospel, we are told that we will be judged according to how we respond to the hungry, the thirsty, the naked, the stranger. As followers of Christ, we are challenged to make a fundamental "option for the poor"—to speak for the voiceless, to defend the defenseless, to assess life styles, policies, and social institutions in terms of their impact on the poor. This "option for the poor" does not mean pitting one group against another, but rather,

strengthening the whole community by assisting those who are the most vulnerable. As Christians, we are called to respond to the needs of *all* our brothers and sisters, but those with the greatest needs require the greatest response.

17. Human rights are the minimum conditions for life in community. In Catholic teaching, human rights include not only civil and political rights but also economic rights. As Pope John XXIII declared, "all people have a right to life, food, clothing, shelter, rest, medical care, education, and employment." This means that when people are without a chance to earn a living, and must go hungry and homeless, they are being denied basic rights. Society must ensure that these rights are protected. In this way, we will ensure that the minimum conditions of economic justice are met for all our sisters and brothers.

18. Society as a whole, acting through public and private institutions, has the moral responsibility to enhance human dignity and protect human rights. In addition to the clear responsibility of private institutions, government has an essential responsibility in this area. This does not mean that government has the primary or exclusive role, but it does have a positive moral responsibility in safeguarding human rights and ensuring that the minimum conditions of human dignity are met for all. In a democracy, government is a means by which we can act together to protect what is important to us and to promote our common values.

19. These six moral principles are not the only ones presented in the pastoral letter, but they give an overview of the moral vision that we are trying to share. This vision of economic life cannot exist in a vacuum; it must be translated into concrete measures. Our pastoral letter spells out some specific applications of Catholic moral principles. We call for a new national commitment to full employment. We say it is a social and moral scandal that one of every seven Americans is poor, and we call for concerted efforts to eradicate poverty. The fulfillment of the basic needs of the poor is of the highest priority. We urge that all economic policies be evaluated in light of their impact on the life and stability of the family. We support measures to halt the loss of family farms and to resist the growing concentration in the ownership of agricultural resources. We specify ways in which the United States can do far more to relieve the plight of poor nations and assist in their development. We also reaffirm church teaching on the rights of workers, collective bargaining, private property, subsidiarity, and equal opportunity.

20. We believe that the recommendations in our letter are reasonable and balanced. In analyzing the economy, we reject ideological extremes and start from the fact that ours is a "mixed" economy, the product of a long history of reform and adjustment. We know that some of our specific recommendations are controversial. As bishops, we do not claim to make these prudential judgments with the same kind of authority that marks our declarations of principle. But, we feel obliged to teach by example how Christians can undertake concrete analysis and make specific judgments on economic issues. The Church's teachings cannot be left at the level of appealing generalities.

21. In the pastoral letter, we suggest that the time has come for a "New American Experiment"—to implement economic rights, to broaden the sharing

of economic power, and to make economic decisions more accountable to the common good. This experiment can create new structures of economic partnership and participation within firms at the regional level, for the whole nation, and across borders.

22. Of course, there are many aspects of the economy the letter does not touch, and there are basic questions it leaves to further exploration. There are also many specific points on which men and women of good will may disagree. We look for a fruitful exchange among differing viewpoints. We pray only that all will take to heart the urgency of our concerns; that together we will test our views by the Gospel and the Church's teaching; and that we will listen to other voices in a spirit of mutual respect and open dialogue.

228

A Perspective on AIDS (1987)

The acquired immune deficiency syndrome (AIDS) epidemic brought significant change to accepted social and medical norms. First detected in 1981, the human immunodeficiency virus (HIV) that leads to AIDS breaks down the body's immune system with fatal results. Initially, the disease was associated with gay men and drug addicts who used "dirty" needles. It intensified animosity toward the gay community (Patrick Buchanan, White House director of communications, said homosexuals had "declared war on nature, and now nature is extracting an awful retribution"). But this attitude softened as HIV spread through blood or sexual contact to infect alarming numbers of heterosexual individuals. To help limit the spread of the virus and calm popular fear of AIDS, the federal government launched an education campaign about the disease and encouraged "safe sex" through the use of condoms. Sexual experimentation and promiscuity declined. With escalating medical costs to treat the disease and few advances toward a cure, AIDS remains a frightening problem. Excerpted here is David C. Jones's 1987 speech about AIDS, which he addressed to medical students at Duke University. Jones is from the North Carolina AIDS Service Coalition.

Questions to Consider

1. Why does Jones argue that AIDS will alter existing health insurance and health care?

2. Why does he believe that HIV antibody testing could lead to blatant discrimination?

3. What six-point proposal does Jones make to change attitudes about AIDS?

4. In what ways have attitudes about AIDS changed? Why?

Too many of my friends have died and far too many more are ill or living in fear. You are being pulled into a maelstrom of controversy about the disease that is killing them. In fact, I believe that Society is setting you up to have to deal with its own doubt, fear and anger. I believe that you are going to have to be the arbiters of some very profound and even radical questions that will shake the very foundations of the delivery of health care as we know it....

First, who will get what care? Some of the ethical dilemmas you will face will be generated by the creeping obsolescence of insurance as we know it. Health insurance as we know it today will not exist twenty years from now. AIDS is not the first but it is the most startling example of a confluence of forces that will change dramatically how we will decide who is going to get what medical care. Let me explain.

We believe that society should share the burden of injury or loss. So we have insurance....

Now comes AIDS. It seems universally fatal, there is not much we can do and care costs a great deal. The financial impact on an insurance company can be great.

The first response of some companies fell somewhere between silly and sinister. My favorite is the letter that one company sent to agents telling them to be suspicious of single men "... in such occupations that do not require physical exertion ... such as antique dealers, interior decorators or florists."

Then there came a blood test to detect antibodies to the virus that causes AIDS also with epidemiological data indicating that large numbers of people with antibodies are infected, and that a growing portion of them are going to die very expensive deaths.

Insurance companies fought for the right to use the antibody test to deny new coverage. Their position is simple and traditional: it identifies a new potential risk....

We are standing on the brink of an explosion of diagnostic capability. This will be possible as a result of breakthroughs in our ability to read and understand our genetic program, and the technological elegance of rapidly evolving new generations of precise, affordable diagnostic systems....

We will be able to run a series of tests and print out the probable health events of an individual. We will have a good picture of what diseases this person is likely to experience naturally, and others that will probably be experienced should certain environmental conditions be encountered.

What this means, based on the structure and management of private insurance today, is that a staggering number of people will be uninsurable and many will be unemployable. We face the very real possibility of creating an entire caste of non-persons, people for whom there is no work, no promise, no place....

SOURCE: David C. Jones, "Perspective on AIDS: Ethical, Socioeconomic and Political Aspects," *Vital Speeches of the Day* 54 (1987): 176–79.

I will go so far as to say that society will not tolerate it. The only question in my mind is how soon people will react. It may be soon as thoughtful people begin to recognize the implications of financing care the way we have always done it when this information is available. Or it may be after millions of people are forced into poverty and we face a cataclysmic reaction from society. How we respond to AIDS now and the problem of a growing number of terminally ill Americans without insurance will tell us a lot about what our future holds.

We will finally be forced to resolve a debate that has been simmering in this country for years. Is good health care a right or a privilege? We were going to have to face up to this sooner or later. AIDS has just made it sooner....

The HIV antibody test represents the first time that medical information has been used widely as the basis for social and political discrimination of an unpopular minority. Society's reaction to homosexuality as a lifestyle ranges from acceptance to scorn. AIDS has even brought forth again the condemnation of those with the astonishing arrogance to claim God's proxy to judge....

But we have to look at the real world in which this disease is spreading. AIDS is not like any other disease. Punitive discrimination does occur, regularly. And now we hear threats of prison. Now we have added fear upon fear. And it is fear that will assure that this system, in this environment, in this state, simply will not work. Fewer people will seek testing, fewer people will know that they are infected, and more people will die from the complications of an acquired immune deficiency.

The members of the AIDS Service Coalition have been dealing with AIDS for a long time. We know how terrible it is and we want to do everything we can to see that no one is ever consumed by it again. We would like to make a specific six-point proposal that should be part of public health policy. We believe it will cause the largest number of people to change the behavior that places them at risk and to seek information, counseling and medical care.

First, a statewide AIDS education program should be the state's first priority. Education is the only hope we have of preventing people from being infected in the first place. Further, people are more likely to seek counseling or testing when they are told that they may have been exposed if they have already received some education about AIDS.

Second, adequate counseling must be available, both before and after testing....

Third, anonymous testing for HIV should continue to be available to all who seek it. It should be the policy of the state to require informed consent before any person is tested, and that every person tested in any setting should be notified of the result.

Fourth, a system of contact notification should be developed that emphasizes voluntary self-referral, with the option of notification by trained AIDS counseling specialists at the state level. Counseling should include both the necessity of informing sexual and needle contacts, and effective and sensitive techniques for notifying others....

Fifth, we must dispel the fear of losing one's apartment or job by making it clear that North Carolina prohibits discrimination based on a positive HIV test or a diagnosis of AIDS.

Sixth, we should reduce the financial burden of AIDS by making alternatives to extended hospitalization available, and thereby make more resources available for controlling AIDS....

... The forces that have been unleashed by AIDS are so powerful that if we do not find a way to harness them productively, and with dignity, we shall all be consumed by them.

All I can really ask you to do is to ask the questions now, over and over, in good faith, within a framework that recognized a respect for people and a commitment to do no harm, a framework that causes us to act in the interests of others and share the benefits and the burdens of what we do. Please deal with them now, while you may still have time.

229

A View on Hispanic Assimilation (1991)

Since the early 1980s, immigration into the United States has increased dramatically. Most of the legal immigrants were Hispanic (from Spanish-speaking countries of Latin America, mainly Mexico) and Asian. Their numbers had swollen to nearly 600,000 per year. In addition, there were illegal immigrants, mostly Mexicans, moving across the border. Many native-born Americans ("Anglos") were alarmed as increasing numbers of immigrants moved into the areas where they lived. The Anglos believed they would become a minority in their own city and that American values would be threatened. Such fears prompted efforts to assimilate the newcomers faster, bar Spanish in public schools, and restrict or prohibit government services provided to the immigrants. Clearly, cultural differences were divisive. In 1991, Linda Chavez published Out of the Barrio, *a study of Hispanics in American society. Chavez served in several federal government posts in the Reagan administration and was the first woman appointed to the Civil Rights Commission. In the selection here, Chavez offers a commentary on the role of Hispanics and of government.*

Questions to Consider

1. According to Chavez, why should Hispanics assimilate?
2. What is the role of government, according to Chavez? Why does she oppose affirmative action programs?
3. Should Hispanics follow the example of previous immigrants to America?
4. In what ways might César Chávez ("César Chávez and La Causa," Document 217) have reacted to Linda Chavez's argument?

Assimilation has become a dirty word in American politics. It invokes images of people, cultures, and traditions forged into a colorless alloy in an indifferent melting pot. But, in fact, assimilation, as it has taken place in the United States, is a far more gentle process, by which people from outside the community gradually became part of the community itself. Descendants of the German, Irish, Italian, Polish, Greek and other immigrants who came to the United States bear little resemblance to the descendants of the countrymen their forebears left behind. America changed its immigrant groups—and was changed by them. Some groups were accepted more reluctantly than others—the Chinese, for example—and some with great struggle. Blacks, whose ancestors were forced to come here, have only lately won their legal right to full participation in this society; and even then civil rights gains have not been sufficiently translated into economic gains. Until quite recently, however, there was no question but that each group desired admittance to the mainstream. No more. Now ethnic leaders demand that their groups remain separate, that their native culture and language be preserved intact, and that whatever accommodation takes place be on the part of the receiving society....

The government should not be obliged to preserve any group's distinctive language or culture. Public schools should make sure that all children can speak, read, and write English well. When teaching children from non-English-speaking backgrounds, they should use methods that will achieve English proficiency quickly and should not allow political pressure to interfere with meeting the academic needs of students. No children in an American school are helped by being held back in their native language when they could be learning the language that will enable them to get a decent job or pursue higher education. More than twenty years of experience with native-language instruction fails to show that children in these programs learn English more quickly or perform better academically than children in programs that emphasize English acquisition.

If Hispanic parents want their children to be able to speak Spanish and know about their distinctive culture, they must take the responsibility to teach their children these things. Government simply cannot—and should not—be charged with this responsibility. Government bureaucracies given the authority to create bicultural teaching materials homogenize the myths, customs, and history of the Hispanic peoples of this hemisphere, who, after all, are not a single group but groups. It is only in the United States that "Hispanics" exist; a Cakchiquel Indian in Guatemala would find it remarkable that anyone could consider his culture to be the same as a Spanish Argentinean's. The best way for Hispanics to learn about their native culture is in their own communities. Chinese, Jewish, Greek, and other ethnic communities have long established after-school and weekend programs to teach language and culture to children from these groups. Nothing stops Hispanic organizations from doing the same things....

SOURCE: Linda Chavez, *Out of the Barrio: Toward a New Politics of Hispanic Assimilation* (New York, 1991), 161–71.

Politics has traditionally been a great equalizer. One person's vote was as good as another's regardless of whether the one was rich and the other poor. But politics requires that people participate. The great civil rights struggles of the 1960s were fought in large part to guarantee the right to vote. Hispanic leaders demand representation but do not insist that individual Hispanics participate in the process. The emphasis is always on rights, never on obligations. Hispanic voter organizations devote most of their efforts toward making the process easier—election law reform, postcard registration, election materials in Spanish—to little avail; voter turnout is still lower among Hispanics than among blacks or whites. Spanish posters urge Hispanics to vote because it will mean more and better jobs and social programs, but I've never seen one that mentions good citizenship. Hispanics (and others) need to be reminded that if they want the freedom and opportunity democracy offers, the least they can do is take the time to register and vote. These are the lessons with which earlier immigrants were imbued, and they bear reviving....

The government can do only so much in promoting higher education for Hispanics or any group. It is substantially easier today for a Hispanic student to go to college than it was even twenty or thirty years ago, yet the proportion of Mexican Americans who are graduating from college today is unchanged from what it was forty years ago. When the former secretary of education Lauro Cavazos, the first Hispanic ever to serve in the Cabinet, criticized Hispanic parents for the low educational attainment of their children, he was roundly attacked for blaming the victim. But Cavazos's point was that Hispanic parents must encourage their children's educational aspirations and that, too often, they don't. Those groups that have made the most spectacular socioeconomic gains— Jews and Chinese, for example—have done so because their families placed great emphasis on education.

Hispanics cannot have it both ways. If they want to earn as much as non-Hispanic whites, they have to invest the same number of years in schooling as these do. The earnings gap will not close until the education gap does. Native-born Hispanics are already enjoying earnings comparable to those of non-Hispanic whites, once educational differences are factored in. If they want to earn more, they must become better educated. But education requires sacrifices, especially for persons from lower-income families. Only a substantial commitment to the education of their children on the part of this generation of Hispanic parents will increase the speed with which Hispanics improve their social and economic status.

Affirmative action politics treats race and ethnicity as if they were synonymous with disadvantage. The son of a Mexican American doctor or lawyer is treated as if he suffered the same disadvantage as the child of a Mexican farm worker; and both are given preference over poor, non-Hispanic whites in admission to most colleges or affirmative action employment programs. Most people think this is unfair, especially white ethnics whose own parents and grandparents also faced discrimination in this society but never became eligible for the entitlements of the civil rights era. It is inherently patronizing to assume that all Hispanics are deprived and grossly unjust to give those who aren't preference on the basis of disadvantages they don't experience. Whether stated or not, the essence of affirmative action is the belief that Hispanics—or any of the other eligible groups—are not capable of measuring up to the standards applied to whites. This is a pernicious idea.

Ultimately, entitlements based on their status as "victims" rob Hispanics of real power. The history of American ethnic groups is one of overcoming disadvantage, of competing with those who were already here and proving themselves as competent as any who came before. Their fight was always to be treated the same as other Americans, never to be treated as special, certainly not to turn the temporary disadvantages they suffered into the basis for permanent entitlement. Anyone who thinks this fight was easier in the early part of this century when it was waged by other ethnic groups does not know history. Hispanics have not always had an easy time of it in the United States. Even through discrimination against Mexican Americans and Puerto Ricans was not as severe as it was against blacks, acceptance has come only with struggle, and some prejudices still exist. Discrimination against Hispanics, or any other group, should be fought, and there are laws and a massive administrative apparatus to do so. But the way to eliminate such discrimination is not to classify all Hispanics as victims and treat them as if they could not succeed by their own efforts. Hispanics can and will prosper in the United States by following the example of the millions before them.

230

Bill Gates and Microsoft (1998)

The most visible and dramatic aspect of the technological revolution in the late twentieth century was the personal computer. The development of the microprocessor—a tiny computer on a silicon chip—paved the way for the personal computer; and as microprocessors became faster and contained more memory, the functions and uses of the personal computer expanded. Gathering momentum in the 1980s, the computer revolutionized almost every facet of life. In the early 1990s increasing numbers of personal computers were connecting to the Internet, a worldwide network of computers and databases. Soon e-mail was replacing the telephone and traditional mail (which some now called "snail mail") services, and Web pages became commonplace. Some individuals called the Internet the "information superhighway." A key individual in the development of the personal computer was Bill Gates. He dropped out of Harvard and, with Paul Allen, formed Microsoft to develop the software to run the hardware of the early personal computers. Microsoft developed many new software programs, often with business applications, and came to dominate the software industry for the personal computer. In March 1998, Bill Gates testified before a Senate committee on Microsoft, its place in the computer industry, and a Department of Justice antitrust suit against his company. His prepared statement is excerpted here.

Questions to Consider

1. How does Gates describe the computer and software industries? What are his examples?
2. On what basis does Gates argue that Microsoft is not a monopoly?
3. What does Gates envision as the future of computers?
4. Should Microsoft face an antitrust suit?
5. In what ways is the impact of the computer similar to that of television in the 1950s ("The Impact of Television," Document 205)?

... Mr. Chairman, in the computer software industry, rapid and unpredictable changes constantly create new market opportunities and threaten the position of existing competitors. The position of a product—no matter how popular—is never secure because it is impossible to know when the next new idea will come along that could render that entire product category less important or even obsolete. Few industries face this kind of intense competitive pressure, even those in other parts of the high technology sector. The computer industry is littered with examples of companies that enjoyed great success for a short time, only to be overtaken by new technologies that better served consumers' needs.

For instance, as inexpensive microprocessors became available in the 1970's, Wang, IBM and others developed computers dedicated to a single task: word processing. Demand for electronic typewriters soon declined sharply, and sales of dedicated devices from Wang and IBM rose sharply. (At one time Wang was nearly synonymous with word processing.) In the 1980s, however, demand for these single-task devices declined dramatically as personal computers became available that could perform a wide range of functions in addition to word processing. In the space of just a few years, Wang went from market leader to bankruptcy....

The advent of the PC industry itself is perhaps the best example of rapid and unpredictable technological change taking established market leaders by surprise. In the 1960s and 1970s, IBM and a few other large vendors such as Sperry Rand, Honeywell, Burroughs, Control Data and NCR were the titans of the computer industry.... The PC was derided by many manufacturers of "big iron" mainframe computers as a "toy" (which it was, at first). IBM and others were slow to appreciate the potential of distributing computing power to individuals. IBM is still a very powerful force in the computer industry. But none of the traditional mainframe or minicomputer manufacturers fully embraced personal computers in a timely way, and many faltered as a result. Today, the computer industry is

SOURCE: U.S. Congress, Senate, *Competition, Innovation, and Public Policy in the Digital Age: Hearings Before the Committee on the Judiciary*, "Prepared Statement of Bill Gates," 3 March 1998 (Washington, DC, 1998), 89–96.

populated by many high volume manufacturers that did not even exist twenty-five years ago, such as Compaq, Dell, Gateway 2000, and Micron Technologies.

The era of hobbyists working in garage operations that nobody ever heard of and developing the next new product to take the industry by storm is not simply a legend from days gone by, it's a story we hear all the time in this industry. Take Scott Cook of Intuit, for example. Scott developed the enormously popular Quicken personal finance software sitting at his kitchen table. And the precursor of Netscape Navigator was designed by undergraduate students at the University of Illinois in Champaign-Urbana who worked for the National Center for Supercomputing Applications....

Microsoft's acute awareness that today's success story could easily become tomorrow's has-been is reflected in the company's stark rallying cry: "Innovate or Die!" Nowhere is that attitude more evident than in Microsoft's response to the emergence of the Internet as a powerful new force in computing. Microsoft has always recognized that there would be a very large network developed to interconnect computers around the world, i.e., the network commonly referred to as the Information Superhighway, but it is no secret that we did not immediately recognize that the Internet would become that network....

The swiftness with which people around the world have taken to the Internet is simply amazing and is powerful evidence that no company in the computer software industry can afford complacency. Microsoft is working hard to identify and pursue the many long-term opportunities that the Internet affords. Virtually everything we do these days at Microsoft reflects our conviction that the Internet is going to continue to grow. I believe that almost everyone in the developed world and huge numbers of people in the developing world will be using the Internet within the foreseeable future. Access to these technologies and the benefits they offer promises to have far-reaching effects on the way we live and work and learn, many of which we cannot even imagine today....

To remain competitive and to continue to provide consumers with high quality, low cost, innovative products, Microsoft and other U.S. software companies must retain the ability to design their products free from government interference. The current case is a good example: the DOJ [Department of Justice] is attempting to require Microsoft to offer Windows without important Internet-related aspects of the operating system, depriving consumers and software developers of the benefits of compatibility provided by a common platform like Windows. If the DOJ succeeds with its efforts to limit Microsoft's ability to improve Windows, software developers will be less likely to create innovative new products that take full advantage of Windows and consumers will be unsure whether applications will work properly with the version of Windows installed on their PC....

In short, while I certainly agree that the government should work to ensure that competition is not stifled by collusion or other plainly illegal activities, I think that the government should be extremely wary of interceding in an industry like computer software that is working so well on its own. As I hope my testimony today has made clear, the computer software industry is not broken, and there is no need to fix it. It is a thriving and vibrant sector of the U.S. economy and the envy of the rest of the world....

Mr. Chairman, let me be very clear on this point—Microsoft does not have monopoly power in the business of developing and licensing computer operating systems. As you know, a monopolist, by definition, is a company that has the ability to restrict entry by new firms and unilaterally control prices. Microsoft can do neither. Software exhibits none of the barriers to entry that characterize traditional industries like mining or manufacturing. A new competitor needs little in the way of physical infrastructure. Distribution costs are low (software can be transmitted around the world nearly instantaneously). The principal assets required to create excellent software are human intelligence, creativity, and a willingness to assume entrepreneurial risk, all of which are in abundant supply in this country. A software product is the copyrighted expression in lines of code of ideas. No one can monopolize new ideas that can be implemented in software.

With regard to pricing, the market pressures we face compel Microsoft to price Windows competitively. In fact, the price of Windows has remained virtually unchanged over the years, while its performance and features have increased dramatically. Today Microsoft Windows is one of the central technologies contained in most new PCs, yet it accounts for less than 3 percent of the cost of a typical PC.

If Microsoft truly had monopoly power, it would be free to increase the prices for its operating systems with no need to innovate. A monopolist is lazy, charging prices above competitive levels for products that are rarely improved because no one else can offer alternative products to consumers. In contrast, Microsoft spends ever larger sums each year on research and development to deliver better operating system technology at affordable prices.

Mr. Chairman, I have been tremendously fortunate to be a part of an incredible industry like computer software during such an exciting period, but I firmly believe that we have only just scratched the surface; the greatest advances in the computer industry are yet to come. And Microsoft is working hard to unleash the power of personal computing to the benefit of everyone. Already we are working on operating systems that will enable personal computers to recognize users when they enter a room, respond accurately to voice and handwritten commands, and serve as highly efficient communication, productivity and entertainment devices. And, of course, we are devoting significant resources to developing the technology that will enable users of the Internet to realize its full potential. There is much more we can and will do to make the Internet more accessible and to give consumers good reasons to want to use it more....

Mr. Chairman, Microsoft will continue to compete vigorously in the computer software industry, listen to our customers, and work hard to create new and innovative products at low prices. If Microsoft fails to keep pace with technological change and is outstripped by its competitors, let it be because we failed to innovate fast enough, not because we were hobbled by government intervention in our efforts to develop new products that meet the needs of consumers....

231

The Changing Demographics of America (1999)

In the period following World War II, the United States experienced the beginnings of a demographic shift that had implications for future generations of Americans. The promise of rising incomes fueled suburbanization, which combined with the desire for early marriage and starting a family to produce the baby boom. The baby boomers, as this large group born between 1946 and 1964 is often identified, have wielded significant influence, in part because of their numbers relative to the rest of American society. In childhood as well as adulthood, baby boomers have helped shape the political, social, and economic landscape of America in the second half of the twentieth century—and by and large, they have enjoyed the fruits of their considerable influence. By the late twentieth century, as the baby boomers neared retirement, some predicted the demise of Social Security and a possible generational conflict between baby boomers and the subsequent generations over taxes, jobs, and resources. In the excerpt here, Thomas G. Donlan, an editor at Barron's, *a business and financial weekly newspaper, offered some commentary on the demographic changes taking place at the end of the twentieth century.*

Questions to Consider

1. Do baby boomers seem selfish?
2. To what extent is it possible to stereotype according to age?
3. What does the author see as having more impact than the baby boomer generation?
4. Why do you think the author is so critical of the baby boomer generation? To what extent is this criticism warranted?

For their whole lives, Baby Boomers have been the 400-pound canaries of American society. The generations of children born between 1946 and 1964 have been the birds who sit anywhere they want, whose whims rule the nation. When they were children, the country moved to the suburbs and forced municipalities to build thousands of new schools. The government built the Interstate Highway system, which let Mom and Dad take them on a new kind of vacation.

When they were teenagers, the country went youth-crazy and idolized idealistic college facilities. When they were young adults, the country changed its banking system to provide credit cards and mortgages so they could go deeply into debt to have it all right then and there. The government changed the bankruptcy laws and eventually taxed everybody to bail out the thousands of lenders who accommodated profligate Boomers. When they reached middle age, Wall Street rebuilt itself to provide mutual funds and brokerage accounts to help them pay off debts and build some wealth. The government created new tax-advantaged retirement accounts and enhanced the attractiveness of the old ones.

What other generation has had its music playing on the radio for their whole lives? There were no big band oldies stations when the Boomers were kids, but every city now has two or three oldies stations playing the Boomers favorites.

What other generation enjoyed a (so far) 17 year bull market, marred only by one big recession and one little one? Their parents weathered three recessions during the Eisenhower Administration alone. Sure, it's coincidence that microchip technology got started when the Boomers were teens, and just good luck for everybody that shrinking transistors made computing and communications ever more powerful, as if on a schedule. But it's no coincidence that the national economy struggled when the Boomers were young and inexperienced, and took off as the Boomers hit their productive stride.

Boomers are frequently condemned, even by their own pundits, as spoiled, self-absorbed and greedy. Some say they were nursed on demand feeding according to the theories of Dr. Spock and they never got over it. But with all their annoying flaws, Boomers in their vast numbers are the best thing that ever happened to the American economy. The demand of 77 million credit-card-wielding consumers, many of them well-educated to demand the best, has driven producers all over the world to do their best on price and performance. And the engineers, scientists, doctors and managers turned out by those expanded schools and colleges have provided the means to design and supply better products and services valued around the world.

That's a trend that ought to continue for as much as two more decades. But it's equally true that Boomers will impose at least one more major shift on the American economy, and this one not for the better. As they retire, the Boomers will convert themselves from producers to pure consumers. Some huge percentage of U.S. cash flow will be devoted to paying their Social Security and their Medicare.

It has never been clear how this will be done. Without changes in the programs, Social Security and Medicare will shoulder aside most other nondefense government spending by the 2030s, or impose huge tax increase on younger generations of working people.

But it has always seemed clear that this would be done, somehow. The Boomers are too many to mess with, and they have always gotten their way.

More recently, we have also heard that the Boomers pose another financial threat, to themselves and other investors. Private retirement savings, though for the most part fully funded, are funded in securities markets, and some analysts have warned that as Boomers tap pensions, they will drain capital from the markets and cause a Wall Street Crash of 2020, or thereabouts.

In a variation on the old Wall Street joke, they ask: Since the generation following the Boomers is so much smaller, who will buy all the securities the Boomers want to sell?

It seems logical, even just, and certainly a bit ironic. If Boomers' saving and investing have driven the market up tenfold from the base of 1982, and even if that goes smoothly for many more years, won't Boomers' dis-saving and disinvesting ultimately tank the market?

Even if demography is destiny, and even if Boomers want to sell in a mad rush, there will be buyers. Foreign buyers, putting newly earned wealth to work in the safest markets in the world. As long as the U.S. government does not do anything to spoil the national economic reputation, Boomers in their millions will be able to sell to foreign investors in even greater millions.

Perhaps more interesting to American trend-spotters, there will be lots of American investors too. The overlooked demographic features of 21st America is this: The baby boom recently ceased to be the most numerous generation in U.S history.

The aging of America has been a widely expected trend, but the 21st century will not be ruled by graying Boomers after all. The Boomers must make way for Generation X and Y, otherwise known as the Birth Dearth and the Baby Rebound.

Generation X followed the Baby Boom and its spokesmen were feeling lost and unloved in the early 'Nineties when they named it. We don't know what Y stands for—neither do they as yet—we just know it follows X.

En masse, Boomers had fewer children, but they also delayed having families, so lots of their kids missed Generation X and are concentrated in the cohorts born after 1980. Joining them in Generation Y are the children of immigrants who came in the large waves of migrants, legal and illegal, arriving here since 1975.

The result is that there are roughly 77 million Boomers, born between 1947 and 1964, 60 million Gen X-ers, born between 1965–1980, and 80 million members of Generation Y, born between 1980–1999. Immigration will continue to swell the ranks of Generation Y for years to come.

If demographics is destiny, then the United States could have a very different destiny than the one we have expected. Perhaps the Baby Boomers will not be permitted to tax Generations X and Y into poverty, or to bind the government to the bidding of the American Association of Retired Persons and its allied groups of lobbyists for greedy geezers.

The first members of Generation Y, including a young man who lived in our house for 18 years, have just arrived at college. Their wings are still wet. They are all promise, all potential. It will take 20 more years for the last members of Generation Y to come of age.

It's their job to find their own definitional cliché, but we note with interest that they are a generation brought up with no illusions of Social Security. As matters stand, they can expect to be taxed heavily to support it, and receive little if any benefit from it. What they do about that will mark them forever.

232

The Issue of Same-Sex Marriage (2001)

Throughout the twentieth century, most gays and lesbians remained silent about their sexual orientation for fear of persecution and violent backlash, although homosexual communities existed in most major cities. Inspired by the Civil Rights Movement, some gays and lesbians began to publicly demand tolerance and hopefully reshape homophobic views. This movement made news when gays at the Stonewall Bar in New York City fought back against a particularly violent police raid in June 1969. In the aftermath of this incident, the Gay Liberation Front made gains by advocating "gay rights" while more and more lesbians and gays "came out of the closet" and argued that their sexual orientation was legitimate. In the 1990s, gay men and lesbians became more prominent in public venues like movies, television shows, and politics, all of which helped dispel some homophobic stereotypes. Despite instances of violence toward homosexuals as well as less-subtle forms of discrimination, increasing numbers of Americans supported gay rights. In 2000, Vermont became the first state to grant legal status to same-sex marriages. As other states considered extending rights to gays and lesbians, Andrew Sullivan, a leading conservative and advocate of gay rights, offered the following editorial on same-sex marriage in The New Republic, *a magazine that covers topics in American politics, culture, and society.*

Questions to Consider

1. According to Sullivan, what are the arguments for and against same-sex marriage?

2. In what ways does Sullivan challenge stereotypical views of gays and lesbians?

3. In what ways is the Gay Rights Movement similar to other similar civil rights movements? Different?

4. What does Sullivan believe will result from same-sex marriage?

5. Have attitudes toward same sex relationships changed since the 1980s ("A Perspective on Aids," Document 228)?

In the decade or so in which same-sex marriage has been a matter of public debate, several arguments against it have been abandoned. Some opponents initially claimed marriage was about children and so gays couldn't marry. But courts made the obvious point that childless heterosexuals can marry and so the

SOURCE: Andrew Sullivan, "Unveiled," *The New Republic* 225 (13 August 2001): 6. Copyright © 2001 by Andrew Sullivan. Reprinted by permission of THE NEW REPUBLIC, © 2001, TNR II, LLC. and the Wylie Agency LLC.

comparison was moot. Others said a change in the definition of marriage would inexorably lead to legal polygamy. But homosexuals weren't asking for the right to marry anyone. They were asking for the right to marry someone. Still others worried that if one state granted such a right, the entire country would have to accept same-sex marriage. But legal scholars pointed out that marriage has not historically been one of those legal judgments that the "full faith and credit" clause of the U.S. Constitution says must be recognized in every state if they are valid in one state....

None of this stopped the Vermont Supreme Court, legislature, and governor from establishing "civil unions," the euphemism for gay marriage in the Ben & Jerry's state. It's almost exactly a year since civil unions debuted, and social collapse doesn't seem imminent. Perhaps panicked by this nonevent, the social right last month launched a Federal Marriage Amendment, which would bar any state from enacting same-sex marriage, forbid any arrangement designed to give gays equal marriage benefits, and destroy, any conceivable claim that conservatives truly believe in states' rights....

Perhaps concerned that their movement is sputtering, the opponents of same-sex marriage have turned to new arguments. Stanley Kurtz—the sharpest and fairest of these critics, summed up the case last week in National Review Online. For Kurtz, and other cultural conservatives, the deepest issue is sex and sexual difference. "Marriage," Kurtz argues, "springs directly from the ethos of heterosexual sex. Once marriage loses its connection to the differences between men and women, it can only start to resemble a glorified and slightly less temporary version of hooking up."

Let's unpack this. Kurtz's premise is that men and women differ in their sexual-emotional makeup. Men want sex more than stability; women want stability more than sex. Heterosexual marriage is therefore some kind of truce in the sex wars. One side gives sex in return for stability; the other provides stability in return for sex.... Both sides benefit, children most of all. Since marriage is defined as the way women tame men, once one gender is missing, this taming institution will cease to work. So, in Kurtz's words, a "world of same-sex marriages is a world of no strings heterosexual hookups and 50 percent divorce rates."

But isn't this backward? Surely the world of no-strings heterosexual hookups and 50 percent divorce rates preceded gay marriage. It was heterosexuals in the 1970s who changed marriage into something more like a partnership between equals, ... All homosexuals are saying, three decades later, is that, under the current definition, there's no reason to exclude us. If you want to return straight marriage to the 1950s, go ahead. But until you do, the exclusion of gays is simply an anomaly—and a denial of basic civil equality.

The deeper worry is that gay men simply can't hack monogamy.... One big problem with this argument is that it completely ignores lesbians. So far in Vermont there have been almost twice as many lesbian civil unions as gay male ones—even though most surveys show that gay men outnumber lesbians about two to one. That means lesbians are up to four times more likely to get married than gay men—unsurprising if you buy Kurtz's understanding of male and female sexuality. So if you accept the premise that women are far more monogamous

than men, and that therefore lesbian marriages are more likely to be monogamous than even heterosexual ones, the net result of lesbian marriage rights is
clearly a gain in monogamy, not a loss. For social conservatives, what's not to
like?

But the conservatives are wrong when it comes to gay men as well.
Gay men—not because they're gay but because they are men in an all-male
subculture—are almost certainly more sexually active with more partners than
most straight men.... But this is not true of all gay men. Many actually yearn
for social stability, for anchors for their relationships, for the family support and
financial security that come with marriage. To deny this is surely to engage in
the "soft bigotry of low expectation.".... [W]ith legal marriage, their numbers
would surely grow. And they would function as emblems in gay culture of a
sexual life linked to stability and love.

So what's the catch? I guess the catch would be if those gay male couples
interpret marriage as something in which monogamy is optional. But given the
enormous step in gay culture that marriage represents, and given that marriage is
entirely voluntary, I see no reason why gay male marriages shouldn't be at least
as monogamous as straight ones. Perhaps those of us in the marriage movement
need to stress the link between gay marriage and monogamy more clearly.... In
Denmark, where de facto gay marriage has existed for some time, the rate of
marriage among gays is far lower than among straights, but, perhaps as a result,
the gay divorce rate is just over one-fifth that of heterosexuals. And, during the
first six years in which gay marriage was legal, scholar Darren Spedale has found,
the rate of straight marriages rose 10 percent, and the rate of straight divorces
decreased by 12 percent....

When you think about it, this makes sense. Within gay subculture, marriage
would not be taken for granted. It's likely to attract older, more mainstream gay
couples, its stabilizing ripples spreading through both the subculture and the
wider society. Because such marriages would integrate a long-isolated group of
people into the world of love and family, they would also help heal the psychic
wounds that scar so many gay people and their families. Far from weakening
heterosexual marriage, gay marriage would, I bet, help strengthen it, as the culture of marriage finally embraces all citizens. How sad that some conservatives
still cannot see that. How encouraging that, in such a short time, so many others
have begun to understand.

27

Age of Anxiety

America's role as the world's lone superpower was accompanied by domestic concerns at the turn of the twenty-first century. The terrorists' attacks on September 11, 2001, caused many Americans to reconsider America's place in the world. Within a twelve-year period, the United States fought three wars (the 1991 Gulf War, the 2003 Iraq War, and the ongoing conflict in Afghanistan) in the Middle East in efforts to remove terrorist threats. And the protracted nature of the wars in Afghanistan and Iraq began to have powerful implications within the United States. At home Congress passed legislation that broadened investigative powers to thwart potential terrorist threats. Immigration continued to be a polarizing issue. In 2008, the world faced a serious financial crisis. That same year, the American people elected the first African American as president of the United States. And an environmental disaster revealed the precarious balance between the need for oil and the need to protect the environment. The following selections reveal some of the themes that defined the time.

233

George W. Bush Responds to the Terrorist Attacks (2001)

Throughout most of American history, the United States has been relatively free of direct military attack or acts of terrorism. The country benefited from this isolation. At the end of the twentieth century, the United States was the wealthiest, most powerful nation on earth. But some had come to loathe the United States and its global influence. One such individual was Osama bin Laden, a wealthy Saudi Arabian who had embraced a fundamentalist, anti-Western view of Islam. Enraged at the presence of American troops in Saudi Arabia following the Gulf War (1991), America's support of Israel, and the spread of American popular culture throughout the world, bin Laden found refuge in Taliban-dominated Afghanistan. From there, he masterminded several terrorist attacks against American interests in the 1990s. By 1998 bin Laden formed an extremist Islamic organization called al-Qaeda (Arabic for "The Base") to recruit, train, and finance fighters who wanted to strike at the United States. On September 11, 2001, nineteen al-Qaeda members hijacked four passenger jets and used them as suicide missiles in a coordinated attack on the United States. Two planes were flown into the twin towers of the World Trade Center in New York City; within two hours, both 110-story buildings collapsed. The third plane smashed into the Pentagon. A fourth plane, headed for Washington, D.C., crashed in a Pennsylvania field after passengers rushed the cockpit. Speaking to the nation a short time after the terrorist attacks, President George W. Bush offered the following response.

Questions to Consider

1. Why does Bush give the Taliban an ultimatum?
2. In what ways does Bush commit the United States to a war on terrorism? To what effect?
3. In what ways does America change after these attacks?
4. Compare and contrast President Bush's remarks with "Woodrow Wilson's Declaration of War Message" (Document 168) and with "Roosevelt's Declaration of War Message" (Document 192). How are they similar? Different?

On September the eleventh, enemies of freedom committed an act of war against our country. Americans have known wars—but for the past 136 years,

SOURCE: "Address of George W. Bush, President of the United States, Delivered to a Joint Session of Congress and the American People, Washington, D.C., September, 20, 2001," *Vital Speeches of the Day* 67 (1 October 2001): 760–63.

they have been wars on foreign soil, except for one Sunday in 1941. Americans have known the casualties of war—but not at the center of a great city on a peaceful morning. Americans have known surprise attacks—but never before on thousands of civilians. All of this was brought upon us in a single day—and night fell on a different world, a world where freedom itself is under attack.

Americans have many questions tonight. Americans are asking:

Who attacked our country?

The evidence we have gathered all points to a collection of loosely affiliated terrorist organization known as al-Qaida. They are the same murderers indicted for bombing American embassies in Tanzania and Kenya, and responsible for the bombing of the U.S.S. Cole.

Al-Qaida is to terror what the mafia is to crime. But its goal is not making money; its goal is remaking the world—and imposing its radical beliefs on people everywhere.

The terrorists practice a fringe form of Islamic extremism that has been rejected by Muslim scholars and the vast majority of Muslim clerics—a fringe movement that perverts the peaceful teachings of Islam. The terrorists' directive commands them to kill Christians and Jews, to kill all Americans and make no distinctions among military and civilians, including women and children.

This group and its leader—a person named Usama bin Ladin—are linked to many other organizations in different countries, including the Egyptian Islamic Jihad and the Islamic Movement of Uzbekistan....

The leadership of al-Qaida has great influence in Afghanistan, and supports the Taliban regime in controlling most of that country....

The United States respects the people of Afghanistan—after all, we are currently its largest source of humanitarian aid—but we condemn the Taliban regime. It is not only repressing its own people, it is threatening people everywhere by sponsoring and sheltering and supplying terrorists. By aiding and abetting murder, the Taliban regime is committing murder. And tonight, the United States of America makes the following demands on the Taliban:

Deliver to United States authorities all the leaders of al-Qaida who hide in your land.

Release all foreign nationals—including American citizens—you have unjustly imprisoned, and protect foreign journalists, diplomats, and aid workers in your country.

Close immediately and permanently every terrorist training camp in Afghanistan and hand over every terrorist, and every person in their support structure, to appropriate authorities.

Give the United States full access to terrorist training camps, so we can make sure they are no longer operating.

These demands are not open to negotiation or discussion. The Taliban must act and act immediately. They will hand over the terrorists, or they will share in their fate.

I also want to speak tonight directly to Muslims throughout the world: We respect your faith. It is practiced freely by many millions of Americans, and by millions more in countries that America counts as friends. Its teachings are good and peaceful, and those who commit evil in the name of Allah blaspheme the name of Allah. The terrorists are traitors to their own faith, trying, in effect, to hijack Islam itself. The enemy of America is not our many Muslim friends; it is not our many Arab friends. Our enemy is a radical network of terrorists, and every government that supports them.

Our war on terror begins with al-Qaida, but it does not end there. It will not end until every terrorist group of global reach has been found, stopped, and defeated....

Our response involves far more than instant retaliation and isolated strikes. Americans should not expect one battle, but a lengthy campaign, unlike any other we have seen. It may include dramatic strikes, visible on television, and covert operations, secret even in success. We will starve terrorists of funding, turn them one against another, drive them from place to place, until there is no refuge or rest. And we will pursue nations that provide aid or safe haven to terrorism. Every nation, in every region, now has a decision to make. Either you are with us, or you are with the terrorists. From this day forward, any nation that continues to harbor or support terrorism will be regarded by the United States as a hostile regime.

Our nation has been put on notice: We are not immune from attack. We will take defensive measures against terrorism to protect Americans.

Today, dozens of federal departments and agencies, as well as state and local governments, have responsibilities affecting homeland security. These efforts must be coordinated at the highest level. So tonight I announce the creation of a Cabinet-level position reporting directly to me—the Office of Homeland Security....

This is not, however, just America's fight. And what is at stake is not just America's freedom. This is the world's fight. This is civilization's fight. This is the fight of all who believe in progress and pluralism, tolerance and freedom.

We ask every nation to join us. We will ask, and we will need, the help of police forces, intelligence services, and banking systems around the world....

The civilized world is rallying to America's side. They understand that if this terror goes unpunished, their own cities, their own citizens may be next. Terror, unanswered, can not only bring down buildings, it can threaten the stability of legitimate governments. And we will not allow it....

Great harm has been done to us. We have suffered great loss. And in our grief and anger we have found our mission and our moment. Freedom and fear are at war. The advance of human freedom—the great achievement of our time, and the great hope of every time—now depends on us. Our nation—this generation—will lift a dark threat of violence from our people and our future. We will rally the world to this cause, by our efforts and by our courage. We will not tire, we will not falter, and we will not fail....

234

A Response to the USA Patriot Act (2001)

In the wake of the September 11, 2001, attacks, the federal government moved quickly to toughen national security. Over one thousand individuals, mostly Arab and Muslim men, were detained and interrogated. Hundreds of non-citizens were summarily deported without due process. Airport security became more rigorous (and soon fell under the jurisdiction of the new federal agency, the Transportation Security Administration), and a more careful screening of applications by foreigners to travel or study in the United States began. Congress passed the USA PATRIOT Act, authorizing law enforcement officials to use broader investigative powers to thwart potential terrorist threats. Such expansion of powers exposes the delicate balance between the need for national security in crisis times and the protection of individual rights under the Constitution and the Bill of Rights. Since its creation in response to the Palmer Raids, which occurred during the Red Scare of 1919–1920, the American Civil Liberties Union (ACLU) has been a staunch advocate of protecting individuals' rights. In the excerpted speech here, Anthony D. Romero, Executive Director of the ACLU, offered the following comments about the USA PATRIOT Act to The City Club of Cleveland, Ohio.

Questions to Consider

1. For what reasons does Romero believe the climate of opinion and tolerance is different from earlier times in American history? What about the Red Scare ("The Red Scare," Document 171)?

2. In what ways does Romero believe the USA PATRIOT Act is a threat to liberties?

3. What is the proper balance between national security and protecting individual rights?

4. Is Romero's "proactive agenda" an appropriate course of action in a time of crisis? Why or why not?

5. How might Ted Nakashima ("Life in a Japanese Internment Camp," Document 193) have responded to this speech?

Amidst such tragedy, there is good news in the form of statements by President Bush and many public officials, who urge Americans to respect the rights of

SOURCE: Anthony D. Romero, "In Defense of Liberty," *Vital Speeches of the Day* 68 (1 January 2002): 169–72.

others and warn that attacks on Arabs and Muslims "will not stand." Although that is exactly what a US President should be saying, the fact is that it has not always been the case. We know from our history that in times of national emergencies government officials have targeted particular groups for harassment or outright discrimination....

Americans have often referred to our country as a "melting pot." That image assumed that all groups who reached our shores eventually assimilated into a larger body, becoming indistinguishable. The image no longer describes what is happening in our country. We now know that people do not in fact "melt" into a larger body, that many groups choose to retain their distinguishing characteristics and identities, and that in turn enriches our country. In that respect, we have grown more tolerant of our differences.

The terrorists apparently took insidious advantage of this tolerance, living in our communities and enjoying our freedoms. Does that mean that those freedoms are somehow at fault? Or that respecting the rights of others is wrong? The answer is an emphatic "No." These fundamental values, established in our Constitution, are the bedrock of our country. They are what truly distinguish us; they are the source of our unique strength; they are our legacy to the world. I also think there is another reason for the greater measure of tolerance and respect we have witnessed so far. That is, that our message—and by "our," I refer to the ACLU and other civil liberties groups—has actually gotten through. We may be the favorite whipping post of conservative editors and the best laugh-line for late-night talk show hosts, but our efforts have not been in vain. Our defense of liberty for over 80 years has succeeded in raising people's consciousness of the Bill of Rights as something more than an appendage to the Constitution. Our efforts have kept the spotlight on these guarantees, reminding people that constitutional principles exist to be exercised, and that they are not subject to the whims of government.

Which brings me to the current debate over the appropriate balance between liberty and security in a time of national crisis. After weeks of negotiation, the USA PATRIOT Act was signed into law last Friday. Notwithstanding the rhetoric and lip service paid to civil liberties by our nation's leaders, the new law gives government expanded power to invade our privacy, imprison people without meaningful due process, and punish dissent.

The ACLU has been in the forefront of those arguing that this is no time for Congress to be pushing through new laws that would seriously diminish our civil liberties. This is a time for reason, not hysteria. The US is facing a serious threat to its security. However, that threat is directed as well to our democratic values, our freedoms, our diversity, our equality.

There are many provisions that simply do not meet the basic test of maximizing our security and preserving our civil liberties.

I would list the following five proposals as among the most offensive:

1. The overly broad definition of "terrorism"—A definition that could easily be used against many forms of civil disobedience, including legitimate and peaceful protest. The language is so ambiguous that it is possible that if an

organized group of peace demonstrators spray painted a peace sign outside of the State Department, they could be charged as terrorists for their actions.

2. Indefinite detention of immigrants based on the Attorney General's certification of a danger to national security—A harmful provision with language so vague that even the existence of judicial review would provide no meaningful safeguard against abuse.

3. Expanded wiretap authority—The new legislation minimized judicial supervision of law enforcement wiretap authority by permitting law enforcement to obtain the equivalent of blank warrants in the physical world; authorizing intelligence wiretaps that need not specify the phone to be tapped or require that only the target's conversations be eavesdropped on. And the new law extends lower surveillance standards to the Internet. Let me explain with regard to the Internet, since it can be rather complicated. Under current law, authorities can require a telephone company to reveal numbers dialed to and from a particular phone by simply certifying that this information is "relevant to an ongoing criminal investigation." This is far less than the probable cause standard that governs most searches and seizures. The new law extends this low level of proof to Internet communications, which unlike a telephone number—reveal personal and private information, such as which Internet sites an individual has visited. Once that lower standard is applied to the Internet, law enforcement officers would have unprecedented power to monitor what citizens do on the Net, thereby opening a "back door" on the content of personal communications.

4. The use of "sneak and peek" searches to circumvent the Fourth Amendment— Under this segment of the legislation, law enforcement officials could enter your home, office or other private place and conduct a search, take photographs and download your computer files without notifying you until after the fact. This delayed notice provision undercuts the spirit of the Fourth Amendment and the need to provide information to citizens when their privacy is invaded by law enforcement authorities.

5. Eviscerating the wall between foreign surveillance and domestic criminal investigation—The new legislation gives the Director of the Central Intelligence the power to manage the gathering of intelligence in America and mandate the disclosure of information obtained by the FBI about terrorism in general—even if it is about law abiding American citizens—to the CIA....

Terror, by its very nature, is intended not only to destroy, but also to intimidate a people; forcing them to take actions that are not in their best interest. That's why defending liberty during a time of national crisis is the ultimate act of defiance. It is the ultimate act of patriotism. For, if we are intimidated to the point of restricting our freedoms, the terrorists have won.

Security and liberty do not have to be at odds, nor put on a collision course. We must act to defend against any assault on civil liberties. However, we should be prepared not only to react, but also to be proactive, offering alternative solutions where feasible.

So what do we do? A proactive agenda has several parts:

First, we need to urge our fellow Americans to think carefully and clearly about the tradeoffs between national security and individual freedom, and to understand that some will seek to restrict freedom for ideological and other reasons that have little to do with security.

Second, we need to stay informed and involved in the current congressional deliberations over anti-terror legislation. We have to let our elected officials know that our eyes are on them....

Third, we must demand that government take the necessary efforts to prevent and punish unwarranted, bigoted attacks on fellow citizens of Arab descent and members of religious minorities, including Muslims and Sikhs.... They are our neighbors, friends, co-workers, not the enemy....

Fourth, we must keep the pressure on other issues. We do not have the luxury of putting other civil liberties on the backburner. We must not lose the momentum on important struggles like the death penalty or electoral reform....

Fifth, we must demand government accountability and responsiveness to civil liberties. The American people have a right to know that our basic protections are in place....

Finally, we should establish guidelines for evaluating new proposals that would affect our basic civil liberties. At the very least, proposed changes to restrict liberty should be examined and debated in public....

The American people must be reassured that constitutional guarantees will apply in times of crisis and tranquility alike....

235

The United States and the World (2003)

Since World War II, the United States has experienced economic expansion that provided job opportunities for its growing population. This economic growth helped shape a society that became increasingly consumer oriented and remarkably affluent. At the same time, American products, technology, and culture were spread throughout the world. Many American citizens enjoyed the fruits of this prosperity and global trade, and they came to believe that the American way of life, its core values and beliefs, and its culture were good for the world. What Americans saw as sharing the benefits of the good life was, however, often viewed as a new form of imperialism. But rather than taking or occupying foreign lands, as happened in an earlier imperialistic impulse, American culture, technology, economic presence, and its military reached into nearly every corner of the globe and seemingly dominated world affairs. In the wake of the September 11, 2001, terrorist attacks, Americans began to question why the country was attacked, and why many in the world held the United States in contempt. In the excerpted article here, Fareed Zakaria, the international editor for the newsmagazine Newsweek, *offered an explanation of America's place in the world.*

Questions to Consider

1. According to Fareed Zakaria, in what ways has the United States come to dominate the world? With what consequences?

2. What positive things does the author have to say about the United States? In what ways is he critical?

3. Compare and contrast the ideas expressed here with those found in George Hoar's "An Anti-Imperialist Perspective" (Document 163) or in Charles Lindbergh's "Isolation from the European War" (Document 191). How are they similar? Different?

Most Americans have never felt more vulnerable. September 11 was not only the first attack on the American mainland in 150 years, but it was also sudden and unexpected. Three thousand civilians were brutally killed without any warning. In the months that followed, Americans worried about anthrax attacks, biological terror, dirty bombs and new suicide squads. Even now, the day-to-day rhythms of American life are frequently interrupted by terror alerts and warnings. The average American feels a threat to his physical security unknown since the early years of the republic.

Yet after 9-11, the rest of the world saw something quite different. They saw a country that was hit by terrorism, as some of them had been, but that was able to respond on a scale that was almost unimaginable. Suddenly terrorism was the world's chief priority, and every country had to reorient its foreign policy accordingly. Pakistan had actively supported the Taliban for years; within months it became that regime's sworn enemy. Washington announced that it would increase its defense budget by almost $50 billion, a sum greater than the total defense budget of Britain or Germany. A few months later it toppled a regime 6,000 miles away—almost entirely from the air—in Afghanistan, a country where the British and Soviet empires were bogged down at the peak of their power. It is now clear that the current era can really only have one name, the unipolar world—an age with only one global power. America's position today is unprecedented. A hundred years ago, Britain was a superpower, ruling a quarter of the globe's population. But it was still only the second or third richest country in the world and one among many strong military powers. The crucial measure of military might in the early 20th century was naval power, and Britain ruled the waves with a fleet as large as the next two navies put together. By contrast, the United States will spend as much next year on defense as the rest of the

SOURCE: Fareed Zakaria, "The Arrogant Empire," *Newsweek,* 24 March 2003, 18–33. © Newsweek, Inc. All rights reserved. Used by permission and protected by the Copyright Laws of the United States.

world put together (yes, all 191 countries). And it will do so devoting 4 percent of its GDP, a low level by postwar standards.

American dominance is not simply military. The U.S. economy is as large as the next three—Japan, Germany and Britain—put together. With 5 percent of the world's population, this one country accounts for 43 percent of the world's economic production, 40 percent of its high-technology production and 50 percent of its research and development. If you look at the indicators of future growth, all are favorable for America. It is more dynamic economically, more youthful demographically and more flexible culturally than any other part of the world. It is conceivable that America's lead, especially over an aging and sclerotic Europe, will actually increase over the next two decades.

Given this situation, perhaps what is most surprising is that the world has not ganged up on America already. Since the beginnings of the state system in the 16th century, international politics has seen one clear pattern—the formation of balances of power against the strong. Countries with immense military and economic might arouse fear and suspicion, and soon other coalesce against them.... At this point, most Americans will surely protest: "But we're different!" Americans—this writer included—think of themselves as a nation that has never sought to occupy others, and that through the years has been a progressive and liberating force. But historians tell us that all dominant powers thought they were special. Their very success confirmed for them that they were blessed. But as they became ever more powerful, the world saw them differently....

... When America had the world as its feet, Franklin Delano Roosevelt and Harry Truman chose not to create an American imperium, but to build a world of alliances and multilateral institutions. They formed the United Nations, the Bretton Woods system of economic cooperation and dozens of other international organizations. America helped get the rest of the world back on its feet by pumping out vast amounts of aid and private investment. The centerpiece of this effort, the Marshall Plan, amounted to $120 billion in today's dollars....

Of course, all these exertions served our interests, too. They produced a pro-American world that was rich and secure. They laid the foundations for a booming global economy in which America thrives. But it was an enlightened self-interest that took into account the interests of others. Above all, it reassured countries—through word and deed, style and substance—that America's mammoth power need not be feared....

In its first year the [George W. Bush] administration withdrew from five international treaties—and did so as brusquely as it could. It reneged on virtually every diplomatic effort that the Clinton administration has engaged in, from North Korea to the Middle East, often overturning public statements from Colin Powell supporting these efforts. It developed a language and diplomatic style that seemed calculated to offend the world....

September 11 only added a new layer of assertiveness to Bush's foreign policy. Understandably shocked and searching for responses, the administration decided that it needed total freedom of action....

... Because of 9-11, it has had to act forcefully on the world stage and assert American power. But that should have been all the more reason to adopt a posture of consultation and cooperation while doing what needed to be done. The point is to scare our enemies, not terrify the rest of the world....

The real question is how America should wield its power. For the past half century it has done so through alliances and global institutions and in a consensual manner. Now it faces new challenges—and not simply because of what the Bush administration has done. The old order is changing. The alliances forged during the cold war are weakening. Institutions built to reflect the realities of 1945—such as the U.N. Security Council—risk becoming anachronistic. But if the administration wishes to further weaken and indeed destroy these institutions and traditions—by dismissing or neglecting them—it must ask itself: What will take their place? By what means will America maintain its hegemony?

For some in the administration, the answer is obvious: America will act as it chooses, using what allies it can find in any given situation. As a statement of fact this is sometimes the only approach Washington will be able to employ. But it is not a durable long-term strategy. It would require America to build new alliances and arrangements every time it faced a crisis. More important, operating in a conspicuously unconstrained way, in service of a strategy to maintain primacy, will paradoxically produce the very competition it hopes to avoid....

There are many specific ways for the United States to rebuild its relations with the world. It can match its military buildup with diplomatic efforts that demonstrate its interest and engagement in the world's problems. It can stop over-subsidizing American steelworkers, farmers and textile-mill owners, and open its borders to goods from poorer countries. But above all, it must make the world comfortable with its power by leading through consensus. America's special role in the world—its ability to buck history—is based not simply on its great strength, but on a global faith that this power is legitimate. If America squanders that, the loss will outweigh any gains in domestic security. And this next American century could prove to be lonely, brutish, and short.

236

A Perspective on Limiting Immigration to the United States (2006)

In the twenty-first century, the numbers of immigrants—both legal and illegal—coming to the United States continued to rise. Alarmed at this increase, particularly among those crossing the border illegally, Congress considered stricter immigration legislation and an amnesty program for those illegal immigrants who were already in the United States. The legislation prompted considerable debate in Congress. Some members opposed any restriction, while others advanced the idea that a high wall be constructed along the U.S.-Mexico border to thwart illegal immigration. Congressman Gary G. Miller (R-CA) offered his views in the debate. Elected to Congress in 1999, Miller represented a district just east of Los Angeles that experienced the impact of recent immigration, as his excerpted speech indicates.

Questions to Consider

1. What reasons does Miller give for supporting stricter immigration laws?
2. What does Miller propose as the solution to the immigration problem?
3. In what ways is Miller referring to globalization and its impact on the American workforce?
4. How might Linda Chavez ("A View on Hispanic Assimilation," Document 229) and Meyer London ("A Speech Against Immigration Restriction," Document 172) have responded to Miller's speech?

When I hear my colleagues, and individuals I consider friends, they get up before us and say, a guest worker program is needed to fill those jobs that Americans will not do, I guess you have to define what are the jobs we are offering Americans. What wages are they offering Americans to work is probably the best question....

Talk to the individual who was a carpenter, who was a plumber, who poured concrete, who did masonry, who was honorably employed by a manufacturing company, that was paid good wages, and you saw this dramatic change start to occur during the recession in California of the 1990s. All of the sudden things were tighter. People started hiring individuals here in this country for a much lesser wage than the American citizen was willing to do that job for.

A good example, I remember seeing dry-wallers being laid off and an illegal being hired. It is not that illegals are bad people. By and large, they are really good people. They are just trying to come here to better their lives. So it is not a matter of race or discrimination. It is just the fact that can the United States accept all the poor that this world wants to send here? And if we decided to do that, why not accept them from India? Why not accept them from Asia? Why not accept them from anyplace in the world and double, triple, quadruple our population if we are just going to be benevolent and accept people who are poor and want to better their lives?

But the problem you have, and this is back to the dry-waller, then you see an illegal hanging dry wall and his wife and kids are going behind him nailing the dry wall off to get the job done quicker so the husband could produce more at a much lesser rate than the American citizen was paid before.

SOURCE: *Congressional Record*, 109th Congress, 2nd Session (11 July 2006), 5028–30.

Now, how do you explain that to the American who was born here, who was educated here, who perhaps does not want to put a suit and tie on to go to work in the morning, who wants to work with his hands in that job that he is very capable of doing, but cannot afford to do for the reduced rate that an illegal is willing to work for? How do you tell that man he cannot support his family, educate his children and cannot afford a home anymore?...

I think we need to go pass a law today, a new law that is strict, enforceable and specific on what we are going to allow and not allow. We need to prove to the American people that we are going to send law-breakers back and we are going to hold employers accountable for hiring people that are here illegally.

Now, one argument that I hear repeatedly is, well, what are you going to do with all the people that came here illegally? They came here for a job, and if there is no job, they will go back home. The government does not need to provide buses. The government needs to remove the incentives that allow people to live here.

There are many. We need to crack down on employers, number one. We need to prohibit access to credit and financial service. We need to prevent illegals from gaining access to food stamps, low-income housing and health care....

Now, we are either a country of laws or we are not a country of laws, and today, we do not enforce the laws of this country at all. This concept we have in the Senate bill of earned citizenship will absolutely bankrupt our social fabric in this country. We cannot spend $50 billion a year, as it is estimated, on those coming to this country who, once they become citizens, are eligible for every program on the social books that we have in this country. We cannot afford it. We should not tolerate it.

Go to California and look at the impact on schools. I have talked to teachers who said they are holding this class back because the bulk of the student body in that class do not speak English. Now, yes, it is a benefit to those kids who are here illegally because they are being educated, but it is a tremendous detriment to the children of American citizens who are being held back because the rest of the class cannot speak English to be moved forward.

Go to an emergency ward in California. You will wait for hours. People go there that are illegal, cannot speak English, for a sprained ankle, for a headache, for a cold, for basic health care. That is not what an emergency ward is for. And who is paying the bill? The people who use the hospital, who are having to subsidize it because they are losing money treating illegals.

We are a compassionate country. There is no doubt about it. If someone is here and they have had an emergency and they need to go to the hospital, they should be treated. You should allow nobody to suffer, nobody to die, but you cannot tolerate 12 to 20 million people coming here with this concept that health care is free, because when they get it they do not have to pay it.

Well, you cannot blame them for that. The people you can blame are the people in this room, for not making sure the laws passed by this Congress are enforced in this country. We can no longer tolerate it. Once again, they are good people that are trying to get here, by and large not bad people. But the American citizen cannot afford it.

It is our responsibility, first of all, to protect and defend our borders. We are not doing it. And we should be concerned about the future of America and American citizens. Hopefully, when this debate continues and enough good people come here and talk about the impact on this country, we will fix the wrong that has occurred and make sure it does not happen again.

237

An Economist
on the Financial Crisis (2007)

Throughout much of the early twenty-first century, the American economy—and portions of the global economy—grew and expanded at dramatic rates. In the United States, the near absence of inflation and remarkably low interest rates helped fuel business growth and consumer spending. In addition, changes in banking laws and lax enforcement of existing regulatory policies allowed some financial institutions to overextend their business practices, often taking actions that resembled a speculative "bubble." Nowhere was this overextension more apparent than in the housing/mortgage industry. Among those who commented on the beginnings of a financial crisis was Princeton University economics professor Paul Krugman, a frequent New York Times *columnist and winner of the Nobel prize in economics in 2008. Below is Krugman's column from December 2007 about the financial situation.*

Questions to Consider

1. In what ways does Krugman describe the financial crisis?
2. According to Krugman, why were regulatory policies not enforced?
3. Does the business community behave as Ayn Rand and Alan Greenspan suggest?
4. What course of action does the federal government take with regard to this financial crisis?

When announcing Japan's surrender in 1945, Emperor Hirohito famously explained his decision as follows: "The war situation has developed not necessarily to Japan's advantage."

There was a definite Hirohito feel to the explanation Ben Bernanke, the Federal Reserve chairman, gave this week for the Fed's locking-the-barn-door-after-the-horse-is-gone decision to modestly strengthen regulation of the mortgage industry: "Market discipline has in some cases broken down, and the incentives to follow prudent lending procedures have, at times, eroded."

That's quite an understatement. In fact, the explosion of "innovative" home lending that took place in the middle years of this decade was an unmitigated disaster.

But maybe Mr. Bernanke was afraid to be blunt about just how badly things went wrong. After all, straight talk would have amounted to a direct rebuke of his predecessor, Alan Greenspan, who ignored pleas to lock the barn door while the horse was still inside—that is, to regulate lending while it was booming, rather than after it had already collapsed.

I use the words "unmitigated disaster" advisedly.

Apologists for the mortgage industry claim, as Mr. Greenspan does in his new book, that "the benefits of broadened home ownership" justified the risks of unregulated lending.

But homeownership didn't broaden. The great bulk of dubious subprime lending took place from 2004 to 2006—yet homeownership rates are already back down to mid-2003 levels. With millions more foreclosures likely, it's a good bet that homeownership will be lower at the Bush administration's end than it was at the start.

Meanwhile, during the bubble years, the mortgage industry lured millions of people into borrowing more than they could afford, and simultaneously duped investors into investing vast sums in risky assets wrongly labeled AAA. Reasonable estimates suggest that more than 10 million American families will end up owing more than their homes are worth, and investors will suffer $400 billion or more in losses.

So where were the regulators as one of the greatest financial disasters since the Great Depression unfolded? They were blinded by ideology.

"Fed shrugged as subprime crisis spread," was the headline on a *New York Times* report on the failure of regulators to regulate. This may have been a discreet dig at Mr. Greenspan's history as a disciple of Ayn Rand, the high priestess of unfettered capitalism known for her novel "Atlas Shrugged."

In a 1963 essay for Ms. Rand's newsletter, Mr. Greenspan dismissed as a "collectivist" myth the idea that businessmen, left to their own devices, "would attempt to sell unsafe food and drugs, fraudulent securities, and shoddy buildings." On the contrary, he declared, "it is in the self-interest of every businessman to have a reputation for honest dealings and a quality product."

It's no wonder, then, that he brushed off warnings about deceptive lending practices, including those of Edward M. Gramlich, a member of the Federal Reserve board. In Mr. Greenspan's world, predatory lending—like attempts to sell consumers poison toys and tainted seafood—just doesn't happen.

But Mr. Greenspan wasn't the only top official who put ideology above public protection. Consider the press conference held on June 3, 2003—just about the time subprime lending was starting to go wild—to announce a new initiative aimed at reducing the regulatory burden on banks. Representatives of four of the five government agencies responsible for financial supervision used tree shears to attack a stack of paper representing bank regulations. The fifth representative, James Gilleran of the Office of Thrift Supervision, wielded a chainsaw.

Also in attendance were representatives of financial industry trade associations, which had been lobbying for deregulation. As far as I can tell from press reports, there were no representatives of consumer interests on the scene.

Two months after that event the Office of the Comptroller of the Currency, one of the tree-shears-wielding agencies, moved to exempt national banks from state regulations that protect consumers against predatory lending. If, say, New York State wanted to protect its own residents—well, sorry, that wasn't allowed.

Of course, now that it has all gone bad, people with ties to the financial industry are rethinking their belief in the perfection of free markets. Mr. Greenspan has come out in favor of, yes, a government bailout. "Cash is available," he says—meaning taxpayer money—"and we should use that in larger amounts, as is necessary, to solve the problems of the stress of this."

Given the role of conservative ideology in the mortgage disaster, it's puzzling that Democrats haven't been more aggressive about making the disaster an issue for the 2008 election. They should be: It's hard to imagine a more graphic demonstration of what's wrong with their opponents' economic beliefs.

238

Barack Obama's Victory Speech (2008)

In 2007, first-term Illinois senator Barack Obama began a presidential campaign that highlighted the themes of "hope" and "change." The campaign had an effective organization and political strategy, a powerful appeal to grassroots supporters, the ability to raise large sums of money and Obama's brilliant oratory. Support for Obama grew, in part because of the faltering American economy, the involvement in two foreign wars and increasing disillusionment with the George W. Bush administration. Barack Obama won the election, becoming the first African American to be president. After learning he won on election day, Obama spoke before a huge rally in Chicago's Grant Park. Below is an excerpt of his victory speech.

Questions to Consider

1. In what ways does his speech address the themes of "hope" and "change"?
2. In what ways does Obama credit the American people for his victory?
3. Why is Obama optimistic about the future?
4. What is the purpose of Obama's commentary about Ann Nixon Cooper?
5. Compare the themes raised in this document with those that appear in "Franklin D. Roosevelt's First Inaugural Address," (Document 182) and Ronald Reagan's first inaugural address ("The Reagan Revolution," Document 224)? What similarities do you notice? Differences?

If there is anyone out there who still doubts that America is a place where all things are possible; who still wonders if the dream of our founders is alive in our time; who still questions the power of our democracy, tonight is your answer.

It's the answer told by lines that stretched around schools and churches in numbers this nation has never seen; by people who waited three hours and four hours, many for the very first time in their lives, because they believed that this time must be different; that their voice could be that difference.

It's the answer spoken by young and old, rich and poor, Democrat and Republican, black, white, Latino, Asian, Native American, gay, straight, disabled and not disabled—Americans who sent a message to the world that we have never been a collection of red states and blue states; we are, and always will be, the United States of America.

It's the answer that led those who have been told for so long by so many to be cynical, and fearful, and doubtful of what we can achieve to put their hands on the arc of history and bend it once more toward the hope of a better day.

It's been a long time coming, but tonight, because of what we did on this day, in this election, at this defining moment, change has come to America....

But above all, I will never forget who this victory truly belongs to—it belongs to you.

I was never the likeliest candidate for this office. We didn't start with much money or many endorsements. Our campaign was not hatched in the halls of Washington—it began in the backyards of Des Moines and the living rooms of Concord and the front porches of Charleston.

It was built by working men and women who dug into what little savings they had to give $5 and $10 and $20 to this cause. It grew strength from the young people who rejected the myth of their generation's apathy; who left their homes and their families for jobs that offered little pay and less sleep; from the not-so-young people who braved the bitter cold and scorching heat to knock on the doors of perfect strangers; from the millions of Americans who volunteered and organized, and proved that more than two centuries later, a

SOURCE: "Transcript of Barack Obama's Victory Speech," 5 November 2008, http://www.npr.org/templates/story/story.php?storyId=96624326

government of the people, by the people and for the people has not perished from this earth. This is your victory.

I know you didn't do this just to win an election, and I know you didn't do it for me. You did it because you understand the enormity of the task that lies ahead. For even as we celebrate tonight, we know the challenges that tomorrow will bring are the greatest of our lifetime—two wars, a planet in peril, the worst financial crisis in a century. Even as we stand here tonight, we know there are brave Americans waking up in the deserts of Iraq and the mountains of Afghanistan to risk their lives for us. There are mothers and fathers who will lie awake after their children fall asleep and wonder how they'll make the mortgage, or pay their doctor's bills, or save enough for college. There is new energy to harness and new jobs to be created; new schools to build and threats to meet and alliances to repair.

The road ahead will be long. Our climb will be steep. We may not get there in one year, or even one term, but America—I have never been more hopeful than I am tonight that we will get there. I promise you: We as a people will get there.

There will be setbacks and false starts. There are many who won't agree with every decision or policy I make as president, and we know that government can't solve every problem. But I will always be honest with you about the challenges we face. I will listen to you, especially when we disagree. And, above all, I will ask you join in the work of remaking this nation the only way it's been done in America for 221 years—block by block, brick by brick, callused hand by callused hand....

So let us summon a new spirit of patriotism; of service and responsibility where each of us resolves to pitch in and work harder and look after not only ourselves, but each other. Let us remember that if this financial crisis taught us anything, it's that we cannot have a thriving Wall Street while Main Street suffers. In this country, we rise or fall as one nation—as one people.

Let us resist the temptation to fall back on the same partisanship and pettiness and immaturity that has poisoned our politics for so long. Let us remember that it was a man from this state who first carried the banner of the Republican Party to the White House—a party founded on the values of self-reliance, individual liberty and national unity. Those are values we all share, and while the Democratic Party has won a great victory tonight, we do so with a measure of humility and determination to heal the divides that have held back our progress....

And to all those watching tonight from beyond our shores, from parliaments and palaces to those who are huddled around radios in the forgotten corners of our world—our stories are singular, but our destiny is shared, and a new dawn of American leadership is at hand. To those who would tear this world down: We will defeat you. To those who seek peace and security: We support you. And to all those who have wondered if America's beacon still burns as bright: Tonight, we proved once more that the true strength of our nation comes not from the might of our arms or the scale of our wealth, but from the enduring power of our ideals: democracy, liberty, opportunity and unyielding hope.

For that is the true genius of America—that America can change. Our union can be perfected. And what we have already achieved gives us hope for what we can and must achieve tomorrow.

This election had many firsts and many stories that will be told for generations. But one that's on my mind tonight is about a woman who cast her ballot in Atlanta. She's a lot like the millions of others who stood in line to make their voice heard in this election, except for one thing: Ann Nixon Cooper is 106 years old.

She was born just a generation past slavery; a time when there were no cars on the road or planes in the sky; when someone like her couldn't vote for two reasons—because she was a woman and because of the color of her skin.

And tonight, I think about all that she's seen throughout her century in America—the heartache and the hope; the struggle and the progress; the times we were told that we can't and the people who pressed on with that American creed: Yes, we can.

At a time when women's voices were silenced and their hopes dismissed, she lived to see them stand up and speak out and reach for the ballot. Yes, we can.

When there was despair in the Dust Bowl and depression across the land, she saw a nation conquer fear itself with a New Deal, new jobs and a new sense of common purpose. Yes, we can.

When the bombs fell on our harbor and tyranny threatened the world, she was there to witness a generation rise to greatness and a democracy was saved. Yes, we can.

She was there for the buses in Montgomery, the hoses in Birmingham, a bridge in Selma and a preacher from Atlanta who told a people that "We Shall Overcome." Yes, we can.

A man touched down on the moon, a wall came down in Berlin, a world was connected by our own science and imagination. And this year, in this election, she touched her finger to a screen and cast her vote, because after 106 years in America, through the best of times and the darkest of hours, she knows how America can change. Yes, we can.

America, we have come so far. We have seen so much. But there is so much more to do. So tonight, let us ask ourselves: If our children should live to see the next century; if my daughters should be so lucky to live as long as Ann Nixon Cooper, what change will they see? What progress will we have made?

This is our chance to answer that call. This is our moment. This is our time—to put our people back to work and open doors of opportunity for our kids; to restore prosperity and promote the cause of peace; to reclaim the American Dream and reaffirm that fundamental truth that out of many, we are one; that while we breathe, we hope, and where we are met with cynicism, and doubt, and those who tell us that we can't, we will respond with that timeless creed that sums up the spirit of a people: Yes, we can.

Thank you, God bless you, and may God bless the United States of America.

239

Editorial on the Nomination of Sonia Sotomayor to the Supreme Court (2009)

Shortly after Barack Obama became president, he had the opportunity to make an appointment to the Supreme Court. He chose Sonia Sotomayor, the first Hispanic to be nominated to the high court. Sotomayor was raised in poverty in a Bronx, New York, housing project, but because of her academic abilities, graduated with honors from Princeton University and received a law degree from Yale University in 1979. She served as prosecutor for the New York County District Attorney's office, practiced law for a number of years, then began a series of federal judgeship appointments. Sotomayor's nomination to the Supreme Court sparked heated debate. Among those who opposed her nomination was columnist Michelle Malkin, who was born in Philadelphia, Pennsylvania, to Filipino parents and graduated from Oberlin College before pursuing a career in journalism. Below is one of Malkin's editorial columns on the Sotomayor nomination.

Questions to Consider

1. In what ways is Malkin concerned over how Sotomayor's "compelling personal story" was part of her nomination?
2. Why is Malkin commenting on how Democrats used Sotomayor's ethnicity?
3. How important is "life experiences" in being a Supreme Court justice?
4. How might Linda Chavez ("A View on Hispanic Assimilation," Document 229) respond to this editorial?

Since when did securing a Supreme Court seat become a high hurdles contest? The White House and Democrats have turned Second Circuit Judge Sonia Sotomayor's nomination into a personal Olympic event. Pay no attention to her jurisprudence. She grew up in a Bronx public housing project. She was diagnosed with childhood diabetes at 8. Her father died a year later.

And, oh, by the way, did you hear that she was poor?

SOURCE: Michelle Malkin, "Not all 'Compelling Personal Stories' are Equal," Copyright © 2009 by Michelle Malkin. Reprinted by permission from Creators Syndicate.

It's a "compelling personal story," as we heard 20,956 times on Tuesday. Sotomayor's a "real" person. Why, she even read Nancy Drew as a young girl, President Obama told us. She's "faced down barriers, overcome the odds and lived out the American dream that brought her parents here so long ago," Obama said.

If Sotomayor were auditioning to be Oprah Winfrey's fill-in host, I'd understand the over-the-top hyping of her life narrative. But isn't anybody on Sotomayor's side the least bit embarrassed by all this liberal condescension?

Republicans are not allowed to mention Sotomayor's ethnicity lest they be branded bigots, but every Democrat on cable television harped on her multicultural "diversity" and "obstacle"-climbing. Obama made sure to roll his r's when noting that her parents came from Puerrrrto Rrrrico. New York Sen. Charles Schumer stated outright: "It's long overdue that a Latino sit on the United States Supreme Court." Color-coded tokenism dominated the headlines, with blaring references to Sotomayor as the high court's potential "first Hispanic."

Missouri Sen. Claire McCaskill—one of the leading Democrats tasked with guiding Sotomayor through the nomination process—carried the "compelling personal story" talking points to the tokenist extreme in an interview on *Fox News*:

> "If you look at what this woman has been through, and the obstacles that she has had to overcome, I think she does have a richly, uniquely American experience that makes her incredibly qualified to pass judgment on some of the most important cases in our country," McCaskill asserted. "Overcoming incredible odds, and I think that is an experience that is new to the courts. There have been a lot of privileged people that have landed on the Supreme Court. The fact that she has lived the life of the common American, trying to grow up in public housing, reaching for scholarships, reaching for the courtroom as a courtroom prosecutor, all of those things will make her a better and wiser judge. And I don't think that is identity politics. I think that is the American experience."

Clever. Challenging Sotomayor's credentials and extreme views on race and the law is not merely anti-Hispanic. It's anti-American!

More significantly, McCaskill waved the high-hurdle card after being asked to defend Sotomayor's infamous statement at a 2001 University of California at Berkeley speech asserting brown-skin moral authority: "I would hope that a wise Latina woman with the richness of her experiences would more often than not reach a better conclusion than a white male who hasn't lived that life." McCaskill actually denied that Sotomayor had made the remarks, then argued the words were taken out of context.

You want context? It's even worse than that sound bite. As *National Journal* legal analyst Stuart Taylor reported, "Sotomayor also referred to the cardinal duty of judges to be impartial as a mere 'aspiration because it denies the fact that we are by our experiences making different choices than others.' And she suggested that companion inherent physiological or cultural differences' may help explain why 'our gender and national origins may and will make a difference in our judging.'" The full speech was reprinted in something called the *Berkeley La Raza Law Journal*. "La Raza" is Spanish for "The Race." Imagine if a white male Republican court nominee had published in a law review called "The Race."

The selective elevation of hardship as primary qualification demeans the entire judiciary. If personal turmoil makes one "incredibly qualified to pass judgment on some of the most important cases in our country," let's put reality-show couple Jon and Kate Gosselin on the bench. Millions of viewers tune in to watch their "compelling personal story" of life with eight children on television. It's a "richly, uniquely American experience" of facing obstacles and overcoming the odds. Get them robes and gavels, stat.

The lesson is that not all compelling personal stories are equal. McCaskill's assertion that "overcoming incredible odds" is "new to the courts" is ridiculous. Is she arguing that Thurgood Marshall, Felix Frankfurter and Sandra Day O'Connor faced lower hurdles than Sotomayor? And how about Clarence Thomas, a descendant of slaves who grew up in abject poverty in the South without a father? His crime, of course, was embracing the wrong ideology. So his incredible set of odds and obstacles don't count in left-wing eyes.

Democrats are eager to celebrate diversity, you see, as long as the diversely pigmented pledge allegiance to the Left for life.

240

Immigration in the 21st Century (2010)

Throughout the 1980s and 1990s, immigrants from around the world poured into the United States, particularly individuals from East Asia and Latin America, with many pushed from their homelands because of widespread poverty and simultaneously lured to America because of the booming economy. A part of this immigration pattern was a rising number of illegal immigrants, who frequently crossed the Mexican-U.S. border near large cities like Tijuana/San Diego, Tucson, Arizona or El Paso, Texas. Alarmed at increasing numbers of illegal immigrants, the United States increased its Border Patrol activities to thwart illegal crossings in these high traffic areas, which only shifted the routes to remote desert areas, like near Douglas, Arizona. In 2000, thirty-two-year-old Ismael and his cousin Silverio left the forested highlands of Guatemala to find work in America. Ismael left behind his wife and four small children, hoping to pull them out of poverty with the wages he would send from America. The following is their story of a border crossing.

Questions to Consider

1. Describe the journey of Silverio and Ismael in crossing the border.
2. What sacrifices did Ismael make?
3. How might Representative Gary Miller ("A Perspective on Limiting Immigration to the United States," Document 236) or Linda Chavez ("A View of Hispanic Assimilation," Document 229) respond to the account below?
4. In what ways could illegal immigration be prevented?

The cousins made their way out of the mountains slowly, on buses overstuffed with passengers and bundles and squawking chickens. Descending through narrow passes, they rode northwest into Mexico, through Chiapas and on into Oaxaca. Past Mexico City and central Mexico they traveled, and on into Chihuahua and finally Sonora.... It took them twenty-five days to go the 2,750 miles to the Arizona line. The two Guatemalans were never beaten up on the road, as migrants often are, but the Mexican police shook them down for money every chance they got.

Once in Agua Prieta—"dark water"—the ragtag factory town across from Douglas, the cousins found themselves in a throng of migrants trying to cross la frontera.... They connected with a coyote.[1]... The smuggler's underling, a *pollero*—"chicken wrangler"—would guide them over the border fence and then through the Arizona desert. A van would be waiting to drive them deep into America. If all went well—a big if—and if their coyote fulfilled his end of the bargain—another big if—the Guatemalan pair could walk to a road and the ride within about five miles. Ismael had no idea of their final destination. "Maybe Los Angeles," he said vaguely.

Five miles sounded like a cinch to young men without cars who had walked miles over the mountains all their lives. They started out at about 7 p.m. on Wednesday, July 19, 2000, in a group of about twenty-five people. Their first hurdle was the border wall in the center of Douglas; its vertical iron bars were fourteen feet high. Spaced a couple of inches apart, the bars allowed breezes to pass through and afforded residents on International Avenue a crosshatched view of Mexico. Painted a pale peach, the fence was meant, halfheartedly, to be attractive.... But for the Douglas homeowners sitting on their porches and in their gardens, the wall looked like prison bars.

Just beyond the central city, though, all pretense of beauty disappeared. The fence was made of sheet metal colored the purples and rusts of a bruise. The sharp-edged panels were military discards, flats that had once been used as helicopter landing pads in the deserts of Kuwait and the jungles of Vietnam. But in the ranch country east and west of town, barbed wire strung between fence posts was the only barrier. A guide wearing gloves could hold open a few strands while the walkers, one by one, did a border limbo, bending over and stepping

---

[1] A coyote is an individual who arranges to guide illegal immigrants across the border. Coyotes are frequently Mexican and are notorious for charging exorbitant fees for their "services."

SOURCE: From *The Death of Josseline: Immigration Stories from the Arizona-Mexico Borderlands* by Margaret Regan, pp. 1–7. Copyright © 2009 Margaret Regan. Reprinted by permission of Beacon Press, Boston.

between the wires. (By 2008 the barbed wire had been replaced by an intimidating wall of metal and concrete.)

The fence wasn't the only military hardware to be negotiated by Ismael, Silverio, and company. High-intensity lights, cameras, and infrared sensors cast Uncle Sam's eye on both sides of the border. Miles out into the desert, mobile surveillance towers were equipped with more of the same. And every few hundred yards along the fence, a Border Patrol agent sat in a big white SUV, his binoculars trained on the line.

No matter. The migrants had already traveled too far, and invested too much, to be deterred. They managed to sneak through the fence undetected and then began the nighttime hike. The land around Douglas is flat, making it attractive to crossers, but it's hazardous. If walkers don't trip on the rocks, they can crash into tree branches or brush their hands against needle-sharp cacti. Ismael's group did get a piece of good luck in the weather. There was a light cloud cover in the evening and even a sprinkling of rain. Yet shortly after beginning their trek *en el otro lado,* "on the other side," Silverio fell ill.

"We were only out one hour and he started to feel bad," Ismael remembered. "He was tired and we sat down to rest." The group didn't bother waiting. The smuggler and the rest went on, abandoning the cousins to the darkness. Survival of the fittest is the typical coyote MO, ... Polleros hustle the travelers to walk fast, even run, and the weak are left behind. Ismael shook his head at the memory. "I had no idea I'd be left," he said. Fortunately, the cousins had paid no money upfront. The guide fee was strictly cash-on-delivery.

The two Guatemalans struggled along on their own. The temperatures were moderate during the night, but by midday Thursday the hundred-degree heat and monsoon's humidity had become unbearable. There was *mucho calor,* Ismael said—"a lot of heat"—and Silverio collapsed. Ismael hoisted him onto his back and tried to make his way back to Mexico. But it was hopeless.

Silverio began to have *dolor de corazón,* Ismael said, clutching his own chest to demonstrate his cousin's heart pain. And *dolor de brazos,* he added, gripping his arms. He laid the young man on the ground and held him, until finally, simply, painfully, Silverio died. It was one month to the day since his twenty-third birthday.

Ismael could have left the body in the dirt and gone on alone. Maybe he could have found his pollero and managed to get past Phoenix, where the Border Patrol presence almost disappears. He didn't, though. Going for help would guarantee his own capture, but Silverio was family. Ismael had to make sure his cousin's body made it home to his parents in Santa Cruz Cajola. And he was in no condition himself to continue the trek. Overcome with grief, overwhelmed by the heat, Ismael was having chest pains of his own.

He trudged a mile out to the road. [and Border Patrol agents captured him]....

An autopsy conducted later by Dr. Guery Flores, the county medical examiner, determined that he had been "a very healthy young man," said Janice L. Fields, Flores's assistant. Silverio was robust, with a well-developed musculoskeletal system." Had he not tried to cross the desert, he wouldn't have died. "The cause of death was exposure," Fields went on. "It doesn't take any time at all in the desert." Chest pains mimicking a heart attack are a common symptom of dehydration, she explained, and sighed. "Unfortunately, yes, we've had a lot of these [deaths]. At this time of year they don't understand how dangerous it is. They've never walked a long distance in the desert. This is a death warrant."

241

Offshore Oil Drilling and the Environment (2010)

America's appetite for oil and the increasing dependency on imported foreign oil prompted oil companies to begin drilling in increasingly remote locations like Alaska. Some companies began drilling in the ocean waters of the continental shelf, a short distance from the shoreline. The public backlash from a platform's major oil spill off the coast of Santa Barbara, California, led to a federal government ban on offshore drilling. Although some states bordering the Gulf of Mexico had been drilling for oil within ten miles of their shore, the federal ban was lifted in 2006. Among those oil companies participating in offshore drilling was British Petroleum (BP), which operated the Deepwater Horizon *platform in the Gulf of Mexico about 130 miles southeast of New Orleans, Louisiana. On 20 April 2010, an explosion destroyed the* Deepwater Horizon *platform and led to a large oil spill. Below is an* AP/Huffington Post: The Online Newspaper *description of the situation one month after the explosion.*

Questions to Consider

1. According to the article, what happened on the Deepwater Horizon oil rig?
2. What actions has British Petroleum taken to stop the problem?
3. What are the environmental concerns about this accident?
4. What should be done about off shore oil drilling?
5. How might Rachel Carson ("Silent Spring," Document 209) or John Muir ("The American Forests," Document 154) have reacted to this selection?

Oil from a blown-out well is forming huge underwater plumes below a visible slick in the Gulf of Mexico, scientists said as BP [British Petroleum] wrestled for a third day Sunday with its latest contraption for slowing the nearly month-old gusher. One of the plumes is "as large as 10 miles long, 3 miles wide and 300 feet thick in spots," the *New York Times* reported. "The discovery is fresh evidence that the leak from the broken undersea well could be substantially worse than estimates that the government and BP have given."

BP, the largest oil and gas producer in the U.S., has been unable to thread a tube into the leak to siphon the crude to a tanker, its third approach to stopping or reducing the spill on the ocean floor nearly a mile below the surface. Engineers remotely steering robot submersibles were trying again Sunday to fit the tube into a breach in a seafloor pipe, BP said.

Oil has been spewing since the rig Deepwater Horizon exploded April 20, killing 11 people and sinking two days later. The government shortly afterward estimated the spill at 210,000 gallons—or 5,000 barrels—a day, a figure that has since been questioned by some scientists who fear it could be far more. BP executives have stood by the estimate while acknowledging there's no way to know for sure.

The *Times* noted:

> BP has resisted entreaties from scientists that they be allowed to use sophisticated instruments at the ocean floor that would give a far more accurate picture of how much oil is really gushing from the well.

"The answer is no to that," a BP spokesman, Tom Mueller, said on Saturday. "We're not going to take any extra efforts now to calculate flow there at this point. It's not relevant to the response effort, and it might even detract from the response effort."

BP also owns a rig that operated with incomplete and inaccurate engineering documents, which one official warned could "lead to catastrophic operator error," records and interviews show.

Two months before the Deepwater Horizon accident, 19 members of Congress called on the agency that oversees offshore oil drilling to investigate a whistle-blower's complaints about the BP-owned Atlantis, which is stationed in 7,070 feet of water more than 150 miles south of New Orleans.

The Associated Press has learned that an independent firm hired by BP substantiated the complaints in 2009 and found that the company was violating its own policies by not having completed engineering documents on board the Atlantis when it began operating in 2007.

Word of huge submerged oil plumes, meanwhile, raised the specter of more damage to the ecologically rich Gulf. It also adds to questions about when large amounts of crude might hit shore.

"It's just a matter of time … and the first significant amount of oil is going to show up around the U.S.," said Hans Graber, director of the University of Miami's satellite sensing facility, who has been tracking the oil slick.

Researchers from the National Institute for Undersea Science and Technology said Saturday they had detected the underwater oil plumes at depths between just beneath the surface to more than 4,000 feet.

Three or four large plumes have been found, at least one that is 10 miles long and a mile wide, said Samantha Joye, a marine science professor at the University of Georgia.

Researchers Vernon Asper and Arne Dierks said in Web posts that the plumes were "perhaps due to the deep injection of dispersants which BP has stated that they are conducting." BP has won government approval to use chemicals on the oil near where it is gushing to break it up before it rises to the surface.

The researchers were also testing the effects of large amounts of subsea oil on oxygen levels in the water. The oil can deplete oxygen in the water, harming plankton and other tiny creatures that serve as food for a wide variety of sea critters.

Oxygen levels in some areas have dropped 30 percent, and should continue to drop, Joye said.

"It could take years, possibly decades, for the system to recover from an infusion of this quantity of oil and gas," Joye said. "We've never seen anything like this before. It's impossible to fathom the impact."

Joye's lab was waiting for the research boat to return so a team of scientists can test about 75 water samples and 100 sediment samples gathered during the voyage. Researchers plan to go back out in about a month and sample the same areas to see if oil and oxygen levels have worsened.

BP has been unable to stop the gusher with huge blowout preventers on the well or by putting a 100-ton box above the flow to trap and siphon it to a tanker on the surface. The latest effort, inserting a mile-long pipe into the largest of two leaks, hit a snag Saturday.

BP chief operating officer Doug Suttles said one piece of equipment, called the framework, had to be brought to the surface and adjusted to fit with the tube.

The framework holds a pipe and stopper. If it works, the tube could capture more than three-quarters of the leak. BP also must contend with a smaller leak that's farther away.

One expert said BP's latest idea seems to have the best chance for success so far. Inserting a pipe into the oil gusher would be easy at the surface, said Ed Overton, a LSU professor of environmental studies. But using robots in 5,000 feet of water with oil rushing out of the pipe makes things much more difficult.

"It's something like threading the eye of a needle. But that can be tough to do up here. And you can imagine how hard it would be to do it down there with a robot," Overton said.

BP is also drilling a relief well that is considered the permanent solution to stopping the leak. It's about halfway done and still months away from being completed. The company also is still considering using a smaller containment dome known as a "top hat," as well as a "junk shot," in which golf balls and rubber would be inserted to try to clog the leak.